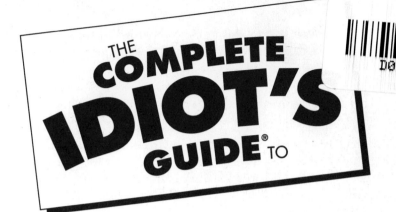

THE
COMPLETE
IDIOT'S
GUIDE® TO

Ancient Greece

by Eric D. Nelson, Ph.D., and
Susan K. Allard-Nelson, Ph.D.

ALPHA

A member of Penguin Group (USA) Inc.

With deep gratitude and abiding love, we dedicate this book to Eric's parents, Dolaine and Betty Lou Nelson, in memory of Susan's parents, James and Priscilla Rowan.

ALPHA BOOKS

Published by the Penguin Group

Penguin Group (USA) Inc., 375 Hudson Street, New York, New York 10014, U.S.A.

Penguin Group (Canada), 10 Alcorn Avenue, Toronto, Ontario, Canada M4V 3B2 (a division of Pearson Penguin Canada Inc.)

Penguin Books Ltd, 80 Strand, London WC2R 0RL, England

Penguin Ireland, 25 St Stephen's Green, Dublin 2, Ireland (a division of Penguin Books Ltd)

Penguin Group (Australia), 250 Camberwell Road, Camberwell, Victoria 3124, Australia (a division of Pearson Australia Group Pty Ltd)

Penguin Books India Pvt Ltd, 11 Community Centre, Panchsheel Park, New Delhi—110 017, India

Penguin Group (NZ), cnr Airborne and Rosedale Roads, Albany, Auckland 1310, New Zealand (a division of Pearson New Zealand Ltd)

Penguin Books (South Africa) (Pty) Ltd, 24 Sturdee Avenue, Rosebank, Johannesburg 2196, South Africa

Penguin Books Ltd, Registered Offices: 80 Strand, London WC2R 0RL, England

Copyright © 2004 by Eric D. Nelson, Ph.D.

International Standard Book Number: 1-59257-273-1
Library of Congress Catalog Card Number: 2004113213

08 07 06   8 7 6 5 4 3

Interpretation of the printing code: The rightmost number of the first series of numbers is the year of the book's printing; the rightmost number of the second series of numbers is the number of the book's printing. For example, a printing code of 04-1 shows that the first printing occurred in 2004.

Printed in the United States of America

Note: This publication contains the opinions and ideas of its authors. It is intended to provide helpful and informative material on the subject matter covered. It is sold with the understanding that the authors and publisher are not engaged in rendering professional services in the book. If the reader requires personal assistance or advice, a competent professional should be consulted.

The authors and publisher specifically disclaim any responsibility for any liability, loss, or risk, personal or otherwise, which is incurred as a consequence, directly or indirectly, of the use and application of any of the contents of this book.

Most Alpha books are available at special quantity discounts for bulk purchases for sales promotions, premiums, fund-raising, or educational use. Special books, or book excerpts, can also be created to fit specific needs.

For details, write: Special Markets, Alpha Books, 375 Hudson Street, New York, NY 10014.

Publisher: *Marie Butler-Knight*
Product Manager: *Phil Kitchel*
Senior Managing Editor: *Jennifer Chisholm*
Senior Acquisitions Editor: *Randy Ladenheim-Gil*
Development Editor: *Jennifer Moore*
Production Editor: *Janette Lynn*

Copy Editor: *Keith Cline*
Cartoonist: *Shannon Wheeler*
Cover/Book Designer: *Trina Wurst*
Indexer: *Heather McNeil*
Layout: *Ayanna Lacey*
Proofreading: *John Etchison*

Contents at a Glance

Contents

Foreword

This book makes a timely appearance as the Olympic Games have once more returned to their birthplace, Greece. Greek culture is the foundation of our modern western society, and many of its values are embedded in the western unconscious. These pages, then, are in part a process of self-discovery.

One can sum up the Greeks in two words, the *agon* and *aretê*, the contest and excelling. Competition is pervasive in the formation of the Greeks' timeless legacy, whether we think of the interaction of individuals in a democracy, or that of atoms within a void. Western politics, science, rhetoric, theater, art, and philosophy emerge from the extraordinary tension between individual and community that characterized the everyday life of Greek *poleis*, or city-states.

The ancient Greeks placed a high value on freedom, human dignity and beauty, and the power of human reason to order and comprehend our world. But their humanism was tempered by a profound sense of the limitations imposed by destiny and mortality. That is the paradox of the Greek tragic worldview. What does it mean to be human? Why do we suffer? Why were we ever even born? Yet there is nobility in the human condition that no Greek god could equal. Oedipus punishes himself and works his own redemption. The hero Odysseus declines the gift of immortality from Calypso and would rather just go home to Ithaca.

The Nelsons, one a Classicist, the other a philosopher, give you a thorough and insightful introduction to not only the essentials but also the essence of Greek history and culture and its legacy. They do so with a balanced perspective, fully aware of the shortcomings of this ancient society as well as its enduring virtues. From the Trojan War to the Italian Renaissance and our present world, the compelling story of the Greeks unfolds in an engaging interrelation of chronology and topics.

A unique feature of this book on the Greeks is the extent to which it incorporates discussion of their significant influence on the Romans throughout, not just in a brief epilogue. It is one of Rome's claims to fame that she preserved and passed on much of the rich culture of the Greeks. Western civilization is in fact the heir of both peoples, and you can continue the story by turning to Professor Eric Nelson's *The Complete Idiot's Guide to the Roman Empire*. We in the United States are the modern Romans, and your journey of self-discovery will then be complete.

—Rochelle E. Snee

Rochelle E. Snee, Associate Professor of Classics at Pacific Lutheran University, is the author of articles on late antiquity in the Greek east and reviews on books covering a wide range of the Greco-Roman world. She is currently completing *The Life of St. Marcian: Greek Text, Translation and Commentary*.

Introduction

> But those that understood him smil'd at one another, and shook their heads; but
> for mine own part, it was Greek to me.
>
> —Casca, from Shakespeare's *Julius Caesar* 1.2.278–80

A working knowledge of Classical Greek language, literature, culture, and history has been the hallmark of an educated and civilized individual for a long, long time. Such was the case when Caesar was assassinated (44 B.C.E.) and when Shakespeare wrote *Julius Caesar* (about 1599 C.E.), and it remains so today. Why is that?

Well, you can't chalk it up to victorious conquest. In fact, the ancient Greeks never really conquered anyone (except themselves, perhaps). For the most part, they were conquered by everyone else: first, (a good part of them) by the Persians, then (most of them) by the Macedonians, then (all of them) by the Romans ... and then (the left-overs) by the Parthians, Goths, Vandals, Turks, and so on. In spite of the conquerors, however, something about ancient Greece persisted.

You can't chalk it up to religious or cultural domination. Christianity and Islam, which eventually dominated most of the pagan world, were often so hostile to Greek pagan culture that they attempted to obliterate its influence, accomplishments, and memory. And yet the legacy and influence of ancient Greece can be found throughout Christian and Islamic texts, histories, cultures, and empires.

You certainly can't chalk it up to easy reading! Greek literature, philosophy, and science—and, above all, the Greek language itself—have perplexed and frustrated students, intellectuals, and citizens of the world since the days of the Romans (who, fortunately, did not stamp them out, like almost everything else that annoyed them). And, as people who have labored through a lot of Greek, let us simply say that the snob appeal alone is not worth the effort.

So, we return to the question: Why has knowledge of classical Greek art, language, history, and culture been a requisite part of a well-rounded education for so long? We would say that successive generations, cultures, and religions found things in the history, literature, and culture of ancient Greece that not only intrigued and challenged them, but that were necessary to their own development, as well. For example, they found a rich and expressive language; subtle, perceptive, and insightful approaches to philosophy, science, mathematics, politics, and medicine; a reasoned exploration of the cosmos, existence, human nature, and knowledge; and some of the best stories ever told! And, yes, they also found biases, prejudices, and misperceptions, and, some-times, they perpetuated them. In any case, even a quick glance at history will reveal that the Hellenized (that is, people who are educated, even indirectly, in Classical Greek learning, literature, and culture) have played pivotal roles in human history. It will also reveal that many people—from Afghan tribal chieftains to American politicians—have laid claim to ancient Greek traditions. In this book, we hope to introduce you to the intrigue of ancient Greece and, even more importantly, help you uncover your own Greek leanings and legacies. Then, in the future, you can smile knowingly, instead of wondering (like Casca) why the Greeks are being mentioned yet again.

To present the ancient world to a modern audience, however, we've found it necessary, at times, to cheerfully embrace inconsistency. For example, given calendars that do not match, we will sometimes show a date as, say 428/7 B.C.E. (to show that the ancient year crosses over the modern ones; not to show that we are confused); given the inconsistency between Greek spellings and (the better known) Latin spellings, particularly of names and places, we will sometimes substitute "ae" (Latin) for "ai" (Greek); and given utterly verbose ancient authors, we will sometimes shorten quotes considerably (while simultaneously attempting to retain the original sense and meaning!). We invite you to join us in the adventure!

What You'll Learn in This Book

Well, you'll learn a lot. Because we're covering roughly 4,000 years of rich and complex cultural history, we've divided the book into five sections. The first section gives you a broad overview (to help you get your bearings); the next three sections cover the major historical periods; and the last section deals with the legacy of ancient Greece, as it was passed on to both the ancient and modern worlds.

Part 1, "All Greek to You?" provides information that is essential for reading and understanding the rest of the book. Besides finding important timelines, you'll get an overarching look at ancient Greek history, literature, and culture. You might find it helpful to familiarize yourself with this section (particularly Chapters 2 and 3), because we will refer to it often in later chapters. Also, for those of you who just can't wait, Chapter 4 will answer your frequently asked questions.

Part 2, "The Bronze Age Through the Archaic Period," takes you from the Bronze Age beginnings of ancient Greece (in the Minoan and Mycenaean cultures), through the formation of complex Hellenic cultures, to the birth of *poleis* (city-states, such as Sparta and Athens). Here, we will set the stage for the Classical period, yet to come.

Part 3, "The Height of the Classical Period and the *Polis*," concentrates on the famous fifth century B.C.E. This section will help you discover the relationship between the two great wars that framed the century (Persian and Peloponnesian), the great personalities that drove it, and the intellectual and artistic accomplishments that still define it.

Part 4, "The Breakdown of the *Polis* to the Death of Alexander the Great," describes the decline of the Classical city-states, the continued development of Classical culture (such as the philosophy of Plato and Aristotle), and the conquests of Philip II of Macedon and his son, Alexander the Great.

Part 5, "The Legacy of Hellas's Legacy," shows the emergence of a new Hellenistic world, which extended from India and Afghanistan to Spain. It also describes how Hellenistic culture was assimilated by Rome and, from there, became part of a world heritage.

Extras

Sidebars provide additional information and insight, and they often expand upon, or clarify, the main text. To make it easier to locate (or identify) different kinds of information, we've included five categories of sidebars:

Lexica

These sidebars help you to understand technical or unusual terms and concepts you'll encounter in the main text. Look here for words and names to drop!

Labyrinths

Here we'll warn you of common or easily acquired misconceptions and provide updates based on new research and discoveries. Look here to sound in-the-know!

Muses

Here's where the ancient Greeks get a chance to speak for themselves. Look to these sidebars for quotations and inspiration!

> **Odysseys**
>
> Here we'll suggest places, from Spain to the steppes of the Himalayas, to go to follow in the footsteps of the ancient Greeks. Look to these boxes for adventure!

> **Eureka!**
>
> These sidebars will provide you with additional information, insight, and little-known modern connections to subjects in the main text. Look here for interesting party conversation!

Acknowledgments

This book is the result of a cooperative effort between two scholars (a male classicist and a female philosopher) who live in the same house, are married, own dueling laptops with different operating systems, and have very different personalities (one, hopelessly, but creatively, random; the other, rigorously, but creatively, precise). And, believe it or not, we enjoyed it, we are still happily married, and we plan to continue working together! So, first and foremost, we must acknowledge and thank one another, for all of the love, support, humor, creativity, insight, and meals (hint: only the classicist cooks).

Our gratitude goes to Randy Ladenheim-Gil and Jennifer Moore, for their patience, assistance, and support, from book proposal to final publication. We thank and acknowledge Norita White, for generously granting us the use of her photographs (even after suffering though our classes!). Our very special, heartfelt thanks go to Rochelle Snee—our friend, colleague, and mentor—for reading over reams of manuscript pages (and noting errors!), for graciously allowing us the use of her photographs, and for writing the foreword to this book. Rochelle still knows more about the ancient world than even Homer himself!

Our thanks and love go to our children and grandchildren—Jody, Erika, Nils, Jared, Camden, and Emilia—for their uncanny ability to simultaneously support and interrupt our grinding schedule. Finally, we gratefully and lovingly acknowledge our parents, to whom this book is dedicated.

Trademarks

All terms mentioned in this book that are known to be or are suspected of being trademarks or service marks have been appropriately capitalized. Alpha Books and Penguin Group (USA) Inc. cannot attest to the accuracy of this information. Use of a term in this book should not be regarded as affecting the validity of any trademark or service mark.

Part 1

All Greek to You?

Are you interested in ancient Greece but can't tell the difference between a *basileus* and a *baklava*? Begin here, and consider this section your general road map for the rest of the book. You'll get an overview of what there is to learn about the ancient Greeks, an Olympian's eye view of some popular topics, and the opportunity to take Greek literature and history out of the labyrinth.

The first chapters put the study of ancient Greece into perspective and break down its major areas. Here you'll find chapters that summarize the ancient Greeks' prolific contributions to literature, philosophy, science, and the arts.

Next, you'll find short answers to some persistent questions about topics such as the Olympics, the Amazons, the Trojan War, women's lives, Atlantis, sexuality, and democracy, and direction on where to look further in this book for more information.

Finally, because understanding Greek religion and mythology is fundamental to appreciating the classical world—both on its own terms and in terms of its influence on our world—this section ends with a chapter that addresses religion and myth.

Beware of Greeks Bearing Gifts—You Might Like Them

In This Chapter

- ◆ The importance of studying the Greeks
- ◆ Why what's past is not passé
- ◆ Where our information comes from
- ◆ A road map of the history we'll cover

Understanding other cultures isn't easy. It's difficult to approach other people on their own terms—to see them and the world through their eyes—without undue prejudices or preconceptions getting in the way. We have to get at them on many levels, and in many honest circumstances, to begin to know them meaningfully. With ancient cultures, the lack of direct communication and the tendency to impose present-day problems, approaches, and attitudes on them in an *anachronistic* fashion further complicates the process.

Because understanding and appreciating ancient civilizations require bringing different kinds of information to bear at the same time, this chapter sets out the framework that we'll need to journey into ancient

Greece. First, we'll establish some overarching ideas and themes to keep in mind along the way. Then we'll find out where our information about the Greeks comes from—how they speak to us—and take a look at a general historical road map of where we're going.

Aren't Greeks for Geeks?

We know from firsthand experience that although ancient Greece has a certain cachet as a subject, it also has a degree of what we might call "the ancient Geeks" factor.

Indiana Jones might have made being an archeologist hero-worthy, but so far "classics professor" brings to mind ... well, never mind. Are there really things—cool things, meaningful things, relevant things—worth learning from these ancient people? Oh, yes.

But before you can make sense of what the Greeks have to offer, you have to tune in to some of the fundamental perspectives that framed their approach to the world. So here are three heroic (if we may say so) concepts for you to keep in mind as we explore. They are, of course, generalizations, but they are necessary for understanding the Greeks and what we might take from them for ourselves.

> **Lexica** _____
>
> **Anachronism,** from the Greek *ana* (meaning "back") + *chron* (meaning "time"), is the error of placing a person, object, or way of thinking back into the wrong time. We also use the word to connote the error of imposing modern ideas or attitudes on peoples, cultures, or beliefs that existed prior to the emergence of such ideas or attitudes.

> **Labyrinths** _____
>
> Where anachronistic tendencies in the last century encouraged us to see the Greeks as "just like us," the trend more recently has been to see the Greeks as "other"—that is, as nothing like us at all. The Greeks *were* quite "other," but the fundamental exploration of what we share with them—most notably our humanity and the cosmos—remains a vibrant link.

The Harmony of a Whole Human(ity)

The Greeks saw humans as a synthesis of what we would now call body, mind, and soul. They accepted that, in order for humans to function well, be happy as humans, and achieve their greatest potential, all aspects of human persons needed nurturing, education and training, and well-ordered expression. Well-being necessitated an integrated harmony of the whole person in every form of activity. To make sense of what the Greeks were about, we'll have to bear in mind their focus on harmony, balance, and the whole person.

Reaching for Excellence Within Limitations

Within this framework of balance and harmony, the ancient Greeks prized the concept of *aretê* (pronounced ah-reh-TAY), or "excellence," in themselves and in all things. When, they asked, was a human/animal/tool at its best, or at the point at which it most fully and elegantly fulfilled its potential and purpose? At what point did it fall short of its potential or exceed its limitations, and with what consequences? Greek literature, philosophy, drama, art, myth, and history revolve around an exploration of these questions. Such a focus also helps to explain the Greeks' celebration of competition, victory, and tragedy.

This drive toward *aretê*, however, was balanced by a realistic, even melancholy, sense of the limitations of humanity, the capriciousness of fortune, and the vicissitudes of fate. Greek sayings such as "know thyself" (i.e., "realize that you are human and know what kind of human *you* are"), "nothing to excess" (i.e., "harmony and balance in all things"), and even "count no man happy until he's dead" (i.e., "there's always time for something to go wrong") give you some idea of the context in which their quest for excellence took place.

Lexica

Aretê (ah-reh-TAY) is a Greek term meaning "excellence," often translated as "virtue."

The Cosmos on Its Own Terms

Although they were a profoundly religious people, the Greeks had a profoundly secular approach to knowledge. Like other people, they wanted to know the origins of things, and to identify the causes of events. To a degree seldom matched before or since, however, they were willing to allow and entertain explanations that grew out of the evidence at hand. What are humans about? Well, let's start with humans and what they do. How does the world work? Well, let's start with how things seem to work around us. How should one live? Well, let's start with people who seem to live well. In this way, the Greeks often found that the best explanation (and the one most likely to be true) best fit and explained the evidence.

This willingness and ability to examine, make sense of, and trust the evidence at hand enabled the Greeks to question traditions, create alternative explanations, and understand the universe in (what they acknowledged was) human terms.

> " " **Muses**
>
> Mortals think that gods are born, wear clothes, speak, and appear like they do. But if oxen, or horses, or lions had hands and could paint or sculpt as humans do, horses would paint horselike gods and oxen the same, each fashioning bodies as their own. For the Ethiopians envision their gods flat-nosed and black, whereas the Thracians theirs as blue-eyed and red-haired.
>
> —Xenophanes of Colophon (c. 550 B.C.E.)

Past, Present, and Future

"Great," you say, "but what does any of this have to do with me? Why does the past, this past, matter? Why not let advanced, modern people, like us, take things from here? Besides, ancient ideas are only right when they agree with what we know now, right?"

"Ahem," we say. "Let's talk a bit about the past, why it's necessary to understand it, and about the Greeks' role in the history of that understanding. Just let us find our large, dark-rimmed glasses. We know they're around here somewhere."

Past Matters

Kidding aside, when we say "the past," we're including not only the events themselves, but also the individual and collective understanding of those events. Over time, people use the past to give meaning to, and draw meaning from, their present. We look back and try to understand what happened in the past, particularly as it explains, clarifies, or determines what is here now. From our present, we anticipate future events, and then look to the past again, to better understand, interpret, or re-interpret the connections. In any event, not only our current circumstances, but also our ideas and cultural assumptions have pasts, and these pasts matter. They are what we have to work with as we go forward into an uncertain future.

Besides, we can never really get away from the past; we can only choose to ignore or deny it. If we try to abandon the past, we still depart from *something*, and if we deny it, we still navigate by negating what went before. What's worse, from which past do we escape? The "past" in this sense is not static and unchanging, but "adapts" to new knowledge, realizations, and perspectives. These adaptations then alter our reactions to, and understanding of, where we are now and where we are going. By ignoring the past, we limit both our present and our future. And yet, that's what we often choose to do.

Ancient Models and Modern Claims

Why do we so often ignore the past? Well, the past has an unpredictable power to affirm, uphold, or upset our present. History, literature, and our own lives are filled with examples of new information about the past transforming—in a heartbeat—everything. New information forces us to change our perceptions and understandings, and these changes can create entirely new claims and obligations. When this happens, the past can turn from a source of steady reassurance to an object of confusion, embarrassment, or resentment. Just think, for example, of Galileo and the Roman Catholic Church. In the early 1600s, Galileo was found guilty of heresy for claiming that the earth revolves around the sun; in 1992, the Catholic Church formally apologized and used Galileo's own terms to affirm the relationship between faith and reason.

All of this helps to explain why maintaining a *particular* understanding of the past has often been more important than developing an *accurate* understanding of it. Even when confronted with new or improved evidence, some people cling desperately to a particular version of the past, and others vehemently attack or dismiss the same version, in order to maintain or undermine its hold on their present. From such extremes come the (sometimes deserved) charges of "revisionist" or "reactionary" or "revolutionary" history. The classical world (both Greece and Rome) remains an important part of these struggles because of its fundamental role in the cultural and intellectual "pasts" of America, Europe, the Middle East, and (to some extent) Africa.

The Wild Hair of the World

Today, although we tend to see the ancient Greeks as the revered ancestors of our modern world, this isn't the whole story. In fact, if we think of the cultural and intellectual heritage of the world as a kind of family tree, the Greeks are a "wild hair" in the mix. In the West, our guiding ideals come from the Judeo-Christian and Roman branches, which intermingled and interposed their own kind of order on the world. Thereafter, the ancient Greeks and their ideas (or, at least, others' ideas of them) entered the mix as a reactionary or revolutionary element to the prevailing order. As such a revolutionary element, the Greeks affected peoples and periods as diverse as the Jews, the Romans, Islam, the Renaissance, the Romantics, and the American Revolution.

How in Hades Do We Know What We Know?

Because even "expert" interpretation of the past is open to question or revision, good experts and scholars do something that is very Greek: They continually return

Lexica

Primary source materials have a direct link to their objects of study. For example, critical editions of Plato's works in classical Greek are considered primary. **Secondary source materials** are a step removed from their "primary" sources. Translations of and commentaries on Plato are "secondary" because scholars have interposed a layer of their own interpretation between the direct evidence (what Plato wrote) and the reader.

to *primary* (not *secondary*) *source materials* in order to let the evidence speak (again) for itself, and to form (and reform) better explanations and interpretations.

Although scholars return to the same sources, the process is exciting and dynamic. It might surprise you to learn just how much more we know about the ancient world today than we did even a few years ago! New discoveries and new technologies bring new evidence to light, and this new evidence—combined with new ideas, interpretations, or perspectives—can lead to improved understandings of material that is centuries, even millennia, old. But where does this material come from? The next three sections will give you an idea of the kinds of things we're working with.

Through the Texts

The Greeks wrote and preserved a staggering amount of material over an enormous period of time: staggering in depth, in breadth, in quantity, and in quality. From epics such as the *Iliad* and *Odyssey* created in the eighth century *B.C.E.* to the *Suda* (an enormous Byzantine encyclopedia of ancient scholarship) in the tenth century *C.E.*, virtually no facet of literature (high or low), science (good and bad), reference material (accurate or otherwise), or personal correspondence (poignant or mundane) went unexplored or unrepresented.

Lexica

Contemporary international scholarship uses **B.C.E.** (Before the Common Era) in place of B.C. (Before Christ) and **C.E.** (Common Era) in place of A.D. (*anno domini*, the year of our Lord) because B.C. and A.D. are neither accurate (Christ was born around 4 B.C.E) nor universally accepted. Also, you'll often see dates written with either **c.** or **fl.** preceding them. The "c" stands for *circa* (or *around, approximately*) and the "fl" stands for *flourit* (or *flourished*).

The texts we have today come from papyri fragments (texts written on flattened leaves of the papyrus plant), which were preserved by quirks of fate, or manuscripts (texts written by hand on animal skin or paper), which were copied and preserved over the centuries. Because errors in copying and interpretation creep into the process over time, no single text (including, for example, biblical manuscripts) is without flaws. Periodically, scholars bring together the best available evidence to establish the most accurate text in critical editions. This process was begun by the Greeks themselves, with Homeric texts (in Athens) in the sixth century B.C.E. and with other classical authors (in Alexandria) in the third century B.C.E. In any case, most of the texts that modern scholars work with come from periods far removed from the texts' original creation.

The discovery of these fragments and manuscripts is ongoing, and sometimes makes for great stories. Papyrus manuscripts, for example, were first recovered from Herculaneum (a city in Italy that was covered by ash during the same eruption that covered Pompeii) in the 1750s, and from sites in Egypt.

In Egypt, old papyrus scrolls were often torn into strips and used to wrap or stuff mummies. In 1899, a Berkeley expedition financed by Phoebe A. Hearst was initially disappointed when it unearthed huge cemeteries of mummified crocodiles (acres of them, hundreds and hundreds of crocodiles) in Egypt. The story is told that, when a worker was digging to find human mummies, he found yet another "worthless" crocodile. Frustrated, he either threw the mummy aside or struck it with his shovel (some even say it bounced off a truck), and the mummy broke open to reveal papyri.

Other crocodiles were opened and papyri was found that contains, besides legal and economic documents, fragments of poetry, fragments of a lost play by Sophocles, quite a bit of Homer, some Virgil, Euripides, and other early literary texts, as well as some painted fragments. The documents are mainly written in Greek, with some Latin and Egyptian demotic, a type of cursive hieroglyphic writing. One of the larger pieces is an early fragment of Virgil, written with a reed quill as a schoolboy exercise. Apparently, a child had to write the excerpt over and over again. Some things never change.

> **Odysseys**
>
> Stop by the Phoebe A. Hearst Museum of Archeology (Berkeley, Kroeber Hall) and say hello to the three remaining, intact crocodiles. Berkeley holds the second largest papyri collection in the United States, dating from the third century B.C.E., most of it highly fragile and waiting in its original packing boxes to be deciphered. There's still a lot to discover—and that's no crock.

From the Stones

The Greeks published public (e.g., laws, decrees) and private (e.g., grave markers) declarations by inscribing them on stone markers set up in public places. Huge numbers of these stone markers still exist, and a large part of what we know for certain about ancient Greek history comes from this evidence.

Greek civic inscriptions, such as the Law Code of Gortyn on Crete (c. 480 B.C.E.), provide valuable information on ancient Greek history and culture.

(Photo courtesy of Norita White)

Out of the Dirt

Speaking of stones, what about all those wonderful ruins, remains, and artifacts scattered from the Black Sea to the Atlantic Ocean? Although things have been lying around the Mediterranean since civilization began, the remains weren't of much interest to people—except as treasure or a source of building materials—until fairly recently. Ancient Greek archeology began in the late 1800s at Troy (in Turkey), in part because of an argument about the past—in this case, whether the *Iliad* was simply Homer's fantasy. Since then, a vast array of monumental buildings, cities, settlements, pottery, sculpture, and implements have come to light for us to uncover, contemplate, and marvel at. Together with the texts, they help fill out the picture of what life was actually like in ancient Greece. Such evidence is also invaluable for giving us some perspective on the lives of people whose voices are not represented (or not represented fairly) in the texts: the lower classes, women, and slaves.

Roman Remains

Artistically, much of what was created in ancient Greece would have been lost if the Romans hadn't conquered Greece and carted back, as war booty, nearly every piece of decent sculpture. Back in Italy, artisans (Greek slaves) churned out full- to pint-sized copies to suit any reasonably affluent Roman household that might want one. A great deal of what we know about Greek art history comes from the study of copies of famous sculptures made during the Roman period. That's why, if you look at pictures in art history books, you'll often find something like "Marble Roman Copy of a Greek Bronze Original" in the credits.

Eureka!

Using digital and multispectral imaging, scholars at Johns Hopkins and Rochester Institute of Technology have recently recovered a long-lost text of the great mathematician Archimedes (third century B.C.E.) from a palimpsest (a manuscript that contains a later text written over a partially erased earlier one). The Archimedes Palimpsest is opening a long-closed window on Archimedes' work in physics, limits, *pi*, and possibly the foundations of calculus.

High-*Technê*

Incredible advancements in technology and in the tools of analysis have contributed to the discovery of new evidence about ancient Greece and given us new information about evidence we already have. Chemical analysis, aerial photography, underwater archeology, multi-spectral imaging, computerized models, virtual-reality simulations, and electronic libraries have revolutionized what, how much, and how quickly we can research. We can now, for example, find ancient coastlines from analyzing satellite images, find and bring up shipwrecks that are thousands of years old, and analyze both the shipwrecks and their cargo for information about the ships, the crews, the materials, and the trade routes they represent.

> **Odysseys**
>
> Ancient historians, classicists, biblical scholars, and archeologists have made wonderful use of the Internet, to the benefit of both scholars and the general public. To get an idea of the amazing things that are just a click away, visit the Perseus Digital Library (www.perseus.tufts.edu), the Internet Ancient History Sourcebook (www.fordham.edu/halsall/ancient/asbook.html), and the Stoa (www.stoa.org), a consortium for electronic publications in the humanities.

A Quick Look at Hellenic History

Ready to dive in? Well, perhaps not just yet. First, let's set up a broad timeline.

The time generally referred to as "ancient Greece" breaks down into several official "ages." You'll need to learn them in order to understand practically any book on the subject and to place some of the major developments into the right context. In addition, you'll need to be somewhat familiar with what went on before (in order to understand how ancient Greece developed) and after these ages (because of the way that ancient Greece's influence was preserved and handed on).

All in all, we're talking about a span of 3,500 years, but it's not as bad as it sounds. We'll give you the breakdown by official names (except for the "Ancient Greece Age," which is definitely *not* an official name), as well as some of the major developments that mark the "ages" and "periods."

The Bronze Age: 3000–1150 B.C.E.

The Bronze Age is named for when civilizations developed bronze (copper and tin) metallurgy. Bronze Ages in Asia, the Middle East, Europe, and Africa differ slightly because these areas developed bronze working at somewhat different times. But for Greece and the Near East, 3000 to 1150 B.C.E. works.

During the "early" Bronze Age (3000–2100 B.C.E.), the inhabitants of the lands surrounding the Aegean began to evolve village and tribal social structures and learned to work in bronze and other metals. These early people were non-Greeks.

During the "middle" Bronze Age (2100–1600 B.C.E.), the Indo-European peoples that we came to know as the "Greeks" migrated into Greece from the north. They displaced or mixed with the indigenous people and became the dominant culture. On the island of Crete, a non-Greek Bronze Age civilization that we know as "Minoan" (after the Cretan King Minos of Greek mythology) flourished and declined, in part due to the destruction caused by the eruption of Thera (modern Santorini).

During the "late" Bronze Age (1600–1150 B.C.E.), the Greeks developed a vibrant and militaristic palace culture. This culture is called "Mycenaean," from the great fortress at Mycenae, said by Homer to be the home of Agamemnon, the leader of the Greeks against Troy. During this period, the Mycenaeans took over Crete, and perhaps waged a war against Troy sometime around 1200 B.C.E.

Lexica

The ancient (and modern!) Greeks called themselves **Hellenes** after a mythological ancestor, Hellen, son of Deucalion. Words with this base (e.g., **Hellenic, Hellenism, Hellenistic**) indicate "Greek" in a broad sense. The word *Greek* comes from Latin.

The Dark Age: 1150–750 B.C.E.

For reasons that are still unclear, the Mycenaean civilization fell into chaos, ruin, and oblivion. Almost everything that we know about this period comes from archeology. The "early" Dark Age (1150–900 B.C.E.) is marked by intense migration and the gradual establishment of small clan settlements. The "late" Dark Age (900–750 B.C.E.) is characterized by the rebirth of a *Hellenic* culture: population growth, new settlements based on trade and expansion, the development of phonetic writing (the alphabet), and the foundation of the Olympic Games (776 B.C.E.).

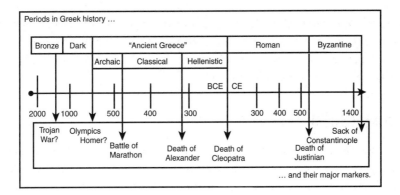

The "Ancient Greece Age": 750–30 B.C.E.

No, this isn't an official age, but it's the time to which the name *ancient Greece* most commonly refers. 750 B.C.E. approximates the time of composition of Homer's *Iliad* and *Odyssey* (the beginning of Greek literature), while 30 B.C.E. marks Cleopatra's suicide and Rome's conquest of Egypt (the end of the Hellenistic kingdoms after Alexander the Great). This unofficial "age" is officially broken down into the following "periods":

- ◆ **The Archaic period** (750–490 B.C.E.) is marked by the development of the city-state, or *polis*. Temple architecture, sculpture, literature, early philosophy, and competitive games all find their genesis during this period in the aristocratic culture that ruled these communities.

- ◆ **The Classical period** (490–323 B.C.E.) begins with the unsuccessful Persian attack on Athens at Marathon and ends with the death of Alexander the Great. During this period, most of the achievements for which ancient Greece in general and Athens in particular are celebrated reached their zenith.

  The first half of the Classical period (the fifth century B.C.E.) is framed by two great wars: the Persian War (490–480 B.C.E.), which the Greeks fought against the invading Persians, and the Peloponnesian War (431–404 B.C.E.), which the city-states of Athens and Sparta (and their allies) fought among themselves. It was during this period that Athens became a hotbed of artistic and intellectual developments and the home of a radical democracy.

  The second half of the period (the fourth century B.C.E.) is marked by the decline and conquest of the ancient city-states by Alexander the Great's father, Philip II of Macedon. Alexander, a brilliant commander, went far beyond his father's planned invasion of Persia to conquer Egypt and the lands stretching eastward to the Hindu Kush. His premature death prevented him, however, from creating a new kind of stable order.

♦ **The Hellenistic period** (323–30 B.C.E.) begins with the death of Alexander the Great and ends with the Roman conquest of Ptolemaic Egypt in 30 B.C.E. After Alexander's death, his generals divided his empire and ruled parts of it as kings. These great Hellenistic dynasties continued to fight with one another for control until Rome intervened and conquered them one by one.

Lexica _____

Koinê (koy-NAY) is the "common" Greek of the late Hellenistic and Roman imperial world. Both the Jewish Septuagint (which became the foundation for the Christian Old Testament) and the New Testament were written in this dialect.

Despite continual fighting between the dynasties, the Hellenistic period is marked by the development of the *cosmopolis* ("city-state of the world")—a world state bound together by Hellenism (Greek language and culture)—and the emergence of art forms, philosophies, religions, and language (the *koinê* dialect) that served the needs of individuals living in this expanded world. It is also the period in which the Greeks began to research, study, and teach their own classical heritage to themselves and to others.

From Rome to the Renaissance: 30 B.C.E. to 1453 C.E.

The Greeks' achievements and influence didn't stop with the Roman conquest. In the West, Rome had already been heavily influenced by Greek thought, literature, and art for more than a century. Hellenistic culture carried on and became an influential part of the Roman Empire. When the Roman emperor Constantine the Great moved the imperial capital to Constantinople in 330 C.E., he set the stage for the continuation of the eastern half of the empire—which retained its Greek language, education, and identification—for another thousand years.

This period is marked, as far as ancient Greece is concerned, by the formation of orthodox Christianity, the emergence of the Byzantine Empire after the loss of the western Roman Empire, and the development of Islamic culture. All of these were heavily influenced by the ancient Greek texts, ideas, and traditions that were passed on to and infused into them, even as pagan culture slowly ebbed and faded away.

In the West, ancient Greece's influence was swept away by a flood of "barbarian" invasions, the loss of knowledge of the Greek language, and the chaos of the early Middle Ages. It wasn't until the eleventh century that Greek translations, texts, and learning were slowly infused back into the West through Islam and Byzantium by exchange, crusade, and conquest.

There isn't any easy way to break up this long period, but here are some of the categories that scholars use to identify the specific aspects that pertain to our topic:

◆ **The Roman Empire** (27 B.C.E. to either 476 or 565 C.E.) marks the end of the Roman Republic and of the Hellenistic period (because Octavian's victory over Antony and Cleopatra brought an end to both). Edward Gibbon identifies 476 C.E. as the year that the West was lost (this has become the traditional date), but the eastern Roman emperor Justinian briefly reasserted control over East and West before his death in 565 C.E.

◆ **Late antiquity** (roughly 200–700 C.E.) is the period during which Greco-Roman pagan culture of antiquity gradually disappeared into the Middle Ages in the West and infused into Byzantium and Islam in the East.

◆ **Byzantium** (565–1453 C.E.) refers to the continuation of the eastern Roman Empire, after Justinian's death and the loss of the western Roman Empire, until Constantinople was taken by the Turks.

The Least You Need to Know

◆ The ancient Greeks valued excellence (*aretê*), harmony and balance, and explanations based on evidence.

◆ Conceptions of ancient Greece have historically played a subversive or revolutionary role in understanding the past and present.

◆ Primary source material about the Greeks comes from a wide variety of textual and archeological sources, as well as from scientific evidence.

◆ "Ancient Greece" usually refers to the time between Homer (c. 750 B.C.E.) and the Roman conquest of Ptolemaic Egypt (Antony and Cleopatra, 30 B.C.E.).

◆ Ancient Greece was influential on the Roman Empire, Byzantium, and Islam. Its influence on western Europe, lost in the Middle Ages, came back through Islam and Byzantium during the late Middle Ages and the Renaissance.

Classical Gas: Ancient Greek Literature and Art at a Glance

In This Chapter

◆ The highlights of ancient Greek literature

◆ Major authors and works of poetry and prose

◆ The ancient Greeks' fascination with the power of the spoken word

◆ How ancient Greek ideals informed their major artistic achievements

The ancient Greeks' contributions to literature, drama, and art are among their most admired and influential achievements. These achievements alone would be sufficient to earn the Greeks a place in humanity's "Hall of Fame." From poetry to prose, epic to epigram, ode to oratory, and sublime tragedy to sidesplitting comedy, the Greeks pioneered (and some would argue perfected) most of the West's literary art forms. In art and architecture, their ability to capture proportion and balance, essential and individual characteristics, and transcendent moments in experience have inspired and influenced centuries of imitation and reaction.

In later chapters, we'll explore these achievements in more depth. Here, however, we'll take a quick look at the ones that you'll definitely need to know something about. In this way, they won't be buried by the details, and you'll be better prepared to understand them within their context when we get there.

Poetry

Eureka!

Ancient poetry wasn't based on rhyme, but on meters (measures) made up of "long" or "short" syllables (two shorts equaled a long). The amount of time it took to say a sound determined whether it was long or short (for example, it takes longer to say the long o of hope than the short o of hop).

As far as literature goes, in the beginning there was the poetic word. Poetic forms, oral in origin, overwhelmingly make up humanity's earliest "serious" literature—religious texts, epic tales, genealogies, and the like. Because of poetry's priority in the transmission of important and sacred information, it retained (and to some extent still retains) the reputation of being inspired and divine, whereas prose was reserved for more worldly human concerns.

For the ancient Greeks, the most important poetic forms were epic poetry, drama (tragedy and comedy), hymns, and lyric poetry.

Epic Poetry

Epic poems are, technically, long poems based on a meter called *dactylic hexameter*. (A dactylic "foot" is *long-short-short*, and hexameter is a "measure" of six.) These poems relate particular episodes of larger, traditional stories called cycles, and both epics and the cycles that contain them concern pivotal events—real or mythological—in a people's history. The epic poems the *Iliad* and *Odyssey*, for example, belong to the Trojan Cycle. These traditional tales explore and explain defining moments, and they answer such questions as "What kind of people are we essentially?" and "What happened at those pivotal moments and why?"

Lexica

Dactylic hexameter, the meter of epic, is based on six measures (*hexa-meter*) of dactyls (fingers). Look at your fingers and you'll see one long and two short segments.

Epics focus on heroic characters whose deeds and choices during these pivotal moments convey cultural values and lessons. Besides the story of the Trojan War, Greek epic cycles cover the mythological history of cities such as Thebes or Mycenae, and they relate the exploits of heroes such as Herakles (Hercules), Theseus, Perseus, and Jason.

Greek (and western) literature begins with two great epics from the Trojan Cycle, the *Iliad* and the *Odyssey*. These works were transmitted from oral to written form sometime around 750 B.C.E. Whether or not a single genius, known to the Greeks (and us) as Homer, is the author of either poem is still the subject of the *Homeric Question*. But, regardless of authorship, the *Iliad* and *Odyssey* are indisputably the "big bang" (so to speak) of western literature. You won't understand the Greeks unless you're familiar with (or better yet read!) Homer, for nearly all of Greek literature (and that which grows from it) stems from, reacts to, or consciously departs from him. We'll give you a brief outline of his stories here.

Lexica

The Homeric Question is whether one author (known as Homer) created the *Iliad*, the *Odyssey*, or both, or if Homer himself is an epic fiction for two (or even a series of) authors.

The *Iliad* takes place in the tenth year of the Trojan War. It begins when the Greek leader Agamemnon insults the hero Achilles. Achilles withdraws from the battle, which causes the Greeks to fail against the Trojans and their hero, Hector (just as Achilles intended). Achilles rejects all pleas to return to battle, but, in order to save the Greeks while still saving face, he finally allows his friend Patroclus to fight in his place. When Hector kills Patroclus, Achilles returns to battle (even though he knows that this will lead to his own death) in a bloody rage. He kills Hector and desecrates his body. Through the intervention of the gods and Hector's father, King Priam, Achilles regains a sense of his own humanity. Fate, mortality, responsibility, effects intended and unintended, as well as the value of life, honor, fame, friendship, nobility, and love are powerfully woven together in this beautifully dark and violent work.

Labyrinths

Neither the *Iliad* nor the *Odyssey* tells the story of the Trojan War. The *Iliad* covers one 40-day episode in the final year of the 10-year war, and the *Odyssey* includes only a couple of minor incidents from the war, while telling the story of one man's long journey home. The rest of the story of the Trojan War (such as the tale of the Trojan horse) is contained or mentioned in other works of literature.

The *Odyssey* belongs to a category of epics called *nostoi,* or "returns," which tell about the return of various Greek heroes from the Trojan War. It tells the story of Odysseus, the wily rogue and king of Ithaca, who struggles to bring himself and his crew home through a gauntlet of fantastic adventures, including a voyage to the Land of the Dead. Bad luck, bad choices, and unfortunate dining decisions cost him his crew and leave him the shipwrecked prisoner of a solitary island nymph, Calypso.

The gods, however, with the aid of a marvelous seafaring people, help him to return home, only to find his wife (Penelope), son (Telemachus), and household under threat from a very unsociable group of suitors (that considers Penelope to be an eligible widow). Disguised as a beggar, Odysseus conspires with Telemachus to clean house and, with the help of Athena, to massacre the suitors. In the end, Odysseus is reunited with Penelope, who has faithfully kept the suitors at bay by guile and denial. Myth, epic, and folktale combine in a story that is at times humorous, at times horrific, and at times utterly human in its examination of choice, responsibility, coming home, growing up, and perseverance.

There were other epic poems from the time of Homer, but these works are either lost or come to us only in fragments quoted by other authors. None were as highly esteemed as the *Iliad* and the *Odyssey*, but other authors, such as the dramatists, took information and ideas from them. Later authors created epic poems as well, but these poems are valued more for their information than their literary merit. An exception is the story of Jason and the Argonauts, the *Argonautica*, written by Apollonius of Rhodes in the third century B.C.E.

Hesiod and Homeric Hymns

The other major figure of early Greek literature is the poet Hesiod (c. 700 B.C.E.), who created two great poems: the *Theogony* and the *Works and Days*. Hesiod was a curmudgeon—sour, dour, and pessimistic—but with good reason: He was cheated out of his inheritance by his brother Perses and the governing magistrate.

The *Theogony* tells of the birth of the gods and Zeus' rise to power, including the story of Prometheus' theft of fire and the creation of Pandora. Besides bringing together earlier traditions, it suggests that Zeus (and justice) will triumph in the end.

Lexica

Didactic means "tending or intending to teach."

The *Works and Days* is a *didactic* poem about work and values. After moralizing to Perses about the need for every man to work for his *own* living, and slamming the "bribe-swallowing" magistrates, Hesiod details the why, when, and how of farm work. This poem contains illustrative myths (Pandora and the "five ages of man") as well.

In addition to the works of Hesiod, we have a collection of hymns (mainly from the seventh and sixth centuries B.C.E.) that were written for and performed at various religious festivals. These hymns, written in Homeric style, contain fundamental myths about Greek gods such as Demeter, Hermes, Apollo, and Dionysus. Their authors also recited Homer's texts for these festivals, and so were called *Homeridai*, or "sons of Homer." Because of these stylistic and artistic connections, the hymns are called the *Homeric Hymns*.

Lyric and Other Poetry

The Greeks created a wide range of poetry that was meant to be sung and accompanied by music and, at times, dance. We generally call this lyric poetry (to be accompanied by the lyre), although it takes many forms beyond true lyric. Such poetry was a facet of aristocratic culture: Aristocrats, including female poets such as Sappho, Corinna, and Praxilla, explored personal viewpoints, celebrated their public and private achievements, and publicly conveyed traditions and ideas through these art forms. Some major forms and authors include the following:

◆ **Monody.** Works to be sung or read by one person. Monody developed into an intensely personal aristocratic poetry that explored, taught, celebrated, and critiqued the personal aspects of love, obligation, hatred, duty, and experience. Poets to look for include Sappho, Alcaeus, Corinna, Praxilla, Anacreon, and Simonides of Ceos.

◆ **Choral lyric.** Works to be performed and sung by choirs at public events such as festivals, funerals, and weddings. Look especially for Alcman, Stesichorus, Ibycus, Pindar, and Bacchylides.

◆ **Epinician.** An *ode* composed in celebration of a victor at a competition (also known as a victory ode). The most famous of these works are composed by the poets Pindar and Bacchylides. Other forms of praise poetry are the paean and eulogy.

Lexica

Ode is a general term for a poetic song.

◆ **Iambic.** A meter (the "foot" is short-long) with a short temper. Aristocrats used iambic poetry to engage in scathing satire, personal attacks, and general criticisms. Look for Archilochus, Semonides of Amorgos, and Solon. Iambic meters were later used by dramatists for writing dialogue in tragedy and comedy.

◆ **Elegiac.** A two-line (couplet) verse based on epic meter, and originally associated with the flute (instead of the lyre). Elegiac poems were the most popular of poetic forms and the most diverse in subject matter. Look for Callinus, Archilochus, Tyrtaeus, Mimnermus, and Simonides of Ceos. A very short elegiac poem is known as an epigram.

Dramatic Poetry and Its Context

The famous forms of Greek drama, tragedy, and comedy, were—quite literally—poetry in motion. They grew out of choral poetry that was performed (sung and

CAUTION

Labyrinths _____

To modern readers, the choral odes of ancient Greek tragedy and comedy often seem confusing and superfluous. They are, however, the foundation from which more familiar dramatic elements (such as dialogue and action) grew.

danced) at agricultural festivals. Over time, poets developed poetic dialogue between individual characters, in addition to the choral songs and dances, to tell their stories.

The famous tragedies and comedies of ancient Greece were produced in Athens during the fifth century B.C.E., and they were part of state-sponsored dramatic competitions during three-day festivals to the god Dionysus. Each day, 15,000 to 17,000 Athenians would gather in the outdoor theater to see a tragic poet and his producer put on three tragedies (plus a satyr play, which will be explained in the next section) in the morning, and a comic poet and his producer put on a comedy in the afternoon. At the end of the festival, a panel of judges ranked the competitors in each category, 1-2-3.

Classical tragedies and comedies weren't originally designed to be timeless literature. The plays were one-time-only productions, written specifically for the Athenians. Indeed, it was illegal until later in the fifth century to reproduce plays for competition. But the best of these works captured timeless and universal themes in such beautiful poetry and stunning drama that they far outlived their intended venue.

Tragedy and Satyr Plays

A tragedy is a play that deals with human suffering. This suffering can be brought on by a variety of factors: lack of knowledge, arrogance, fate, unintended or unexpected consequences, a capricious universe, or just plain bad luck. In any case, the suffering (as far as the characters of the drama are concerned) is inescapable and inordinate. Plots generally came from the epic cycles, but sometimes (like with Aeschylus' *Persians*) they came from historical moments that were thought to be weighty and monumental enough for the tragic stage.

Eureka! _____

It is traditionally held that, about 534 B.C.E., the poet Thespis first wrote and performed a part separate from the tragic chorus. He became the first "actor," and this is why we sometimes refer to stage actors as thespians.

Tragedies had a maximum of 3 actors (speakers) and a chorus of 12 that carried out the dialogue, song, and dance. Extras played silent roles (like soldiers or slaves). Tragedies were produced in sets of three, all by a single playwright. A satyr play is a short and lighthearted play (a kind of comic relief, which followed the trilogy of tragedies and had a similar theme) that features a chorus of half-men, half-goat creatures called satyrs.

There were many tragic poets, but three achieved lasting fame:

◆ **Aeschylus** (c. 525–456 B.C.E.) was the first great Athenian tragedian. He introduced the use of a second actor, and wrote more than 70 tragedies famous for their grandeur, depth, and (even to the Athenians!) nearly incomprehensibly thick imagery. Aeschylus died in Sicily, writing plays for the ruler of Syracuse. We have only a handful of his works, the most famous of which is the *Oresteia* (the plays *Agamemnon*, *Libation Bearers*, and *Eumenides*), the only complete tragic trilogy to survive.

◆ **Sophocles** (c. 496–406 B.C.E.) was (and is) the most famous of the tragic poets and the tragedian *par excellence* for nearly everyone from Aristotle forward. Sophocles wrote more than 100 plays in his long and productive career, many featuring monumental heroes and heroines. His most well-known plays, known as the *Theban Plays* (*Antigone*, *Oedipus the King*, and *Oedipus at Colonus*), are from the Theban Cycle and about the family of Oedipus.

> **CAUTION**
>
> **Labyrinths**
>
> Although the Theban Plays are usually read as if they go together, each play belongs to a different, and widely separated, trilogy. *Antigone* (last in dramatic chronology) was produced first in 441 B.C.E., *Oedipus the King* around 426 B.C.E., and *Oedipus at Colonus* (produced posthumously by Sophocles' grandson) in 401 B.C.E.

◆ **Euripides** (c. 485–406 B.C.E.) was the most radical of the three great tragedians and wrote plays that challenged the accepted limits and conventions of the Athenian stage. His vivid portrayals of emotion and female characters, his questioning of traditional ideas and values, and his characters' use of rhetorical argumentation made him a figure of controversy in his day and a favorite of many modern critics. Some of his most famous plays include the *Medea*, *Bacchae*, *Hippolytus*, and *Alcestis*.

Comedy Old and New

Ancient Greece is famous for two very different kinds of comedy. Comedies known as "Old comedy" were produced in Athens during the same time and for the same festivals as were the great tragedies. Old comedy uses fantastic ideas (such as escaping Athens to a bird-city in the sky, or going to Hades to bring back a good poet from the dead) to attack real problems and real people (who were sitting in the audience!). It is aggressive, satiric, and shockingly brazen, and its often obscene humor advocates change. Only one playwright, Aristophanes (c. 450–385 B.C.E.), survives. His most famous plays include the *Clouds* (featuring Socrates), *Birds*, *Lysistrata*, and *Frogs*.

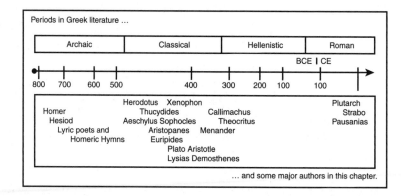

> ### Eureka!
>
> Aristophanes' play *Lysistrata* features the women of Greece, who take over the state treasuries and go on a sex strike to force their warring, pig-headed husbands to make peace. It isn't long before it's too hard for the men to go on and peace is restored. A worldwide network of theater and community groups (in 59 countries and all 50 U.S. states) organized 1,029 readings of this funny and famous play on March 3, 2003, to protest the pending invasion of Iraq. (www.pecosdesign.com/lys/about.html)

"New comedy" was produced for a very different world order in the fourth and third centuries B.C.E. New comedy is "situation comedy," and uses representative characters and their foibles to cajole, chagrin, and reassure the audience into realizing that certain norms really are necessary and good. New comedy is the source for most popular comedy from Shakespeare to *The Simpsons*.

The most famous playwright of this style was Menander (c. 344–292 B.C.E.), but only one complete play, the *Dyskolos* (the "Grouch"), survives. Other plays were adapted by the famous Latin comic writers Plautus and Terrence.

Periods in Greek literature …

Archaic	Classical	Hellenistic	Roman

BCE | CE

800 700 600 500   400   300   200 100   100

Homer
Hesiod
Lyric poets and
Homeric Hymns

Herodotus Xenophon
Thucydides   Callimachus
Aeschylus Sophocles   Theocritus
Aristopanes Menander
Euripides
Plato Aristotle
Lysias Demosthenes

Plutarch
Strabo
Pausanias

… and some major authors in this chapter.

The Power of Prose

Poetry had the authority of tradition and (sometimes divine) inspiration from the oral past. Even with the advent of writing, prose was for lists (of rules, of jars in the palace storeroom, and of other such things) and other mundane human concerns—if you had something to write on. However, the ancient Greeks turned this lack of received authority into a strength. Freed from the constraints of traditional authority, prose became the literary medium for human inquiries that were based on the authority of experience and reason: history, philosophy, and rhetoric. Eventually it also became the medium for literature based openly on human imagination: fiction.

Here, we'll deal a bit with history and philosophy texts *as literature.* There's more in Chapter 3 on these subjects as inquiry.

History or Histrionics? The Dramatic Past

Greek history emerged from its epic roots at the same time that the great tragedies were being performed and rhetoric was beginning to flourish. Authors used the conventions of epic, drama, and rhetoric to create vivid, literary, historical narratives. Although what emerges is often gripping, it is rarely "historical" to the degree that we might hope for. Here are some things to look for in the two foundational authors:

- **Herodotus** (c. 480–420 B.C.E.) wrote to investigate and explain the causes and outcomes of the Persian War. Because he called his work *historia,* or "inquiry," he has been called the father of history. His work, however, is epic and dramatic in scope. As in epics and dramas, fate, the gods, and human character are central players; great characters (some anachronistically placed for effect) play their heroic or tragic roles on the stage of human events. For these reasons, Herodotus was also called the father of lies by those who demanded more accuracy or who disagreed with his claims and ideas.

- **Thucydides** (c. 460–400 B.C.E.) fought in and wrote about the Peloponnesian War, and he is the father of "scientific" history. (That is, he claims to write only about that which he either knows firsthand or has verified.) His stark and concise style is the intentional antithesis of Herodotus' dramatic style. But there is one area in which Thucydides admits taking liberties: in his renditions of the rhetorical speeches given by historical characters. Here, he brings rhetoric to bear on history and its players, and he uses it brilliantly (sometimes creating speeches, sometimes adapting what was actually said) to portray what he saw as timeless historical truths at work in human events.

Odysseys
If you visit Herodotus' hometown of Halicarnassus (modern Bodrun, Turkey, right across from the Greek island of Cos), you can enjoy a nice promenade with the father of history, visit Bodrun's fine Underwater Archeology Museum, and see the site of one of the "wonders of the ancient world": King Mausolus of Caria's (c. 377–353 B.C.E.) burial monument, the Mausoleum. Earthquakes and crusaders damaged and dismantled the structure, but it's still worth a visit.

Examples, Experts, and Guides for the *Idiotes*

Prose also became the medium for the development of literary forms both about and by specific individuals: biography, memoir, and treatises on specific subjects (like the one you're reading!). Biography was a natural development of history and the Greeks' interest in character. As all aspects of public and private life became objects of study and subjects of applied theory, experts (both recognized and self-proclaimed) created works about them. Here are four representative authors of such works, widely separated by time:

- **Xenophon** (c. 430–354 B.C.E.) stands at the beginning of these developments. He was an eclectic Athenian aristocrat and mercenary who was banished from Athens and spent his remaining years among the Spartans. His historical works include the *Hellenica*, which follows Thucydides' work, and the *Anabasis*, a memoir of his adventures as a mercenary in the East. He wrote idealized biographical works and memoirs about Socrates, the Persian king Cyrus, and the Spartan king Agesilaus. Xenophon also published works on politics, household management, public finance, horsemanship (on which he was an expert), and hunting.

- The authors **Strabo** (c. 64 B.C.E.–21 C.E.) and **Pausanias** (second century C.E.) helped to address a growing world consciousness. Strabo published a geographical description of the world of his day, and Pausanias brought the traveling public one of the first great forerunners to the travel guide: *Descriptions of Greece*.

- **Plutarch** (c. 46–120 C.E.) was a Greek teacher, diplomat, and *prolific* author (more than 270 works are attributed to him!) under the Roman Empire. He chose to convey his philosophical, religious, scientific, political, and literary wisdom mostly in the form of dialogues or diatribes (the *Moralia*), but he is best known for his paired biographies of famous Greek and Roman statesmen, called the *Parallel Lives*.

Philosophic Dialogues and the Search for Truth

Socrates (c. 469–399 B.C.E.) may be a pivotal figure in Greek philosophy, but he wrote nothing down. We wouldn't have any real idea of what he was about if not for the philosophical dialogues of Plato (c. 428–348 B.C.E.), Socrates' pupil and admirer. Fortunately for Socrates, Plato was a gifted writer (as well as, presumably, a good conversationalist).

Plato created literary dialogues that show Socrates engaging, challenging, and quite often annoying important and influential people of his day. Some dialogues show Socrates speaking on (and on), while his listener seems to say little more than "Yes, Socrates," "Certainly, Socrates," or, with some reluctance, "Apparently, Socrates." But the dialogues are brilliant literature in and of themselves: descriptive, witty, observant, and dramatic.

Works that are well known for their literary as well as philosophical contributions are the *Euthyphro, Apology, Crito,* and *Phaedo* (dialogues covering Socrates' trial and execution), the *Symposium* (the drinking party at which Socrates discusses the nature of beauty and love with the likes of the comic poet Aristophanes and the renegade aristocrat Alcibiades), and the *Republic* (in which Socrates discusses the nature of justice as it pertains to both humans and the ideal city). Plato is also famous for his creation and use of myth, metaphor, and allegory in philosophy: the "Allegory of the Cave" and the "Myth of Er" (in the *Republic*), as well as the myth of Atlantis (in the *Timaeus* and *Critias*), are particularly fine examples.

The Power of Persuasion: Rhetoric and Rhetoricians

The ancient Greeks celebrated the spoken word, and some of their best literature features characters speaking in their own voices. They were fascinated by the ability of language to convey the thoughts and emotions of the speaker, and the power of language to affect the thoughts and emotions of the hearer.

A cultivated ability to speak well was admired as early as the *Iliad*. However, with the development of democratic courts and assemblies in the fifth century B.C.E., effective communication became a necessary skill for successful participation in the state. Teachers took up the task of teaching the art of persuasion, and Greek literature of the period is full of references to, criticism of, and reverence for it. The study of the theory and practice of effective communication (in oral or written form) became known as rhetoric late in the fifth or early in the fourth century B.C.E., and rhetoric remained an indelible part of Greco-Roman education, which was passed on to the Middle Ages and the Renaissance.

> **Muses**
>
> The spoken word is a mighty lord who, though having a minute and invisible body, can do works that are godlike: expel fear, wipe away grief, instill pleasure and enhance pity.
>
> —Gorgias, *Helen*, 8–14

Rhetorical compositions, whether working speeches or compositions of a more fictional nature, make for wonderful literature. Here are some famous authors and examples to look for and to keep in mind:

- **Gorgias** came to Athens from Sicily in 427 B.C.E. and created a stir with his use of language and argumentation. His most famous work is *The Encomium of Helen*, in which he argues that Helen is morally blameless for the Trojan War.

- **Demosthenes** (384–322 B.C.E.) was the most famous speaker of antiquity. He was vehemently opposed to the interests of Philip II of Macedon, and his speeches concerning his own activities in this regard (such as the *Philippics*, *Olynthiacs*, and *On the Crown*) are his most famous. Demosthenes' worthy opponent, the orator **Aeschines** (c. 390–after 330 B.C.E.), is also someone to look for.

- **Attic orators.** We also possess a collection of other well-known Athenian orators. (Because Athens is in Attica, they are called "Attic Orators.") The most famous of these is the orator **Lysias** (c. 459–380 B.C.E.).

Rhetorical speeches were also delivered in public ceremonies as carefully crafted showpieces or as demonstrations of extemporaneous rhetorical genius. The most famous of these (such as those by **Aristides**, c. 129–189 C.E.) come from a period of Greek literary revival, in the second century C.E., called the Second Sophistic.

The Popular Press: Novella and Other Fiction

From the late fifth century B.C.E. onward, the development of writing for communication in Greece not only brought forth prose works of "serious" literature, but also literature that appealed to an increasingly literate public. And what does the public want? Socratic dialogues? Aristotle's *Physics*? Plutarch's *Moralia*? We think not. They want romance, adventure, buxom (yet virtuous) maidens swooning over misunderstood bad boys, oracles, miracles, exotic lands, thrills, chills, and spills—essentially the same things that you'll find at the checkout stand today.

The roots of the romantic novel come from such writers as Xenophon of Ephesus (probably before 263 C.E.), and probably developed from the semi-historical, semi-mythical accounts of legendary heroes and famous men that were popular during the first century B.C.E. The novels that we have—about five of them—come from the second century C.E. Whereas Xenophon of Ephesus wrote what is often considered to be the weakest of the existing novels, you'll find everything you're looking for in Chariton's *Chaereas and Challirhoe*, Heliodorus' *An Ethiopian Tale*, Longus' *Daphnis and Chloe*, and Achilles Tatius' *Leucippe and Clitophon*.

Art and Sculpture

Besides their literary legacy, the ancient Greeks created artistic works that captured the imagination and admiration of generations. These works illustrated many of the concerns and themes that pervaded the culture of their day and provide us with an enriched understanding of what the Greeks were about.

Vase and Mural Painting

The artistic and technical evidence left by pottery is often the most complete and useful we have for understanding ancient cultures. We use pottery to date archeological sites, track cultural influences, and chart trade routes. The functional and beautiful designs of the vessels themselves, as well as the pictures and designs glazed onto them, create an aesthetic window into a culture's creativity and artistic concerns. The pottery of the ancient Greeks is a visually stunning record of their historical development, and often the only visual record we have of their daily lives.

Labyrinths _____

Neither the serene white buildings nor the marble statues that we associate with Greek and Roman sculpture originally appeared as they do today: Buildings such as the Parthenon were brightly painted, and sculptures were painted and (often) robed.

Greek pottery has three main phases that you should know:

- ◆ **The "geometric" period** (Dark Age into early Archaic period). During this time, Greek artists moved from creating intricate geometric designs to including primitive, but powerful, depictions of animals and group scenes.

- ◆ **Corinthian and *black figure*** (middle Archaic period). The city of Corinth was a trading powerhouse in perfume and pottery. It developed a distinctive decorative style called black figure. This style was adopted, developed, and perfected by the Athenians, who captured the market by about 550 B.C.E.

Black figure pottery is dramatic and clean. Its themes move, along with the concerns of literature of the Archaic period, from mainly mythological and epic motifs early in the period to more personal scenes of aristocratic life.

Lexica _____

Black figure was a technique where the figures (such as designs or people) were painted in black silhouette and the details cut through them into the red clay. **Red figure** was the opposite: The figures were left red against a black background with details painted in with a fine brush.

- ◆ ***Red figure*** (late Archaic period, c. 530 B.C.E, onward). The Athenians developed this method to allow for more artistic control and expression, and it eventually supplanted the black figure technique. Mythological motifs remain strong, but there are also a large number of scenes showing men and women of all social classes and occupations at home, at work, and at play. For the most part, these images are our only window into domestic life and the lives of women.

Artistically, red figure pottery is about humans in action and it reflects the Classical period's consideration of the ideal human figure in motion and in space. Landscapes and other accompanying figures, such as animals, receive little attention by comparison.

Odysseys

If you go to the ruins of Mycenae (the city of Agamemnon) in southern Greece, you'll find the earliest example of western monumental sculpture, the famous Lion Gate.

As artistic focus moved toward the exploration of individuality (features) and emotion, artistic innovation and impetus moved away from and out of pottery (which didn't lend itself to such material) and into sculpture and murals (wall painting), where new techniques and mediums made depictions of these elements more effective. No murals survive, but we do know that realistic expression and emotion, shadow and depth, and movement were artistic elements.

Sculpture

The Greeks are most famous, artistically, for their sculpture. Greek *freestanding* sculpture gets revitalized in the Archaic period under Egyptian influence. Stylized and stiff *monumental* statues of young men and women (*kouroi*) in stone or bronze gradually give way to figures that are more realistic and accurate. In the same way, the figures of *relief sculpture* showing mythological scenes on temples became more accurate, detailed, and animated.

Lexica

Kouroi are **monumental** (life-size or larger) statues of men (*kouroi*) or women (*korai*). **Chryselephantine** statues are monumental statues made of ivory (for flesh) and gold (for drapery) over a framework of wood. These statues were finished on all sides, or **freestanding. Relief sculpture** projects from, but is not free from, the background from which it has been cut.

From the mid-fifth century B.C.E. (following the Persian War) into the fourth century B.C.E, Greek sculpture underwent a creative explosion. Artists developed new techniques in marble and bronze to create realistic works that captured the essential characteristics (harmony, balance, and proportion) of their subjects in movement or physical tension. They also brought these skills to bear in the grand relief and *chryselephantine* sculptures that adorned temples such as the Temple of Zeus in Olympia and the Parthenon in Athens. In the Hellenistic period, sculpture explored how to portray and convey the unique qualities of individuals (both kingly and common) and particular emotions.

Some important names in sculpture are ...

- **Myron** (mid-fifth century B.C.E.) created dramatically realistic bronzes. Athenians said his bronze cow on the Acropolis was often mistaken for a real animal. His *diskobolos* ("discus thrower"), known to us through Roman copies (such as at the *Museo Nazional* in Rome), has been one of the most admired sculptures since antiquity for its capture of tension and movement.

- **Phidias** (c. 490–430 B.C.E.) created the most famous grand sculptures of antiquity. He directed and supervised the sculptural development of the Parthenon. His great creations are the 30-foot-high bronze statue of Athena on the Acropolis, and the chryselephantine statues of Athena Parthenos (38 feet) and of Zeus (42 feet) for their temples in Athens and Olympia, respectively. This last statue, his masterpiece, was regarded as one of the "wonders of the world." No original work survives, though there are small copies of his Athena Parthenos.

- **Polycleitus** (working from 452–405 B.C.E.), a younger contemporary of Phidias, had an immense popularity during and after his lifetime. He specialized in statues of Olympic victors, and numerous Hellenistic and Roman copies of his work survive. He worked mainly in bronze, but he also carved statues in marble and made the chryselephantine statue of Hera for the temple at Argos.

- **Praxiteles** (mid-fourth century B.C.E.) was renowned for his ability to capture emotion and intimacy in supple figures. These attributes are apparent in the famous Hermes Carrying Dionysus, discovered at Olympia in 1877, and copies of Aphrodite of Cnidos (at the Vatican), which was the first sculpture to show Aphrodite naked.

- **Lysippus** (mid-fourth century B.C.E.) was admired for his lithe figures, detail, and ability to capture an individual subject in a momentary look or gesture. He was the only sculptor allowed to depict Alexander the Great. His works survive in copies, such as Hermes with the Sandal at the Louvre.

The Least You Need to Know

- Greek literature and art follow, respond to, and reflect similar currents in Greek thought and culture.

- Greek poetry includes epic (the *Iliad* and *Odyssey*), hymns, drama (tragedy and comedy), and many varieties of personal and public lyric poetry.

- Greek prose developed into literature of human intellectual exploration such as history, philosophy, science, rhetoric, and fiction.

- To understand the ancient Greeks, you have to be familiar with (and better yet read!) Homer.

- The artistic and technical evidence left by pottery is often the most complete and useful we have for understanding ancient cultures.

- The Greeks are most famous, artistically, for their sculpture.

Chapter 3

Classical Analysis: Greek History, Philosophy, Science, and Architecture at a Glance

In This Chapter

- Major Greek intellectual trends from the Archaic period through the Hellenistic period
- Important figures of ancient Greek philosophy, history, science, and architecture
- The major Greek philosophical schools

Besides being famous for their inspired literature and poetry, the ancient Greeks are renowned for intellectual achievements and approaches that helped create the foundations of western science (natural and social), medicine, philosophy, and architecture. They also influenced the development of Islamic thought. As western and Islamic culture mingled with world culture, this influence continued to spread.

But there is more to the ancient Greeks than the influences they had on our past. The kinds of questions that they asked—"What are the causes, origin, and nature of being, reality, and movement?" "What can we know and how can we know it?" "How should one live?"—are relevant in all times and ages. More importantly, their approach to inquiry and the spirit in which they answered these questions remain remarkably fresh, insightful, and productive.

We would leave you with the wrong impression, however, if we tried to reduce these areas and figures to sound bites. So, let us begin by giving you some guidance in understanding their projects—what they were trying in the main to do and what they were primarily concerned with—and by discussing their major accomplishments.

Think About It: Philosophy

From our experience, the word *philosophy* seems to strike terror in the hearts of students, numbness in the minds of adults, and a degree of hostility in nearly everyone that is seldom evoked by other disciplines. If any of this describes you, please take comfort in the fact that philosophy has evoked similar reactions since, at the very least, the time of Socrates. But, don't get *too* comfortable. The idea that philosophy is a nit-picking, pointless mind game that is intended to confuse and irritate good people may be reassuring, but it is pure nonsense. Philosophy was—and, very importantly, remains—a process of rigorous inquiry and structured argumentation through which human assumptions, opinions, and beliefs can be revealed and examined. It was—and is—the attempt to ground human knowledge in truth, to formulate coherent and consistent systems of belief, and to understand what it means to live an ethical, authentic, and meaningful human life. Its willingness to pursue questions that challenge our preconceptions and beliefs, and to entertain answers that threaten our personal understanding of the world, often creates deep discomfort. But, given an opportunity, the discomfort tends to give way to a deeper and enriched understanding of ourselves and the cosmos.

Before we take a look at the history of this full-contact sport, let's break down philosophy into three major areas of inquiry that occupied, to various degrees, the ancient Greek philosophers. Each is listed by its current name, its area of concern, and the kind of question it addresses:

Eureka!

The term *metaphysics* comes from the placement of an Aristotelian manuscript by Hellenistic scholars: "after" (*meta*) his work on "physics" (*physica*). Because of the relationship in ideas between the *metaphysics* and the *physics*, *meta* (as in metatheory or metalogic) has come to indicate a larger context into which ideas or phenomena can be fitted and through which they can be explained or justified.

◆ **Metaphysics (existence, being, and reality).** What is the nature of being and reality?

◆ **Epistemology (knowledge).** What can we know and how can we know it?

◆ **Ethics (living well and flourishing as a human).** How should one live? (Not, as is often the case in modern ethics, What should one do?)

Are these questions settled? Well, let's get started.

Presocratic Philosophy

Presocratic (coming before Socrates) philosophers are also called "natural" philosophers because they were concerned with the nature of reality, the physical world, and explanations for change (movement, mutation, and so forth). In our terms, their projects were primarily metaphysical/scientific (What is the origin and composition of the universe, and how does it function?) and epistemological (Should we rely on our senses or on our reason to gain knowledge of ourselves and our world?), and they come out of the movement we know as Ionian rationalism (since several of the Presocratic philosophers came from Ionia). In some cases, such as with Democritus (and later, Epicurus), their conclusions also led to ethical considerations. For more information on natural philosophy, see Chapter 10.

In natural philosophy, we see two of the fundamental assumptions that pervade Greek thought coming to bear on the natural world. The first is the belief that, if we wish to understand something thoroughly, we must understand its beginning or origin. The second is that a reasoned explanation of the causes (*aitia*) of things is both possible and profitable. Some of the natural philosophers' explanations and conclusions may seem a bit odd, but bear in mind that we have only very small fragments or secondhand paraphrases of their writings. Other explanations and conclusions, such as early versions of atomic and evolutionary theory, might be surprisingly familiar. Here are some of the major figures and their areas of inquiry:

> **Lexica**
>
> *Aitia* (or *aetia*) is the Greek word for "reason/cause," as in (a)etiology, the study or history of cause and effect. Causes were a major concern not only for the Presocratics, but also for the historians Herodotus and Thucydides.

◆ **What's the matter?** Early Presocratics sought to identify a primary material substance of the universe. Thales (fl. 585 B.C.E.) thought it had to be a liquid (water), Anaximander (c. 610–546 B.C.E.) a "limitless" substance (he also believed that all life comes from the sea and that the present forms of animals evolved by means of adapting to their environments), and Anaximenes (fl. 546 B.C.E.) a vapor (air).

Eureka!

Because Anaxagoras (c. 500–428 B.C.E.) taught that the sun is a red-hot stone and the moon is made of earth, he was the first philosopher to be tried and condemned on charges of impiety. He was saved by Pericles and went into exile. Galileo met similar resistance when he reported that the moon's surface looked imperfect (rather than divinely perfect) through his telescope.

Labyrinths

Democritus' atomism is different from modern atomic theory, and his view of humans (body and soul are composed of atoms) seems to eliminate the possibility of free choice. According to Democritus, perception occurs when atoms from objects strike the sense organs, which in turn strike atoms of the soul. Death is merely the dissipation of soul atoms when the body atoms no longer hold them together.

◆ **Spare change?** Nothing comes from nothing, and Being, the One, already *is*. Yet change is all around us. Thus, Parmenides (fl. c. 485 B.C.E.) concluded that change, or becoming, is an illusion. In contrast, Heraclitus (fl. 500 B.C.E.) embraced change as a constant movement between opposites within an ordered, reasonable cosmological system. For Heraclitus, "It is not possible to step twice into the same river."

◆ **A composite universe?** In the Classical period, similar questions and concerns (i.e., about the composition and workings of the universe) were addressed by more sophisticated theories—ones that include more than one primary substance and add forces that combine and separate the different materials, creating various forms. Empedocles (c. 484–424 B.C.E.) postulated four elements, earth, air, fire, water, and two forces, love and strife; Anaxagoras (c. 500–428 B.C.E.) postulated an infinite number of material particles or "seeds"; and Democritus (c. 460–370 B.C.E.) postulated an infinite number of tiny "un-cut-ables," *atomoi* or "atoms," that combine in different patterns to form the material objects of the observable world). These philosophers all developed complex theories that had scientific and ethical implications and outgrowths.

Personal Trainer

As the center of political and intellectual thought, classical Athens drew experts to town who claimed to be able to teach the "skills" (*technai*) that young men needed to think, speak, and live successfully. These experts came to be called Sophists (literally, "wise-guys" or "learned experts"). For the most part, the Sophists were more concerned with practical success than with either speculation or natural philosophy. Sophists generally held that knowledge is situational or relative, and they used rhetorical argumentation to point out contradictions in traditional values and knowledge.

They argued that these traditions were grounded more in "convention" (*nomos*) than in "nature" (*physis*). Traditionalists saw the Sophists' teachings as a challenge to their authority and values, whereas Socrates and Plato saw the Sophists and their pupils, at least for the most part, as ignorant of what they were claiming to know and to teach.

Despite bad press, the Sophists were popular and influential in their day. Of the fifth century B.C.E., Protagoras (c. 490–420 B.C.E.) and Gorgias (c. 483–376 B.C.E.) are the most famous (and treated by Plato in dialogues that bear their names); of the fourth century B.C.E., Isocrates (c. 436–338 B.C.E.), the rhetorician who created a kind of cross between a school and a public relations firm for clients in Athens, is particularly noteworthy.

From the Top Down: Socrates, Plato, and Neoplatonism

Both the natural philosophers and the Sophists undermined traditional authority and revealed knowledge with their speculative approach (natural philosophers) and association of reason with human endeavors (Sophists). Socrates and Plato, however, equated reason with the divine, and worked to establish a new kind of revealed truth from which all other truth derived. Their ideas, as well as the dualism (mind/body) that these ideas imply, were radical in their day, and they became influential on all further philosophical trends and on early Christianity.

Socrates (c. 469–399 B.C.E.) is famous for his method of "conversation" (*dialektos*) and "cross-examination" (*elenchus*) in coming to, and deepening one's understanding of, the truth. His project, however, was the condition of the soul, which he associated with pure reason and held to be immortal, and he was deeply interested in the question "How should one live?" He sought the universal definition of qualities that improve the soul—such things as virtue, justice, and piety—by questioning and challenging the people (Sophists, politicians, poets, and various experts) who claimed to have, or understand, or teach them. Plato, the Cynics, the Stoics, and the Epicureans all looked to Socrates as their intellectual founder in some way.

Lexica

Dialektos ("conversation") describes a process of synthesis and analysis used to derive understanding. With Aristotle, it became associated with logical argumentation and, in the medieval period, with logic itself.

Socrates called his method (using questions-and-answers to draw out logical inconsistencies) **elenchus** ("cross-examination").

Muses

Socrates busied himself with ethical matters and neglected the world of nature entirely. But seeking the universal in these ethical concerns, he fixed thought for the first time on definitions.

—Aristotle, *Metaphysics* 1.6

Plato (c. 428–348 B.C.E.) is far more difficult to describe. For Plato, the kind of knowledge that Socrates was seeking—indeed, all knowledge that is infallible and of the *real*—is knowledge of universal concepts and ascertainable only by pure reason. Whereas particular situations change, the concept of, say, goodness remains the same, and it is in reference to this stable concept that we judge particular situations to be good. Like Socrates, Plato suggests that the intellectual soul (that is, the rational element in humans) exists prior to birth and survives death.

When the soul is embodied, it already possesses knowledge of universal concepts, but this knowledge must be drawn out, or recollected, through education, reflection, and speculation. For Plato, true knowledge can never be achieved through sense perception of the material world because some concepts (such as the conclusions of mathematics) cannot be apprehended through sense perception and because sense perception can be deceptive and illusory. Because Plato's epistemology is nearly impossible to separate from his metaphysics, although his project centers on knowledge, it involves the existence and apprehension of universal concepts, a developing theory of human psychology and the human soul, and implications for living a full and ethical life.

Plato's interests, however, went beyond pure speculation and theory. Dismayed by Socrates' execution, Plato envisioned an ideal human society (in the *Republic*), ruled by philosopher kings (and, perhaps, queens), in which all human beings would live and work in accordance with (and limited by) their intellectual and physical capacities. Only those individuals who had attained knowledge—philosophers like himself and Socrates—would be entrusted with a comprehensive understanding of, and control of, the society. Plato knew well the power of metaphor and myth in establishing the "divine" truths and traditions that he criticized, and he skillfully used many of these same elements to convey his own ideas and to imbue them with authority.

Plato's views and ideas continued to evolve throughout his lifetime and, as a result, there is no static Platonic philosophy. Indeed, scholars still study the order of his works to better understand the development of his thought. He established a school in Athens (the Academy) that endured until 529 C.E., when it was closed by the Roman emperor Justinian. The late Hellenistic development of Platonism, Neoplatonism, was extremely influential on early Christian thought (especially on Augustine). Its chief proponent was Plotinus (c. 205–270 C.E.).

From the Bottom Up: Aristotle and the Peripatetics

Aristotle (c. 384–322 B.C.E.), Plato's most famous pupil, is also the most difficult to summarize. Although he studied under Plato, Aristotle came to sharply disagree with Plato's ideas, and he remarks, "While both are dear, piety requires us to honor truth above our friends." About 343 B.C.E., Aristotle was called to Macedon by King Philip II to tutor his son, the future Alexander the Great, and several years later, when Alexander became his father's regent, Aristotle returned to Athens and founded his own school, the Lyceum. Philosophers associated with the Lyceum were called Peripatetics. Aristotle published a large number of works, but these texts are lost. Today only portions of his lecture notes remain—yes, *The Complete Works of Aristotle* are his lecture notes! His most famous works concern ethics, politics, metaphysics, rhetoric, and poetics, but other works branch out into nearly every area of human inquiry and experience.

In *very* general terms, if you think of Plato's project as involving eternal and unchanging knowledge, you might think of Aristotle's project as involving actualizing potential, or becoming. For instance, he saw purpose and potential in everything from inanimate objects to human beings to planetary movements, and he sought to identify and understand the ways in which this potential could be (or was) actualized, or fulfilled. He argued that one's method of inquiry must be appropriate to the subject matter at hand, and he utilized logic, experience, experimentation, practical judgment, and speculation accordingly. (For example, try experimenting on an abstract idea or using untested speculation on a ruptured appendix ... and see how far you get!)

> **Eureka!**
>
> Aristotle, like many professors, paced around when he lectured. That's how his followers came to be called Peripatetics (*peripatetikos* means "meanderer"). Stoics and The Garden (a term for Epicureans) got their names from meeting places (the Stoa Poikile in Athens; Epicurus' garden), whereas the Cynics (*kunikoi* means "dogs") were probably named from the habitat and habits of the infamous Diogenes of Sinope.

For Aristotle, knowledge of such things as mathematics relies on universals, but living well and flourishing as a human being relies on both particular facts and the appropriate use of generalizations and principles. He was deeply concerned about ethics and politics, and he wrote the first systematic ethical treatise (the *Nicomachean Ethics*). He also thought carefully and, in our terms, scientifically about how to accurately categorize the objects of inquiry and how to secure knowledge (or, at times, right opinion) about them. He had a brilliant and exacting mind, and he is the father of botany, zoology, physics, linguistics, logic, literary criticism ... and the list goes on.

Aristotle's project was carried on by Hellenistic scholars, such as his pupil and successor Theophrastus (c. 372–288 B.C.E.), who began specialized work and research in individual areas. Much of this work was done by scholars at the famous Museum and Library of Alexandria. In the early Middle Ages, Aristotle's work was preserved and commented upon by renowned Arab philosophers, and his influence on later medieval philosophy was so great that St. Thomas Aquinas refers to him simply as "The Philosopher."

Epicureans, Stoics, Skeptics, and Cynics

During the late Classical and Hellenistic periods, individuals found themselves adrift, often searching for a sense of control over an increasingly complex and impersonal world. Several philosophical movements developed in reaction to this changing world, and their projects all center on an individual state of "composure" or "inner quietude" (*ataraxia*). The following philosophies gave personal control back to individuals through particular understandings of the universe, human nature, and the relationship between the two:

◆ **Epicureans** believed that the cosmos and nature are merely atoms at work. From their perspective, there is no immortal soul to save, no divine plan or purpose to ascertain, and no religious claims to fret over. Epicureans sought to live in accordance with this understanding of the universe by seeking moderate pleasures in this life. They defined pleasure as the absence of pain (both emotional and physical), and they advocated "natural" pleasures, or those most likely to lead to contentment and repose. Their chief philosopher was Epicurus (341–270 B.C.E.), whose writings exist mainly in the form of letters. The Roman poet Lucretius (c. 94–55 B.C.E.) also wrote a long poetic work (*On the Nature of Things*) on Epicurean philosophy.

◆ **Stoics** believed that human beings can control only one thing: their own reactions. However, in opposition to the Epicureans, they argued that a divinely rational principle, not the random swerving of atoms, determines the cosmos and events (even those that seem terrible). Stoics argued that virtue, rather than pleasure, is the chief good, and they sought a state of calm by living virtuously and rationally in accordance with cosmic order, or with natural law. The originator was Zeno (c. 336–265 B.C.E.). Stoicism was especially appealing to the Romans. The statesman Cicero (106–43 B.C.E.), Seneca (4 B.C.E.–c. 65 C.E.), and the emperor Marcus Aurelius (121–180 C.E.) wrote works on Stoic philosophy.

◆ **Skeptics** claimed that human reason is incapable of providing us with knowledge about the substance of things, and that we can only know how things appear to us, through our senses. Because the same things appear differently to different people, dogmatic claims about what is true or right are always incomplete and capable of contradiction. (Every thesis has its antithesis.) In such circumstances, the best thing to do is maintain an attitude of suspended judgment and, in so doing, attain a state of imperturbable calm. Their originator was Pyrrho (c. 360–270 B.C.E.).

◆ **Cynics** claimed that virtue is wisdom, but this wisdom is expressed in negative terms: It is independence of all possessions and pleasures, the absence of desire, and freedom from wants. The Cynics argued that virtue (as complete independence) is sufficient by itself for happiness. They held that money, power, and passions are not truly good, and that suffering, poverty, and contempt are not truly evil. Virtue consists primarily in seeing through traditional values and, although virtue/wisdom is teachable, it requires little study or contemplation. The wise man stands beyond whatever laws and conventions he rejects, and he cannot be harmed by so-called evils. Living self-sufficiently and independently, focused only on what he truly needs (which is very, very little), the virtuous man lives happily. The most famous Cynic was Diogenes of Sinope (c. 400–325 B.C.E.), who claimed that humans need no more, and should act no differently, than other animals. His brazen behavior (including living in a barrel!) gave the movement its hero and, probably, its name. However, the founder of the school was Antisthenes (c. 445–365 B.C.E.).

> **Eureka!**
>
> Diogenes of Sinope became infamous for his actions (urinating and masturbating in public) and his attitude. A story is told that Alexander the Great once paid him a visit to ask if there was anything he could do for him. Diogenes, who was sunning himself, looked up and dryly replied, "Yeah, step aside. You're blocking my sun."

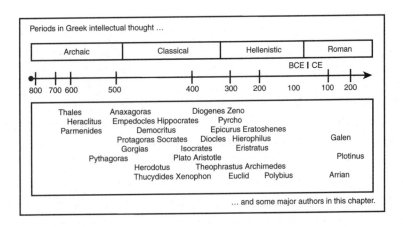

Periods in Greek intellectual thought …

| Archaic | Classical | Hellenistic | Roman |

BCE | CE

800 700 600   500   400   300   200   100   100   200

Thales   Anaxagoras   Diogenes Zeno
   Heraclitus   Empedocles Hippocrates   Pyrcho
Parmenides   Democritus   Epicurus Eratoshenes
          Protagoras Socrates   Diocles Hierophilus   Galen
          Gorgias   Isocrates   Eristratus
     Pythagoras   Plato Aristotle   Plotinus
          Herodotus   Theophrastus Archimedes
          Thucydides Xenophon   Euclid   Polybius   Arrian

… and some major authors in this chapter.

Let's Make History

The project of recording Greek history has roots in epic poetry (to preserve, explain, and interpret the past) and in Ionian rationalism (to develop reasoned explanations that are based on observation). Although precursors to history came through the Presocratics and the travel descriptions of Hecataeus of Miletus, Greek history developed in the fifth century B.C.E. in order to preserve, explain, and interpret the following two great wars:

♦ **The Persian War (490–480 B.C.E.).** The customarily fragmented Greeks unified (for the most part) to achieve a remarkable victory over the Persians. In the process, the underdog Athens and its democracy came to prominence as a naval power. This war was the subject of Herodotus of Halicarnassus (c. 484–425 B.C.E.).

♦ **The Peloponnesian War (431–404 B.C.E.).** Greece was torn apart by a brutal war fought by Athens and Sparta (and their respective allies), which resulted in Athens' eventual defeat. This war was the subject of the Athenian Thucydides (c. 460–400 B.C.E.).

> **Muses**
>
> I, Herodotus of Halicarnassus, here set forth my investigation [*historia*], so that human actions may not fade with time, nor the magnificent accomplishments done by both Greeks and barbarians be forgotten, and, among other things, the reasons [*aitia*] why they fought each other.
>
> —Herodotus, 1.1

> **Eureka!**
>
> *Historia* is Greek for "research" or "investigation," and it was first applied by Herodotus to the events and causes (*aitia*) of what we now call history.

Classical History: Looking for Causes and Diagnosing Cases

Herodotus and Thucydides wrote under the influence of the intellectual currents of their day as these currents applied to the general tone of their subject material. Both sought to preserve events and to explain their causes (*aitia*), and both claimed to provide rational explanations for the causes based on reliable (or supportable) evidence.

Herodotus identified the driving force of history with the interplay of events and character (both personal and ethnic). To illustrate this interplay, he used all the literary tools at his disposal—dramatic dialogue, tragic and epic characters, and grand description—to remarkable effect. He was an engaging storyteller and entertainer. He would have been great, we're sure, at a party! Although he was a rationalist, he was also a traditionalist in many ways: traditional notions of fate, the gods, justice, and suffering color his work.

Thucydides was influenced by the more radical scientific and medical theories of his time. He identified the driving force of history more deeply (and more darkly) with a human nature that is motivated (and can be manipulated) by fear, honor, self-interest, and power. This nature forms the basic nature of human societies. When stressed by illness, conflict, or civil strife, predictable individual and collective behavior results. History is, in this way, a set of case studies that can be analyzed to develop a set of symptoms yielding both a diagnosis of past/present events and a prognosis of future events.

 Muses

These revolutions were the cause of many terrible things in the cities, as happens (and always will) as long as human nature remains constant; though degrees of savagery and, according to circumstances, specific cases will vary somewhat from the general rule.

—Thucydides, 3:82

Biographies, Insights, and Inspiration: Trends from the Hellenistic Period Through the Roman Empire

In the Hellenistic period, historians—following the model of Xenophon (c. 430–354 B.C.E.)—turned toward works of smaller scope: histories of individual cities, or histories of the lives of individuals themselves (biographies). Many of these works were written by specialists, and they were intended to entertain their readers as well as promote their subjects. Most of these works are lost, although some survive in fragments. Influenced by the rhetorical trends of their day, the authors sometimes sacrificed factuality for readability, and they attempted to give readers psychological insights into their subjects. The prolific writer of biographies (and much else), Plutarch (c. 46–120 C.E.), exemplifies this trend in the Roman period.

One exception to this Hellenistic trend is the historian Polybius (c. 203–120 B.C.E.), who attempts to explain another epic subject: the rise of Rome. Polybius was a well-born Greek who, as a captive, spent the second half of his life in the company of Rome's elite during a time of vast conquests. In his *Universal History* (covering 220–144 B.C.E., only parts of which survived), he analyzes Rome's successes as a result of a "mixed" constitution (an Aristotelian idea), and he sees Roman stability as being undermined by some of the same natural forces that Thucydides and the Stoics saw at work. Polybius' somber, pragmatic, and unromantic approach to history can also be seen in the last great Greek historian, Arrian (fl. second century C.E.), who wrote (among other works) a history of Alexander called the *Anabasis*.

Practical Matters: Science and Medicine

Greek science developed to establish working models, based on rational explanations, to explain, predict, and utilize natural phenomena. Because we've already described some of this progression from the natural philosophers to Aristotle's formulation of the sciences, we'll concentrate here on three areas that haven't been mentioned yet: medicine, mathematics, and mechanics.

Healers and Humours: Medicine

All societies possess medical knowledge, traditions, and practices that seek to cope with universal human experiences of illness, injury, suffering, and death. Because explanations for these experiences sometimes overlap with religion, healers often mediate the boundaries of a culture's physical and spiritual realms. Ancient Greece always had a variety of medical practitioners. Medical doctors appear in the *Iliad* and in Herodotus, and we know that, throughout antiquity, towns had home-grown herbalists, midwives, and folk-doctors.

Specialists of the Classical period traveled from town to town treating the ill and the wounded, and they had to compete for business and reputation. Like the natural philosophers, they endeavored to explain the causes of medical illness in terms of mechanistic, physical (not spiritual) processes. They believed that when the natural movement of fluids and vapors (the humours) within the body become blocked, excessive, or unstable, illness results. They attacked traditional folk-practitioners as superstitious quacks and laid great stress on hygiene and diet. As medical theories developed into schools of thought (just as schools of philosophy did) in the later Classical and Hellenistic periods, the schools attacked each other.

> **Muses**
>
> The so-called 'sacred' disease [epilepsy] seems to me not at all more divine or sacred than other diseases, but has a nature from which it originates like the rest of the afflictions. People concoct the idea of its divine origin out of ignorance and wonder because it is so different from other diseases ... But if it were divine because it is wonderful there would be many 'sacred' diseases, not just one; for, as I will demonstrate, there are others no less marvelous which nobody deems sacred.
>
> —*On the Sacred Disease*, 1

The most famous physician of antiquity is Hippocrates of Cos (c. 460–377 B.C.E.), who was known to both Plato and Aristotle. In actuality, however, we know little about him, his life, or his writings. His fame comes from good press (from his home island of Cos) and from becoming, like Socrates, a figure from whom later thinkers claimed intellectual descent. Other famous physicians include Diocles of Carystus (fourth century B.C.E.), and Hierophilus of Chalcedon and Eristratus (both third century C.E.). The most influential was Galen of Pergamum (129–210 C.E.), the personal physician of the Roman emperor Marcus Aurelius. Galen's voluminous works on medical history, philosophy, anatomy, physiology, and therapeutics codified Hippocrates as the "good physician" of the West and remained the basis for European medicine until the 1800s.

Labyrinths

　　Neither the collection of writings known as the Hippocratic Corpus (an anonymous collection of Classical and Hellenistic medical texts) nor the Hippocratic Oath can be securely linked with the actual Hippocrates.

Number Rules

Humanity's fascination with patterns and numbers, and its attempt to use them to comprehend the natural world (especially in astronomy), goes *far* back, well before the Greeks. The Greeks took the beginnings of their scientific knowledge from Egypt and the Near East. Their own approach, however, evolved in concert with the intellectual trends that we have seen at work in philosophy and history. It moved from a search for origins and primary substances in the Archaic period, to the development and application of more sophisticated theories in the Classical period, to the further development of specialized forms in the Hellenistic period.

Presocratic philosophers noted recurring or predictable patterns and relationships in geometric forms and harmonic ratios, which led, in turn, to two avenues of inquiry: 1) Is the world governed by abstract mathematical principles or not (speculative mathematics)? and 2) How can we use this knowledge to do something practical (applied mathematics)? The following is one such inquiry:

- ◆ **The universal formula.** The ancient Greeks' fascination with mathematics (particularly geometry) is a component of their focus on proportion, balance, and harmony. These ideals led some philosophers to attempt to describe the cosmos in idealized mathematical form, and their projects involve explaining both the relationship between number and perceptible objects or properties and the significance of this relationship. The most famous of these philosophers is Pythagoras (c. 571–497 B.C.E.), who is steeped in legend but nonetheless credited with discovering the numerical ratios that determine the principle intervals of the musical scale. Later Pythagoreans developed a geometric solution to quadratic equations and the famous Pythagorean Theorem.

Pythagoras claimed that number is the primary source of reality, and that investigation and contemplation of the nature of reality will lead to a kind of salvation for the soul. His views on the mathematical nature of reality, which bridged religion and mathematics, were highly influential on Plato's work. But other philosophers, in turn, had to develop mathematical models for their own conceptions of the physical universe. Epicureans, for example, whose universe contained an element of chance, had descriptions of atomic interactions that begin to approach chaos theory; and the Stoics, who had a very different idea of the universe, developed their own supportive theories, including physical, logical, and ethical aspects.

The Greeks of the Archaic and Classical periods encountered irrational numbers (such as the square root of two) in geometric forms (particularly spheres, cones, curves) and contemplated concepts of infinity and infinitesimals. In exploring the abstract relations of natural forms, the Hellenistic Greeks made significant advances in geometry and forged paths into abstract algebra and calculus. The most famous authors are as follows:

♦ **Euclid (fl. c. 300 B.C.E.).** Euclid wrote works of elementary (*Elements*) and higher geometry. His work is still taught as Euclidean geometry.

♦ **Archimedes of Syracuse (c. 287–212 B.C.E.).** Archimedes developed the geometrical "method of exhaustion" to approximate *pi* and explore the concepts of limit and infinity. His work, newly recovered in a recent manuscript, anticipates calculus.

♦ **Apollonius of Perga (c. 262–190 B.C.E.).** Apollonius, the last great geometer, wrote the fundamental work on conics. It survives partly in Greek, partly in Arabic translations. In astronomy, he may also have been the inventor of eccentric circles and epicycles.

Eureka!

Other Greek authors have been influential on later giants of mathematics. Fermat (as in Fermat's Last Theorem) was inspired by the problems of Diophantus' *Arithmetica* (fl. 250 C.E.); Descartes by the proofs of Pappus (fl. 300 C.E.).

Number Works

In theorizing about the makeup of the cosmos and the place of the senses, some Greek philosophers had to describe the way that senses such as vision (optics) and sound (acoustics) worked (or didn't). Aristotle was the first to create a systematized theoretical approach to physical science (physics), and most subsequent work in physics was aimed at exploring the properties of physics.

This doesn't mean, however, that the Greeks were only interested in theory! Greeks quickly began to make use of mathematical and geometric formulas for practical purposes. Thales (fl. 585 B.C.E.), for example, used sun and shadow to calculate a pyramid's height, and he is said to have accurately predicted the eclipse of the sun on May 23, 585 B.C.E. Eratosthenes of Cyrene (c. 275–195 B.C.E.) used similar means to calculate the circumference of the earth. Moreover, Greek architecture, city planning, and sculpture depended upon an understanding of geometric formulas and ratios, as well as an understanding of mechanics.

The greatest name in ancient Greek mechanics (and, arguably, the greatest mathematician of antiquity) was the Leonardo da Vinci of antiquity, the eccentric Archimedes of Syracuse (c. 287–212 B.C.E.). Archimedes was primarily interested in pure mathematics, but he was also a prolific inventor. (He is credited with such things as the planetarium, automated toys, washing machines, the compound pulley, the water screw, and automatic door openers.) His work led to other developments in the use of compressed air and steam. He died in Syracuse's fall to the Romans, whom he had helped keep at bay with his huge ballistic catapults.

Standing Order: Greek Architecture

The project of architecture is the design and creation of space (by controlling elements that define it) that mediates a relationship between humans (who inhabit the defined space), the building (the defined space), and the environment (the space around the building). The general Greek perspective that there is an essential framework of balance, proportion, and harmony lying behind natural phenomena (an idea that we've already seen in their literature, philosophy, medicine, and art) manifests itself spectacularly in their monumental architecture. These buildings, an expression of mathematical proportion and harmony, have continued to interest and inspire architects through the ages.

Monumental Order: Greek Temples

Both the Minoans and the Mycenaeans were monumental stone architects, but their knowledge was lost through the Greek Dark Age. The Greeks relearned these skills from the Egyptians (who had been constructing monumental buildings and urban infrastructure for a *long* time) during the eighth century B.C.E. The Greeks, however, based their stone structures on earlier forms constructed of wood, and by the end of the eighth century B.C.E. the Greek temple as we know it was well established. Its form remained unchanged throughout antiquity, although the following three "orders" of temples (based on their columns) developed and were sometimes used to express variations of the temple's themes of stability, order, and balance:

- **Doric.** The Doric order conveyed a solid majesty using thick columns with shallow flutes resting directly on the floor, and featuring a simple capital.

- **Ionic.** The Ionic order conveyed graceful charm by using slender and deeply fluted columns resting on a base, and featuring a delicate scroll-like capital.

- **Corinthian.** The Corinthian order was more decorative and playful than the Ionic by way of an ornate capital carved to resemble an acanthus leaf.

The most famous temples are probably those of Olympian Zeus at Olympia (not standing) and the Parthenon in Athens (mostly intact). However, there were hundreds of other famous temples whose ruins are scattered all around the Mediterranean. Some, such as the Temple of Aphaia at Aegina (c. 480 B.C.E.), have become famous for the sculpture that adorned them.

Order in the House: Other Buildings and Urban Planning

As the Greek *polis* ("city-state") evolved and developed, so did buildings that housed and helped define its activities; most were erected around the central marketplace, or *agora*. The most famous of these structures are the *theater* (for watching plays) and the *stoa* ("a portico," open on one wall, with shop spaces along the other—think a strip mall with a columned, covered walkway).

In the Classical period, city planning, like everything else, became the subject of study. Hippodamus of Miletus (fifth century B.C.E.) developed the grid layout for new cities and was commissioned by Athens to design its port of Piraeus. It was in the Hellenistic period, however, when Greek cities were being built from the Aegean to the Indus, that this model for urban development took hold.

The Least You Need to Know

- Ancient Greek philosophers—notably Socrates, Plato, and Aristotle—influenced the development of western philosophy, science, religion, politics, and ethics, and their work is as relevant today as it was during their lifetimes.

- Greek history developed in the fifth century B.C.E. in order to preserve, explain, and interpret two great wars: the Persian War (Herodotus) and the Peloponnesian War (Thucydides).

- Ancient medical practitioners endeavored to explain the causes of medical illness in terms of mechanistic, physical (not spiritual) processes, predominantly as the natural movement of fluids and vapors (the humours) within the body.

◆ The ancient Greeks' fascination with mathematics (particularly geometry) is a component of their focus on proportion, balance, and harmony. These ideals led some philosophers to attempt to describe the cosmos in idealized mathematical form, and they led to the development and application of sophisticated mathematical and geometrical theories.

◆ The general Greek perspective that there is an essential framework of balance, proportion, and harmony lying behind natural phenomena manifests itself spectacularly in their temples.

◆ As the Greek *polis* evolved and developed, so did buildings that housed and helped define its activities; most were erected around the central marketplace, or *agora*. The most famous of these structures are the theater and the *stoa*.

Chapter 4

Greek FAQs: Hot Topics in Brief

In This Chapter

- The Trojan War in mini-series
- The Olympics then and now
- Losing and finding Atlantis
- Women's lives, sexuality, and eroticism in context
- The *dêmos* in Athenian democracy

As you can see from the previous two chapters, there is a great deal to discover, learn, and know about ancient Greece. But what if you don't want to jump in and risk drowning in the details? Not to worry. You already have a general overview of the periods, literature, and intellectual trends of ancient Greece. Now we'll take a look at some perennially interesting topics. Here you're likely to find a few things that already interest you and, hopefully, others that you'll want to learn more about. *Then* armed with the general road map and some scenic detours, we'll proceed on a more substantial and chronological journey through ancient Greece.

Keep in mind that although even frequently asked questions are complex and require detailed answers, the replies in this chapter are *very* concise. So there is more information on these topics in later chapters, and Appendix A points the way to further reading and surfing. Keep in mind, as well, that these topics are of interest to people today because they are relevant to and impact many things that people care about today.

The Trojan War

Homer's *Iliad* and *Odyssey*, the lost epic *Kypris*, and vase paintings show that the Trojan Cycle (i.e., the many tales that, together, tell the story of the Trojan War) developed by the 700s B.C.E., and western literature since that time shows that it has never lost its luster as a subject. In fact, the story of the Trojan War has occupied the western mind and imagination in a way that few other stories, with the exception of the narratives of the Bible, ever have. Indeed, a tremendous amount of western literature engages these two sources—the Bible and the Trojan Cycle—and similar questions have been asked about both narratives since antiquity. When it comes to the story of the Trojan War, we tend to ask: At what point is it literature, and at what point history? What is the real story? What does it tell us? What does it mean? You'll find more on Homer in Chapter 9.

What's the Story?

It's a *long* story. But in essence, this is it:

- ◆ **Gods lose, and boy gets, girl.** A sea nymph, Thetis, is destined to have a son greater than his father. To protect themselves and the status quo, the gods arrange for Thetis to fall in love with the mortal hero Peleus, one of the Argonauts. Everyone is invited to the wedding—except the goddess Eris (Strife). Strife crashes the party and deposits a gift with a mysterious tag: "To the fairest." An argument over the gift breaks out between the goddesses Hera (woman/queen), Athena (wisdom/prowess), and Aphrodite (sex/desire). The gods (wisely) won't touch this one with a 10-cubit pole, and they have a mortal judge which of the goddesses is "the fairest." (For more on this, keep reading.) Peleus and Thetis have a son: Achilles.

- ◆ **Boys get girls.** In Greece, the courtship of two beautiful, rich, and powerful twin sisters, Clytemnestra and Helen (who is really a daughter of Zeus), takes place. The suitors, chiefs from all over Greece, are reluctant to compete for Helen (and so become a target of the others) until they all swear an oath to uphold and defend whomever Helen picks. Helen and Clytemnestra marry the powerful brothers Menelaus (Sparta) and Agamemnon (Mycenae), respectively. One suitor, Odysseus, marries Penelope (and they become the hero and heroine of Homer's *Odyssey*).

◆ **Wrong boy gets girl.** Across the Aegean, Alexandros (a.k.a Paris, a prince of Troy) is chosen to judge the "fairest" contest. Each goddess offers him something in exchange for a decision in her favor, and Alexandros declares Aphrodite, who offers him the most beautiful woman in the world, the winner. There is only one problem: Helen is the most beautiful woman in the world and she's married to Menelaus. Somehow (kidnapping? divinely inspired love?), Helen ends up in Alexandros' boat and on her way to Troy.

◆ **Boys go to get girl.** Agamemnon calls on the Greek chiefs to uphold their oath, and he assembles a fleet. However, the fleet is stranded on the island of Aulis, and it remains stranded until Agamemnon sacrifices his daughter Iphigenia. Once at Troy, the siege drags on for 10 years, and the two sides fight their way to a bloody standstill. Finally, the Greeks contrive to take the city. They build a great wooden horse (the mascot of Troy), fill it with hidden fighters, leave it at the city walls, and sail away in feigned hopelessness. The Trojans, after a fateful debate, take the horse into the city. At night, the Greek ships return, the fighters pour out of the horse, and they open the gate. There is a vicious and bloody slaughter. Troy falls, the Greeks divide the spoils, and they sail home.

The battlefield of Troy from the walls of the ancient city.

(Photo by Eric Nelson)

♦ **Girls get boys back.** Few of the heroes make it back easily, safely, or happily. Helen wins Menelaus back, but they spend five years trying to get home. Clytemnestra gets Agamemnon back—by killing him in his bath with an axe—for sacrificing their daughter to the war. Penelope gets Odysseus back, but only after his 10-year journey home and yet another slaughter—this time, in her own home.

What's the Truth?

The truth? Well, we're not sure, even when it comes to questions as fundamental as "Was there a Troy?" and "Did a Trojan War between Troy and the (Mycenaean) Greeks take place?" The ancient Greeks generally accepted Homer's account and authority, but even they placed the Trojan War around 1200 B.C.E. In that case, about 400 years of oral tradition preceded the first written accounts, which leaves a lot of room for the loss of historical accuracy (and we're not sure that historical accuracy was the point of the cycle in the first place). In more modern times, Homer was often considered little more than a fanciful storyteller until Heinrich Schliemann, an amateur archeologist/treasure hunter, excavated both Troy (Hissarlik, Turkey) and Mycenae (Greece)—in part to support Homer's authority—and reignited an ongoing debate about the past.

If there *was* a Troy, it was probably the generally accepted site of Hissarlik (western Turkey). The archeological levels identified as Troy VI and Troy VIIa are the ones most often suggested as candidates for the Homeric city. Each fits the general time period, and each has some features that fit Homer's description, but neither level is a perfect match. Although the earlier level, Troy VI, appears to have been destroyed around 1300 B.C.E. by earthquake, rather than by human force, it has massive walls like those described by Homer. Level VIIa, which was destroyed around 1200 B.C.E. by fire, seems to have been poor in comparison, leaving many archeologists reluctant to identify it as Homer's Troy.

As for a Trojan War between Troy and the Greeks, we're on even shakier ground. There are some Hittite records that may support an attack on Troy. However, the whole region was coming under attack, possibly by Greeks, possibly by people migrating down the Danube, possibly by both, and possibly by others. This instability continued well into the Dark Age. You'll find more on these ages in Chapters 7 and 8.

The Trojan Cycle may stem from many general traditions wrapped anachronistically around a single city. On the other hand, we do know that oral tradition preserves some historical details, and that the *Iliad* preserves such things as a long catalogue of

Greek cities (some long gone by Homer's time) that sent ships to Troy. But even if there was a Greek expedition against Troy, this event alone wouldn't guarantee that other details are historically accurate. In any case, it's difficult to be unbiased: Homer's stories are so vivid and compelling that people seem to wish them to be one way or the other, fact or fantasy.

The Olympics

The modern Olympics take their name from an ancient pan-Hellenic athletic competition that was held every four years beginning in 776 B.C.E. The ancient festival was the most famous of four major competitions, and it has significant differences from (and a few similarities to) its modern namesake. You'll find more on the ancient Olympics in Chapter 10.

When, Where, and What Were the Ancient Olympics?

Competitive sports were a feature of Greek religious festivals, which were held in honor of various gods and heroes. These games celebrated achievement, excellence, and the divine moment of victory. The Olympic Games, held in honor of Olympian Zeus, were part of a religious festival at the temple sanctuary of Olympia in the Peloponnesus (southern Greece). This sanctuary was one of the oldest and most hallowed in Greece. A number of traditions surrounded the origins of the Games and variously claimed that they were founded by Zeus himself or by the hero Herakles (Hercules), or that they were founded to commemorate the death of the hero Pelops.

The religious festival was held during the second full moon after the summer solstice (July or August) and lasted up to five days. (If you've been to Greece at this time of year, you might wonder how the competitors ever survived without Gatorade—it's hotter than Hades.) For three months prior to the Games, a general truce was declared, which allowed competitors and spectators to travel safely from their homes to the Games, even through enemy territory.

Who Participated and What Went On?

Only Greek men who were free (that is, not slaves) could participate in the Olympics, but "Greek" was defined broadly. The ancient Greeks defined Greekness linguistically and mythologically: If you could speak Greek and provide some plausible explanation from myth/history as to your connection to Greek traditions, you were Greek (as far as the Olympics went). Competitors came from as far away as the Black Sea, Spain,

CAUTION

Labyrinths _____

The marathon is not an "Olympic" event. However, Plutarch (c. 50–125 C.E.) relates a story (which has no basis in either fact or myth!) that, in 490 B.C.E., a messenger ran from the plain of Marathon to Athens (26 miles), announced the Greeks' victory over the Persians, and promptly dropped dead.

and Africa, and they were protected by the general truce. Women were restricted from participating and training and (mostly) from being spectators.

Competitors trained 30 days before local judges, who decided which participants would be allowed to compete. The original competition was the footrace. Over time, other individual events were added, including fighting events (boxing, wrestling, and the *pankration*, or "all-out brawl"), equestrian events (riding and chariot racing), and track and field events (running, discus and javelin throwing, jumping, and the pentathlon). All of the competitions were done in the nude.

Only the winner of each event was recognized (no silver or bronze finalists). Each winner received a laurel crown and the right to erect a commemorative statue at Olympia. That was all. Back home, however, victors often received considerable civic privileges (such as free meals), public adulation, and other perks that made being a victor *very* desirable and *very* profitable. Because of these privileges, bribes, cheating, game-fixing, and rule-bending were a dark underbelly of the Games.

Were the Competitors "Amateurs"?

Not really. The stakes and rewards were far too high. Competitors had professional (and highly paid) trainers, under whom they spent a great deal of time preparing for competition, just as athletes do now. Many athletes also competed at other events and festivals, and some achieved celebrity status, as well as an athletic "career" of sorts. Money drove the equestrian events. Just as it takes wealth and/or sponsors to compete in equestrian events and auto racing today, only wealthy aristocrats had the means to fund and enter elite horses and professional chariot drivers in the Games.

What's the Connection with the Modern Olympics?

There is more of an idealistic connection than a realistic one between the ancient and modern Olympics. For example, although the ancient Greeks might not speak in these terms, an outsider *might* remark that the Games, at their best, used athletic competition to celebrate human excellence and to reinforce common cultural bonds that supercede war and conflict. In this way, the Baron de Coubertin (who established and promoted the modern Games) might have gotten things right. At their worst, the ancient Games were marred and manipulated by nationalism, politics, money, and personal ambition in ways that would be all too recognizable today. In practice, however, the specifics of the ancient Games—that is, the participants (male), scope (Greeks), events (more limited), venue (a fixed location), and purpose (religious celebration)—differ markedly from their modern counterpart.

And did the Games include amateurism and competition for their own sakes? Not the ancient Games, at least.

The Myth of Atlantis

Nearly everyone has heard the name Atlantis, and most people identify it, vaguely, with some fabulous city located somewhere in some ocean. But where? Once you begin to search for Atlantis, you'll find people who argue very passionately that Atlantis is located in, among others, the following:

Turkey	Antarctica
South America	Crete
Indonesia	Bimini
Santorini	Just about anywhere

So, let's begin our search by discussing parts of the Atlantis myth. You'll find more about Minoan Crete (a favorite for the source of the story) in Chapter 7.

What's the Story?

The story of Atlantis is told by Plato in his dialogues *Timaeus* and *Critias*. Plato describes Atlantis as a large island, roughly the size of northern Africa, located in the Atlantic Ocean. According to the dialogues, once upon a long, long time ago, Atlantis controlled the western Mediterranean. When it attempted to conquer the rest of the region, it was defeated by the ancestors of the Athenians, who liberated the people of the western Mediterranean and saved the others from conquest. More than 9,000 years before the time of Socrates, both Atlantis and the ancestors of the Athenians were destroyed in a deluge. Fortunately, the ancient Egyptians preserved the story of the Athenians' noble ancestry, as well as detailed descriptions of both Atlantis and its utopian culture.

Does this story raise an eyebrow? Well, consider Plato's description of the transmission of the tale:

According to the dialogues, this 9,000-year-old story came from a very old, mysterious Egyptian priest, who told it to …

Solon, the Athenian poet, sage, and statesman in about 600 B.C.E. Solon told it to …

a friend, who told it to …

… his grandson. When he was 90, this man told it to …

his 10-year-old grandson (Critias), who told it 15 to 20 years later to …

Socrates (in order to entertain him) in the late 400s B.C.E.

Plato, however, who would have been a teenager or young man at the time, didn't write down the conversation (assuming that he didn't create it) until roughly 30 to 40 years later.

Does that sound dependable? Not really. Nevertheless, enough ink has been spilled trying to establish the veracity of that old Egyptian's tale to sink several island paradises.

What's the Fuss?

The fuss is about the authority, power, and intrigue of the past. As noted in Chapter 3, Plato created myths both to communicate his ideas and to imbue them with a kind of traditional authority. With Atlantis, Plato may have done his job just a little *too* well. Our best evidence suggests that people have been trying to find an historical Atlantis ever since the time of Plato, in order to establish Atlantis as an alternate source of civilization and history, and as a utopian culture.

The fuss is also about money. Expeditions, lectures, archeological digs, museum exhibitions, and the like require enormous financial support and public interest, and generating this kind of support and interest often depends upon capturing the human imagination. Atlantis has been raised from the seafloor, again and again, in order to capture all of these things.

What's the Truth?

The evidence suggests that Atlantis is a myth, written into the *Timaeus* and *Critias* to give the ideas in these dialogues historical authority and majesty. By precedent and analogy, such authority might have minimized, undermined, or offered an alternative to an accepted tradition that connected Athens' greatness to its role in defeating the Persians (during the invasions of 490–480 B.C.E.) and to its democracy. Whatever his purpose, Plato includes two traditional authorities that were well respected by the Athenians: 1) Egypt, the civilization that the Greeks considered the most ancient, and 2) Solon, the Athenian lawgiver whom the Athenians considered a wise sage. Moreover, Plato gives the story a line of oral transmission that was at least as reliable as Homer's.

When the *scholarly* debate returns to an historical source for Atlantis, it centers on where Plato might have gotten his ideas in the first place. Some believe that Plato used bits of folklore, and that this folklore included tales about the destruction of Minoan Crete, which was rocked by the eruption of Thera (Santorini) in the 1600s B.C.E. Others propose that Solon picked up the story while traveling in Lydia (Turkey), where an ancient city near Mount Sipylus had fallen into a lake during an earthquake. These views, however, may have been colored by a desire for the Minoans to serve the same kind of utopian or alternative historical role that Atlantis might have served (we'll talk more about the Minoans in the next chapter), and by very selective reading of the story.

Still, Plato may have had real sources of inspiration for his story that were close to his own time and close to home. For a long time, Greek and Phoenician seafarers had known of far-off islands and shoals in the Atlantic, and their tales may have given him the idea (just as sea exploration provided mythic settings for works such as *Gulliver's Travels* and *The Island of Dr. Moreau*). More strikingly, the Greek city of Helike was destroyed by an earthquake and seismic wave, and it sank into the Gulf of Corinth in 373 B.C.E. (during Plato's lifetime). Later writers tell us that you could sail over and look down on parts of the city through the water, so Plato could have been inspired by this contemporary catastrophe.

> **Odysseys**
>
> You can explore the remains of the ancient Achaean city of Helike (both on land and by boat) on the southern Gulf of Corinth, southeast of modern Aigion.

Behind the Men's World: What About the Women?

A good deal of recent scholarship, which has been pioneered and propelled by *feminist* scholars, focuses on the lives of people who rarely appear in traditional accounts (written by men for men) or feature in the study of the past (undertaken mostly by men for men): women, slaves, and other marginalized groups (foreigners, homosexuals, and so on). This scholarship attempts to understand these groups on their own terms, through their own eyes and, in so doing, to correct mistakes and undermine claims based on *patriarchal* ideas about *sex* and *gender*. Because ways of thinking that led to the codification of patriarchal ideas and ways of thinking that call these ideas into question can both trace their roots to ancient Greece, scholarly research and debate have been very fruitful and very fractious. You'll find more on women's lives in Chapters 9, 16, 21, and 23.

> ### Lexica
>
> Although there is no single feminist approach to scholarship, **feminist** scholars tend to agree on some core ideals of feminism (e.g., that males and females should have equal political, economic, and social opportunity, voice, and value).
>
> **Patriarchy** is the human social interaction and organization that results from consciously and unconsciously conceiving of and ordering human affairs to privilege males and male authority—from Greek *patr* ("father") + *archy* ("rule").
>
> **Sex** is a biological distinction (male or female); **gender** is a conception, composed of social and cultural assumptions and expectations, regarding what male or female persons, behaviors, and roles are and should be.

What Did the Ancient Greeks Think of Women?

In general, the literature of ancient Greece portrays women as naturally inferior and subordinate to men. Women are often characterized as emotional, irrational, unstable, manipulative, sexually charged, untrustworthy, and powerless. Although women could live well, they could not achieve excellence to the degree that a male, being fully rational and quintessentially human, could. Indeed, even the female body was, at times, conceptualized as a deviation of the ideal male form.

What Were Women's Lives Like?

In general, from birth to death, "good" women of the Classical period lived in a world of their own, separated from the men by boundaries and borders that were controlled by the men. This world was within the limits of the *oikos*, or "household." In her teens, a girl was married to a man twice her age, and then moved from her household to an *oikos* ruled by the mother of her husband. She received little, if any, education; she could not inherit; and she had no legal status outside of being the property of her husband.

Of course, evidence from lives of real people (grave markers, vase paintings, papyri fragments) tell a more complicated and interesting tale, and traditional ways of thinking were challenged, as well as promoted, in literature and by philosophers. What we lack, however, are women talking in their own voices and from their own authority, and this void creates tremendous difficulties in accurately reconstructing and adequately understanding their lives. The process is further complicated by the fact that we must sift through evidence that has already been filtered through men, and we must avoid imposing our own ideas, anachronistically, on women of that time.

What Roles Did Women Have in Ancient Greek Culture?

It appears that women had higher status and broader social roles in the Dark Age than they did in the Archaic period, when the confines of their world narrowed during the development of the Greek *polis*, or "city-state." Ironically, democracy was one of the worst things to happen to women in ancient Greece, because it sharply politicized gender and sexuality. For example, in an aristocracy, although aristocratic women were considered inferior to aristocratic men, an aristocratic woman might have a higher status than a male peasant. But in a democracy, where all *men* are equal (e.g., male citizens of Athens), all women (e.g., even female citizens of Athens) were held inferior to all men. Athens excluded everything female from the political world of the *dêmos* ("a territory and its free inhabitants," primarily citizen males and their property). Women had no public roles, except those that involved communal religious worship, and few chances beyond public festivals to participate even informally or indirectly in public life. Opportunities for women broadened again in the expanded world of the Hellenistic period, but women never did achieve—and never have achieved—equal value and status.

Muses

"But since I have to mention something about womanly excellence for those who will now be widows, everything I can say is summed up in this: Your great glory is not to become less than your natural temperament, and the least of excellence is hers who has any reputation—good or bad—among men."
—From the Funeral Oration of Pericles (Thucydides 2.45)

Spartan Women and Those Amazing Amazons

Our picture of women in ancient Greece comes primarily from Classical Athens, but two groups of women, one real, the other largely mythical, stand out in opposition. These are the women of Sparta and the Amazons. As an integral part of Sparta's unique social organization—which maintained local supremacy by bearing, raising, and training the best fighting men anywhere—Spartan women were educated and trained, held property, could have multiple husbands (polyandry), and, unlike Athenian women, were active (not passive or indirect) participants in Sparta's private and public life.

Labyrinths

There is little evidence of Amazon women with one breast removed. The story seems to be a Greek legend that dramatized the Amazons' rejection of strictly "female" roles and their willingness and ability to embrace "male" ones.

Eureka!

The discovery of a man and woman, both with weapons, buried with an infant in southern Ukraine, and of burials of female Pazyryk warriors on the Okok Plateau (between Mongolia and Kazakstan), suggest that there were nomadic tribes in which women fought on horseback and held high status. Such tribes might be the source of the "Amazons."

The Amazons, a semi-nomadic tribal society composed exclusively of women, appear throughout Greek literature and myth from Homer (eighth century B.C.E.) to Strabo (second century C.E.). As fierce warriors who rejected any subjugation by men, the Amazons fascinated the ancient Greeks (particularly the Athenians), who used them to exemplify the barbarian antithesis of their own beliefs about gender and civilization. In Greek, their name means "breastless," and it was attributed to a practice of cutting off or maiming a breast to aid in fighting (for instance, holding a shield or using a bow). Herodotus connects them with the Scythians and locates them in Eurasia (around the Black and Caspian seas), and recent archeological finds may support him, insofar as there appear to have been nomadic societies in which women were warriors and achieved high status *alongside* men.

The Amazons have been a powerful symbol and potential source of historical empowerment for feminist and lesbian writers and thinkers, as well as a source of fascination for many people. (Again, alternate pasts have potential for the present.) However, how much of the Amazons' existence (as the Greeks portrayed it) is historical, and how much is the creation of the Greek mind, is an ongoing debate.

Sexuality and Eroticism

The ancient Greeks left an exuberant and reasonably comprehensive record of sexuality and eroticism, which has been a continuing source of fascination, revulsion, and reassessment. It remains central to considerations of sexuality in psychoanalysis, literary criticism, cultural studies, feminist theory, and queer theory.

Before going further into sexuality and eroticism, however, let us first ask you to set aside, for just a moment, your own assumptions about the human body, sexual expression ("natural," "normal," or otherwise), and the nature of sex itself. Many of these assumptions come from "pasts" (e.g., Judeo-Christian and Victorian traditions), and from other cultural ideals, beliefs, and conventions that either cohere with or strain against these pasts. Because the ancient Greeks were not influenced by these same conventions and systems of belief, most of them would neither recognize nor agree with the assumptions that depend upon them. So if you wish to accurately and adequately understand ancient Greek sexuality and eroticism, you'll find it helpful to suspend judgment and set aside highly personal or culturally dependent views, at least for the moment. That said, it is important to know that the ancient Greeks did not consider the body or sex to be "sinful" (that is, these things were not, on their own, a source of guilt or shame) or extraneous to human identity.

Also human sexuality seems to be a complicated, layered expression of both essential (inherent and consistent) and constructed (created and manipulated by culture over time) elements. Because humans are individual members of socio-biological groups, these elements exist on both individual and communal levels. Various scholars emphasize one element over the other, and some try to make human sexual behavior fit overly restrictive essentialist or constructionist explanations. Because of this trend, most of what you read about the Greeks and sex will be heavily slanted, one way or the other.

What Do We Know About Ancient Greek Sexuality and How Do We Know It?

The ancient Greeks have a well-earned reputation for sexuality and sensuality: Sensual, sexual, and erotic content appears in myths, literature, philosophical works, statues, vase paintings … everywhere. Given a culture that celebrated human development, experience, and excellence, and that saw the body and sex as essential human elements, this isn't surprising. However, it isn't always easy to decide, especially from our vantage point, exactly when something (or even which element of it) is intended to be sexually charged. The most obviously *erotic* or *pornographic* material comes from vase paintings, which show a full spectrum of sexual practices. In addition, we also get information about sexual practices from a variety of texts, particularly the comic plays of Aristophanes, which are filled with sexual innuendo and satire.

Elsewhere we get information about how the ancient Greeks viewed sexuality and desire from discussions that range from personal accounts (for example, lyric poetry) to philosophical works (such as Plato's *Symposium*) to philosophical/scientific texts (such as Aristotle's *On the Generation of Animals*).

> **Lexica** _____
>
> Although the terms **erotic** and **pornographic** are notoriously difficult to define, they generally refer to sexually explicit materials intended to arouse the viewer. Fine distinctions between them often depend on whether the material is seen as aesthetic, humane, and acceptable (erotic) or visceral, inhumane, and unacceptable (pornographic). But subjective distinctions are difficult to separate from personal taste or political agenda and nearly impossible to apply.

Because of the Greeks' gender-separate and patriarchal culture, we know the least about the sexual life of women. Most of the texts are written by males (although we do have lyric poetry written by women), from a male perspective and male-centered approach, and with the intention of being exclusively masculine by definition.

What About Homosexuality?

Human sexual desire and practice have never been strictly *heterosexual* or strictly *homosexual*. Instead there seems to be a continuum of human sexual desire and practice, one that includes subtle degrees of appreciation, attraction, and avoidance. The ancient Greeks assumed that it is both natural and normal for human beings to find other human beings erotic, and that eroticism is not limited to members of the opposite sex. In practice, their culture allowed for homoerotic expression between males and between females in relationships, literature, and art that extends beyond modern definitions of gay, straight, or bisexual. These expressions surprise and challenge our ideas and assumptions, whether they come from literature (such as Sappho's female homoerotic poetry), history (the Sacred Band, a famous fighting unit made up of homosexual lovers), or other sources.

> **Lexica** _____
>
> The English terms heterosexual and homosexual have Greek roots. To describe sexual relationships, they are used here in the customary sense: **heterosexual** (from Greek *heter*, "other") refers to male-female relationships, and **homosexual** (from Greek *homo*, "same") refers to male-male and female-female relationships.

However, the Greeks generally frowned on homosexual orientation in adult males, because it challenged popular ideas that linked "maleness" with penetrating (versus being penetrated) and with being the active (versus the passive) sexual partner. Just as we know very little about the world of women, we know very little about female homosexual relationships within that world.

What Is Pederasty, and ... Why?

The most famous and infamous homoerotic cultural practice associated with ancient Greece is pederasty. Pederasty was a practice that encouraged an intensely emotional and erotic (and ideally supportive and instructive) relationship between a twenty-something male (the "lover" or *erastes*) and an adolescent male (the "beloved" or *eromenos*) in order for the younger male to mature under the guidance of his older partner. Similar female relationships may also have been encouraged.

In idealized form, the sexual dimension of this relationship ended with the younger partner's entrance into adulthood (although some relationships continued beyond that point). This practice is actually fairly common in human history. It appeared in aristocratic Greece in the sixth century B.C.E. Its acceptance declined in the fifth century B.C.E., but remained a facet of Greek culture, particularly in Sparta, throughout the Classical period. You'll find more on the development of pederasty in Chapter 9.

It is clear that pederasty was *supposed* to be good for the beloved's development as a man and that it included sexual aspects. However, supporters and critics often characterize the relationship in a one-dimensional or overly restrictive manner, either as strictly platonic or as exploitive and pedophilic, and, sometimes, as just plain silly. In practice, though, the evidence (and human experience) argues that individual relationships run the gamut from one extreme to the other, again along a continuum, and that they include elements that defy easy or comfortable classification. Given the ages of the participants and the general nature of human relationships that involve sexual contact, all overly restrictive descriptions of homoerotic behaviors and relationships in ancient Greece are likely to be inaccurate or incomplete.

Politics and Democracy

The ancient Greeks are famous for their politics and constitutions, and for the ways they thought about and approached political organization. We get such distinctions as *oligarchy, aristocracy, monarchy, tyranny,* and *democracy* from them. Athens, of course, is famous for its radical democracy, which is generally cited as the source for modern participatory democracies. However, there are significant differences between then and now, and between the various Greek city-states of the time. You'll find more information about the development and workings of Athenian democracy in Chapter 14.

What Kinds of Political Systems Did the Greeks Have?

Each Greek city-state, or *polis*, developed its own kind of constitution (political arrangement by consensus) during the Archaic period, and these arrangements fell broadly into the following categories, all with the suffix *archy*, which means "rule by":

- **Monarchy (*mono*, "one").** Although the city-states abandoned rule by hereditary kings, a popular leader (a *tryannos*, or "tyrant") might establish one-man rule. The general long-term outcome of such arrangements gave tyrannies their bad name.

- **Aristocracy (*aristo*, "the excellent").** Aristocracies were governed by men chosen from (and by) hereditary aristocrats.

- **Oligarchy (*oligo*, "the few").** Oligarchies were governed by a few select men, whose selection did not depend upon birth but upon wealth, influence, and power.

- **Democracy (*demo*, "the people").** Democracies permitted all people (here, *people* means all free citizen males over a certain age) some measure of participation in the political system.

Was Athenian Democracy Like Modern Democracies?

The democracy in Athens was in some ways more participatory, and in other ways much more exclusive, than modern democracies. First, only males of good standing, who were born of a citizen mother and father, could participate in public, legal, and political life. Women, foreigners, persons of questionable parentage, and, of course, slaves had no place or voice in political life, except to the extent that they could influence a citizen to work or intercede on their behalf.

However, for citizens, there were many political opportunities, obligations, and responsibilities. Besides being permitted to speak and vote in the "assembly" (*ekklesia*), an Athenian citizen was likely, in his lifetime, to serve the council that prepared business for the assemblies (perhaps on its governing board, perhaps even holding the keys to the state treasury), and to hold other offices (e.g., city commissioner, port supervision, and tax collection). These offices were determined by lot and restricted to those men who had not already served. Inexperience was no excuse: Officials were reviewed and audited at the end of the year, and they were fined if their accountability was questionable. In the law courts, Athenian juries made up of 200 to 500 (or more) citizens heard and decided cases on a case-by-case basis. Of course, the men who lived in more rural areas were less able to participate than those who lived in and around a city. But even then, citizens attended to all of the village and local business. You'll find more details on the citizens' lives in Chapter 16.

The Least You Need to Know

♦ Although the ancient Greeks generally accepted the Trojan War as historical, we do not have conclusive evidence that Troy existed or participated in a war with the (Mycenaean) Greeks.

♦ The modern Olympics take their name from an ancient pan-Hellenic athletic competition, held in honor of Olympian Zeus, which took place every four years beginning in 776 B.C.E.

♦ Although many people argue for an historical Atlantis, our best evidence suggests that Atlantis is a myth either created or retold by Plato.

♦ In general, the literature of ancient Greece portrays women as naturally inferior and subordinate to men, and women of the Classical period generally lived in a world of their own, within the limits of their households.

♦ Ancient Greek culture allowed for homoerotic expression between males and between females in relationships, literature, and art that extends beyond modern definitions of gay, straight, or bisexual.

♦ The democracy in Athens was significantly different from modern democracies in that it was both more participatory and more exclusive.

By Zeus! Ancient Greek Religion and Mythology

In This Chapter

- Definitions and distinctions in and among myths

- The character of Greek myth

- An overview of the ancient Greek gods and Greek religion in practice

- Understanding how the Greeks themselves and others interpreted their myths

To understand ancient Greek literature and culture, it's necessary to understand the importance and influence of religion and myth. In general, religion and myth help to mediate the relationship between human beings and the divine and to explain the place of humans in the cosmos. Because the Greeks generally conceived of these things very differently than we do now, it will be helpful to begin with an examination of myth in general, and then move to Greek myth in particular. This way you'll better understand some of the Greek religious perspectives and practices in context.

Mythology is a fascinating subject, and Greek mythology is particularly entertaining. Besides, both the myths themselves and the ancient Greek approach to myths have important legacies.

What's in a Myth?

Myth has a myriad of definitions. For our purposes, we'll adapt the definition used by scholar Walter Burkert and say that "Myths are traditional cultural tales that address matters of collective concern." But bear in mind that this short definition has limits built into it, because not all stories or tales are myths.

In order to become *traditional*, stories must be entertaining or engaging (boring or unimportant stories do not survive this process) to a culture generally. Moreover, these stories must entertain or engage a culture across generations, through time. Finally, to become traditional, a story must *do* something, or perform a function (such as explain natural phenomena or teach moral lessons), and it must perform this function through time.

Mythology is the study of the functions, origins, and meanings of myths, and traditional stories are often separated into three categories by the focus of their concerns and the primary means of their transmission.

CAUTION

Labyrinths _____

Although myths primarily originate and evolve in oral form, they can become codified (fixed in written form) and transmitted in texts. And although a picture is not a myth, myths can be represented in pictures. (The myth is the narrative that the picture references.)

The Human Plane: Folktales

Folktales are generally passed on orally, and they address individual issues of collective concern on a human scale (fears of the unknown, moral and ethical action, psychological development). It's generally obvious that these stories do not make historical claims, because they are often set in no-time ("once upon a time") and no-place ("far, far away"), and that they are not religious texts. Although fantastic elements abound (witches, talking beasts, and so on), they rarely feature gods or goddesses. Folktales are highly entertaining, and are frequently dark and violent.

The Past: Saga

Sagas are traditional tales that address historical issues of collective concern for a particular people, such as: "Who are we?" "How did we get to be who we are?" "What were the defining moments, and who were the defining people in that history?" Epic poetry belongs to this category. Sagas originate in oral form, but are, at times, written down and, after the story is fixed, they become quasi-historical documents (like the *Iliad*). Other traditional elements are often part of sagas (for example, there are a lot of folktale elements in the *Odyssey*), but it is clear that these stories make historical claims for and about a people.

The Big Picture: "Myth" Proper

Myth, with a capital *M*, is generally reserved for traditional tales that address metaphysical issues of collective concern. These tales often seek to explain the essential workings and meaning of the universe and human life. Myths generally assert authority by invoking a link to the divine (though direct inspiration) and by portraying gods and goddesses acting or speaking for themselves.

Setting the Stage: Living in and to the Limits

Before going on, we need to set up a conceptual model—a stage, so to speak—to help make sense of the ways that human, divine, and cosmic forces play themselves out in ancient Greek myth and religion. Although such a model is simplistic, to be sure, it will serve as a base from which we can develop a more sophisticated understanding.

In general, the Greeks had a cyclical, rather than a strictly linear, approach to time and human affairs. They saw cycles in both natural and human events (from individual lives to the workings of civilizations) that, like the natural and unchanging cycles of the seasons, have recognizable patterns and are, in some ways at least, determined by cosmic nature, human nature, fate, or the gods. This perspective might seem pessimistic—perhaps suggesting that humans aren't going anywhere, in the big sense, and that we're not in control. In other ways, it might seem liberating—perhaps freeing us from attempting to control uncontrollable elements, and encouraging us to better understand, adapt to, and accept the cycles of which we are a part. And, in many ways, it might seem profoundly realistic.

Within this cyclical universe, the range of possible human experience is limited by such extremes as human good and evil, human happiness and unhappiness, and human success and failure. Each individual is governed by his or her physical, intellectual, and emotional capacities, and human experience is an expression of the development, exercise, and loss of these capacities through time. Certain individuals exceed others in particular capacities, but most human experience and expression fall within general, recognizably human, parameters for such things as good and evil, achievement and failure, and happiness and suffering. Those people who significantly exceed these parameters are, to the Greeks, heroes. The gods, as we'll see, exceed the limits further still.

Live and Learn

For the Greeks, living well and developing one's potential for excellence required exploring one's limits and limitations as an individual and as a human. Much of Greek literature investigates this dangerous endeavor, fraught as it is with the potential for error and regret, and finding those limits was not a painless task. Overestimating one's capacities and abilities was considered arrogance, and grossly overestimating them (to the point of wanton arrogance) was considered *hubris*. Consciously failing to develop, underestimating, or under-representing one's talents and capacities was, well, a kind of cowardice and dishonesty. From this perspective, if pride is understood as having and expressing appropriate esteem for one's own abilities and accomplishments, then it is *not* a vice. And if humility is understood as failing to adequately credit or acknowledge one's own achievements and talents, then it is *not* a virtue.

Lexica

Hubris means wanton arrogance, and it often manifests in grossly inappropriate (and often violent) actions or attitudes.

Eureka!

Even in the face of "divine madness" (*atê*)—that is, temporary insanity brought on by the gods—the ancient Greeks believed that they (not the gods) must make reparations for whatever actions they took at the time. In the *Iliad*, Agamemnon admits that he was mad when he angered Achilles, and he offers Achilles an abundance of gifts as reparation.

The No-Win Scenario: Pessimists Are Always Pleasantly Surprised

For the ancient Greeks, human experience and existence were always subject to forces beyond human control—fate, the gods, a capricious universe, or other natural forces—that could end, or alter the meaning of, one's life in a heartbeat. So Greek literature and thought were often occupied by the question of how to live well in the face of such events, and even in the face of such possibilities. Greek truisms such as "Count no man happy until he is dead," and "Learning comes through suffering" acknowledge an unpredictable universe, the idea that there is always time for something to go wrong, and the notion that the most profound realizations are often found in life's failures.

However, in such a universe, the focus can also shift to living nobly in the shadow of tragedy, and in spite of the vicissitudes of fate, and to taking full responsibility for one's own actions and attitudes (whatever the moods of the gods or the state of the universe). And it can include a celebration of those rare moments when human activity goes exactly right. The Greeks' celebration of and fascination with victory in competition are, in part, a celebration of the kind of human achievements that are, in some sense, complete and everlasting.

Gods in Our Image? An Anthropomorphic Polytheism

The Greek gods were *anthropomorphic*—that is, they were like humans in every way (physically, emotionally, intellectually) except three: They didn't work (although they had hobbies and avocations), they didn't die, and they were vastly more powerful. Otherwise, they fought, loved, and suffered; they liked some people better than others; and they had individual personalities and character traits. They were neither *omniscient*, *omnipotent*, nor *omnipresent*. But because the Greeks were *polytheistic*, the universe was full of divine beings and presences. There was always someone, or something, around.

Lexica

Anthropomorphic means created in human form.

Polytheistic means having or pertaining to many gods.

Omniscient means all-knowing; **omnipotent** means all-powerful; **omnipresent** means everywhere at once.

Olympians and Titans

The primary gods of Greece had their own dynastic history in which each generation achieved dominance by succession and by force. The ruling generation included Zeus, his brothers and sisters (Hera, Poseidon, Hades, Demeter, Hestia), and some of Zeus' divine (Apollo, Ares, Artemis, Athena, and Hermes) and semi-divine (Dionysus, and eventually the hero Herakles) children. With Zeus as king, they occupied Mt. Olympus as the Olympians.

The Olympians had achieved dominance over the previous generation, the Titans. The chief Titans, Cronus and Rhea, were the mother and father of Zeus and his siblings. The Titans, in turn, had achieved dominance over the primal pair Gaia (Earth) and Uranus (sky). All of these gods had their own places in the cosmos, although some had been cast into

Labyrinths

This is by no means a comprehensive list of major gods! Hesiod's *Theogony* tells how hundreds of gods emerged and descended from the first gods: Chaos, Gaia, Tartarus, and Eros.

prisonlike Tartarus. (You might think of Tartarus as the basement or garage of creation: the place where you put everything that you don't use anymore, and don't want cluttering up the house, but just can't get rid of.)

On the trail to Mt. Olympus, the home of the Olympian gods.

(Photo courtesy of Norita White)

Here's a list of the Olympian gods and goddesses, their Roman equivalents, and their general domains.

Greek	Roman	Domain
Zeus	Jupiter, Jove	King of the gods, justice, the air
Hera	Juno	Queen of the gods, Zeus' wife, women
Poseidon	Neptune	God of sea, waters, horses, and earthquakes
Hades	Dis	King of the underworld
Demeter	Ceres	Grain and vegetation
Hestia	Vesta	Home and hearth
Athena (also Pallas Athena)	Minerva	Wisdom, strategy in war, weaving, and handicrafts
Aphrodite	Venus	Desire, attraction, and love

Greek	Roman	Domain
Hephaistos (or Hephaestus)	Vulcan	Fire, blacksmiths, potters
Hermes	Mercury	Boundaries, messengers, thieves, business
Ares	Mars	War
Artemis	Diana	The wild, newborns, young women
Apollo	Apollo	Knowledge, medicine, music
Dionysus (also Bacchus)	Bacchus	Vitality, wine, mystic experience, ecstasy
Herakles (or Heracles)	Hercules	Hero famous for strength and perseverance

Minor Gods and Things That Go "Bump" in the Night

In and among the major gods and humans lived minor divinities, all descended in some way from the major gods. Some, like the god Pan (a god of animals and forest) and the Muses (goddesses of inspiration and song), had wide-ranging domains. Others were extremely local: Each prominent natural feature (river, lake) had its local guardian deity. Other minor gods lived in and personified these environments, such as the nymphs (female nature spirits) and satyrs (half-goat, half-human, male nature spirits).

Below the minor divinities was a class of unnamed, vague, and murky divine presences that the Greeks referred to as *daimones*.

> **Eureka!**
>
> The Greek word *daimon* could refer to a wide range of vague and unnamable spirits (one word for happiness is *eudaimonia*, "having a good *daimon*"), but it tended to be used for creepy and potentially harmful things, which is where we get the English word *demon*. Socrates, however, trusted his personal *daimonion* ("divine voice") implicitly.

Where Do We Fit In?

Humans shared the cosmos with these various divine beings and intermingled with them in a way that necessitated relationships of some kind. Sometimes these relationships were personal and special (like the one between Odysseus and Athena), for the gods and goddesses liked (and sometimes loved) specific individuals, cities, or places. Other times, the relationships were quite distant and detached. In order to secure divine favor or even indifference, humans had to offer something. Thus, in a system that included bribes, bartering, and offering payment for services rendered, there was always some obligatory ritual or respectful gesture to perform so as not to anger or offend the divinities.

However, although the gods might have cared about humans and about our relationships with them, humans were ultimately inconsequential both to the gods and to the universe. The universe was not created for humans, and humans were not created for some special role in the universe. The gods did not create humans in order to love or be loved by them. Although the gods occasionally argued with each other on behalf of mortals, or even interfered with one another's plans for the sake of mortals, in general humans were not worth the effort or the trouble. Most of the time, the gods reached a point where they said, "What are we doing?" and left the mortals to their sorry fate.

The only myth in which a god displays affection for humans in general concerns Prometheus, who stole fire from Zeus for the sake of humans. However, even this myth is more about Prometheus' feud with Zeus than his regard for human beings. When Zeus and Prometheus made up, they left humanity to cope with the mess. More frequently, the gods engage in a kind of indirect tit-for-tat by punishing each other's favorite mortals, while still meeting for a cold glass of ambrosia during happy hour.

Sources of Greek Myth and Religion

Greek religion was not a religion of the book—there is no sacred authoritative text to reference, like the Bible or Koran—and religious practices were inconsistent from place to place. Consequently, our knowledge of myths and religious practice comes from a variety of sources (nearly all Greek literature contains some religious and mythological references), none of which are strictly religious. In addition, the Greeks' inclusive, rather than exclusive, approach to religious practice and belief meant that the views represented in these sources were constantly changing.

Mix and Match: Syncretism and Assimilation

If the universe is populated with divinities, and if gods can be known in different guises from place to place, one has to be open to *cult* practices other than one's own. However, the ancient Greeks looked for areas of commonality between various beliefs and practices, and they tended to see similarities and analogies as indications of common gods. For example, if another culture worshipped a sky god X instead of Zeus, the Greeks tended not to ask "Which of us is really correct about the sky god?" Instead they tended to conclude, "Zeus is worshipped as X among those people." Over time, the Greeks assimilated and incorporated the myths, beliefs, and practices of people they conquered or had contact with into their own mythological or religious systems. This process is called *syncretism*.

> **Lexica**
>
> **Cult** is a term used to indicate an organized system of traditions and ritual used in religious worship of any god or deity. **Syncretism**—from Greek *syn* "together" + *cret* "mix"—is the process of blending different cultural beliefs and customs into a synthesis that incorporates elements of each.

> **Muses**
>
> From what I heard at Dodona, the Pelasgians originally worshipped the gods without titles or names ... which they learned from the Egyptians ... and later passed on the names to the Greeks. But whether these gods were born or always were, and what form they have, hasn't been known, so to speak, until yesterday ... it was Homer and Hesiod (only 400 years ago, I believe) who gave our gods their individual genealogies and attributes.
>
> —Herodotus, 4.53

Secular Scripture

What we have to work with, then, are countless references to evolving gods, religious practices, customs, and beliefs in all of the literary and artistic forms that we have covered in Chapters 2 and 3. Many of these sources reflect a traditional core of beliefs. There was, however, no definitive "Hellenic" scripture, no set of codified beliefs that served as a litmus test for whether someone was a believer, and no authoritative description of a god's personality or character. Although this lack of dogmatism allowed for flexibility of practice, opinion, and critique, it also made room for incoherent and inconsistent traditions, something that put paganism at a disadvantage as philosophy and religion began to demand stricter adherence and conformity to systematic principles.

Practice What You Preach: Practice and Belief

Because Greek (and Roman) religion was based on a polytheistic universe in which gods had individual personalities and relationships (close and personal, or impersonal and distant) with people and places, religion focused on *orthopraxy* rather than *orthodoxy*. In other words, it was imperative, for both individual and public religious acts, that the proper rituals were performed properly. These rituals generally involved gestures of respect, a prayer, and an offering of some kind. When traveling from place to place, one would not ask "Do you believe in Zeus?" or "What do you believe about Zeus?" Instead, one would ask "How do I perform the rituals to your god(s)?" or "How is Zeus worshipped here?" To ignore rituals or to perform them improperly was to court disaster by offending the god(s), and rituals that went badly were taken to be very bad omens. This is not to say that Greek religion can be reduced to such a slogan as "Just do it," but at times it can come close.

> **Lexica**
>
> **Orthodoxy**—from Greek *ortho* "right" + *dox* "opinion"—places emphasis on correct belief. **Orthopraxy**—from Greek *ortho* "right" + *prax* "action"—places emphasis on correct ritual action.

Cultivating Cults

There were religious rituals to be performed in every sphere of human activity. Household and individual gods were honored in the home and in private, local shrines to divinities needed tending, and state cults honored the major and local gods. Some states had special relationships with particular gods (such as Athens with Athena) and, if so, the celebrations of these gods were the focus of great festivals (such as the Panathenaic Festival in Athens). The proper maintenance of public cults and rituals was the responsibility of hereditary guilds of priests. There were, however, no official priestly castes.

Getting the Word: Oracles and Divination

How does one know the gods' will? Well, first one has to ask. There aren't many ancient Greek versions of an Old Testament prophet, who knocks on (or down) the door with a message from God. But, if one wanted to ask a question of the gods directly, there were traditional means of getting an answer through priests at specific temples or shrines. These responses (and the institutions that handled them) were known as oracles. One went to an oracle, and after performing the appropriate rituals and sacrifices, asked the question. A response was interpreted by the priests from divine signs in natural phenomena (such as a voice in the rustling of leaves, or in fire, or on water) or by direct communication through prophetic utterance.

There were oracles all over the Greek world, but only a few were famous throughout it. The most respected of the oracles were the temple of Zeus at Dodona and the mountain shrine of Pythian Apollo at Delphi. At both, individuals and states could consult the god about every-thing from the mundane (Should I marry? What should I do about my inheritance?), to the serious (Should we go to war? Why is there a plague?). Although there were a variety of means to gain the answers, getting them straight from Apollo's prophetic priestess, the Pythia, was the most prestigious.

> **Odysseys**
>
> Delphi is still one of the most popular and haunting destina-tions for visitors to Greece. But come prepared with good shoes and plenty of water! The steep, rocky, mountain site is well worth exploring, but you have to climb a steep hill to enjoy the stunning views and to get to the stadium!

If you didn't have the time, or opportunity, to travel to an oracle, there were local specialists who would assist you in reading omens. Omens were signs sent by the gods in such things as dreams, occurrences, or the flight of birds. In a polytheistic world, the potential for divine communication was everywhere, and the Greeks were con-scious of omens all around them. Many omens were commonplace and easy to read (a quick sneeze = good; tripping out the door on a journey = bad; omens on the right = good; omens on the left = bad), but others required professional assistance to inter-pret safely. You could also go to these specialists with questions about the future and have them do a reading for you (from the way that special dice fell to the appearance of the guts of a sacrificial animal).

Just for Me: Personal Experience and Mystery Religions

Consulting oracles and watching out for omens weren't the only forms of religious communication. There were also cults that allowed individuals to communicate di-rectly with the divine. For example, mystery cults emphasized direct experience and communion with a benevolent divine figure who cared directly about the individual believer. Through secret rites and rituals (such as baptisms and shared meals), ecstatic experiences (visions, talking in tongues), or being allowed to gain "secret" knowledge, initiates gained the sense of divine favor in this life and the next.

The most famous of these cults in the ancient world was the Eleusinian Mysteries. In the Hellenistic and Roman periods, the mystery cults of Isis and Mithras grew and, in part, were assimilated into Christianity. The worship of other gods, such as Dionysus and Cybele, also focused on individual charismatic expression and experience. These rites were called *orgia*. The healing cults of Asclepius, such as at Epidaurus, facilitated personal communication with the god as a part of individual therapy.

Curses! Love Potions! Voodoo Dolls! It's M-a-g-i-c

Finally, Greek religious practice was full of what we might call magic. However, the term *magic* was so often reserved for religious practices of which writers disapproved that scholars have largely abandoned delineating magic from religion (at least when discussing the ancient world). *Very* broadly, magic entails rituals and practices by which individuals bring about some intended result. Folk magic, spells, charms, love potions, tablets on which one wrote curses (and threw into wells), dolls in the shape of one's enemies (to which one did bad, bad things) were all part of the Greek world. Charms and incantations against the "evil eye" (a look that can inflict harm) abounded—and are still prevalent—throughout the Mediterranean. There were also various specialists (both male and female) that one could go to for assistance in making charms and potions and in casting spells for various purposes.

Let's Think About That: Greek Introspection and Examination of Traditional Beliefs

The ancient Greeks began to examine their religious beliefs and traditional stories at the same time they began examining natural phenomena and history, and they held divergent opinions about the meaning of myths and the truth(s) of religion. If you were to walk up to various ancient Greeks and ask them if Cronos *really* castrated his father and swallowed his children, for example, you would get answers as varied as those you might hear today if you asked people if Adam and Eve *really* existed and were thrown out of the Garden of Eden.

In the Classical period, the authority of traditional knowledge was a raging concern in Athens. Traditionalists accused the Sophists, natural philosophers, and rhetoricians of undermining and weakening this authority, and so they did. But in examining traditional beliefs and stories, the Greeks of the late Classical period and the Hellenistic period developed approaches for explaining the origins, causes, and purposes of myths that are still in use today.

It's a Social Disease

Some modern interpretive systems envision myths as traditional stories that establish, explain, and maintain social charters, customs, and beliefs, or that arise alongside rituals that accomplish these same purposes. These views have their roots, or at least analogies, in antiquity. Although Plato and Epicurus wouldn't have agreed on many things, they both viewed traditional religion and myth as instruments of social education, training, and control. However, they also believed that many of these traditions were based on and perpetuated untruths.

Plato argued that some myths and traditions should be discredited or abandoned, and that they should be replaced with (new) myths and traditions, ones that taught appropriate lessons and helped maintain the appropriate social order. On the other hand, Epicureans saw religion and myth as social instruments that were used to control people by perpetuating groundless fears (for example, fears of death, the unknown, and divine wrath). To be free of such fears, as well as free from the individuals and institutions that sought control through them, one merely needed to comprehend the material nature of the universe and the implications of that nature. The Skeptics and Cynics agreed, but saw the "truth" of the matter differently.

> **Muses**
>
> Our greatest anxiety arises by thinking heavenly bodies are blessed and immortal, and yet have desires and actions and motives inconsistent with those beliefs; and by dreading some everlasting misery as envisioned by myths ... reduced to dread, not for any good reason but by a vague irrational foreboding.
>
> —Epicurus, *Letter to Herodotus*

It's an Historical Disease

Other modern approaches see myths as traditional stories that preserve history in a convoluted fashion. Nevertheless, one can recover historical truths or facts from the myths, with the proper method of understanding. This historical approach to myth has its roots in Greek history (Herodotus was already doing it), and particularly in the work of Euhemerus of Messene (fl. 300 B.C.E.). Euhemerus was influenced by the view that religious worship proceeded, historically, from *deifying* celestial phenomena to deifying beneficial humans, and he noticed how Alexander and the Hellenistic rulers of his day were becoming gods. Euhemerus claimed to have found an inscription on the island of Panchaea (in the

> **Labyrinths**
>
> Interpretive models are useful tools for extracting meaning from myths, but none is without flaws. Models that depend upon allegory, for example, all make terrific sense as long as you accept their symbolic codes. However, the meanings, formulation, and sources of the codes are difficult to verify or authenticate outside of the models themselves.

Lexica _____

To **deify** is to make something or someone into a god or divine being. **Euhemerism** is an approach where myths are thought to contain historical facts that have been amplified and exaggerated in an historical process of transmission.

Indian Ocean; another kind of Atlantis) that showed that the Greek gods were really rulers of long ago who had also become deified and the subjects of myths. For him, both the origins and causes of myth are to be found in history, and this approach is known as *euhemerism*.

Euhemerus was very influential among Christian writers who hoped to identify immoral acts in myths with immoral pagan culture; and for many people today, the urge to try to tease history out of myths is still strong.

It's a Linguistic Disease

The Greeks also speculated that there might be some kind of underlying or hidden meaning to traditional stories, and if one could find the key to unlocking that meaning, the stories might make sense.

The Stoics, who thought that the entire cosmos is the result of a rational principle, looked for rational explanations in myths as symbols. Others looked for symbolic

Lexica _____

Allegory is an approach where it is thought that myths are, or contain, symbolic elements that must be interpreted metaphorically in order to be correctly understood.

meanings that were more psychological in nature. This metaphorical interpretation of myth, where the elements of the story (or even the story itself) are not what they appear to be but a symbol for something else, became known as *allegory* ("expressing it differently"). Modern psychoanalytic and Jungian interpretive approaches, for example, rely on allegory, as do others, such as semiotics and structuralism, at least in part.

The Least You Need to Know

- Myths are traditional cultural tales that address matters of collective concern.
- Mythology is the study of the functions, origins, and meanings of myth, and traditional stories are often separated into three categories: folktales, sagas, myths.
- The Greeks recognized major gods and goddesses, minor divinities, and numerous vague and unnamed spirits.
- Our knowledge of myths and religious practice comes from a variety of sources, none of which are strictly religious.
- The Greeks developed approaches for explaining the origins, causes, and purposes of myths that are still in use today.

Part 2

The Bronze Age Through the Archaic Period

If you want to understand the ancient Greeks, you can't just arrive in Athens, poke around the Parthenon, and call it a day. Classical Greek culture didn't emerge from a vacuum. It developed over centuries in the shadows of ancient and complex civilizations, such as Egypt, and it was entwined with the development of other fascinating cultures, such as the Minoans, the Phoenicians, and the Persians.

Distilling some of the rich and complex history of the Mediterranean, this section takes you from the Bronze Age birth through the Archaic adolescence of ancient Greece. We peer into the Dark Age and Archaic period to discover the rational and humanistic foundations of classical Greek literature and culture (such as the Olympic Games), and witness the development and maturation of two influential, but very different, city-states: Athens and Sparta.

Chapter 6

Where in the Hellas? Ancient Greece and Its Neighbors

In This Chapter

- ◆ The geography of ancient Greece
- ◆ Ancient Greek settlements around the Mediterranean
- ◆ Other peoples of the ancient Greeks' world
- ◆ Civilizations influential on ancient Greek culture and history

Ancient Greek civilization and culture developed in a part of the world rich in complex civilizations, some already ancient—and others long gone—by the time of Homer (eighth century B.C.E.). Egypt and Mesopotamia (Sumerians, Akkadians, Babylonians) provided the fertile soil on which the great civilizations grew, and around which other influential civilizations—such as the Minoans (on Crete), the Hittites (in Anatolia), and the Mycenaeans (in Greece)—grew and declined. These civilizations collapsed into the Dark Age, from which an eruption of cultures (the Assyrians, Jews, Phoenicians, Persians, Lydians, Greeks, Etruscans, and finally, the Romans) began a westward march. The purpose of this chapter is to set the development of ancient Greece into the context of some of these other cultural histories from the tenth through first centuries B.C.E.

Why the Greeks, a people never politically unified, inhabiting resource-poor and geographically fragmented lands on the edge of major civilizations, became what they did is still something of a mystery and a cultural Cinderella story. To some degree, the Greeks made lemonade from lemons: Their lack of natural resources and geographically inaccessible homelands made them less of a target of conquest (by others and each other) and allowed for their independent and idiosyncratic development. Their material circumstances, which were marginal, and their interconnection with other cultures, which was substantial, seemed to promote and focus their remarkable cultural and intellectual energy.

The Hellenic World

It's not as easy as you might think to identify "ancient Greece" in terms of geography. Greek culture was, throughout its history, always on the move. Even the ancient Greeks, while looking to mainland Greece as the Greek heartland, recognized a migratory past. The first migrations into the Balkan Peninsula occurred around 2000 B.C.E. and, as other migrations took place, Greeks spread to the Aegean islands (where they also encountered and assimilated preexisting *Cycladic* cultures) and around the Mediterranean. Many lived in colonies founded by migrants, and even those on the mainland recognized that indigenous people, known to them as *Pelasgians*, had been there before their arrival (although some Greeks, like the Athenians, claimed to be indigenous).

Lexica

Cycladic refers to the islands of the central Aegean (e.g., Paros, Delos, Naxos).

As mentioned in Chapter 4, the Greeks tended to identify themselves linguistically rather than geographically or racially. They identified early settlements and migrations based on three main categories of dialects. The Aeolic and Ionic dialects came from central Greece (Attic, the dialect of Athens, is an Ionic variation), and they probably represent the earliest migrations and settlements. The Doric dialect came, according to Greek tradition, from a later invasion of Greeks who settled in both northern and southern Greece. All of these dialect groups are represented in the proliferation of colonies and settlements that started in the ninth century B.C.E. By the sixth century B.C.E., Greek settlements and cities could be found from the Black Sea to Spain, with primary concentrations around the Aegean, and in southern Italy and Sicily. We'll start, however, from mainland Greece and work out in all directions to situate the Greeks in the Mediterranean and to give you an idea of the lay of the lands.

A Patchwork Homeland

The ancient Greeks generally recognized Hellas as those lands stretching roughly from somewhere in Macedonia south through the Peloponnesus. The whole region consists of relatively small areas suitable for farming and settlement that were isolated by incredibly rugged terrain and coastlines. Regions were dominated either by clan families and royal warlords (such as in the north and west), or the dominant regional city-state (such as Thebes, Athens, or Sparta in the center and south). No one region, however, was rich enough in resources to sustain populations or materials that were sufficient to conquer and control the rest—at least not for long.

Muses

The wrongs that the Greeks suffered from the Spartans and from us were at least the works of true-born Greeks; one might think of them as terrible mismanagement by legitimate heirs ... but Philip [II of Macedon] ... is not only neither Greek nor related to them, but he's not even a barbarian of anywhere to speak of. He's a rogue from Macedonia, where one never has—and never will—be able to buy even a decent slave.

—Demosthenes, *Philippic 3*, 30–31

Northern Greece

Northern Greece was inhabited by people whom many southern Greeks regarded as barely Greek. Northwest Greece, along the Adriatic, was called Epirus (part of modern Albania). This wild area wasn't unified until the late Classical period by the Macedonian kings. The most famous Epirote king was Pyrrhus, whose *pyrrhic victories* over the Romans in Italy helped lead to Rome's invasion of Macedon.

Lexica

A **pyrrhic victory**, named for the "victories" of King Pyrrhus of Epirus over the Romans, is a victory won at excessive cost, or one that involves staggering losses (and, possibly, eventual defeat).

Labyrinths

If you're looking around for "authoritative" information on Macedonia, be aware that the *ancient* argument over whether Macedonia is, or is not, Greek rages on in *modern* geopolitics (further complicated by the re-naming of the Former Yugoslav Republic of Macedonia) in competing publications (both private and governmental) and on Internet sites.

Northeast Greece was known as Macedon (or Macedonia; the terms are interchangeable when referring to the ancient world), a vast territory of tribal lands divided between a horseshoe of rugged highlands and broad lowland plains. Macedonians recognized a royal family, but it wasn't until Philip II (Alexander the Great's father) that they were really united. To the west was Chalcidice, a large peninsula with three arms projecting down into the Aegean. This was an area rich in silver mines, and an area of contention between Athens and Sparta in the fifth century B.C.E., and between Athens and Macedon in the fourth century B.C.E.

South from Macedonia and over more mountainous terrain were the broad and rich plains of unruly Thessaly, loosely organized into a federation of powerful clan families. The Thessalians were particularly powerful in the sixth century B.C.E., and in the fourth century B.C.E. under the "overlord" (*tagus*), Jason of Pherae. The Thessalians were Dorians; a pre-Dorian population of Aeolic speakers remained in Achaea Phthiotis, just south of Thessaly.

Central Greece

Central Greece extends, in a gentle arch, along the mountainous northern side of the Gulf of Corinth and southward into Attica. To the far west was Acarnania, which remained only marginally Greek throughout these ages, then Aetolia, a mountainous region loosely held together by the Aetolian League, whose members became extremely powerful in the third century B.C.E. Aetolia's chief city was Calydon, famous in Greek myth for the "Calydonian Boar."

East of Aetolia were the lands of Phocis, which included the sanctuary of Delphi. East of Phocis was Boeotia, mainly an agricultural district, whose major city was Thebes (of Oedipus fame). On the eastern border of Boeotia and over Mt. Parnes lay Attica, a region of small plains, good silver mines, and excellent marble and clay. Athens was always the dominant city here. Along the northeast coasts of both Boeotia and Attica lay the enormous island of Euboea, which Athens dominated for most of the Classical period.

> **Odysseys**
>
> Kephallonia, an island off southwestern Acarnania, is often identified as ancient Ithaca, the home of the hero Odysseus.

Southern Greece

Southern Greece is connected to the mainland by the narrow Isthmus of Corinth, named for the flourishing trade city there. The lands below the isthmus are known as the Peloponnesus, or "Island of Pelops" (a mythological hero). With few good harbors, a virtually inaccessible interior, and surrounding districts isolated by mountains, the Peloponnesus maintained some of the most distinctive cultures in Greece.

The interior was known as Arcadia, a wild and mysterious region where pre-Greek and pre-Dorian refugees had retreated from successive migrations and settled. Along the north (the southern coast of the Gulf of Corinth) lay Achaea, whose chief city, Helike, may have been the inspiration for Plato's Atlantis (see Chapter 4). The Achaean cities (the Achaean League) became very powerful in the third century B.C.E.

The western Peloponnesus was known as Argolis, from the city of Argos. This area was rich in history, myth, and culture. Besides being the home of Helen, the Argolid contained the cities of Mycenae and Tyrens (the home of Herakles). Argos was always sandwiched between Corinth and Sparta, and maintained a stubborn but fragile independence.

The lands south of the Argolid were known as Laconia, dominated by the city of Sparta. To the west of Laconia (the southwest Peloponnesus) and over the ridges of Mt. Taygetus, lay the fertile lands of Messenia. The Spartans conquered this territory in the seventh century B.C.E., occupied it, and turned most of its inhabitants into *helots*, or "serfs." Messene was the chief city; the Mycenaean city of Pylos (home of the Homeric king Nestor) remained in ruins until the Athenians fortified it in the Peloponnesian War in order to outflank the Spartans. The eastern Peloponnesus was known as Elis. This remote area, famous for its horses, was largely uninvolved in Greek history except for its supervision of the Olympic Games.

From Sea (Aegean) to Sea (Black) to Sea (Eastern Mediterranean)

From the tenth through seventh centuries B.C.E., Greeks migrated from the mainland and settled throughout the islands and along the shores of the Aegean, Black, and eastern Mediterranean seas. These settlements became great cities and, in some cases, their own regional powers. What's more, some of these settlements, nestled on the edges of other great civilizations, became the source of the Archaic period's literary, cultural, and intellectual developments.

The Aegean

The earliest Greek migrations occurred in the chaos of the Dark Age. Aeolic speakers from central Greece migrated and founded the city of Mytilene on the island of Lesbos and colonized the northern coast of Anatolia (now western Turkey). This area was known as Aeolis. Ionic speakers colonized the southern coast of Anatolia and islands such as Samos; this area became known as Ionia. Among these, Doric speakers colonized islands such as Crete, Cos, and Rhodes. From these early settlements, Greeks went on to further establish colonies on Cyprus, along the Black Sea and northern Africa, and in the western Mediterranean.

The Black Sea

The trade routes from the Black Sea have always been historically important. As Greek city-states grew in population, grain, which was difficult to grow in the poor soil, was a necessary import from these areas. Athens, in particular, depended upon grain shipments, because Attica could not produce enough food for its population. Greek colonies settled all around the Black Sea, and their contact with the peoples of these areas is the source of myths about the Amazons, the Golden Fleece, the Argonauts, and Medea.

One city of note is Byzantium (often called Byzantion, its Greek name), on the Bosporus and Golden Horn. This strategic site, at the confluence of Europe and Asia, has remained important to the Greeks (Byzantium), the Romans (*Nova Roma*, or "New Rome"), Byzantines (Constantinople), and Turks (Istanbul).

The Eastern Mediterranean Sea

Greek traders shared the sea lanes with the Phoenicians, who were busy establishing trading settlements in Cyprus, northern Africa (Carthage), Sicily, Sardinia, and Spain. Besides settlements in Cyprus, the Greeks established two influential cities, one by trade agreement with the Saite Pharaohs in Egypt, Naucratis, and one in present-day Libya, Cyrene. Each developed its own unique culture. Naucratis, besides providing trade goods, was an important exporter of Egyptian influence on the Greeks, and was eventually surpassed by Alexandria. A cluster of cities (Cyrenaica) developed around Cyrene, and it became especially influential as a center of culture in the Hellenistic period.

Magna Graecia and the West

After their initial migrations, Greeks colonists headed west and established a number of cities in southern Italy (as far north as Naples; ancient Greek *Neapolis*, or "New Polis"), on Sicily and Corsica, and in modern France and Spain. Greek settlements were so prolific in Italy and Sicily that this region was sometimes known as *Magna Graecia*, or "Big Greece." Conquered by the Romans in the third century B.C.E., these cities continued to thrive until many were put to rest by malaria in the early Middle Ages, leaving their impressive ruins for later travelers to marvel at.

> **Odysseys**
>
> Some of the finest ancient Greek ruins you can visit are in Magna Graecia (Italy and Sicily). Two particularly impressive sites are the temples of Poseidonia (modern Paestum, south of Naples), and Akragas (modern Agrigento, in Sicily), the home of the Pre-socratic philosopher Empedocles.

Southern Italy

Greek colonies encircled the boot of southern Italy, and many of these cities remain vibrant centers of Greco-Italian culture even today. Particular cities to note are Taras (also known as Tarentum, modern Tarento), which put up stiff resistance to the Romans (including bringing Pyrrhus over from Epirus), and Neapolis (Naples). Other important cities included Croton, Thuri, Locri, Rhegium, Poseidonia, and Cumae.

The magnificent Doric Temple of Hera at Paestum (ancient Poseidonia).

(Photos by Eric Nelson)

Sicily

The rich and strategic island of Sicily was colonized by both Phoenicians and Greeks, with the Phoenicians occupying the western portion of the island's coast. The dominant city of the island was Syracuse, whose famous tyrants became the patrons of both Aeschylus and Plato. Other particularly noteworthy cities were Akragas, Gela, Leontini, and Naxos. Sicily was conquered by the Romans, along with the rest of Magna Graecia, in the third century B.C.E.

Western Mediterranean

Greek colonists continued into the western Mediterranean. Their major settlements were at Alalia, on Corsica, and at Massalia (modern Marseilles). Others were attempted along the Spanish coast and past Gibraltar. But two powerful seafaring rivals, the Etruscans (who controlled the lands and waters off northwestern Italy) and the Carthaginians (who were already heavily into the west), kept further expansion from happening and, in the case of Alalia, forced the Greeks to abandon their settlements.

Meet the Neighbors!

The Mediterranean was not an empty frontier. Wherever the Greeks went, they encountered other peoples, whom they referred to as *barbaroi* (that is, people who go "bar-bar-bar," another linguistic identification). Sometimes these were tribal societies that were, by Greek standards, primitive. The Greeks recognized other societies, like the Egyptians, as advanced, and still others, like the Phoenicians and Etruscans, as competitors.

When the Greeks arrived in boats to found a city, they needed to establish control over their site. Their plans weren't always well-received by the locals, but just as with major development projects now, they weren't always unwelcome either. Eventually all sides had to come to some kind of cooperative agreement or at least grudging acceptance. In some locations and circumstances, the locals and settlers intermarried and created a kind of common culture. Other times, the Greeks faced opposition and established their colonies by conquest. If the Greeks were successful, the surrounding peoples were subjugated and enslaved, or they fled the area. No matter which way it went, however, after colonies were established, the Greeks found themselves having to deal with other powerful cities, tribes, and advanced cultures, and many times they became the object of attack and conquest themselves. Now that we have the Greeks situated in the Mediterranean world, we'll meet some of these tribes, kingdoms, and cultures and see who the ancient Greeks connected with and how.

> **Eureka!**
>
> Barbarian comes from Greek *barbaroi*, which means, "people who don't speak Greek" (and, therefore, sound like they're saying "bar-bar-bar-bar" at you). Because the Greeks identified their language as the mark of a superior culture, *barbaroi* were generally regarded as inferior (although they could be noble) savages.

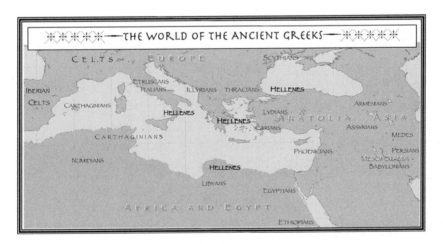

To the North

As we've said previously, the Greeks weren't entirely convinced that the Macedonians qualified as Greeks, but this question of status was often a function of whether the Greeks wanted the Macedonians in or out of a particular equation. Beyond Macedonia, however, there were people whom none of the Greeks would have included as Greek, but whom they recognized as distinctive peoples.

Above and around Macedonia were Indo-European tribal peoples known as the Illyrians, Paeonians, and Thracians. The Illyrians occupied the lands south of the Alps from the Adriatic to the Danube (essentially modern Albania and Bosnia); the Paeonians were a smaller set of this larger group. The Macedonians and Romans both had trouble with these peoples. The Thracians, with whom the Greeks had more contact, were the people who occupied the lands east of the Illyrians and between the Danube and Aegean (essentially modern Bulgaria). The Greeks had contact with about 20 different tribes, which they both feared and disdained for their savage fighting and barbaric practices, such as human sacrifice, tattooing, and (believe it or not!) eating butter. (Even today, it is considered uncouth in various areas to use butter—rather than olive oil—on one's bread!)

> **Odysseys**
>
> The Thracian coast had a number of Greek settlements, particularly the town of Abdera (modern Bouloustra), home of the philosophers Leucippus, Democritus, and Protagoras. Despite its legacy, *Abderite* was a jeer used by the ancient Greeks for "boony-boy" or "hick" because Abdera was *so* far out in the sticks.

Beyond the Thracians were the Scythians, fiercely proud, independent, and brutal nomadic tribes that ranged on horseback around the lands of the Black Sea (today mostly in southern Russia and Hungary). Female Scythian warriors may be the source of the Greeks' conception of the Amazons (see Chapter 4). The Scythians traded war booty with the Greeks for pottery and metal goods.

Near East

When the Greeks occupied the coast of Anatolia (modern Turkey), the Hittite Empire (c. 1750–1200 B.C.E.), which had occupied this area, had already fallen. In its place, the Lydian empire—whose king Croesus (as in "rich as Croesus") was made famous by Herodotus—had a run from the seventh through sixth centuries B.C.E. and had important cultural and military involvements with the Greek settlements, mainland Greece, Egypt, and Persia.

Working along the southern Anatolian coast, other interesting cultures include the Carians, the Lycians (whose culture was *matrilineal* and *matronymic*), and the Cilicians. South, along the coast of present-day Lebanon and Syria, came the Phoenician cities of Biblos, Sidon, and Tyre. It was from these cities that Phoenicians colonized parts of Cyprus, and founded Carthage (near modern Tunis) in about 800 B.C.E. The Carthaginians went on to develop their own western Mediterranean naval empire, with colonies in Sicily and Spain, which nearly defeated Rome.

Lexica _____

Matrilineal means that bloodline is traced through the mother, not the father. (Through the father is patrilineal.) **Matronymic** means that one uses one's mother's name to keep track of one's birth (e.g., Susan Priscillas-daughter, Eric Bettysson).

Eureka! _____

It's worth pausing here to recognize the Phoenicians for their influence on and connections with the Greeks. They were preeminent traders and seafarers: Herodotus reports that they circumnavigated Africa for Pharaoh Necho, and some assert that they reached England. Moreover, it was the Phoenician alphabet, adapted by the Greeks to their own language, that made Homer and the literary genesis of the Archaic period possible.

Into Africa: Egypt and North Africa

By the time of ancient Greece, Egypt was the remaining elder of the civilizations that arose around the Fertile Crescent and Nile Valley. The Sumerian, Akkadian, Hittite, and Babylonian kingdoms had come and gone. But Egypt, which comprised a unification of the Upper and Lower Nile under a single king (Pharaoh), had survived several reincarnations that we know as the Old (c. 2600–2100 B.C.E.), Middle (c. 2000–1700 B.C.E.), and New (c. 1550–1100 B.C.E.) kingdoms. Although Egypt was conquered and ruled by the Assyrians (c. 671 B.C.E.), Persians (c. 525 B.C.E.), Greeks (332 B.C.E.), and Romans (30 B.C.E.), its underlying culture remained as immovable as the pyramids. The occupying forces and rulers left their marks in relatively shallow relief upon the monolith below.

Labyrinths _____

The period of Greek rule over Egypt is known as Ptolemaic from the line of Macedonian pharaohs established by Alexander the Great's general Ptolemy, who controlled Egypt after Alexander's death. The Ptolemaic dynasty ended with the death of Cleopatra in 30 B.C.E.

Egypt was in close contact with the Bronze Age cultures of the Minoans and Mycenaeans, about which we'll learn more in the next chapter. In the Dark Age and Archaic period, Egyptian contacts with Greece re-emerged, first through Phoenician trade, and then through the use of Greek mercenaries by Egyptian pharaohs in the seventh and sixth centuries B.C.E. It was during this time that the pharaohs allowed the Greeks to establish their mercantile trade city of Naucratis on the Nile Delta, and Greeks settled Cyrenaica (Cyrene and Apollonia). From then on, the histories of Egypt and Greece are entwined by the various dynastic struggles and invasions of this ancient land. Naucratis, in particular, served as a conduit for Egyptian influence upon Greece.

> **CAUTION**
>
> ## Labyrinths
>
> *Ethiopian* in Homeric, Archaic, and early Classical literature indicates dark-skinned people who live far away, such as Africans and Indians. From Herodotus onward, however, Ethiopia indicates Africa.

Beyond Egypt, the Greeks were aware of dark-skinned peoples of the Upper Nile, whom they referred to as Ethiopians. Greek traders and mercenaries were in contact with Ethiopia from at least the seventh century B.C.E., and under the influence of Ptolemaic Egypt the Ethiopian city of Meroë became partially Hellenized. Along the coast of Africa, the Greeks in Cyrenaica intermingled with the Berber tribes of that region, but had relatively little contact with the other peoples, such as the Moors, along the Phoenician-dominated western coast.

West and Far West

In Magna Graecia, the Greek colonists of the Archaic period were uneasily sandwiched between the Carthaginians and the Etruscans, who combined to drive the Greeks from Sardinia in 535 B.C.E. Carthage was settled about 800 B.C.E. by Phoenicians, and it became a maritime empire whose outposts included settlements on western Sicily and in Spain. The Etruscans, whose origins are a matter of dispute, dominated northern Italy from Pisa to Naples by 500 B.C.E., and jealously guarded their territory and coastal seas. A combined force of Greeks and Phoenicians defeated the Etruscans in about 470 B.C.E., which crippled the already unstable Etruscan hold on central Italy.

> **Odysseys**
>
> Etruscan cities and remains can be found throughout northern Italy, but Tarquinia, Rome, and Cerveteri are particularly noteworthy sites. The waters between Italy and the islands of Corsica, Sardinia, and Sicily are still known as the Tyrrhenian Sea after the Etruscans, who were known to the Greeks as *Tyrrheni*.

From the fifth century B.C.E. onward, Magna Graecia's history is bound up with the rise of Rome. Rome's conquest of southern Italy and Sicily in the third century B.C.E. brought it into conflict with, and led to the conquest of, Macedon and other Hellenistic kingdoms. We'll examine this complicated history in Chapter 24.

Eastern Orientation: Assyria and Persia

The rich, complicated, and bloody history of Mesopotamia is the subject for an entire shelf of books, but as far as the ancient Greeks go, you have to know something about both the Assyrians and the Persians in order to understand Greek history. The Assyrians were a Semitic people, whose brutal conquest of the Middle East and Egypt (c. 900–612 B.C.E.) established an organizational framework of subject territories (satrapies) under governors (satraps) appointed by the Assyrian king.

The satrap oversaw the collection of tribute, as well as other military and judicial matters pertaining to the empire. Local kings or ruling bodies were under the satrap's jurisdiction. This system of organization incorporated mercenaries and foreigners, which involved Greeks in the affairs of these kingdoms, and it set the stage for later empires. The Assyrian empire came to an end when the Medes and Babylonians combined to defeat them and take their capital, Nineveh (modern Mosul, Iraq).

The Persians, an Indo-European people closely related to the Medes, established an empire under Cyrus the Great with a capital at Persepolis (near modern Shiraz, Iran) that, by the sixth century B.C.E., included Lydia, Egypt, and lands stretching east to India. In the late sixth and early fifth centuries B.C.E., the Persians turned to the unruly lands of the north and west and launched unsuccessful attacks on Scythia and Greece (the Persian War recorded by Herodotus) that galvanized classical Greece and Athens. Although unsuccessful, the Persians remained influential in the outcome and aftermath of the Peloponnesian War. By playing the Greeks one against the other, they regained control of a fair share of Greek Asia and Cyprus by the early fourth century B.C.E., just about 50 years before being invaded and conquered by Alexander the Great.

Muses _____

The historian Xenophon served as a mercenary from 401 to 399 B.C.E. under the Persian Cyrus the Younger (against his brother Artaxerxes II), and he had this to say about Cyrus:

Whenever [Cyrus] was on campaign and was likely to be seen by many, he invited his friends around and held earnest conversations with them to show that he respected them; as a consequence, from everything I have heard, I warrant that no one was ever so esteemed by so many, either Greeks or barbarians.

—*Anabasis* 9.28

Odysseys

Darius (521–486 B.C.E.), whose forces attacked the Athenians at Marathon, was instrumental in improving the Persian Empire's organization and infrastructure. One can still follow parts of his famous 3,000-mile Royal Road from Susa (modern Shush, Iran) to the Lydian capital Sardis (modern Sart, Turkey) and to the ancient Greek port city of Ephesus (Turkey). Pony express riders could travel the whole route in about two weeks.

Although Greek sources, and most western history, tend to portray the Persians in terms of an oriental, despotic culture that was completely separate and opposite from the Greeks, the Greeks and Persians were, in fact, heavily intertwined with and influenced by each other throughout their histories. Although the Greeks definitely saw the Persians as different, they also gave them a great deal of begrudging respect, and they recognized their achievements in ways that distinguished them from other barbarians. Alexander (to the dismay of some Greeks) synthesized Persia's imperial organization and culture with Greek culture, generating a new mix of Persian and Greek elements, which created the Hellenistic world and has been influential ever since.

The Least You Need to Know

- Even the ancient Greeks, while looking to mainland Greece as the Greek heartland, recognized a migratory past.

- Three main categories of dialects (Aeolic, Ionic, and Doric) delineated and represented early settlements and migrations that the Greeks recognized in their own times.

- The ancient Greeks generally recognized Hellas as those lands stretching roughly from somewhere in Macedonia south through the Peloponnesus.

- From the tenth through seventh centuries B.C.E., Greeks migrated from the mainland and settled throughout the islands and along the shores of the Aegean, Black, and eastern Mediterranean seas.

- By the time of ancient Greece, Egypt was the remaining elder of the civilizations that arose around the Fertile Crescent and Nile Valley. The Sumerians, Akkadians, Hittite, and Babylonian kingdoms had come and gone.

- You have to know something about both the Assyrians and the Persians in order to understand Greek history.

Chapter 7

Bullish on the Bronze Age: The Minoans and Mycenaeans

In This Chapter

- ◆ The discovery of Troy, the Mycenaeans, and the Minoans
- ◆ The marvelous Minoan civilization
- ◆ The Minoans and their myth
- ◆ The rise and fall of Mycenaean Greece

Now that we've set the ancient Greeks into their geographical context and into the context of the cultures that surrounded and influenced them, it's time to tell their story in more detail. In order to do this, we must begin in the Aegean Bronze Age with two spectacular cultures, one non-Greek and the other Greek: the Minoans of Crete and the Mycenaeans of Greece.

The Minoans and Mycenaeans are the ancestors, so to speak, of ancient Greece, in historical, cultural, and modern conceptual terms. The discovery of the ancient Minoan and Mycenaean civilizations ignited a renewed interest in, and scholarly reassessment of, ancient Greece. In this chapter, we'll begin with the "discovery" of these cultures (an exciting and intriguing story in and of itself!), and we'll progress to what we know of these important precursors to the Greeks of the historical periods.

Homeric Discoveries

The story of the discovery of the Minoans and Mycenaeans goes back, like western literature (see Chapter 2), to the narratives of Homer and the Bible. Eighteenth-century scholars generally held the opinion that ancient texts were imaginative works of primitive minds with no historical value. But when Egyptian hieroglyphics were deciphered in the early nineteenth century, biblical archeologists searched Egypt and the Middle East for evidence that the Bible is, in fact, an accurate source of historical information. Although they were unsuccessful in Egypt (little, if any, evidence corroborates, for example, Moses and the Exodus), they were more successful in other areas, unearthing cities and settlements recorded in the Old Testament. Since then, the subsequent successes, failures, and complications of biblical archeology have led to fierce debates, which are often further complicated by the personal preconceptions and doctrinal approaches of the participants.

Elsewhere a search involving the works of Homer was beginning to take place. Heinrich Schliemann, an eccentric and restless German, who happened to be a self-made millionaire, turned to the *Odyssey* for solace. Spending time on the modern island of Ithaca, he began to use Homeric texts and local traditions, like Biblical archeologists use the Bible and religious traditions, as a guide to digging up Odysseus' world. When he found artifacts, Schliemann decided to embark on his own epic quest: the discovery of Troy and Mycenae.

> **⚠ CAUTION**
>
> **Labyrinths**
>
> Archeological finds and artifacts connected with the Old and New Testaments are often quickly embroiled in controversy, because claims about their meaning tend to be pronounced preliminarily by people who are deeply invested in certain perspectives. The "Ossuary of James," which first appeared to be the burial box (for bones) of Jesus' brother, but which now appears to involve forgery, is just one recent example.

Schliemann's Discovery of Troy and Mycenae

In 1870, Schliemann went to Turkey, where he began excavating the hill of Hissarlik with John Calvert, an Englishman who partially owned the property. Between 1872 and 1873, Schliemann unearthed the gates of a substantial city, and discovered what he was primarily looking for: treasure. He unearthed a substantial horde of gold, silver, and bronze objects, which he was certain belonged to King Priam's Troy.

Although Schliemann had an agreement with the Turkish government to split any finds, he smuggled the treasures out of the country, and some have only been recently rediscovered. (See Chapter 4 for more information on Troy.)

Schliemann, *persona non grata* in Turkey after smuggling out the treasures, next negotiated with Greece to excavate Mycenae under stricter supervision. There, he unearthed buildings, burials, and treasures. Some of his most spectacular finds were stunning gold death masks, one of which he proclaimed the mask of Agamemnon himself. Convinced that he had found both the city and the bodies of Agamemnon and Clytemnestra, Schliemann set out to excavate Tiryns, Ithaca, Marathon, and eventually Troy again (under the very watchful eye of the Turkish government!). He made archeological finds, but didn't unearth any more of the kind of treasure, palaces, or stunning artifacts that most interested him. He died in 1890, leaving the face of Aegean archeology forever changed and, fortunately, in the hands of more careful archeologists.

> **Eureka!**
>
> Schliemann's "Treasure of Priam" was smuggled out of Turkey, first to Greece and other locations, and finally to Berlin. A Nazi curator gave it to the victorious Russians to protect it from looters, and it remained in secret, as war plunder, at the Pushkin Museum until 1993.

> **Labyrinths**
>
> Heinrich Schliemann is a complicated figure, vilified by some as a treasure-seeking megalomaniac (he ruled his house in Athens like a Homeric king: only Greek was spoken and he renamed his servants after Homeric characters), and lionized by others as a visionary and larger-than-life pioneer of archeology.

Evans and the Discovery of Knossos

Schliemann's discoveries, in combination with subsequent archeological work, inspired Arthur Evans, the keeper of antiquities at the Ashmolean Museum of Art and Archaeology at Oxford, to begin excavations of his own. Evans began excavations in Crete at Knossos, a site that had been of interest to archeologists for some time. There, he and his teams unearthed a spectacular palace complex, which was advanced far beyond and quite unlike anything seen previously. There were multistory buildings, vibrant frescoes, Europe's first paved road, written records in two related scripts, and indoor plumbing! He named the culture "Minoan" after the mythical King Minos of Crete, the son of Zeus and Europa.

Eureka!

Minoan and Mycenaean art and artifacts are full of pictures of bulls—bull sacrifices, bull-jumping games, and bulls in the fields—which were religiously and politically symbolic animals. Greek myth also connects Crete with bulls. Zeus, in the form of a bull, kidnaps Europa and brings her to Crete; their son, Minos, constructs the Labyrinth (a complex maze) at Knossos to contain the half-bull, half-human monster, the Minotaur.

A look at the ruins of the multistory Minoan palace at Knossos.

(Photo by Eric Nelson)

No Cretans: Minoan Civilization and Culture

Evans' discovery of an advanced, but previously unknown, Bronze Age culture rocked the archeological world. His imaginative, partial reconstruction of the site at Knossos has met with both admiration and condemnation, however, because it tended to fix Evans' vision of Knossos, which was in part the product of his own creative impulses and biases, as canonical. Nevertheless, the art, architecture, and evidence all suggest that the Minoans had a distinctive and individual culture, with substantial creative resources of their own, and that they were highly influential on the Bronze Age Greeks, whom we know as the "Mycenaeans."

Origins and Language

Crete is a huge island, situated evenly between the continents of Asia, Africa, and Europe, with enough room to accommodate migrations from many places. The origin of the Minoans is something of a mystery, however, in that there is no obvious migration of people from any one area that we can point to as the ancestors of the Minoans. It's probable that peoples from Anatolia, other islands, Egypt, and northern Africa were already on the island when Minoan culture developed during the Pre-Palatial period (c. 2600–1900 B.C.E.). Generally, it's now thought that the most substantial portion of the island's population came from Anatolia, because of both proximity and some similarities between early Minoan and Carian (southern Anatolia) cultures.

It would be helpful if we knew which language the Minoans spoke, but we don't. Palace records, imprinted onto clay tablets in a script known as *Linear A*, date from about 1800 B.C.E. This script, probably inspired by Egyptian *hieroglyphics*, developed from *pictographs* into an elaborate *syllabic* script that we have yet to decipher. Unfortunately, we simply don't possess enough Linear A tablets to determine which kind of language it represents. However, it is generally thought that the Minoans spoke a West Semitic dialect. Until a sufficient number of documents are found, or some kind of bilingual document turns up (such as the Rosetta Stone), we won't know for sure. Linear A was adapted by the Mycenaeans to their own language, which was Hellenic, when they conquered Crete in the fifteenth century B.C.E. This script is known as *Linear B*, and it has been translated.

Labyrinths

Evans quickly unearthed numerous artifacts at Knossos and, unfortunately, accurate records of very important data (such as where and at what depth written tablets were found) were either lost or never compiled. It even appears that, later, Evans tweaked some of this data to fit his own claims for dating.

Lexica

A **hieroglyphic** script uses pictures, or **pictographs,** to represent words, like the bumper sticker "I [heart] my [picture of a breed of dog]." If the symbols are **syllabic,** they represent syllables such as "ba" or "po."

Linear A is the system of writing on clay tablets used by the Minoans c. 1800 to 1450 B.C.E.; **Linear B** is an adaptation of Linear A by the Mycenaeans to their own language c. 1450 to 1200 B.C.E.

Periods and Palaces

Based on archeological evidence, Minoan history is broken down into several periods. These periods follow the rise of Minoan civilization, including the formation and development of a palace culture, through its gradual decline and domination by the Mycenaeans. The degree to which this domination came about by conquest, agreement, natural disaster, or some combination of these factors is unknown. The periods (we've used approximate dates, since there is some controversy about specific dates and dating) and their general developments are as follows:

♦ **Pre-Palatial period (c. 2600–1900 B.C.E.).** Agricultural settlements on Crete developed along with trade between Egypt and Anatolia. With an increase in population, there was the appearance of social stratification (concentration of wealth and power) and the emergence of trades in pottery and metalworking.

♦ **Old Palatial period (c. 1900–1700 B.C.E.).** Sometime around 1900 B.C.E., Crete underwent a profound transformation. Regional palaces emerged (such as at Knossos, Phaistos, and Zakros) as political, economic, and religious centers, and smaller versions of these centers could be found throughout Crete. This change was fueled and supported by organized control of the surrounding lands, and by an explosion of trade between the Minoans and the rest of the Mediterranean. The greatest of these palaces was located at Knossos, but whether Knossos was the "capital" of a unified island, or only the largest (and probably most influential) member of a loose federation of Minoan states, is unknown. Linear A was developed at this time for the management of palace affairs and business.

> **Odysseys**
>
> Although centrally located Knossos (and the nearby Museum at Heraklion) is the most famous destination for travelers interested in the Minoans on Crete, don't overlook other wonderful sites on Crete, which include Phaistos (southern coast), Malia (northern coast), and Kato Zakros (eastern coast).

♦ **New Palatial period (c. 1700–1450 B.C.E.).** Sometime around 1700 B.C.E., regional earthquakes leveled a sizeable part of Crete (and the Aegean), but an even more vibrant palace culture emerged in its aftermath. (If you visit the grand palace of Knossos today, you will be walking through the palace of this period.) The Minoans seem to have been at the hub of what has been called the "first international age," in which trade links were established between the cultures of Europe, Asia, the Near East, and Africa.

More than international trade exploded in this period, however. Sometime around 1630 B.C.E., the island of Thera, which sat on an active volcano, blew its top with more force than Krakatoa (which erupted in 1883, on the Indonesian

Island of Rakata). We'll explore the impacts of this explosion soon, but the shadow (quite literally) that this eruption cast over the entire eastern Mediterranean was certainly a factor in the decline of the Minoans. It was a gradual decline, however, and it ended with the destruction of the palace centers about 1450 B.C.E.

◆ **Post-Palatial period (c. 1450–1100 B.C.E.).** When the dust finally settled over the ruins of the New Palatial period, we find the Mycenaeans in possession of Crete. The Mycenaeans incorporated and adapted the palace culture of the Minoans, and there was a brief flourishing of Knossos, which had considerable influence on Mycenaean centers, such as Pylos, in southern Greece. This is the period in which, besides adapting Minoan organization, art, and architecture, the Mycenaeans adapted the Minoan Linear A script to the Greek language in a version that we call Linear B. When the Mycenaean civilization crumbled, what was left of Minoan civilization went with it.

Culture, Society, and Trade

It is important to remember that, although you can read a great deal about Minoan culture and society, we have no (usable) written records from them. They left no texts and no history—nothing in their own words. Moreover, we have no written records by their contemporaries that are about them. What we know, we surmise from archeological and pictorial evidence (vases, frescoes), from comparison and contrast with cultures that had contact with the Minoans, and by way of comparison with other human experience. All of these mechanisms have limitations, so the best arguments incorporate evidence from all of them. Even then, however, we are still in the realm of forensic imagination rather than deductive certainty.

Still, we *think* we know this much: Palace structures and economies (such as those found throughout the Mediterranean in this period) require intense and prolonged concentrations of regional economic and cultural resources at a particular site. Moreover, to survive and flourish, they must support and control economic, social, military, and religious structures and organization. History and experience suggest that this was accomplished by way of stratified

> **Muses**
>
> [King] Minos was the first we know of to establish a navy and dominance over what is now called the Hellenic sea. He controlled the Cyclades, on which he established the first colonies, and expelled the Carians and appointed his own sons as rulers; all this, it seems, to put down piracy in those waters as best he could and secure revenues for his own purposes.
>
> —Thucydides, 1.4

societies, which were controlled and managed by an elite class (priests, kings/queens). The elite class controlled religious and military affairs, a corps of specialized workers (scribes, tradesmen), and the production and distribution of resources in the surrounding lands. Elites used the wealth gained from surplus production (taxes, tribute) and the control of valuable natural resources (such as mining) for trade purposes and to build, protect, and develop both the palaces and the societies that went with them.

CAUTION

Labyrinths

Some people theorize that the Minoans worshipped a "great goddess," a common feature of the—supposedly kinder and gentler matriarchal or gynocentric—cultures of pre-Bronze Age Europe and Asia. Although popular in appeal, these claims have been complicated by further analysis and evidence and, in some cases, the "great goddess" hypothesis has been abandoned altogether.

The Minoan Old and New Palatial periods have the archeological features necessary for us to generally conclude that Minoan Crete must have had many of the social and cultural features that elsewhere accompany them. And, for the most part, the remaining evidence bears out this conclusion. Some anomalies, however, are worth mentioning. For instance, there is a relative lack of fortifications and, scattered around Crete, there are important buildings of the New Palatial period that don't fit neatly into any of our residential or palatial categories. So, many aspects of Minoan culture remain a mystery (e.g., were the buildings villas of the nobility?) and suggest that some parts of Minoan culture may not match our preconceptions or analogies.

Minoan religion appears to be goddess-centered, in that the preponderance of deities represented by icons and in images are female. Judging from artistic scenes, female priestesses held positions of honor and prestige in Minoan society. We have representations of elaborate processions, sacrifices, and dances. Palace centers had shrines in their complexes, but the principle sanctuaries appear to have been on mountaintops and in caves. Religious symbols, including animals, double axes, and stylized motifs, all of which are poorly understood, abound. All in all, they paint a picture of a society that was enthusiastically religious.

Arguments about the Minoans center on questions concerning the humanitarian quality of their culture. For example, how much control did the elites exercise over the rest of the population? How "elite" were the rulers, and was the society more egalitarian in some fashion than others? And what position did women hold within the society? For, although the surrounding palace cultures often featured militaristic, brutal, patriarchal, and oppressive social organizations, the differences in Minoan art and architecture seem to hold out the hope that the noble achievements of a civilization might have been accomplished without ignoble means.

Beautiful Dreamer: Minoan Art and Architecture

The art and architecture of the Minoans *are* distinct: distinctly beautiful, graceful, functional, and compelling. Their multistory palace structures—which feature light wells, good ventilation, open courtyards, complex indoor drains and plumbing, aesthetic (versus strictly strategic) placement, and multiple entrances—emerge from the landscape like artfully arranged stacks of cardboard boxes. Their art, on pottery and in magnificent frescoes (from Knossos and sites such as Akrotiri, on Thera, modern Santorini), is worthy of any modern gallery. Charming nature motifs; lithe young Minoans engaged in boxing, bull-jumping, fishing, and religious rituals; and even a few scenes of naval conflict and village life paint a picture of a remarkably exuberant and intriguing people.

A graceful seascape from the "Queen's Room" at Knossos.

(Photo courtesy of Norita White)

Wouldn't It Be Nice? Making Myths of the Minoans

Such intrigue has led to conjecture about the Minoans and, for some, to characterizations of their society as a utopian and alternative model for civilization (one that allows for advanced civilization without its less-"civilized" features). Generally, the conjecture runs something like this: Minoan settlements lack the same defensive features and fortifications that we see in other societies, so perhaps the (cooperative) Minoans had little to fear from one another or outside forces. Minoan settlements on the islands seem to be mostly trading posts, rather than colonies, so perhaps the (peaceful) Minoans were not obsessed by conquest. Female images and nature scenes abound, so perhaps the (egalitarian) Minoans avoided the dominance model of other patriarchal cultures and celebrated, rather than subjugated, females and nature in a reverence for life.

Unfortunately, further excavations at Knossos and other Minoan sites do not support such an uncomplicated picture, nor do they suggest that the Minoans were entirely different from their neighbors and the rest of humanity. Nevertheless, scholarly consideration of evidence for defensive fortifications, island outposts, weapons production and trade (the Minoans appear to have been influential in developing arms technology), social structure, and human sacrifice (including grisly remains) is often obscured by polarized debate. Such debate often seems geared to protect the Minoans' place in a particular view of history rather than to discover their actual place in it. In any case, be aware that the Minoans seem, from their very beginning, to have been the inspiration for myths of all kinds.

Thar She Blows! Thera and the Minoans

In about 1630 B.C.E., the volcanic island of Thera (modern Santorini), which faces the northern coast of Crete, blew its top in a massive volcanic explosion of the kind that occurs (thank the gods) only about once in 10,000 years. Besides sending out tidal waves (some up to 50 feet high) that would have obliterated coastal settlements in several directions, ash showered (up to 10 feet deep) over parts of the Aegean. Plumes of ash, carried by the winds, reached as far away as the Black Sea and the Nile Delta, and affected weather and crop patterns in the whole Mediterranean basin.

Thera and Atlantis: Snow Job or Pumice Job?

In 1967, excavations on Santorini led to the discovery of "a Minoan Pompeii"—a city covered and preserved by ash from Thera's eruption. Initially, the eruption of Thera was linked chronologically to the downfall of the New Palatial complexes on Crete (in about 1450 B.C.E.), and romantically to Plato's myth of Atlantis. The sudden destruction of the Minoan culture, whose brilliant remains were easy to romanticize, seemed to fit with the sudden destruction of the idealized culture of Atlantis. It was argued that, in telling the story of Atlantis, Plato must have used remnants of folk traditions about the Minoans that were otherwise reflected in Greek myths and traditions (such as one finds in myths of Zeus, Europa, Minos, Theseus and Ariadne, and Daedalus and Icarus).

> **Odysseys**
>
> Don't neglect to visit one of the most dramatic sites in Greece: the island of Santorini (Thera). Besides the beauty of gleaming white towns clinging to the sides of the ancient volcano, you can enjoy the haunting excavations of the Minoan city of Akrotiri (covered, like Pompeii, by ash).

Greek myth traditions, however, don't support an idealized picture of the Minoans, for King Minos' Crete was a cruel empire (with human sacrifice, one might add). But, it has been countered, if Minoan civilization was suddenly and catastrophically destroyed, it is possible that the Minoans, who could not speak for themselves, have been inaccurately rendered by people unfamiliar with their actual culture and history. Even given this possibility, the location of Minoan Crete doesn't fit with Plato's placement of Atlantis in the Atlantic Ocean (see Chapter 4). Nevertheless, the urge to suggest a link between Minoan Crete and Atlantis has both retained a powerful hold on the imagination and helped to popularize Minoan studies.

 Muses

And upon [the shield] the famous strong-armed smith created an elaborate dancing circle, like the one that Daedalus made long ago for lovely-haired Ariadne in the spaces of broad Knossos; young men and women, sought for their beauty with gifts of oxen, were dancing there, holding hands at the wrist.

—Homer, *Iliad* 18.590–594, the Shield of Achilles

Warlords of the Walls: Mycenaean Civilization and Culture

Mycenaean refers to the Bronze Age Greek civilization that flourished from about 1600 to 1200 B.C.E. Mycenaean culture followed the path of other cultures of the time, with the development of centralized palace economies and their accompanying social, military, and religious structures. There were major settlements at Thebes, Athens, Tiryns, Mycenae, and Pylos, and many others could be found throughout central and southern Greece, the coast of Anatolia, and, eventually, Crete.

The Mycenaeans seem distinctly different from their Minoan neighbors. Their culture was more obviously warlike (their decorative arts feature far more violence), and they engaged in both trade and piracy. Also their architecture differs in ways that might imply significant differences in cultural organization and character.

Eureka!

Mycenaean fortifications were built with cut and dry-fit stones of such size that later Greeks thought the mythical Cyclopes must have had a hand in their construction. These walls are still referred to as "cyclopean."

The Mycenaeans built gargantuan fortifications (which, in later times, became the subject of myth) and grandiose tombs, such as the massive *tholos* ("beehive") tombs of

Lexica

A tholos is a monumental stone burial chamber cut into a hillside in the shape of a conical beehive (*tholos*). It had a processional entrance with huge bronze doors. A **megaron** is a large interior hall, with a large, circular, raised hearth and a chimney vent in the center. Megarons have a portico entrance at one end, a small anteroom at the other, and four pillars around the hearth to support balconies and the roof.

Mycenae. These practices seem more in keeping with the egoistic rulers of the Near East and Egypt than with the Minoans of Crete. The architectural spaces that the Mycenaeans designed for communal and societal functions were also different. Whereas the Minoans designed around open courtyards, the Mycenaeans focused on the *megaron* (or "great room," a kind of king's hall).

On the other hand, it is rarely easy to maintain stark contrasts between the Minoans and Mycenaeans, especially if they are based on such differences alone. If we formulated claims about other societies, using only the same kinds of limited evidence that we have about the Minoans, a surprising number of despotic regimes might end up classified as "utopian" or qualify for Atlantis. Indeed, the Mycenaeans grew and flourished, in part, by becoming closely intertwined with, and influenced by, the Minoans over several centuries. Gradually, the Mycenaeans usurped the Minoans' place in trade and dominated their homeland, but by then they had adopted (and adapted) Minoan organization, art, and written script. Teasing out the similarities and differences, and sorting out the influences and incorporations, and then making distinctions based on them, will remain a process that is both extremely difficult and subject to revision.

A Mycenaean tholos tomb—the "Tomb of Clytemnestra"—from Mycenae.

(Photo courtesy of Norita White)

Origins and Language, Periods and Palaces

Just as with the Minoans, the origin of the Mycenaeans is something of a mystery. But, from Linear B tablets recovered from Pylos and Knossos, we know that the Mycenaeans spoke an early form of Greek, and that they worshipped most, if not all, of the same major Greek gods that the later Greeks recognized. Also, with the Mycenaeans, Bronze Age Greece transformed from an agrarian backwater to a palace-economy power. Mycenaean history breaks down into three phases:

- **Early (c. 2000–1600 B.C.E.).** Hellenic peoples migrated into Greece and settled there. Agrarian settlements developed, which then followed the progression of other Mediterranean cultures: there were increases in population, the development of trade and contacts with other complex civilizations, and the evolution of a more centralized and hierarchical social and political system. During this time, the Minoan's developed contacts with the islands of the Aegean and with the Mycenaeans.

- **Middle (c. 1600–1400 B.C.E.).** Following the eruption of Thera (c. 1630 B.C.E.), Mycenaean power and influence sharply increased. Evidence from burials suggests that Mycenaean leaders solidified their control over surrounding territories, expanded their trade contacts throughout the Aegean, and greatly increased their power, wealth, and status relative to the elites of other cultures. Chariots, probably imported from the Hittites of Anatolia, made their appearance around 1600 B.C.E., as a military innovation (of little use in mountainous Greece) and a mark of prestige. About 1500 B.C.E., grand tholos tombs began to appear, and by 1450 B.C.E. the Mycenaeans were in control of Knossos. Mycenaean settlements, like those at Miletos and on Rhodes, became powerful presences in the region. The artifacts from Schliemann's famous excavations at Mycenae come from this period.

- **Late (c. 1400–1200 B.C.E.).** During this time, the Mycenaeans reached the zenith of their power in Greece, Crete, and the coast of Anatolia. Minoan influence in this period, seen in comparisons between Knossos and Greece, is so apparent that scholars initially thought that the Minoans had conquered the Mycenaeans, not the other way around! The Mycenaeans were particularly involved with the Hittites, and they appear in Hittite records as the

> **CAUTION**
>
> **Labyrinths**
>
> Ancient "trade" in this period occurred primarily between, and under the strict control of, palace centers in the form of "gift exchanges" as a part of embassies, weddings (dowries), and other official occasions. There was little, if any, private enterprise. Palace economies controlled the resources to make and outfit ships and to fill their holds.

Ahhiyawa, which is probably the root of *Achaean* (Homer's generic term for "Greek"), and *Millawanda* (probably the Mycenaeans of Miletos). There is also good evidence for their direct contact with Egypt. Besides evidence of trade goods, Mycenaean settlements are listed among the "subject" peoples of the pharaohs (though "subject" includes "people who give the pharaoh gifts" according to the trade system) of this period.

Palace Culture and Society

At its height, the Mycenaean palace system was a complex social, military, and economic organization that generated and maintained great power and wealth. The Linear B texts, especially those unearthed at Knossos and Pylos, give us a good idea of how it worked. At the top was the *wanax*, or "lord." Under him, high-ranking officials such as the *lawagetas* (probably "commander" or "heir designate"), the *telestai* (possibly "priests" or "baronal landholders"), and *korete* (probably "regional administrators") oversaw the collection, production, and protection of palace resources. These officials received their lands from the *wanax* and, in return, gave him their service and a share of their resources. Military enforcement and raiding for the kingdom seem to have been the job of a "military caste," the *hequetai*. Villages were under the supervision of the "local magistrate," or *pasireu*.

The palace was a beehive of activity and accounting. Masons, potters, carpenters, weapons makers, goldsmiths—specialists of all kinds—worked under the supervision of the elite and the careful eye of scribes, who noted and inventoried everything from a dented tripod to a finished chariot. Textile production, from carding wool to the embroidery of finely woven fabrics, was a large part of the palace economy, and where women mostly worked. Metalwork, pottery containing plain and perfumed oils, and textiles appear to have been the Mycenaeans' major trading items (although these are the items most easily preserved by time), which they traded for exotic and luxury goods and spices, copper and tin, and other desirable commodities.

> ### Odysseys
>
> The Mycenaean site of Pylos is a good place to contemplate both the end and the legacy of the Mycenaeans. Here, in the fires that consumed the palace, the scribes' temporary clay records in Linear B were hardened into permanent documents that provide a window into what Mycenaean palace life was like.

Then, shortly after 1200 B.C.E., probably within the span of two generations, the powerful Mycenaean world came to a sudden and fiery end. The palaces of central and southern Greece, from Thessaly to the tip of southern Greece, were destroyed and never rebuilt. Some centers, such as Mycenae and Tiryns, seem to have attempted a recovery, but were destroyed again shortly thereafter. Knossos, too, fell. Beyond the Mycenaeans, the Hittite empire also fell, and just as mysteriously. Cities throughout Anatolia and Syria were destroyed and burned, including, apparently, Troy.

Whatever happened, by 1100 B.C.E. the Mycenaeans had abandoned some of their most fertile territory in Greece and fled east and west. They left ruined palaces, depopulated lands, and a mysterious void in Greek history that has never been quite filled or explained. But that is where we'll pick up again in the next chapter.

Labyrinths

Almost all dates in Mediterranean archeology are established by comparison with Egyptian and Anatolian artifacts, which have their own accepted chronology. Recently, highly controversial proposals that radically revise these dates would place the fall of the Mycenaeans closer to 900 B.C.E. than to 1100 B.C.E. If correct, this dating would erase the long "Dark Age" that followed the collapse of Mycenaean civilization.

The Least You Need to Know

◆ The Minoans and Mycenaeans are the ancient progenitors, so to speak, of ancient Greece, in historical, cultural, and modern conceptual terms.

◆ Based on archeological evidence, Minoan history is broken down into several periods: Pre-Palatial (2600–1900 B.C.E.), Old Palatial (1900–1700 B.C.E.), and New Palatial (1700–1450 B.C.E.).

◆ Although you can read a great deal about Minoan culture and society, we have no (usable) written records from them, and they have been the inspiration for all sorts of myths.

◆ Mycenaean refers to the Bronze Age Greek civilization that flourished from about 1600 to 1200 B.C.E.

◆ At its height, the Mycenaean palace system was a complex social, military, and economic organization that generated and maintained great power and wealth.

◆ Shortly after 1200 B.C.E., the powerful Mycenaean world came to a sudden and fiery end.

Chapter 8

The Mysterious "Dorian Invasion" and the Obscurities of the "Dark Age"

In This Chapter

- ◆ Explanations for the mysterious fall of the Mycenaeans
- ◆ The Dorian invasion and Sea-Peoples controversy
- ◆ Lighting up the Dark Age
- ◆ Linking Homer to the Bronze and Dark Ages

As we said in Chapter 7, the reasons for the fall of the Mycenaean civilization are still unknown. Moreover, until recently, the collapse left a 400-year void in Greek history, from about 1150 to 750 B.C.E., known as the "Dark Age" of Greece. At one end, a rather *homogeneous* Mycenaean civilization seems to go into a shredder and, four centuries later, a much more *heterogeneous* Archaic Greek culture emerges. It isn't until the Hellenistic period that a similarly homogenous "Greek" common culture is re-established.

Until fairly recently, the Dark Age occupied a kind of hallowed and untouchable place in Greek history. Without written records, developed archeological sites (such as the palace centers), or other obviously reliable evidence, it seemed that the Dark Age was destined to remain a mystery. Careful and thoughtful scholarship, however, has begun to piece together this period with evidence from archeology, linguistics, comparative analysis with other cultures, and Greek traditional sources (such as Homer). What scholars have found are only shards, tiny pieces of the overall puzzle, but this puzzle is slowly, but surely, coming back together.

Now, instead of darkness and discontinuity, the Dark Age has a form that gives us some historical continuity between the Mycenaeans and the Archaic period—even if we are still missing many details. In this chapter, we'll tell you which pieces of the puzzle we have, and give you an idea of what scholars think might go into the remaining blank spots.

Fire and Sword or Rock 'n' Roll? The Sudden Fall of the Mycenaeans

We know this much: The Mycenaean centers were destroyed. But why? Until fairly recently, the pervasive theory about the fall of the Mycenaeans came from ancient Greek tradition, which claimed that, in remote antiquity, a race of Dorians (so-called because they spoke a Doric dialect), the *Heracleidai* ("the descendants of Heracles"), invaded and conquered parts of Greece. Scholars theorized that the Dorians represented an influx of Greeks who—perhaps motivated by the rich prize of the palaces or driven out of their own homelands by invasion—attacked and burned the Mycenaean centers.

A similar theory came from Egyptian reports of attacks by "land and Sea Peoples," which occurred during the same time that the Mycenaean centers suffered attack. Perhaps, it was thought, the "Sea Peoples" who were bold enough to attack Egypt, were also responsible for the destruction of the Mycenaean palaces. However, recent evidence has called into question these explanations, at least in their simpler forms. Excavators, for example, have advanced the idea that earthquakes (rather than attack) caused the initial destruction of the centers at Mycenae and Tiryns. Other scholars have wondered if social or civic unrest might have rocked the Mycenaean social, economic, and civic order and led to its collapse. Some have looked to internal forces, noting that Mycenaean wealth was increasingly gained by upper-class control and exploitation of both material resources and the people that utilized them in production. Perhaps the people below the elite class rebelled.

Still other scholars have looked to external factors that might have undermined the tightly structured systems of the Mycenaean palace economy: disruptions in trade, ecological changes (brought on by drought or deforestation), or the inability to adapt to changing markets. We'll examine all of these theories in a bit more detail below, after we go over the evidence.

CAUTION

Labyrinths _____

As indicated in Chapter 1, we often look to the past to understand our own present and our possible future. The application of modern theories (from Marxist to economic to systems collapse theories) to the fall of the Mycenaeans shows how "new" tools of analysis also often reflect attempts to understand history in terms of contemporary concerns and perspectives.

Trouble in Paradise?

There's good evidence that a sense of foreboding hung over the Mycenaean palace centers in the thirteenth century B.C.E. In Mycenae, Tiryns, and Athens, significant defensive improvements—such as enlarged walls, storage areas, and underground water systems—suggest that these palaces were in a hurry to prepare themselves to survive prolonged sieges. Although each of them survived initial attacks, only Athens appears to have survived in the end.

In addition, there is evidence that someone began to construct a huge fortification wall across the Isthmus at Corinth, and this evidence is equally suggestive. Such a massive construction project, whether initiated by one or more centers, represents the kind of outlay of expense and energy not undertaken unnecessarily. The object of the wall was presumably to seal off the Peloponnesus from land invasion from the north, which seems to indicate a well-anticipated threat from that direction.

In the south, Linear B tablets at Pylos mention "watchers by the sea," which has been taken to indicate coast guards, on lookout for anticipated attacks from that direction. Whichever ways the Mycenaeans were looking, they didn't have long to wait.

And the Walls Came A-Tumblin' Down

Over the next century to century and a half, bad things began to happen. In central Greece, Mycenaean settlements in Phocis (e.g., Krisa) and Boeotia (e.g., Thebes) were destroyed and, in some cases, abandoned. The citadel at Athens was burned. However, the city may have remained in the hands of its defenders, and there is evidence of a refugee population.

Eureka!

Athenian tradition proudly held that it alone survived the invasions of the late Bronze Age, and served as a refuge for others. Although archeological evidence suggests that Mycenaean Athens was destroyed in this period, it also suggests that the city was not abandoned like other Mycenaean sites.

In southern Greece, things were even worse. Both major (e.g., Mycenae and Tiryns) and minor settlements throughout Corinth and the Argolid were destroyed by fire, although a massive earthquake might have initiated the fires. The same thing occurred in Laconia and, in Messenia, the palace at Pylos was burned and abandoned. In the wake of these calamities, the once-populous and -fertile lands of the Peloponnesus suffered an almost unimaginable loss of population. By the eleventh century, for example, Lefkandi (near Tiryns), a significant Dark Age settlement, supported a mere 15 people.

Relics of Mycenaean conquerors ... soon to become refugees. A boar's tusk helmet from the Museum of Herakleion, Crete, dated 1450–1300 B.C.E.

(Photo by Eric Nelson)

Where did the Mycenaean populations go? Well, in short, anywhere but the palace centers. By land, increased tombs in Arcadia and Achaea suggest that many refugees from the Mycenaean centers fled to these rugged regions and stayed there. By sea, similar findings on the Ionian islands, Cyprus, and sites on Crete indicate substantial arrivals of refugees during this time. One place they didn't go was Knossos—that palace suffered its final destruction in this same period.

> **Muses**
>
> Odysseus also put on his head a helmet made of a leather cap. Inside, many leather straps crisscrossed tightly back and forth, while on the outside, the white teeth of a gleaming-tusked boar were sewn skillfully one next to another.
>
> —Homer, *Iliad* 10.261–264

Did Mycenaean Civilization "Fall" or "Fall Apart"?

Can these multiple events be attributed to one cause, or were there separate causes for individual events—perhaps ones that can be unified or better explained by identifying and understanding the underlying common features? Well, that's what everyone is trying to figure out.

As we said, the traditional view is that some outside force invaded and brought down the Mycenaean world. This view is suggested by ancient traditions and, to some extent, supported by the evidence. Recent approaches haven't abandoned these traditional views altogether, but they tend to identify underlying forces, which were common to Mycenaean palace and/or Bronze Age Aegean cultures, that brought about individual collapses at specific Mycenaean sites.

Who Turned Out the Lights? The Dorian Invasion and Sea-Peoples Controversy

No one questions the fact that many Mycenaean settlements were burned and abandoned. Instead, the questions remain focused on who, when, and why. If there was an invasion, it seems that a considerable outside force would have been needed to bring about this level of destruction. The usual suspects have been either the Dorians, suggested by ancient traditions, or the Sea Peoples, identified in Egyptian records. Both of these suspects were favorites of nineteenth- and early-twentieth-century explanations, and such explanations still have a considerable presence in books on Greek history. Let's look at each in turn.

The Dorian Invasion

A fault line of Mycenaean destruction and depopulation stretches from north to south, and the waves of refugees fleeing the Mycenaean centers flow east (by sea) and west (by land). So it's not unreasonable to attribute these events (especially given both tradition and history) to an invasion from the north. The construction of defenses at Corinth, for example, seems to indicate preparations for just such an invasion. Until quite recently, a massive Dorian invasion was the commonly accepted cause of the Mycenaean collapse and depopulation.

Although these destructions occurred in a kind of geographical line, however, further research shows that they happened out of the expected sequence for an explanation based on either invasion or migration. Moreover, to date, there is no good evidence from Thessaly or Macedonia of substantial forces moving through these areas into Greece. In addition (and quite significantly), a linguistic case can be made that the Doric dialect is, in fact, the dialect of the common Mycenaean people. If true, evidence that was once thought to indicate Dorian migrations *into* Greece and the islands is really evidence of the flight of preexisting Mycenaean refugees *out of* the population centers. In other words, the linguistic evidence might suggest that Dorians didn't invade Mycenae at all; instead, Doric-speaking Mycenaeans might have fled their own homes and cities.

The Sea Peoples

On the other hand, the Linear B references to "watchers of the sea" at Pylos might indicate that the Mycenaeans feared attacks from that direction. Again, the primary suspects have been the Dorians and the mysterious Sea Peoples, whom Egyptian records state were wreaking havoc on Egypt, the Middle East, Anatolia, and Cyprus in the late thirteenth and early twelfth centuries B.C.E. Tradition holds that the Greeks amassed a force to lay siege to, plunder, and destroy Troy. Perhaps the Sea Peoples similarly attacked Mycenaean sites along the same north-south axis as each one became an opportunity for plunder. Visual depictions of naval ships (mostly on pottery), together with a number of hilltop "fall-back" sites built on the islands during this period, seem to confirm that attacks from the sea were increasing.

However, there is no agreement as to who the Sea Peoples were, where they came from, or where they went. Scholars now think that the chaos brought on by both the Sea-People attacks and the Dorian migrations was just as likely to be a result of the Mycenaean collapse as it was a cause of it.

It Was Self-Destruction

It has also been suggested that no good evidence for outside forces destroying Mycenae exists, because the forces both defending and attacking the palace centers were composed of Mycenaeans. It's possible that the Mycenaeans waged war with one another, destroying different centers at different times. Greek traditions say that various Homeric heroes (such as Agamemnon and Odysseus) faced unrest and opposition when they returned home from Troy, and other traditions, such as those concerning Thebes, recall civil war. Some scholars believe that these stories come from a time of inter-Mycenaean conflict.

Hellooooo? Is Anybody Home?

There are, however, problems reconciling any of these explanations with the overall evidence of Mycenaean collapse. Particularly troubling is the fact that the palace centers and their lands were abandoned by their inhabitants *and* their supposed attackers. If the Mycenaeans waged war against themselves, why didn't the victors occupy the palaces and continue with a Mycenaean way of life? If someone else conquered them, why did the Mycenaeans flee in large numbers either to remote areas or the islands, and why didn't the conquerors occupy the palaces?

It remains difficult to imagine that *somebody* didn't occupy the former Mycenaean lands. Evidence, however, has been difficult to come by. Some changes in burial practices, a cruder form of unburnished pottery, and what appear to be seasonal huts (such as *pastoral* peoples use) have been found here and there. This meager evidence has led some scholars to wonder if a substantially less-advanced pastoral culture (which would leave little trace) occupied these lands. But the evidence for such a claim is inconclusive. The pottery, for example, may turn out to be a kind of low-grade Mycenaean pottery, which was used simply because the people who remained in the area could create it. Pastoral practices, which took hold in regions like Messenia, but not in others such as Attica, may be the result of local adaptation rather than occupation.

Labyrinths

Mycenaean centers weren't entirely abandoned. The numbers, however, appear to be unimaginably small—perhaps one tenth—in comparison to what was there before and what the land would support.

Lexica

Pastoral refers to organizations based on herds (such as cattle and goats) and herding. Agrarian, on the other hand, refers to organizations based on farming and agriculture.

What Rocked the Boat?

Many people think that individual cases of Mycenaean collapse, which may be particular to a site or region, were nonetheless brought on by some kind of common instability. Whether the root of this instability can be traced to the Mycenaeans themselves, to interference by other peoples, or even to natural phenomena is the object of theories that move beyond invasions or migrations. Let's look at a few of them.

You Say You Want a Revolution

The Pylos Linear B tablets indicate that things were not running smoothly at the palace. Taxes were late, materials were in short supply, and craftsmen were lacking. So there is the possibility of an internal revolution against the Mycenaean elite, and pottery scenes from the period just following the palatial collapses may indicate such a scenario. Animals that symbolized the elite in Mycenaean times, such as lions and sphinx-animals, appear in playful settings that seem to mock their former emblematic functions. Two theories about the origin of a social revolution are as follows:

- **Power to the people.** The Pylos tablets indicate that the Mycenaean elite increasingly exploited the peasant and craftsman classes, which led to a revolution of the people. However, there is no adequate explanation for why this revolution took place all over the Mycenaean world, why the palaces were not rebuilt, or where the revolutionaries went.

- **Chariots a-fire.** Some scholars note that both Mycenaean and Hittite cultures were organized to support, and be protected by, a tightly structured hierarchy of military elites. As the chariot-based hierarchies were defeated and their cities conquered in the thirteenth and twelfth centuries B.C.E., so this argument goes, the social structures depending upon them would have collapsed by force or by foresight.

It's the Economy

Some scholars think that the Mycenaean collapse was precipitated by a collapse in trade. As noted, the Linear B tablets in Pylos indicate that materials and people—both crucial to the palace economy—were in short supply. Elsewhere in the Aegean, the Sea Peoples were disrupting trade and possibly contributing to the downfall of the Hittite empire by destroying the trading city Ugarit. These factors may have caused or contributed to the downfall of the Mycenaeans in the following ways:

◆ **No fuel for the fire.** If the centers were unable to maintain their trading links and wealth, the materials upon which the whole palace system depended would evaporate. Leaving the now-purposeless structure dangerously idle might have caused the instability that brought the palace centers down.

◆ **The economic dinosaur.** Other scholars postulate that, because the Mycenaeans became overspecialized, they were unable to adapt to changing markets or harvest conditions, especially when the commodities upon which their economy depended for trade failed or became less valuable. If true, the Mycenaeans may not have been able to meet the needs of their growing populations, which led to the collapse.

Mother Nature's Child

Other scholars postulate that environmental disasters, either natural or man-made, brought about regional instability in social and economic structures. Two avenues of investigation into such causes are as follows:

◆ **Where have all the flowers gone?** There are some indications of severe climate shifts (both droughts and wet periods) during the time of population growth, which may have destabilized the entire region's harvests. The increase in Mycenaean populations both in Greece and on the islands may have led—as it has elsewhere—to deforestation and soil erosion. In combination with erratic weather and crop patterns, this may have led to famine and social chaos.

◆ **Bad germs, not bad germination.** Over human history, one thing that is known to devastate populations and empty once-fertile lands is the experience and fear of epidemics. It's also true that each "international" age leads both to an international exchange of goods and services and to an international exchange of plagues and pestilences. It's possible that the first international age initiated just such a series of epidemics and plagues. If harvests were bad, poor nutrition and famine may have contributed to the virulence of the illnesses. Although we don't have epidemiological evidence from this period, the increase in the practice of cremation might indicate a response to death by disease.

It's the System, Man

Combinations of all these theories have been incorporated into approaches that see in the Mycenaeans an example of "systems collapse." You might think of a systems collapse as something that happens to either a race car at full speed or an old car at any speed. In a highly complex, interconnected, and stressed system such as a race car going 200 miles per hour, it only takes one little thing to go wrong to put enough strain on the other systems to blow everything apart. If you've had an old car, you've probably noticed that things limp along as long as everything works. Then, when one *little* thing goes wrong—clink, clank, clunk—everything seems to crumple. The other systems are so worn out that they can't withstand any additional strain.

There were more than enough potholes and pings, all of them discussed above, for the Mycenaean machine (whether it was a roadster or a rust bucket) to fail. How this happened, and in what order, is still a matter for research.

Shots in the Dark: What Do We Think Was Going On?

Okay, let's recap. At the height of their power and population, Mycenaean palace centers suffered some kind of stress, and there are indications that they anticipated attack. Within about a century, once-powerful centers were burned and abandoned. Their populations fled into the rugged terrain of Arcadia and Achaea, into parts of Attica, or to Mycenaean settlements on islands like Crete, Cyprus, or Rhodes. Although the islands continued to fare better for a while, they too, eventually, suffered destruction.

Mini-My: 1200 to 1050 B.C.E.

Initially, what was left in the aftermath was a period (called sub-Mycenaean) during which people carried on Mycenaean customs and organizational structures, though on a *much* smaller scale. There was hardly any new building in brick or stone, but there is evidence that the inhabitants that remained at sites such as Mycenae, Tiryns, and Athens attempted some reconstructions before giving up.

Foreign trade virtually disappeared, along with some of the kinds of specialized work (such as in metal and ivory) that depended upon imported materials. Mycenaean pottery continued to be made, but the scenes began to change. Figures such as lions, once the symbols of the elite class, become playful subjects on vases.

From Palace to Village: 1050 to 900 B.C.E.

By the end of the twelfth century B.C.E., the sub-Mycenaean period had given way to the Dark Age. Writing was lost, regions drifted into isolation, and, as these separated populations began to develop, characteristic differences between them became more pronounced. Pastoralism took hold in different areas in Greece, and a new kind of pottery decoration (still glazed on Mycenaean ceramic styles)—composed of concentric circles or wavy lines, called protogeometric—emerged. The use of iron developed, in part, because of the lack of copper and tin.

There is evidence of some social, as well as artistic, continuity, with the Mycenaean past. It seems that the village settlements of this age retained the Mycenaean *pasireu*, or "village chief." As communities developed, the *pasireu* acquired elevated status, and distinctive buildings and burials were associated with him and his family. Eventually, what was a minor official in the Mycenaean system was remembered by Homeric epic and classical Greek language as a king, or "*basileus*."

> **CAUTION**   **Labyrinths**
>
> If controversial proposals that redate the fall of the Mycenaean civilization downward to about 950 B.C.E. become accepted (based on redating Egyptian pottery), the darkest part of the Dark Age will be virtually erased.

From Village to *Polis:* 900 to 750 B.C.E.

The two primary questions about the late Dark Age have to do with its roles in the formation of the Greek *polis* ("city-state") and in the transmission of Mycenaean culture to Archaic Greek culture. Whereas it used to be thought that there was a discontinuity, or a radical break, between the Bronze and Dark Ages, and between the Dark Age and Archaic period, the advances in scholarship that we've just described show that there was, in fact, much more continuity than previously realized.

By about 900 B.C.E., the dust of the collapse of Mycenaean civilization had settled and the regrowth of Greek civilization had begun. Populations began to increase, trade began to be reestablished, and, as evidenced by burials, there was an increasing amount of wealth and social stratification. A new style of pottery decoration (called geometric) developed, and Athens and Corinth began to emerge as exporters of distinctive pottery styles.

There is also evidence from this period that Greek culture was once again on the move. Evidence comes from traditional accounts of early settlements, from archeological sites of temporary settlements, and from a growing abundance of offerings at religious shrines and sanctuaries that were in use since the Bronze Age. Many of these sanctuaries were initially without buildings (only a precinct, a place for sacrifice, and a place to leave offerings or dedications), but toward the end of this period permanent structures began to be built. When such evidence is combined with textual evidence from both Linear B and later literature (such as the Homeric hymns), it appears that there was a considerable degree of religious continuity from the Mycenaeans through the Dark Age.

As this growth occurred, Greek regional centers (e.g., Athens) and their surrounding countryside (e.g., Attica) had to develop forms of social, economic, and political interaction. It used to be thought that the people of the regional center exerted control over people in the countryside. Archeological and anthropological evidence, however, suggest that it was, in fact, the opposite. The regional center built and fostered regional identity, but was controlled largely by the countryside (which tended to prefer a more distributive power structure). And, as neighboring Greek regional communities were developing their own particular structures, they were also interacting and competing with each other. And such interactions and rivalries among neighboring regions can promote the development of similar political and social structures. Thus, we now think that the particularly Greek institution of the *polis* was the result of processes that started well back in the tenth century B.C.E.

Homeric Dark Age Culture and Society

The other major question about the Dark Age concerns the degree to which we can learn about Mycenaean or Dark Age culture and history from Homer's *Iliad* and *Odyssey*. And why does that matter? Well, in part, because it goes back to questions about Troy. Was the Trojan War one of the last great events of the Mycenaean world, after which things started to unravel? Or are fragmented cultural memories of the chaotic end of the Bronze Age wrapped around a single city? Can we, like the Greeks, use Homer to track history back through the Dark Age to Priam's palace, or does Homer's insight end in a Dark Age cul-de-sac? Well, here's the short answer.

In many ways, the Homeric world of Odysseus and Agamemnon, the world of the *basileus*, seems to leap from the late Dark Age world as we find it in archeological evidence and see it portrayed, with all of its warriors and ships, on geometric vases. We also know that oral traditions preserve evidence of events, cultural values and habits, economic and political institutions, and other "facts" of history. The apparent amount of continuity through the Bronze and Dark Ages suggests that some of Homer's account preserves such facts. Sorting out *which* facts belong to *which* period, however, and to what degree Homer is either a Dark Age or Mycenaean creation, is very complex. For example, burials at Lefkandi reveal a culture that might well have influenced Homer's imaginative world, but other contemporary burials in places such as Eleutherna (on Crete), Salamis (on Cyprus), and

> **Eureka!**
>
> Homer's "Catalogue of Ships" in the *Iliad* is a kind of "list poetry" used by oral cultures to preserve historical records. By Homer's own time, many of the places that he names were no longer significant and some didn't even exit. This may indicate that the epic tradition preserved—even if some cities were added later—credible evidence for an ancient Trojan War.

at Argos (in Greece) seem to emulate it and, perhaps, indicate an ongoing tradition. The same could be said for several vase paintings, which may—or may not—illustrate scenes from the Trojan Cycle well before Homer's time. In short, which elements of Homer are the chicken, and which are the egg, are still scrambled.

Whatever lay behind, with the end of the Dark Age, the Greeks were about to head down a spectacular road.

> **Muses** _____
>
> Those living around Thaumakia and Methone ... and Meliboia and Olizon, sent seven ships under the leadership of Philoctetes ... Those holding Trikke, terraced Ithome, and Oichalia ... were led by the sons of Asclepius, Podaleirius and Machaon in thirty hollow vessels; those holding Ormenius and the spring Hypereia and Asterion and the white peaks of Titanus were led by Eurypylus ... in forty black ships.
> —From Homer, *Iliad*, 2.716–737, the "Catalogue of Ships."

The Least You Need to Know

♦ Until recently, the Mycenaean collapse left a 400-year void in Greek history, from about 1150 to 750 B.C.E., known as the Dark Age of Greece.

♦ Evidence for a continuous (though evolving) Hellenic culture between the Bronze Age Mycenaeans and the Archaic Greeks has been strengthened by recent study of the Dark Age.

♦ Until fairly recently, the pervasive theory about the fall of the Mycenaeans came from ancient Greek tradition, which claimed that, in remote antiquity, a race of Dorians, the *Heracleidai* ("the descendants of Heracles") invaded and conquered parts of Greece.

♦ Some scholars have wondered if social or civic unrest might have rocked the Mycenaean social, economic, and civic order and led to its collapse.

♦ By the end of the twelfth century B.C.E., the sub-Mycenaean period had given way to the Dark Age: Writing was lost, regions drifted into isolation, and pastoralism took hold in many parts of Greece.

♦ The two primary questions about the late Dark Age have to do with its roles in the formation of the Greek *polis* and in the transmission of Mycenaean culture to Archaic Greek culture (including Homeric epic).

The Archaic—and Aristocratic—Big Bang

In This Chapter

- ◆ A cultural explosion
- ◆ The formation of the *polis*
- ◆ Aristocracies, oligarchies, and ever-popular tyrants
- ◆ Colonies and colonization
- ◆ Archaic society, the rules of warfare, and the Greek alphabet

Although many questions still surround the fall of the Mycenaeans, the Dark Age that followed isn't quite as dark as it was once thought to be. Archeology, linguistics, pottery, and anthropology have provided us with examples of cultural continuity from the thirteenth through the ninth centuries B.C.E. However, as the Greeks emerged from the Dark Age, the stage was set for a remarkable explosion of Greek colonization, one that created new political and economic structures, and that fostered the development of Archaic Greek culture.

This period of explosive growth is sometimes called the "Archaic renaissance," but the characterization is somewhat misleading, at least insofar as what might be implied by the term *rebirth* (renaissance). Hellenic culture underwent profound transformations in the Archaic period—transformations that went well beyond a rebirth—that provided foundations for the Classical period that cannot be securely linked to earlier ages.

In this chapter, we'll trace the developments of the Archaic period (750–490 B.C.E.) by concentrating on colonization, the aristocratic social structure that characterizes the period, and the effects of this social structure on the beginnings of the *polis*, or Greek "city-state." We'll discuss cultural achievements of this time in Chapter 10, the Olympic (and other) Games in Chapter 11, and Athens and Sparta (the two most famous city-states) more fully in Chapter 12.

Light at the End of the Tunnel

By the ninth century B.C.E., the Greeks had regained cultural momentum. There was an increase in both population and social stratification, and burials indicate a growing social, political, and economic hierarchy. Objects found in the burials show that some families were able to control enough land to trade surplus goods for imported items, and to gain a considerable amount of wealth in comparison with others.

Trade began to be reestablished around the Aegean, and with Anatolia and Egypt, thanks in large part to the Phoenicians—who had developed trade routes in response to the needs of the Assyrian Empire. The Phoenicians, along with Mycenaean settlers in the Dark Age, had colonized parts of Cyprus, and from there they established trade routes and settlements along the northern coast of Africa, in Sicily and Sardinia, and along the southern coast of Spain. In the following centuries, the Greeks followed in the Phoenicians' wake by creating colonies of their own and by developing their own written communication based on the Phoenician alphabet. The Hellenic world was transformed by the impact of both the Greek colonies and the Greek alphabet.

Lexica

Idiotes means "private individual" (gives new meaning to the *Complete Idiot's Guide* series, doesn't it?), and *syncrasis* means "mixture." **Idiosyncratic** indicates a mixture of (eccentric) characteristics that are unique to a particular individual (or group). The negative connotations of "idiot" come from its use for people who are just a bit *too* unique.

This transformation was particularly remarkable in that the Greeks were, to a large extent, left to their own *idiosyncratic* development for the next three centuries. In the west, Italy and Sicily had large areas of land available for colonization. The Phoenicians were primarily traders, not colonists or colonizers, and they didn't attempt to interfere with the Greeks' expansion until their economic interests were threatened. By then, the earliest Greek colony in Magna Graecia (Pithecusae) was two centuries old.

In the east, the collapse of the Hittite and Assyrian empires left the coasts of Anatolia and the Black Sea largely open to Greek colonization. Egypt, relatively weak and involved in internal conflict, allowed the Greeks to settle Naucratis and Cyrenaica. The Macedonians and Romans were still a long way off, chronologically. Rome, for example, spent the same period developing from a bunch of mud huts into a Latin city just barely free of the Etruscans. So, for nearly the entire Archaic period (roughly 250 years), no empire was around—in any direction—to squelch the emerging Hellenic culture, which allowed it to become both highly developed and widely disseminated.

> ### Odysseys
>
> You can visit the site of Pithecusae, the earliest Greek colony of this period (c. 750 B.C.E.), on the northwest tip of the delightful island of Ischia. It's just a short boat ride from Naples, a relative latecomer to Greek colonization (470 B.C.E.). On the way, you'll pass by the second-oldest Greek colony, Cumae (c. 740 B.C.E., now a suburb of Naples), on the mainland facing Ischia.

All Together Now? *Synoikism* and the Formation of the *Polis*

As mentioned in Chapter 8, regional centers and their surrounding countryside were developing social, economic, and political interconnections in the late Dark Age. These interconnections, however, were developed and controlled by the elite families who held most of the land and wealth, and who made up the "local councils and chiefs" (*basileis*). By the eighth century B.C.E., many regions had worked out cooperative arrangements, whereby the *oikoi* ("households") of a "city" (*polis*) and the *oikoi* of its "surrounding territorial communities" (*dêmoi*) were incorporated into one political structure. The Greeks called this process *synoikism*, whereby all members had common citizenship as *politai* ("*polis* members"), as if they belonged to one *polis*.

As regions formed political units, they also formed a sense of regional identity with their respective *poleis* ("city-states"). The appearance of permanent buildings at regional shrines, the construction of monumental temples, and a sense of regional borders during the Archaic period are signs of the Greeks' developing sense

> ### Lexica
>
> **Oikos** is the Greek work for "household," which included the family, property, real estate, slaves, and animals. **Synoikism** (from the Greek *synoikismos*, "having *oikoi* together") is the process of forming disparate communities into one political unit. **Politai** is the Greek word for "members (or citizens) of a *polis*."

of regional affinity. How extensively the surrounding region bonded to its *polis* was often a determining feature in how powerful the *polis* became. Attica, for example, which surrounded Athens, was a huge area in contrast to most other regions that identified with a single *polis*.

The regional forces that cooperated in forming the *polis* also had to both organize and control the larger territory and preserve and promote their own self-interests. They accomplished both objectives by reducing the power of the royal families and by increasing the power and participation of the broader aristocracy. They made the *basileus* a (more) ceremonial figure by dividing his former powers among several magistrates, and they gave councils of aristocratic elders an increased ability to oversee governmental and legal affairs. The degree to which these reforms succeeded in disseminating the power of the royal families varied from *polis* to *polis*, but, in general, by the seventh century B.C.E., Greek cities were controlled by aristocratic oligarchies or tyrannies.

New Rules: Aristocracies and Oligarchies

By breaking up the powers of the *basileus*, the aristocrats were able to create magistracies that suited the needs of their particular *polis*. The kinds of magistrates (typically called an *archon* "leader" or a *prytanis* "presiding official") evolved and multiplied as states became more complex. None of these officials held executive control of the *polis*, however, and their powers were further limited by a yearly term of office.

Labyrinths

The term *aristocracy* (*aristokratia,* "rule by the best") doesn't appear in the Archaic period. It appears as a kinder, gentler term for oligarchy in the Classical period.

Lexica

Archon (plural *archontes*) is a term for "leader," and **prytanis** (plural *prytaneis*) for "presiding official." Both were common terms used for magistrates of a *polis*.

Long-term control of the state was held by an aristocratic council, made up of former high magistrates, which drafted laws and made decisions that affected the whole state. These decisions were sometimes passed to a "general council," or *boulê*, to ratify. Because only a few members of a few aristocratic families controlled the outlying regions, the magistracies, the council, and the *boulê*, this form of government could not be considered representational. In fact, the Greeks came to call this form of government *oligarchia*, or "rule by the few." However, by the end of the sixth century B.C.E., and in response to pressures from other citizens upon whom the *polis* depended for economic and military existence, most oligarchic states had become more representational. Nevertheless, aristocrats (and states such as Sparta) periodically tried to reestablish oligarchic rule in various *poleis* throughout the Archaic and Classical periods.

New Old Rules: Tyrants and Tyrannies

Another feature of Archaic Greek *poleis* was the emergence of tyrannies, which often arose in opposition to the aristocratic oligarchies. A "tyrant" (*tyrranos*) was a sole ruler who seized control of the state by force. But tyrants weren't all bad. Although tyrants sometimes used forces from outside supporters to achieve initial control, they depended upon at least tacit support at home to overcome opposition and achieve long-term success. This support came from disaffected aristocrats and other citizens (such as those who made up the army) who had been shut out of the oligarchic system.

Labyrinths

Tyrants could be ruthless, but the term *tyrannos* was not originally a negative word. In fact, tyrants were often popular and populist leaders. Bad press, the tendency of power to corrupt, and attempts by tyrants to turn tyrannies into hereditary monarchies all contributed to the negative sense of the word.

The degree of resentment that both groups—excluded aristocrats and other citizens—harbored against the ruling aristocrats can be seen not only in the way that the ruling aristocrats were treated by successful tyrants, but also in the ways that the tyrants sought to cater to the other citizens. Tyrants drove out or killed powerful aristocrats, confiscated aristocratic property, and curbed aristocratic privileges. They also encouraged limited citizen participation in the affairs of the city. And they engaged in public works (building projects, fostering trade, creating public festivals and events) that provided work for underemployed citizens and fostered a sense of pride in their cities. Ironically, these strongmen did a great deal to create both civic centers and a common sense of identity among all classes, which not only (intentionally) undermined the aristocrats' hold, but also (unintentionally) fostered democratic developments in the Classical period.

Muses

[Periander, tyrant of Corinth] sent a messenger to Thrasybulus [tyrant of Miletus] inquiring how best to administer his city. Thrasybulus took the messenger outside the city into a field of grain; there, as he walked and questioned the messenger about his mission, Thrasybulus kept hacking off grain stalks that he saw growing above the rest and throwing them away … then he sent the messenger back without comment … Periander understood the act, and grasped that Thrasybulus was telling him to eliminate the most eminent citizens.

—Herodotus, 5.92

The Greek tyrants were some of the most colorful and influential people of the Archaic period. We'll discuss the tyrants of Athens, Peisistratus and his sons Hippias and Hipparchus, in Chapter 12, but some other famous tyrants that you'll want to know about are …

- **Cypselus** (c. 655–625 B.C.E.) and his son **Periander** (c. 625–585 B.C.E.) **of Corinth** came from a disaffected branch of Corinth's royal family, the Bacchiads. Both dramatically increased their city's economic power. Periander was famous for constructing a "stone trackway" (*diolkos*) across the Isthmus of Corinth (about 6 kilometers, or 3.72 miles, wide), which allowed ships and cargoes to be hauled between the Saronic and Corinthian gulfs.

- **Pheidon of Argos** (c. seventh century B.C.E.) was a *basileus* who became a tyrant. He is supposed to have created a standardized system of weights and measures for the Peloponnesus.

- **Cylon of Athens** was a would-be tyrant. He attempted to use his popularity as an Olympic victor to stage a coup in 632 B.C.E., with help from his father-in-law, Theagenes, tyrant of Megara.

- **Cleisthenes of Sicyon** was from a long line of tyrants going back to Orthagoras, who took power c. 665 B.C.E. Cleisthenes ruled c. 600–570 B.C.E. Besides making Sicyon one of the most powerful cities on the Gulf of Corinth, he arranged for the marriage of his daughter Agariste to the Athenian noble Megacles. Their son, also named Cleisthenes, created the foundational reforms that made Athenian democracy possible, and their descendants in the fifth century B.C.E. include Pericles and Alcibiades.

- **Polycrates of Samos** was a colorful pirate who took power c. 540 B.C.E. He made Samos into a naval power and a center for the arts, and he undertook many public works. He was lured off the island by the Persian satrap Oroetes and crucified.

Colonies and Colonization

If anything characterizes Greek activity in the Archaic period, it's colonization. There was an intense outpouring of settlers from Dark Age settlements in Greece and along the Anatolian seaboard during this time. Colonization was the most intense from about 750 to 500 B.C.E., during which time the Greeks established cities from the eastern end of the Black Sea to Spain. Besides spreading Hellenic culture, the new colonies presented opportunities for the emergence of new *poleis*. In the following sections, we'll describe the colonization movement and discuss some of its causes and effects.

Go West (and East, and South, and North), Young Man

The Euboeans were the pioneers of the colonization movement, establishing six colonies along the Italian and Sicilian coasts (from Pithecusae to Catana and Rhegium) in the eighth century B.C.E., but other settlements from the Peloponnesus (Achaea and Sparta) and Corinth soon followed. Phocaea (modern Foça, Turkey) established Massilia (modern Marseilles, France) in 600 B.C.E., and from there other outposts in Spain.

In the seventh and sixth centuries B.C.E., other large colonizing movements went into the Black Sea, Africa, and Egypt. The shores of the Black Sea were primarily settled by Aeolians and Ionians from the cities of Miletus (near modern Izmir, Turkey) and Megara (Greece). Cyrene, the major Greek colony in Libya, was originally founded about 630 B.C.E. by colonists from the island of Thera. The city prospered, and later issued an invitation for other Greeks to join it. Soon other colonists arrived from the Peloponnesus and other

Labyrinths

Greek expansion in the central and western Mediterranean was halted in the mid-sixth century B.C.E., when the Carthaginians and Etruscans, who combined to protect their own interests, forced the Greeks to abandon their colony at Alalia on Corsica.

Dorian areas to found several cities that made up Cyrenaica. About the same time as the founding of Cyrene, the trading port of Naucratis was established on the Nile Delta. For some time, the Greeks had been active in Egypt as traders and as mercenaries for the pharaohs, who apparently allowed them to establish a commercial base about 620 B.C.E. Settlers came from many different cities, and Naucratis served as an important melting pot of Greek and Egyptian ideas and influences throughout the Archaic period.

Growing Pains, Economic Gains

But why did this translocation and settlement occur on such a large scale? People don't normally pick up and leave a place without having compelling reasons. These reasons usually involve either a need/desire to escape from something at home or a need/desire to obtain something that home can't provide. Colonization, which requires social and political organization, is often brought on by compelling social and political problems.

In Archaic Greece, a variety of factors combined to make migration and colonization viable options for individuals and communities. Population growth spread family inheritances too thin to sustain family members. Also, although there was always enough arable land to sustain native populations, an effective land shortage was created by the concentration of land into the hands of a few powerful families during the late Dark Age. These groups, who had controlled the best pasturelands, made a profitable transition to farming. In contrast, more poorly positioned families were left with marginal lands on which to farm. Through the production of surplus goods, the upper-echelon families were also in the best position to cultivate and exploit trade opportunities for raw materials (mostly metals) and luxury items.

This led to a period of intensified social stratification. At the bottom of the economic ladder, poor families fell into landless servitude to the wealthy; in the middle, families of moderate means found themselves stretched thinner and thinner; at the top, even though burgeoning trade, improved farming, and increased control contributed to the wealth of some, the pressures from both overstretched inheritances and increased competition among aristocratic clans had a negative effect on others. So people from all sectors of Greek culture came to have compelling social, political, and economic reasons for seeking out new horizons and opportunities.

Children of the Mother City

The process of founding a "new colony" (*apoikia*) involved the whole community. Once the decision to send out a colony was made, the original city, or *metropolis* ("mother city") had to determine where the colony would go. This involved both practical planning and reconnoitering, as well as receiving the appropriate go-ahead from the gods at oracles such as Delphi. A "founder" (*oikistês*) was then chosen to lead the expedition. The *oikist* was always a member of a prominent family, for this was a position of great prestige and power. He not only led the community to the new site, but also laid out the site in every detail—defenses, religious sanctuaries, home and farm sites—for the colonists. As ruler of the new colony, he also became its guardian hero and was honored with a shrine after his death.

> **Lexica**
>
> A **metropolis** was the "mother-city" of the colony. The leader of the colonists and "founder" of the colony was called the *oikistês*, or *oikist*.

Colonization provided opportunities for all sectors of society—some on the new site and others generated by the ongoing economic relationship between the colony and its metropolis. All colonists received homestead plots (*kleros*). These plots were the main draw for the poor, because they provided a unique opportunity for lower-class families to regain self-sufficiency and to participate in the life of the colony. Middle-class families were drawn by the prospect of good land and by new opportunities for tradesmen and craftsmen. The wealthy were enticed by the possibility of becoming big fish in very new ponds, and by the opportunities that this kind of positioning afforded.

There were, however, substantial risks for the colonists. There was no coming back: Although the colony and metropolis retained an affiliation, colonists generally lost their citizenship in the metropolis unless some prior agreement had been made. On site, besides the hardships of building a city from scratch, the Greeks often faced opposition from the indigenous populations, from other competitors such as the Phoenicians and Etruscans, and, at times, from other colonies sent out by rival cities. It's no wonder the evidence indicates that not all colonists were willing participants. And in nearly all cases, those who left and those who stayed behind could be virtually assured that they would never see one another again.

> **Muses** _____
>
> If the colonists establish a settlement, any later colonist who joins them shall have a share in its citizenship, honors, and unassigned land. But if, after five years of trying, they cannot secure the colony and the Therans cannot aid them, the colonists may return to Thera without fear and regain their citizenship and their property. However, if anyone refuses to sail when sent by the city, let him be executed and his property confiscated. And let anyone who harbors such a person—be it his father or son or his brother— suffer the same.
>
> —From the Foundation Oath of Cyrene (c. 630 B.C.E.)

Rebirth or Birth? Archaic Society

The written and artistic evidence from the Archaic period paint a picture of an intensely developing culture. Often these developments were driven by the class that had privileged economic and social positions through the Dark Age, and by the tension between its traditional and emerging modes of life. During such times of transformation, it's not surprising that people seek to establish some kind of individual or communal identity. In Archaic Greece, aristocrats sought to both define themselves as Hellenes and distinguish themselves from other

> **Labyrinths** _____
>
> Not all regions became centered on a *polis*. Some (such as Thessaly, Aetolia, Boeotia, and Phocis) formed leagues (federations) to act in cooperation when necessary. The peoples of such regions were known as *ethnê* ("nations," "peoples," or "clans"). Another kind of Archaic federation that crossed ethnic lines was the *amphictyony* ("association of neighbors"), which protected a common shrine such as Delphi.

sectors of Greek society. And both objectives required them to link themselves with, and differentiate themselves from, the traditions of the past. We will examine some of their remarkable cultural accomplishments in the next chapter. Here we'll take a quick look at the social classes of the Archaic period and at some of the forces that helped to balance them, one against the other. We'll begin with the aristocrats, and with their contribution to a growing pan-Hellenic identity, and then move to other classes and groups of Greek society.

Hey! We're Hellenes! Pan-Hellenic Consciousness

While regional identities were being formed by the development of the *polis*, aristocrats also had Homeric and other traditions linking them, by birth and by heroic exploits, to one another. As aristocratic power and prestige were eroded and challenged, the aristocrats sometimes found (not surprisingly) that they had more in common with each other (e.g., noble birth going back to the Homeric world, oligarchic values and ideals) than they did with the people under them. This sense of class identity contributed to a vibrant exchange of aristocratic culture and to the establishment of pan-Hellenic events such as the Olympic Games.

These events were (and remained) venues for displaying traditional aristocratic excellence (individual martial or artistic prowess in celebration of aristocratic heroes). However, such events also contributed to a growing sense of Hellenic identity among all Archaic Greeks. Yet, because this sense of identity was emerging in concert with the expansion and development of disparate Archaic settlements, something interesting happened. Hellenic identity came to be based not on geography (whether one came from Greece), but on language (whether one spoke Greek) and mythology (whether there was a past that could be linked to accepted traditions).

The Good, the Bad, and the Many

The aristocracy traced its lineage back to Homeric heroes and the gods, which gave to its members a special place in history and a hereditary right to rule. Aristocrats further sought to distinguish themselves by framing their birth and their values as those of the *kaloi k'agathoi* ("beautiful and good people"), and by defining themselves as those who pursued the proper intellectual, political, and military ideals with *aretê* ("excellence"). In contrast, others who fell short of these qualifications or ideals were labeled *hoi kakoi* ("bad and evil people"). Because, by definition, there could only be a few *oligoi*, the common folk from whom the aristocrats sought to distinguish themselves were referred to as *hoi polloi* ("the many").

Eureka!

The Archaic aristocratic name for the masses—*hoi polloi*—remains a term for common people (with a similarly derogatory connotation) today.

Archaic elites were positioned to take advantage of opportunities to display *aretê* and to win honor and power in the developing *polis*. However, although aristocrats endeavored to consolidate their hold over their respective *poleis* and regions, their ability to exercise control became contingent upon broader citizen participation. In fact, the very survival of the *polis* came to depend upon a certain leveling of power within the *polis* and on the development of ideals of *aretê* that included, at least to some degree, common citizens.

Pressure from the Rank and File: The Citizen/Soldier Hoplite

Changes in warfare began to undermine the fiercely exclusive aristocratic culture, and they contributed to demands for broader public participation in the *polis*. Tactics changed from loosely ranked groups of fighters to the use of *hoplites*, "specialized heavy infantry" who fought in a "disciplined formation," the *phalanx*. Effective pha-

lanxes depended upon the commitment of many citizens, not merely a few well-armed aristocrats and their supporters, and so the *polis* came to depend upon the commitment and cooperation of the middle ranks of citizens (who could afford the equipment).

Men fought as a unit, which created a public forum for distinction that was open to all participants. The relationship between the state and the hoplite orders was often the determining factor in whether a *polis* became an oligarchy (an alliance of aristocrats and the hoplites), a tyranny (a strongman and the hoplites), or a democracy (the hoplites and the lower orders). These alliances could—and often did—change quickly.

Lexica

A **phalanx** is a fighting formation of shoulder-to-shoulder hoplites, usually about eight deep. Phalanxes attempted to break each other's formation by killing the front rows and by using their own phalanx like a bulldozer. As ranks collided, the front rows first stabbed overhead with spears and then slashed at each other with swords, while the rear rows attempted to push their formation through the other and break its ranks.

Eureka!

Hoplite armor consisted of a bronze helmet, breastplate, greaves (shin and knee protectors), and the *hoplon,* a "1-meter diameter bronze-over-wood round shield." The *hoplon* was worn across the forearm (elbow at the center) so that it protected both the wearer and the man to his left. The gear was heavy (about 70 pounds), cumbersome, and hot. No wonder the most arduous race at Greek games was the race in full armor! In addition, the hoplite carried a long and heavy stabbing spear and a short slashing sword.

Alpha to Omega: The Development of the Alphabet

Another development that fostered both the aristocratic culture of the Archaic period and its counterbalances was the development of writing. Sometime in the ninth century B.C.E., the Greeks adapted the Phoenician *alphabet*, which was familiar throughout the Mediterranean, to their own language.

> **Eureka!**
>
> **Alphabet** comes from the first two Phoenician symbols (alph, bet) that the Greeks adapted. You can still see some of the original pictographs in the forms of capital letters. Turn an *A* over and you'll see the horns of the *alph* ("ox"); turn a *B* on its side and you'll see a *bet* ("house"); and you can still see the waves of the *mun* ("water") in an *M*.

The Phoenician symbols represented a language in which every syllable starts with a consonant. The symbol for *bet* ("house"), for example, meant the sound of "b," the symbol for *mun* ("water"), the sound of "m." There were no symbols for vowels, because vowels were predictable once you knew the consonants in a word and the word's placement in a sentence. The Greeks took several symbols to represent vowels (which were not predictable), and created the first completely alphabetic writing, in which each symbol stands for a separate sound.

Letter		Name	Pronunciation	
A	α	alpha	ă	(as in *hop*)
B	β	bēta	b	
Γ	γ	gamma	g	(before γ, κ, μ, ξ, χ = ng)
Δ	δ	delta	d	
E	ε	epsilon	ĕ	(as in *let*)
Z	ζ	zēta	sd	(as in *wisdom*)
H	η	ēta	ē	(as in *pair*)
θ	θ	thēta	t-h	(as in emphatic *top*)
I	ι	iōta	ĭ	(as in *peep*), ī (*keen*)
K	κ	kappa	k	
Λ	λ	lambda	l	
M	μ	mu	m	
N	ν	nu	n	
Ξ	ξ	xi	x	(= ks)
O	o	omicron	ŏ	(as in *gut*)
Π	π	pi	p	
P	ρ	rhō	r	(rolled or trilled)
Σ	σ	sigma	s	(as in *sing*)
T	τ	tau	t	
Y	υ	upsilon	ŭ	(as in French *tu*)
Φ	φ	phi	p-h	(as in emphatic *pot*)
X	χ	chi	k-h	(as in emphatic *kit*)
Ψ	ψ	psi	ps	
ω	ω	ōmega	ō	(as in *low*)

The development of writing allowed for an explosion of Archaic culture, and writing itself served important civic and social functions at a critical time in Greek history. It gave aristocrats a way to communicate with one another and to form a Hellenic sense of shared history. It also allowed them to establish their regional traditions as a part of their respective *poleis* and to promote their ideals as those of the state.

However, writing also encouraged broader civic participation and helped provide a counterbalance to aristocratic privilege and authority. When written records of important laws and agreements were created and displayed in public, for example, it strengthened the sense that all citizens had rightful roles in common public endeavors. Moreover, writing counterbalanced the authority of oral tradition, which rested in aristocratic hands, by allowing these traditions to be codified in texts that could be referenced and debated by anyone who could read.

The Least You Need to Know

- By the ninth century B.C.E., the Greeks had regained cultural momentum: There was an increase in population, social stratification, and economic hierarchy.

- As regions formed political units, they also formed a sense of regional identity with their respective *poleis*.

- In general, by the seventh century B.C.E., Greek cities were controlled by aristocratic oligarchies or tyrannies.

- If anything characterizes Greek activity in the Archaic period, it's colonization.

- Changes in warfare began to undermine the fiercely exclusive aristocratic culture, and they contributed to demands for broader public participation in the *polis*.

- Sometime in the ninth century B.C.E., the Greeks adapted the Phoenician alphabet, which was familiar throughout the Mediterranean, to their own language.

10

A Cultural Explosion: Archaic Literature, Art, and Architecture

In This Chapter

♦ The effects of an emerging regional and pan-Hellenic consciousness on Archaic Greek expression

♦ Archaic foundations for Greek literature in the works of Homer and Hesiod

♦ The growth of individual consciousness and authority in lyric poetry and Presocratic philosophy

♦ Developments in Archaic painting, sculpture, and architecture

In the Archaic period, the combination of a developing sense of Hellenic identity, the competing social and cultural tensions inherent in the development of the *polis*, and the proliferation of Greek settlements throughout the Mediterranean provided inspiration and material for advancements in literature, philosophy, art, and architecture. And the introduction of a phonetic alphabet fueled the intensity, creativity, and pervasiveness of these advancements. Although Hellenic culture remained, like other ancient cultures, largely oral in nature, it became much more widely literate than others. A growing number of individuals used writing to communicate within and between social classes about a wide range of public and private topics.

In this chapter, we'll explore the ways that Archaic literature developed from and responded to various traditions, and the ways in which it held an ongoing dialogue with the past and with itself. Works built upon claims of traditional authority (Homer and Hesiod) were some of the first great literary creations. However, the authors were not priests who possessed unassailable knowledge, but individuals whose claims could be analyzed and discussed. This fact, combined with the pervasiveness of writing, encouraged both individual expression and works based on the personal authority and experience of the authors.

These works provide us with an astounding window into the minds and experience of the Archaic Greeks, and they include everything from discussions of public events and politics to declarations of love to philosophical explorations. Sometimes, such as in the development of Ionian rationalism, these explorations led away from received tradition and to new ways of thinking and new kinds of authority.

We'll also see how regionalism, as well as other political and economic developments, influenced Archaic painting, sculpture, and architecture. In the next chapter, we'll explore how a sense of pan-Hellenic identity resulted in the establishment of competitive festivals such as the Olympic Games.

CAUTION **Labyrinths** _____

The traditional view was that reading and writing were confined to the elite classes. Recent archeology in Attica, however, indicates that Greek shepherds had mastered the craft enough to scrawl graffiti (such as "I was here" and "Megakles is hot"), and suggests that a base level of literacy was reached by individuals in even the lowest classes of Greek society.

Archaic Literature

In the Archaic period, Greeks produced literary works of enormous range and scope, including monumental epics, religious hymns, intensely personal reflections, public celebrations, and political critiques. And whereas works from the Classical period are the most widely recognized today (except, perhaps, for Homeric epics), Archaic literature is not only beautiful and compelling, but often the source from which classical authors drew inspiration and material. In addition, Archaic authors, which include a woman (Sappho), represent more classes, regions, and political stances than do those of other periods, and they provide a fascinating look into both the diversity and the commonalities of ancient Greece.

Blind Bard? Homeric Questions and Answers

Literary history is often marked by authors who master influential traditions, ideologies, and techniques, and then combine the strongest elements of each with new traditions, new ideologies, and new techniques to create monumental works that become (in turn) the bedrock of a new age. In western literature, one thinks of authors such as Virgil, Dante, Chaucer, and Shakespeare in this vein. Similarly, Homer's *Iliad* and *Odyssey* appeared like literary supernovae out of the Greek Dark Age and represented the culmination of one sophisticated literary tradition (oral) and the beginning of another (literary). But exactly how these works were composed, and by whom, and when, is still a matter of intense debate. Tradition ascribes them to a single literary genius, a blind bard from Ionia (both Smyrna and Chios claimed him), known as Homer. Modern scholarship, however, falls into two general camps around the Homeric Question: unitarians (who believe a single author composed one or both works) and separatists (who believe the *Iliad* and *Odyssey* are the product of multiple authors).

What the preponderance of evidence shows is that the bulk, if not the whole, of the text of both epics was created in the last half of the eighth century B.C.E. out of traditional oral poetry that had been passed on from the late Bronze Age through the Dark Age. By technique, the poetry was formulaic—that is, the oral poet composed each piece using a metrical poetic language of traditional phrases, expressions, and entire scenes that fit the meter (dactylic hexameter). Performances developed and expanded upon a scene taken from an epic cycle, whose general events were known to the audience. To a degree, you might think of an oral poet as a sophisticated jazz or blues artist, who has a store of traditional licks, riffs, and changes from which to compose, improvise, and expand on standard tunes (e.g., "As Time Goes By") that audiences recognize.

The advent of writing in Greece allowed someone—or some ones—to expand and develop the stories of Achilles' rage (the *Iliad*) and Odysseus' homecoming (the *Odyssey*), both in complexity and on a scale previously unthinkable. Performances, after all, are limited by the performer's stamina and memory and the audience's attention. With writing, poets had the ability to stop and start, revise and recast, and extend and develop pieces into works that were previously impossible to produce.

Muses

Biographical details about ancient authors are generally unreliable because they have been lifted from their works. For example, Homer's reputed blindness probably comes from this passage in the *Odyssey* (8.62–64): "Soon the herald returned, leading the skilled bard. Aye, the Muse cherished him and gave him both good and evil; for while she took his eyes, she gave him sweetness in song."

Eureka!

You'll find a synopsis of the Trojan War in Chapter 4 and summaries of the *Iliad* and the *Odyssey*, along with more information on Homer and the Homeric Question, in Chapter 2.

However, writing also brought an end to the evolution of these epics. By the sixth century B.C.E., for example, Homer—whether blind bard or pure blarney—became the canonized foundation of a growing Archaic literary movement. Here, both because it's too cumbersome to keep qualifying what we mean by "Homer" and because, personally, we like the idea of a single author, we're going to refer to the author of both the *Iliad* and the *Odyssey* as Homer, especially now that you know what we mean.

The Bible of Hellas

Homer's *Iliad* and *Odyssey* are sometimes referred to as the "bible" of the ancient Greeks, but that title must always be qualified. As we said in Chapter 5, the Greeks had no religious text that they considered authoritative in the way that Christians consider the Bible to be authoritative, or Muslims the Koran. But, like the Bible and the Koran in other cultures, Homer's works provided the Greeks with a traditional history and narrative from which they could draw a common identity, and to which they could refer and relate. And just as many Christians look to the Bible for moral guidance, many Greeks considered Homeric texts a source of moral examples and ideals. Others, however, saw them as the source of morals and ideals that needed to be rejected. Whichever point of view they took, the ancient Greeks had to deal with the *Iliad* and the *Odyssey*, and they often used them as a point of reference and a source of material.

Homer's works are told from the point of view of the elite class (that is, chiefs, heroes, and other elites), and this class included both the main characters of the stories and the traditional audiences of epic poetry. In the Archaic literature that followed, however, the perspectives of more ordinary individuals, both those within and those outside of this elite circle, began to be represented, often in response to the Homeric world.

Odysseys

By tradition, Homer came from either Smyrna (modern Izmir, Turkey) or the island of Chios (Greece). Other tales connect the famous bard's life with Pylos, Ithaca, Argos, Colophon, and Athens.

Scholars debate which elements of Homer's works are historically accurate and the degree to which we can learn from them. Some contend that Homer's narrative—particularly insofar as it shows the ways that the characters act and interrelate—tells us more about late Dark Age society than about earlier periods or events. Others argue for Homeric elements that go back to Mycenaean times by emphasizing the role of oral poetry and oral formulae in preserving and passing on knowledge and historical details. Whatever the case, for more than 2,700 years, the *Iliad* and *Odyssey* have remained ongoing sources of inspiration, exploration, and debate regarding history, heroism, the relevancy of human relationships, and the nature of the divine.

Tell It Like It Was (and Is): Hesiod's *Theogony* and *Works and Days*

Shortly after Homer composed the *Iliad* and *Odyssey*, another poet, Hesiod, composed works that also became foundational for later Greek literature. According to his poetry, Hesiod's family immigrated from Aeolian Cyme (modern Turkey) to Boeotia, near Mt. Helicon. After his father died, Hesiod's brother Perses bribed the local *basileus* ("king" or "chief") and cheated Hesiod out of his share of the family inheritance, which left him to toil for himself. In contrast, Perses' new and improved share of the inheritance allowed him to live it up for a while. However, it isn't altogether clear to what degree this information is accurate and to what degree it might have been invented by Hesiod to give his didactic poetry authority. Still, most scholars are inclined to take him at his word.

> **Eureka!**
>
> Mt. Helicon became a metaphor for poetic inspiration, in part because of Hesiod's claim that the Muses appeared to him there and taught him the *Theogony*. It was the home of the Muses, and the location of the springs of inspiration (Hippocrene, Pirene, and Aganippe) associated with the flying horse, Pegasus.

What *is* clear is that Hesiod critiqued the emerging aristocracy by writing from the point of view of those who were being squeezed out of, or denied access to, aristocratic privileges. Rather than glorifying aristocratic ideals, Hesiod set aristocratic claims into a larger context and defined *aretê* ("excellence") and value in terms that could include all landed citizens. In the *Theogony*, for example, three generations of gods struggle for power and dominance. The first (Ouranus) relies on power, and the second (Cronus) on power and craftiness. The third (Zeus), however, achieves and maintains dominance through power, craft, the sharing of privileges, and the establishment of justice. By setting up Zeus—the founding father of aristocratic lineage, privilege, and power—as the guarantor of justice, Hesiod calls purely aristocratic ideals into question. Moreover, in the *Works and Days*, Hesiod ennobles the toil of the farm, not the battlefield; the renown of one's accomplishments in the village, not in the *megaron* (a large interior hall); and the divine favor shown to the farmer through wealth in harvest, not wealth in gold.

Muses

From [Pandora] comes the evil race of women, who live among men as a nagging burden and share only wealth, not want, well ... whosoever avoids their malice, not wishing to marry, finds himself in old age without any son to care for him ... and even if he does marry a good and prudent wife, he spends his life trying to cope with her inconstant nature; but he who marries one of the bad ones lives continually plagued by troubles of mind and heart without a cure for his sorrow."

—Hesiod, *Works and Days*, 590–612.

Hesiod's works are important and noteworthy in many ways, both good and bad. On the positive side, the *Theogony* is the first ancient Greek religious text, and it shows similarities to other near-eastern religious theogonies (such as the Babylonian *Enuma Elish*). His works are also the first to be claimed by their author (Homer never mentions himself), and the first in which the author's own experience is an acknowledged source of knowledge and authority. More negatively, Hesiod's works are profoundly *misogynistic*. From his use of the myth of Pandora to his pronouncements on wives, Hesiod portrays women, at best, as a zero-sum gain for men and, at worst, as treacherous, self-serving, and a drain on the resources and accomplishments of heroic farmers. Certainly some of the tenor and tone of this misogyny emerge from Hesiod's own personal vindictiveness, but misogyny itself was also a product of his culture. During the Archaic period, the areas and opportunities open to women became progressively restricted, and other authors (such as lyric poets and even Homer, particularly in the *Odyssey*) portray women in an unfavorable, though not so spiteful, light.

Lexica

Misogynistic—from Greek *miso* "hatred for" + *gyn* "woman, wife")—means displaying hatred for or toward women.

Labyrinths

We possess very few complete lyric poems. Most of our lyric poetry comes from fragments that were preserved on torn papyri and short sections that were quoted by other authors.

Poetry Slam: Lyric Poetry

Shortly after Homer and Hesiod, the Archaic period experienced a burst of creative energy, which was fostered and expressed by the authors of lyric poems. The subject matter of lyric poetry covers a wide range of human experience, from intensely private sexual encounters to public events and moral exhortation, and so it is impossible to cover all of the subjects and styles here (see Chapter 2). However, it is important to note that Archaic poets were important forces of social change and consciousness. Authors responded as individuals to Homeric (i.e., aristocratic) ideals and to the political and social tensions of their times. For example, Homer's works portray an excellent man as one who is a doer of fine deeds on the battlefield and a speaker of fine words among his peers. But written poetry allowed individuals to record and spread their ideas throughout Hellas, and to discuss deeds of all kinds— good or bad, noteworthy or sorry, heroic or cowardly. Moreover, lyric poetry gives us some of the few insights we have into the personal and internal lives of individual authors, and it is the only literary form in which women, such as Sappho, Praxilla, and Corinna (the last two are from the Classical period), speak in their own voice. Here are some selections from Archaic poets as they react to …

♦ **Homeric ideals:**

"Some say a battalion of horsemen, some say armies on the march, and some say ships at sail; but I say the fairest thing on the dark earth is the face of the person one loves … Anactoria, gone from me …." Sappho of Lesbos (sixth century B.C.E.)

"Not for me a tall long-legged captain strutting in his curls and trimmed beard; no, give me a stump of a man set squarely on his short legs, who, full of heart, stays where he plants them." Archilochus of Paros (seventh century B.C.E.)

> **Eureka!**
>
> The homoerotic poetry of Sappho of Lesbos is the origin of the modern term *lesbian*. The island of Lesbos had a reputation for female homoeroticism even during Sappho's own time.

♦ **Class struggle within the *polis*:**

"The *polis* will not gain better governance from [an aristocratic athlete]; it gets small pleasure from an Olympic victor. This doesn't make the treasury of the *polis* rich." Xenophanes of Colophon (sixth century B.C.E.)

"They have deposed the noble helmsman, who knew what he was doing … and plunder the cargo indiscriminately. The ship-hands and porters lord it over the great … let this be my secret message to the nobles, but any low-life with half a brain can decode it." Theognis of Megara (sixth century B.C.E.)

♦ **Life in general:**

"The dim-sighted god of Wealth never came through *my* door saying, 'Hey, Hipponax, I'm giving you a windfall!' No, he's a dim-wit." Hipponax of Ephesus (sixth century B.C.E.)

"Wine, my dear boy, and truth." Alcaeus of Mytilene (sixth century B.C.E.)

Rational Revolution: Ionian Rationalism and Presocratic Philosophy

During this time, an intellectual revolution was also taking place, which began with Presocratic philosophers who lived in Ionia (thus, Ionian Rationalism). This revolution emphasized human reason, sensory observation, and speculation, and it paved the way for the development of philosophy, science, medicine … and the list goes on. Here we'll give you a brief description of Presocratic philosophy and leave you with some intriguing Presocratic fragments.

As mentioned in Chapter 3, Presocratic (coming before Socrates) philosophers are also called "natural" philosophers because they were concerned with the nature of reality, the physical world, and explanations for change (movement, mutation, and so forth). However, it's important to note that both names (Presocratic and natural) may be misleading in one sense, in that they seem to suggest a kind of unity or agreement among philosophers who reached startlingly different conclusions. Yet, there is one thing that the Presocratics share, which distinguishes them sharply from earlier thinkers, and that is their focus on human reason. All of the Presocratic philosophers made a distinctly human attempt to comprehend the world, using human reason and relying on human sensory observation and contemplation. Prior to this intellectual revolution, ancient thinkers predominantly used mythological stories of the gods to explain the origins, composition, and workings of the universe, as well as to explain the place of human beings within that universe.

Today we have only fragments of Presocratic discourses, along with quotes from, and discussion by, later writers (for example, Aristotle, in the first book of his *Metaphysics*). But the fragments are fascinatingly suggestive, and the work of these philosophers has had a lasting impact on the history and development of philosophy. For instance, it is nearly impossible to fully comprehend certain passages in Plato without knowledge of the Presocratics; Aristotle studied them closely and discussed them at length; and it appears that the Stoics were influenced by Heraclitus and the Epicureans by Democritus. For a closer look at the individual philosophers, see Chapter 3. Here we will leave you to think over a few fragments:

> "Among those who say that the first principle is one, movable, and infinite is Anaximander of Miletus, son of Praxiades, the pupil and successor of Thales. He said that the principle and element of all things is the infinite, and he was the first to apply this name to the first principle. He says that it is neither water

nor any other of the things called elements, but some other nature, from which came all the heavens and the worlds in them." (Anaximander c. 610–546 B.C.E., quoted by Simplicius)

"No man knows or ever will know the truth about the gods or about everything I speak of, for even if one chances for the most part to say the truth, still he would not know; but everyone thinks he knows." (Xenophanes, c. 570–478 B.C.E.)

"The teacher of many is Hesiod. People believe that he knew many things, that man, who did not even know day and night: they are one." (Heraclitus, fl. 500 B.C.E.)

"Only one way remains for us to tell: that it is. To this way there are many signposts: that what *is* is without beginning, indestructible … without end … Nor will the force of credibility ever admit that anything grows out of what is not except what is not … And the decision of the matter rests herein: either it is or it is not." (Parmenides, fl. c. 485 B.C.E.)

"Nature and instruction are similar, for instruction transforms a man and, in transforming, creates his nature." (Democritus, c. 460–370 B.C.E.)

Archaic Art and Architecture

The Archaic Greeks also expressed both private and public ideals—beautifully and prolifically—in art, sculpture, and architecture. In fact, the artistic achievements of the Archaic period are among the most splendid and impressive of ancient Greece, surpassing, for many, even those of the Classical period.

Sculpture

In Greek sculpture of the Archaic period, we see significant achievements in the exploration of the human form. Notable examples of this exploration were life-size, freestanding sculptures of naked "young men" (*kouroi*) and draped "young women" (*korai*), and the sculptures that adorned the pediments and entablatures of temples. These artistic developments were interconnected with the economic and political developments of the time. As regions consolidated wealth and power, they established and embellished regional and city sanctuaries using knowledge, models, and materials brought in and made possible by trade and exchange.

An Archaic kouros.

(Photo courtesy of Rochelle Snee)

An Archaic korê.

(Photo courtesy of Rochelle Snee)

Kouroi and *korai* statues were costly grave monuments or sanctuary dedications. In the early Archaic period, the Greeks took their models, as well as the techniques in bronze and marble that went with them, from the Egyptians. Wealthy families commissioned and set up the monuments to honor the person represented by the statue, as well as the family itself. Sometimes they included an inscription at the base that told who dedicated the statue and who made it.

Temple sculptures, which depicted scenes from mythology, underwent significant advancement during the late Archaic period as well. Monumental temples constructed during the period provided magnificent venues for sculptors and painters to both explore and expand their crafts. Whereas the traditional uses and poses of *kouroi* and *korai* encouraged restraint, the subjects of temple sculpture encouraged narrative and movement, for which relief carving was particularly well suited.

> **Eureka!**
>
> Artisans initially created *kouroi* and *korai* using traditional proportions and stiff poses (e.g., arms along the side, feet together or the right foot slightly extended, and a blissful "Archaic" smile). They began to portray more realistic features, expressions, and movement in the sixth century B.C.E. For more on sculpture and sculptors, see Chapter 2.

The beautiful late Archaic temple sculpture from the Temple of Aphaia in Aegina, now in the Glyptotech, Munich, Germany.

(Photo by Eric Nelson)

Architecture

During the Archaic period, architectural forms and structures were also developed that met the emerging needs and identity of the *polis* ("city-state"). Monumental temples, expressions of prestige for regions and *poleis* ("city-states"), came into being early in the period. Other public buildings and spaces grew to meet the economic, political, and military needs of the *poleis*. As trade increased between regions and their

Labyrinths _____

Greek statues and buildings were brightly painted. Carving and finishing techniques used by Archaic artisans (vertical strikes with point chisels and the use of abrasives) created stone surfaces that took pigments well. Later artists began to exploit the translucent qualities of polished marble.

cities, and between cities themselves, the *agora*, or "marketplace," was enhanced with "covered colonnades" (*stoa*) and buildings for councils, citizens, and officials to carry on business.

For the physical training of the citizenry, upon which hoplite fighting depended, public "spaces for exercise" (*gymnasion*) and "wrestling" (*palaistra*) became regular features of every Greek city early on. The "*theatron*," or theater, became a fixture of the *polis* in the late Archaic and early Classical periods as a venue for the dramatic performances and competitions of the time.

Greek temples took their characteristic shape in the ninth and eighth centuries B.C.E. as small wooden structures. As regional power and identity developed with the *poleis*, temples began to increase in size and splendor. In the seventh century B.C.E., the Greeks adapted Egyptian building techniques and learned to cut, move, build, and finish architectural limestone and marble. These buildings were adorned with sculpture and painting. Despite using new materials, however, they retained the shape and many of the features of the old wooden buildings. Although the overall form of the temple remained constant, two distinctive Doric and Ionic orders of columns developed. (For more on these orders, see Chapter 3.)

Painting

The temples and public buildings of the Archaic period provided vast spaces for artists to paint vivid mythological and patriotic scenes that were still famous centuries later. Unfortunately, these works are lost. Consequently, what we know about Greek painting during this period comes from high-end Corinthian and Attic ceramics,

Eureka! _____

Corinth was the export capital of pottery (and perfume) in the early Archaic period, but the Athenians captured the market from them by 530 B.C.E. The suburb of the *Cerameicus* (i.e., "Pottstown") was named for and devoted to pottery production and metallurgy.

whose exquisite shapes and elaborate scenes were made possible by the demand of burgeoning trade and wealth in this period. Like sculptors and other artists, good vase painters were well known and proud of their work. They often signed their pieces and gave them a dedication (and sometimes added a taunt to a rival painter).

Archaic vases follow many of the same artistic and intellectual currents that can be traced through sculpture and literature. In general, a geometric representation of epic themes, along with motifs taken from trade with the east, gave way to the depiction of Homeric and aristocratic characters as real people. In much the same way that Greek literature and philosophy shows a growing interest in understanding humanity on its own terms, Greek art shows an increasing interest in portraying the lives of real people in varying situations—with a particular, though not exclusive, focus on the elite class. For more about the history of pottery painting (including black and red figure pottery styles), see Chapter 2.

The Least You Need to Know

◆ Although Hellenic culture remained, like other ancient cultures, largely oral in nature, it became much more widely literate than others.

◆ In the Archaic period, Greeks produced literary works of enormous range and scope, including monumental epics, religious hymns, intensely personal reflections, public celebrations, and political critiques.

◆ Shortly after Homer composed the *Iliad* and *Odyssey*, another poet, Hesiod, composed works that also became foundational for later Greek literature.

◆ Shortly after Homer and Hesiod, the Archaic period experienced a burst of creative energy, which was fostered and expressed by the authors of lyric poems.

◆ The Presocratic philosophers made a distinctly human attempt to comprehend the world, using human reason and relying on human sensory observation and contemplation.

◆ The artistic achievements of the Archaic period are among the most splendid and impressive of ancient Greece, surpassing, for many, even those of the Classical period.

Go for the Gold! The Games of Ancient Greece

In This Chapter

- ◆ Competition and ancient Greek culture
- ◆ Ancient Greek sporting events and training
- ◆ The formation of pan-Hellenic games in the Archaic period
- ◆ The Olympian (Olympic), Nemean, Pythian, and Isthmian games

Ancient Greek culture was intensively competitive. Nearly every public event, whether held within a particular *polis* ("city-state") or as a pan-Hellenic festival, featured *agones* ("contests") and *athla* ("prizes"). As long as there was a range of abilities—in sports, poetry, singing, drama, dancing, you name it—there was a competition to establish the best. Even the structure of political and legal debate lent itself to a vigorously competitive atmosphere.

Athletic competitions appear as part of Greek culture from at least the Dark Age onward. For example, in the *Iliad*, they are included in the funeral celebration of the hero Patroclus, and Homer portrays them as customary for such an event. In the Archaic period, both pan-Hellenic competitions, like those at Olympia, and regional competitions, like the Panathenaic festival in Athens, were established in conjunction with religious festivals as a regular part of Hellenic culture. In this chapter, we'll examine some of the roles played by competition in ancient Greek culture, and then focus on the athletic events and competitions for which ancient Greece is famous.

We Compete: Sport and Identity

The Greeks wanted to define, understand, experience, and demonstrate excellence in the skills that they considered essential to human expression and achievement. And a serious examination of excellence, whether in human beings per se or in particular human skills, will result in the establishment of some standard or standards (of good, better, best, and their opposites). The Greek standards of excellence, which incorporated the skills that an excellent human being should be able to perform well, led naturally toward competitions in many areas. In addition, Greek ideas of harmony and balance contributed to an appreciation of style, form, and function, particularly in athletics.

Eureka!

Greek myth is full of competitions, such as a weaving contest between the goddess Athena and the mortal Ariadne, and a flute-playing contest between the gods Apollo and Pan (judged by King Midas). These contests had disastrous results for the mortals involved (the gods were not good losers): Athena beat Ariadne and then transformed her into a spider (well, spiders *are* excellent weavers), and Apollo changed Midas' human ears into ass ears for judging Pan superior.

Individual Eyes on the Common Prize

Organized competition within groups can also provide the kind of outlet for aggression and tension that will, hopefully, solidify and intensify group cohesion. Although some forms of individualism can threaten a group, certain skills and abilities can be valuable enough to the group to be worthy of individual expression and emulation. And organized games and contests can identify and focus on these skills and abilities, and they can be a way of saying, "As a people, we value x, y, and z. So, if you want to be recognized by us as a cool, skilled, and worthy individual, you must do x, y, and z well." In this way, competitions can foster a sense of shared values and common identity. In ancient Greece, competitions nurtured, depending on their venues, both regional and pan-Hellenic identity, even as they fostered and encouraged rivalry.

Moreover, to the ancient Greeks, the experience of victory (or loss) was closely connected with ideas of the divine. (One only has to watch pregame prayer huddles, or skyward pointing by victorious competitors, or speeches during award ceremonies to see that this connection remains strong today.) In ancient Greece, competition occurred in conjunction with religious festivals, and to compete was to celebrate the gods and, hopefully, experience their favor in the outcome of the events.

Perhaps the value of the experience helps to explain why the initial prizes for victors at the major events seem so paltry in comparison to modern prize money (a wreath and the right to put up a statue of oneself). However, once home, a victor's status brought him rich rewards and privileges. (Again, if you think of commercial endorsements, speaking engagements, and the faces on cereal boxes, these kinds of rewards and privileges still attach to "amateur" athletes.) In regional competitions, the actual prizes for winning were more lucrative, and particularly during the Hellenistic and Roman periods, athletes could earn substantial prizes at city games.

> **Muses**
>
> "Water is best, and gold, like fire burning in the night, outshines the most eminent of wealth; but if you, my heart, wish to sing of prizes won, seek no star more radiant in the deserted upper air than the sun, and let us not sing a contest better than the Olympian."
>
> —Pindar, *Olympian* 1.1–7

> **Eureka!**
>
> By the early sixth century B.C.E., Athenian legislation granted Olympic victors rewards and privileges amounting to hundreds of thousands of dollars (in contemporary terms).

Healthy Competition?

Competition, however, can also be divisive in that it puts people in their place, or ranks them, according to a scheme and set of rules established by a particular group. It distinguishes winners from losers, competitors from spectators, and members of the excellent class from nonmembers who must watch and learn.

The pan-Hellenic competitions that were established in the Archaic period celebrated aristocratic traditions and skills, as well as individual achievement. These contests were established and conducted, in part, to maintain the traditions and values passed

Lexica

An **agon** was a struggle (hence "agony") in contest for an *athlon* ("prize"). Those who competed came to be called athletes.

on through Homeric and aristocratic culture. In contrast, contests (such as the Athenian dramatic festivals and dance competitions) held within a *polis* often included events in which groups, rather than individuals, competed, in part to establish and promote more democratic ideals of excellence. Regardless of whose values were being promoted, however, the Greeks never lost their taste for an *agon*.

Labyrinths

"Amateur" emerged among the upper classes in the late 1800s C.E. as a term for "gentleman sportsman." The first amateur athletic associations were formed to allow gentlemen to compete without having to mix with (or lose to) competitors from lower classes or professional athletes. These exclusive associations quickly sought to define amateur sport as true sport, amateurs as true sportsmen, and ancient Greek sports in their own image.

Women and Competition

The competitive nature of Greek culture entered into the restricted lives of women only to a degree. Although there are myths involving such things as weaving competitions, women had few opportunities for public expression, except for dances and processions at public festivals. Although famous female characters were often portrayed on stage during dramatic competitions at Athens, only male actors were allowed to play the roles. Athletic competitions—as a form of male expression in which participants competed in the nude—generally excluded the direct participation of women.

Nevertheless, there were a few opportunities for women to compete with one another and with men. At Olympia, for example, divisions of girls, young women, and women competed in footraces at separate games in honor of Hera, the *Heraia*, and there were similar footraces at other games and festivals.

Females did not compete in the nude, as did the males (although Spartan women worked out in the nude alongside men in the *gymnasion* and *palaistra*), but wore a short (A-line) running dress. Their race was also slightly shorter in distance. Women could also enter horses and teams in the equestrian events (as owners, not as jockeys or drivers) and win a prize at the major festivals. The most famous of these women was Kyniska, daughter of the Spartan king Archidamus. She was not only the first woman to win an Olympic victory (in the chariot races, c. 396 B.C.E.), but she was also reportedly the first Greek woman to breed horses.

Outside of athletics, there were a few artistic competitions in which girls competed together with boys, and women together with men. This appears to have been the case in the original musical competitions at Delphi. There is also some evidence that, based on this precedent, women may have competed in other events as they were added to the Pythian Games at Delphi. In any case, musical competitions in which both sexes could participate gradually became a feature of some city competitions in later periods.

> **Eureka!**
>
> Another example of girls competing comes from a Spartan dance called the *bibasis*, in which the object was to jump and touch the feet to the buttocks as many times as possible. An epigram records that one girl, the champion, had a thousand touches. Today it might read: "I Kicked Butt at the *Bibasis*."

As far as being spectators, women were excluded or included depending on the venue and, interestingly enough, on their marital status. In Olympia, for example, married women were barred from watching the competition (with the exception of the priestess of Demeter) on pain of being thrown off a cliff, but unmarried women were allowed to watch. This exclusion led a Spartan woman named Callipateira to dress as a male trainer in order to watch her son compete. When her son won, she leapt over the barrier to greet him and her cloak fell away. And, well, everything was revealed. Although the judges spared her life (her father, three brothers, and a nephew had been Olympic victors), a few rules were changed. From then on, both athletes and trainers were required to attend the games in the nude. Similar, though not identical, practices were followed at the other games, and the Pythian Games were presumably the most inclusive of women.

Getting in the Game

All male citizens underwent physical training as a part of their education as boys and young men. Training took place in the *gymnasion* and *palaistra* under the watchful eye of trainers (who were also disciplinarians and beat their charges with sticks for infractions or errors) and public officials. Young men also received training in weaponry and hoplite tactics, and the Greeks engaged in several kinds of ball games (throwing and catching games, ball-dodging games) for fun, exercise, and skill.

Physical training and athletics were only part of what took place at the *gymnasion*. It was also where young boys (and young girls, in Sparta) received their initial training and education in music, dance, mathematics, grammar, and reading, as well as where young men received their initial training in warfare. This education was designed to comprehensively prepare young Greek males to appreciate, practice, and, eventually, master numerous skills.

No Sweat Suits Required

Although a backpack might have come in handy, young men didn't need many supplies. No workout clothes were required at the *gymnasion* or *palaistra*, since training took place in the nude. An athlete needed to bring his own *aryballos* ("a small jug for olive oil"), a *stlengis* or strigil ("a kind of curved scraper"), and a sponge. These items were attached together by a string, so that they could be hung on hooks on the walls.

Eureka!

Greek athletes used dust from various kinds of materials (e.g., terracotta or clay) to regulate body temperature and control sweating. According to one author (Philostratos), yellow dust added a particularly attractive sheen to good bodies.

To prepare for training, an athlete first rubbed his body down (or had someone else do it) with olive oil from his *aryballos* (Roman moralists were particularly suspicious of this step, and claimed that it made the body soft and wimpy), and then covered himself with a fine dusting of sand. After training, the trainee scraped the film from his body with the *stlengis* and finished cleaning up with water and his sponge.

Some of the equipment that was needed for training was present, but enthusiasts, like today, often preferred to bring their own personal items.

Advanced Training

Enthusiasts, or athletes who hoped to prepare for competitive venues like the Olympic Games, could hire various kinds of personal trainers. These trainers included *paidotribes* ("event trainers"), *gymnastes* ("exercise trainers"), and *aleiptes* ("sports therapists" who oiled and massaged the muscles).

Trainers not only supervised athletes' technique and training, but also provided them with strict regimens (training schedules and diet) and placed restrictions on things such as sex. There was a great deal of debate concerning, and criticism of, these regimens among the Greeks, especially from outside the sports arena. Both medical texts and philosophical works criticize trainers for being willing to compromise—and even harm—athletes' health in the pursuit of victory. (Today, we need only think of the controversy surrounding the tender age of female gymnasts in the modern Olympic Games, or the use of performance-enhancing drugs, to understand this debate.)

Other authors complain that specialized athletic regimens exalted useless skills at the expense of intellectual ability and true health.

We know that athletes were hiring personal trainers and specializing in particular events since the sixth century B.C.E. At Olympia, where competitors swore an oath that they had properly trained for their events, training was an expected part of preparation and participation from the beginning. And although authors tell a few stories of victors who were fresh from the farm, the fact that these stories are presented as extraordinary argues that most competitive athletes were the product of training.

If an individual couldn't afford training, but was nonetheless a particularly good prospect for bringing his city a victory, the city might underwrite the training. In later periods, as athletics became more specialized and professional (in the sense that athletes trained for specific events in order to compete for prize money), training became even more essential to winning.

> **Muses**
>
> It's clear to everyone that athletes have never dreamed of mental blessings. In the first place, they are so weak—in the head—that they scarcely know they have a brain; by gorging themselves on so much flesh and blood they keep their brains fouled to the point that they can't think straight and are as mindless as brutes.
>
> —Galen, *Exhortation for Medicine*

The Thrill of Victory, *Agon*, and Defeat: Competition from Poetry to the *Pankration*

So, what events did competitors train for? Well, some of the events we describe in the following section, such as track and field and equestrian events, will be familiar. But competitors also trained for such events as flute playing, lyre ("*kithera*") playing and singing, dancing (for example, the *pyrrhiche*, a "war-dance performed by a group," fully armed, in competitions), and torch racing (a race that required just enough speed to keep the torch lit).

Let the games begin.

> **Labyrinths**
>
> Torch races were a feature of Athenian and other city competitions, but not a part of the Olympic Games. Lighting the flame at ancient Olympia and relaying the torch to a modern Olympic stadium began in 1936, as a way to glamorize the Games in Berlin.

Track and Field

Many of these events featured skills that warriors originally needed on the battlefield (running, jumping, throwing), and they were similar to track events today. A sprint of a *stade* ("192 meters") was the oldest event at Olympia, and it took place in (and lent its name to) the *stadion*, where the *stade* was laid out. Other track events also took place in the *stadion*, where viewers and participants admired athletes for their style and grace, as well as for their speed or endurance. The events included …

Eureka! _____

Athletic programs have a long history. There were many manuals on athletic training in the ancient world, though only one, Philostratos' *On Gymnastics* (c. 230 C.E.), survives.

- ◆ **Running.** Ancient runners didn't run around the *stadion*; instead, they ran back and forth like swimmers in a pool. Running events were multiples (up to 24) of the *stade* (192 meters). The most grueling running event, the *hoplitodromos*, was a two- or four-*stade* race in full hoplite armor.

- ◆ **Discus.** Competitors whirled around and threw a saucer-shaped discus for distance and accuracy. Sizes of discuses varied between men's and boys' divisions.

- ◆ **Javelin.** The javelin was a short throwing spear (about the height of a man). It had a leather throwing thong attached at the balance point to increase distance and accuracy.

- ◆ **Long jump.** Athletes used "weights" (*halteres*) made of stone or lead, which they swung out in front of them when they jumped and then behind them (at which point they were dropped) when they began to descend, to increase the length of their jumps.

The hillside stadion *at Delphi.*

(Photo by Eric Nelson)

Put 'em Up, Lay 'em Down

In addition to the track events, there were field events that tested contestants' abilities in hand-to-hand combat. A competitor had to be tough—very tough—to engage in these events. Although men and boys competed separately, there were no weight divisions. Opponents were chosen by lot until a single victor emerged. We're not entirely sure where these events took place. Some think that they took place in front of the Temple of Zeus, but others think that they occurred, like the track events, in the *stadion*. The events were …

- **Boxing.** There were no rounds, and no ring, in ancient boxing. For this reason, ancient boxing required quite a bit more defensive strategy than modern boxing. It appears that fighters concentrated on head blows, rather than on the body, and that open-handed blows were common. Boxers fought until one man was knocked out or admitted defeat. Instead of gloves, boxers wrapped "leather thongs" (*himantes*) around their knuckles and forearms.

- **Wrestling.** Wrestlers fought standing up, and sought to throw or force their opponents' shoulder, hip, or back to the ground three times. Only biting and grabbing the genitals were illegal holds.

> **Eureka!**
>
> One of the most famous boxers, Melankomas of Caria (Olympic victory 49 B.C.E.) never landed a blow. He was famous for his ability to avoid being struck, and for defending himself until his opponent gave up in exhaustion and frustration. A man of famous beauty, strength, and endurance, Melankomas ended his career undefeated, without ever striking a blow.

> **Eureka!**
>
> The most famous wrestler was Milo of Croton, who won six Olympic victories from 540 to 516 B.C.E. Milo was also famous for his showy demonstrations of strength and for his appetite. It is reported that he once ate an entire bull in one day!

A relief of wrestlers about to tangle.

(Photo by Eric Nelson)

- **The *pankration*.** *Pankration* means something like "all-out brawl," and the event was a combination of wrestling and kick-boxing. It was the most vicious of contests, and the gloves were indeed off. Combatants fought bare-knuckle with few restrictions; only biting and gouging (eyes, nose, and mouth) were illegal, and the event occasionally ended in the death of a competitor.

- **The *pentathlon*.** The *pentathlon* was a combination of five events: running, discus, javelin, long jump, and wrestling. Pentathletes were greatly admired for their comprehensive abilities and their well-proportioned physiques.

Horsing Around

In the equestrian events, the elite (kings, tyrants, and the ultra-wealthy) competed for both honor and victory. In fact, because it was the owner of the horses (not the jockey or driver) who won the victory and the prize, these were the only events in which one could win without actually competing. Much like today, the "sport of kings" took *big* money to house and train the horses, jockeys, and (chariot) drivers. The races took place on a track that went around the *stadion,* and there were separate races for mature horses and foals. The events were …

- **Horse racing.** Jockeys raced (without stirrups and in the nude!) for six laps (about 4½ miles at Olympia) around the *stadion.*

- **Chariot racing (two and four horses).** The chariot races were thrilling, but very, very dangerous. Imagine hooking a racing wheelchair (without the front wheels, but with a railing) behind two or four race horses, standing on it, and shouting "Hyah!" If that isn't enough, imagine careening around the track at full tilt, surrounded by other careening yahoos, for (at Olympia) 12 laps (about 9 miles). Thankfully, you don't have to imagine everyone in the nude (charioteers wore a tunic). There was also an event at Olympia in which two mules pulled a cart, but the event was discontinued by 440 B.C.E. for its "lack of dignity." (We like to think of this event as the origin of the tractor pull.)

The Games of Greece

Now that we've looked at competition in ancient Greek culture, athletics, and training, and some competitive events, we'll give you an overview of the major pan-Hellenic festivals that were established during the Archaic period: the Olympian (Olympic), Nemean, Isthmian, and Pythian games. These games came to make up a yearly circuit of athletic festivals that were attended by athletes and spectators from throughout Hellas. In addition to the spectacle of competition, the festivals were a place for national rivalries, intrigue, politicking, networking, and personal promotion. Additional material on the Olympics can be found in Chapter 4.

It's Your Funeral: The Olympic Games

The Games at Olympia, located in the Peloponnesus, were the oldest and most venerable of the games, having been established (according to tradition) in 776 B.C.E. Through various myths, the Games' origins can be traced back to Zeus, or Herakles (Hercules), or the hero of the Peloponnesus, Pelops (who won a chariot race against King Oenomaus to marry the king's daughter, Hippodamia).

Labyrinths _____

Although the Olympics were originally restricted to free Greek males, they were opened to Roman citizens when Rome conquered Greece in 146 B.C.E. (Much later, the Roman emperor Nero won a chariot race, even though he fell off.) Eventually, when Roman citizenship was granted to all the provinces, all citizens of the Roman Empire could compete.

The Games took place within the "sacred precinct" (*temenos*) at the sanctuary of Zeus. The most important religious areas within the precinct included the "sacred grove" (*altis*), the temples of Zeus and Hera, and the great altar of Zeus. Over time, various cities constructed treasuries and other temples; four oracles were added; and thousands of statues, altars, and dedications filled the area. Facilities for the events (e.g., the *stadion* and *hippodrome*) and arenas for training (e.g., the *xystos* arena for track, the *tetragonon* for field) were also built within the precinct.

Official buildings, baths, and accommodations for priests, judges, athletes, trainers, and pilgrims also grew up, spilling over the boundaries of the *temenos* in the Hellenistic period. You can get an idea of the eventual extent of the games from the size of the *stadion*, which held about 40,000 spectators!

Footraces were the sole events at Olympia until the eighteenth Olympiad, when the pentathlon and wrestling were added. By the fifth century B.C.E., the games had a program, which began with a sacred procession of athletes and *Elean* officials along the Sacred Way to Olympia (a two-day journey). A large crowd would gather in Olympia and await their arrival. Athletes would register for the games, and both athletes and judges would swear public oaths that they had trained properly and

Lexica _____

The **Eleans** were people from Elis, a plain in the western Peloponnesus in which the city, also called Elis, was founded about 471 B.C.E. Because Olympia was closer to the city of Pisa than to the city of Elis, there was intermittent struggle between the two cities for control of the Olympic Games.

would compete or judge fairly. Five days of ceremonies and competition followed, probably according to this schedule:

- **Day 1.** Opening sacrifices and rituals; competition to determine heralds (announcers) and trumpeters (to signal events)

- **Day 2 (or 3).** Boys' *stadion* and field events

- **Day 3 (or 2).** Ceremonies in honor of Pelops; pentathlon and equestrian events

- **Day 4.** Sacrifice of a *hecatombe* (100 oxen) to Zeus; men's track and field events

- **Day 5.** Final ceremony and announcement of victors, followed by a feast

The site of the games was controlled by the Eleans, who made up the priests, "judges" (*Hellenodikai*), and other officials who ran the festival and oversaw the competition. The Eleans vigorously promoted the festival, sending heralds throughout Greece to proclaim the "sacred truce" (*ekecheiria*), and fined or barred from competition those (such as the Spartans in 420 B.C.E.) who violated it. They also supervised the initial training and cuts, administered fines, and disciplined participants. Although the Eleans maintained a reputation for fairness, their hold on the games didn't go unchallenged: the neighboring city of Pisa (in Arcadia) succeeded at least twice (c. 665 and 364 B.C.E.) in taking control of them. The second time, the Eleans counterattacked during the games themselves, turning the festival into a battleground. The Roman dictator Sulla took the treasuries and moved the games to Rome in 85 B.C.E., but the games returned to Olympia until the Christian Roman emperor Theodosius I ended them as a form of pagan worship around 391 C.E.

> **Odysseys**
>
> The sites of the pan-Hellenic festivals still make splendid destinations for visiting. The most difficult trek is at Delphi: The *stadion* is a steep hike up the hill, and the hippodrome for the equestrian events lies far below in the valley.

Other Major Pan-Hellenic Venues

Due in part to the prestige of the Olympian Games, other regions instituted similar festivals at religious sanctuaries in the sixth century B.C.E. These festivals were organized by those who held regional power in the Archaic period and who were also seeking broader recognition among their fellow Hellenes. The Nemean Games (Argos) and the Isthmian Games (Corinth) were organized by rulers of powerful *poleis*, and the Pythian Games (Delphi) were organized by a federation of *ethnê* ("territorial peoples").

All the games became major festivals at which Greeks celebrated a common Hellenic culture and engaged in significant cultural, political, and economic exchange. The Nemean, Isthmian, and Pythian games occurred in a different year than the Olympian Games, which created a kind of pan-Hellenic circuit for competitors and spectators. Originally, the Nemean Games occurred in the valley sanctuary of Nemea, which lay near the city of Cleonae in the northern Peloponnesus. By tradition, they celebrated Zeus and originated from one of Herakles' twelve labors, the conquest of the *Nemean lion*. However, the games emerged as a pan-Hellenic festival around 573 B.C.E., when Argos took them over and enlarged them on the Olympian model. The Nemean Games took place every two years, on the second and fourth years of the Olympiad.

The *Pythian* Games took place at the famous mountain oracle shrine of Delphi (in central Greece), which was sacred to Apollo. Originally a musical competition held every eight years, the festival was expanded in 582 B.C.E., when the shrine was conquered (from the neighboring city of Crisa) by an *amphictyony* ("league of neighbors") led by Thessaly. Athletic and equestrian events were added (though the hippodrome had to be put in the valley, because Delphi clings to the mountainside), and the festival was moved to every four years, on the third year of the Olympiad. Music continued to play a prominent role even after the changes, and the Pythian Games became second in importance to the Olympian Games.

The Isthmian Games took place at Corinth every two years, on the second and fourth years of the Olympiad. They were founded c. 581 B.C.E. by the tyrants of Corinth, and they included Olympic-style competitions. Although there was less pomp and circumstance at the Isthmian Games, they were a popular destination for competitors and spectators—particularly because Corinth was the pleasure capital of Greece (think Vegas or Miami Beach) and easy to reach by boat.

Lexica

The **Nemean lion**'s skin was impregnable, but Herakles used his great strength to strangle and kill the beast. He then skinned it with its own claws and wore the hide and head as a cloak.

The word **Pythian** comes from the serpent Pytho, which Apollo killed in order to found the shrine at Delphi. ("Pythian Apollo" refers to Apollo in conjunction with the Delphic shrine.)

Eureka!

Victors at the pan-Hellenic festivals received crowns of leaves that were sacred to the god in whose honor the festivals were held:

Olympian Games [Zeus]: olive

Pythian Games [Apollo]: laurel

Nemean [Zeus] and Isthmian [Poseidon] games: wild celery

The Least You Need to Know

- Ancient Greek culture was intensively competitive.

- Athletic competitions appear as part of Greek culture from (at least) the Dark Age onward.

- All male citizens underwent physical training as a part of their education, but the competitive nature of Greek culture entered into the restricted lives of women only to a degree.

- We know that athletes were hiring personal trainers and specializing in particular events since the sixth century B.C.E.

- The games at Olympia were the oldest and most venerable of the games, established (according to tradition) in 776 B.C.E.

- Besides the Olympic Games (Olympia), the major pan-Hellenic festivals included the Nemean Games (Argos), the Isthmian Games (Corinth), and the Pythian Games (Delphi).

Two to Tango: Athens and Sparta

In This Chapter

◆ The development and growth of Sparta into the foremost power of Archaic Greece

◆ Sparta's unique culture

◆ Archaic Athens and the tyranny of Peisistratus

◆ Democratic developments from Solon to Cleisthenes

As the Archaic period progressed, regional development predominantly took place along two organizational lines. Some areas organized around a central *polis*, or "city-state" (like Athens), and other regions were organized into loose confederations of *ethnê*, or "tribe" (such as Boeotia and Thessaly). In addition, as the hereditary aristocracies lost power, three different power structures emerged: oligarchy (control by a few men), tyranny (domination by a sole ruler who seized power, generally from the oligarchs), and democracy (where power rested in the citizens of a *dêmos*, or "territorial precinct"). At various times in the Archaic and Classical periods, most Greek states experienced each form of government, and the legacy of their experience profoundly shaped the political and cultural history of the West.

In this chapter, we will examine the development of two famous and influential, but very different, *poleis*, Sparta and Athens. Sparta's unique oligarchic system—with its strict militarism, rigid conservatism, and unusual social practices—was both admired and feared by the Greeks. Xenophobic (or fearful of strangers), proud, and paranoid, Sparta's warrior culture—with all of its strengths, rigidity, and dependence upon subjugation—has been both praised and criticized throughout history. Sparta's unique culture developed primarily in the Archaic period, and remained fairly consistent thereafter. So in this chapter, we'll spend more time discussing Sparta than Athens and, in the following chapters, Athens will receive the lion's share of the discussion.

Lexica

A *dêmos* (plural *dêmoi*) is a territory and the people (often restricted to the free males, or citizens) who live in it. While the term came to be used by aristocrats (probably in the seventh century B.C.E.) as a term for "commoners" or "the masses," it retained its more inclusive sense (i.e., "the whole people") in legal inscriptions.

An *ethnos* (plural *ethnê*) is a group of people who share a common identity and territory, such as a tribe.

Athens, like several other Archaic *poleis*, vacillated for a time between oligarchy and tyranny. In the sixth century B.C.E., however, Athenian reforms set the stage for a radical democracy that vested an astounding degree of civic power in the citizens. The development and refinement of these reforms, along with Athens' rise as Greece's preeminent sea power, occurred in the fifth century B.C.E. The two powers, Athens and Sparta, combined their strengths in the early fifth century B.C.E., to help repel the Persian invasion but, shortly thereafter, they became embroiled in a bitter conflict to impose their individual visions upon Hellas.

Unit Cohesion: The Development of Sparta

Both the essence of Sparta's allure and its unique ability to horrify seem to be located in Sparta's fierce and fearful discipline. Spartan freedom and independence were maintained through absolute commitment to military strength and a disciplined adherence to their unique social and political organization. In turn, this commitment to military strength and discipline was reinforced—on the one hand, by a sense of superiority and a practice of exclusivity and, on the other hand, by a fearful distrust of "inferior" peoples and city-states. Ironically, the Spartan system relied upon placing strict limitations on the independence and freedom of both their neighbors and themselves. Yet, by committing their state resources to raising, training, and fielding an elite military force, a relatively small number of Spartans were able, for centuries, to subjugate the surrounding Greeks, maintain their territorial integrity, and produce the most feared fighting force of antiquity.

Ancient Sparta

The *polis* of Sparta lay in the central, southeast section of the Peloponnesus, in the region of Laconia (Spartans were also called Lacedaimonians or Laconians). The site occupied a narrow valley along the Eurotas River, between two north-south mountain ranges and about 25 miles inland from the nearest sea port. The location was easily defensible, given its limited access from the sea and the ruggedness of the surrounding mountains, but it was also essentially landlocked. However, this landlocked character became a feature of Sparta's mentality and culture, such that Sparta concentrated on land forces and agriculture, while distrusting the sea and trade.

> **Odysseys**
>
> If you visit Sparta (perhaps to see the temple of Artemis Orthia), remember that Sparta always remained a "Spartan" *polis*, with only a few public buildings and modest private homes. As the historian Thucydides remarked (1.10): "If Sparta were deserted and only temples and foundations remained, people long hence would seriously question whether its power ever really lived up to its fame."

> **Muses**
>
> The Laconians (i.e., Spartans) were famous for being terse (hence laconic) and unimpressed by rhetoric:
>
> The Samian refugees arrived in Sparta and made a long speech to the authorities concerning their great need. The Spartans responded that they couldn't understand their request, since the speech had gone on so long that they had forgotten what the first part of it was about. The next day, the Samians simply brought a bag, held it up, and said, "The bag needs grain." "The bag," the Spartans replied, "was unnecessary"; but they decided to help them. (Herodotus, 3.46)

According to tradition, the Spartans belonged to the race of Dorians, which invaded and settled during the late Bronze Age and early Dark Age. Whatever the truth about the Dorians, during the early Archaic period, four or five villages combined, or underwent a *synoikism*, to create the Spartan *polis*. The combined villages developed an oligarchic system of government, with a "council of elders" (*gerousia*) that prepared business for ratification by the assembly and performed judicial functions. To counterbalance this aristocratic body, the Spartans also created an "annually elected body of five magistrates" (*ephoroi*). This body of magistrates had powers over the entire citizenry and the job of upholding Sparta's unwritten code of law.

Lexica

The ***gerousia*** ("body of elders") was a council of 28 men, each over 60 years old, and the 2 kings. Election to the *gerousia* was for life, and it was the highest honor for a Spartan.

The ***ephoroi*** ("overseers") were an annually elected board of 5 adult citizens, each over the age of 30. *Ephors* had executive political and judicial power over the *gerousia*, assembly, and kings in order to maintain adherence to Spartan laws and customs.

But unlike other instances of *synoikism*, the chiefs of two of the main villages (the Dark Age *basileis*) retained powerful roles and became, as dual kings, leaders of the oligarchic *polis*. Although the kings could not determine policy, and although they were subject to both the laws and the *ephors*, they were religious leaders, members of the council, and supreme military commanders in the field. The kings came from two royal households, the Agiads and the Eurypontids, which claimed descent from Herakles and remained rivals throughout Spartan history.

First Among Unequals: Spartans and the *Perioikoi*

Like other *poleis*, Sparta faced the challenge of a dwindling land base for a growing population. Instead of enlarging through further *synoikism* or turning to colonization, however, Sparta took a different tact. It conquered the immediately surrounding lands and subjugated the peoples as *perioikoi*, or "dwellers-around." Although the *perioikoi* were Greek, they were not incorporated into the Spartan *polis* (as they might have been in other areas of Greece as part of *synoikism*). They were granted some local autonomy, in that they retained self-governed communities, but they were required to serve as *hoplites* in the Spartan military and to pay taxes to a *polis* in which they had no status as citizens.

The status of the *perioikoi* seems to have resulted from Sparta's intensely clannish focus on bloodline as a mark of identity and status. Throughout their history, the Spartans viewed themselves as an

---

Lexica

Perioikoi ("dwellers-around") were second-class "half-citizens" who served in the army and had limited legal and property rights (but no political rights). *Perioikoi* could work as craftsmen and traders. **Helots** (from the Greek word for "capture") were Spartan serfs and the object of systematized subjugation.

---

ethnically distinct class that needed to remain pure. Intermarriage with foreigners was forbidden, and any attempt to broaden Spartan ranks was resisted (even when their population fell to disastrously low numbers in the Classical and Hellenistic periods). Indeed, even the founding of Sparta's only major colony, Taras, seemed to involve strict ethnic distinction. (That is, it was founded by Spartans of suspicious bloodlines who had been deprived of their full citizenship.)

Hell on the Helots

Most of the richest land in Laconia was in the hands of the Spartan aristocracy. In response to pressure for more land, Sparta conquered the fertile region of Messenia (the First Messenian War c. 730–710 B.C.E.). The victory gave Sparta control of roughly 40 percent of the Peloponnesus and a population that dwarfed its 8,000 to 10,000 man army. Some of the Messenians, particularly those who lived along the coast and were useful to the Spartans for trade purposes, became *perioikoi*. The rest, however, were reduced to *helots* and systematically subjugated. In fact, the status of the helots was unique in ancient Greece: They were Greeks subjugated by Greeks and they were the property of the *polis* (rather than the property of individuals, like other slaves).

> **Lexica**
>
> **Helots** (from the Greek word for "capture") were Spartan serfs and the object of systematized subjugation.

As Spartan serfs, the helots lost all rights. While their farms were apportioned to Spartan citizens, the helots themselves were forced to work their former lands and to provide the new owners with half of their harvests. Other helots were put to work as menial servants in Spartan households. Worse yet, in order to sustain the degree of superiority necessary to justify violent and brutal subjugation, the Spartans encouraged communal hatred and fear of the helots.

Helots were compelled to wear distinctive dogskin caps as a mark of their lower status, and they were forced to endure public beatings. They were also forced to endure public humiliation (such as forced public drunkenness) and, thereby, to demonstrate their own inferiority and serve as examples of wrongful behavior to the Spartan youth. Yet, for a helot, demonstrating good Spartan virtues (physical strength, courage, discipline, and so on), or standing out from the crowd, was life-threatening. A secret police force, the *krypteia*, spied on them and eliminated any who posed a potential threat. Even the most average helot was in continuous danger, because ambushing and murdering helots was part of a Spartan male's training. Finally, each year, the *ephors* (who ran the *krypteia*) formally declared war on them, thereby sanctioning and

Lexica _____

The *krypteia* ("secret society") was a secret police force that identified and assassinated subversive, or potentially subversive, helots. All Spartan youths were enrolled in this society for a time.

Spartiatai were full Spartan citizens. *Spartiates* were barred from all professions except soldiering.

justifying the murder of any helot—in the eyes of the state and in the eyes of the gods.

Sparta had resolved its food and land problems, and it had become the largest (3,000 square miles, far larger than Attica) and wealthiest *polis* in Hellas. This status was, however, held together by a relatively small number of *Spartiates*. (Perhaps 1 in every 20 people was a full citizen.) Yet, the Spartans were victorious in another regional war, the Second Messenian War c. 640 to 630 B.C.E. This war appears to have influenced, or necessitated, further adaptations in Spartan culture in the sixth century B.C.E. that were designed to ensure Spartan domination of the region.

Spartan Culture

Spartan culture was organized for one purpose: to promote, develop, and maintain Sparta's fighting force. Economic development and trade were left to the *perioikoi*. From boyhood until the age of 60, Spartan males were trained as warriors, and they were forbidden to engage in any form of work except soldiering. The roles of Spartan females were to bear strong, healthy children and to value and support only those Spartan males who adhered to and exemplified the Spartan warrior character and code. Discipline, endurance, austerity, courage, and, above all, dedication and conformity to Spartan customs and traditions were beaten, starved, encouraged, ingrained, and drilled into both sexes from birth.

Males lived in all-male barracks from the age of 7 until, at minimum, the age of 30, and their physical appearance was distinctive: Spartan males shaved their moustaches, but wore the long hair and beards of Archaic aristocrats. Married males under the age of 30 could visit their wives only secretly (that is, by going AWOL), and they were beaten if caught.

At age 20, citizen males sought admittance to one of the Spartan "communal meal groups," or *sussitia*. Each *sussition* consisted of roughly 15 members, who voted on whether to admit or reject a candidate. Once admitted, each member was required to attend meals and to contribute a standard portion of produce (from his land, which was worked by the helots) to help feed the group. Failure to contribute resulted in expulsion, shame, and loss of full citizenship (as did cowardice and failure to be admitted to a *sussition*).

No Kidding

At birth, Spartan boys were examined by state officials for any signs of weakness or deformity that might compromise their ability to reach peak physical performance. Those who failed the tests were killed, and those who passed were allotted one of the 9,000 *kleroi* ("parcels of farmland"). At age seven, boys were taken from their mothers to begin the *agôgê*, or training regimen. At the barracks, they were attached to a *sussition*, whose members became the boy's mentors, examples, and trainers. Boys called all older members *patêr* ("father") to emphasize attachment to the group rather than to a particular family. Homosexual pairings between older and younger males were also officially encouraged. Pederasty was a feature of the Doric Greek cultures of Crete, the Peloponnesus, and Boeotia, and it was thought to encourage emotional bonds, expressions of love (including physical) between generations of comrades, and, in Sparta, patriotic spirit. However, pederasty was controversial, even in Classical Greece (and it was never pervasive among the Ionians, whom the Dorians considered too soft and wimpy for the practice). See Chapter 4 for more on the practice of pederasty.

The *agôgê* was not, however, fun and games. Boys were rigorously trained and disciplined. They were kept silent and allowed only one outer garment (and no shoes) year-round. They slept on reed beds, underwent routine hazing (which was intended to toughen them up), and exercised naked in all weather. They were systematically underfed and starved, to encourage them to steal food. If they were caught stealing, however, they were beaten and disgraced for their ineptitude (that is, for getting caught).

Stealth and cunning were further encouraged by enrolling boys in the *krypteia*, the secret society charged with eliminating suspicious helots. Given only a dagger and field rations, older boys were sent out to survive in the wild by stealing from and murdering helots. If they successfully completed the *agôgê* and were admitted as a member to a *sussition*, males became *homoioi* ("equals") … and the cycle continued.

> **Eureka!**
>
> Spartan boys were taught to follow orders and endure hardships, and they feared disgrace above all else, including death. Plutarch tells the story of a Spartan boy who stole a fox cub and hid it beneath his cloak. The cub began to bite, and to eat away the boy's insides, but rather than reveal his theft, the boy collapsed and died without making a sound.

> **Lexica**
>
> **Homoioi**, or "equals," were full-rank Spartan citizens of age. The **agôgê**, or "path, education" was the 13-year training program that Spartan boys (except for royal sons) received in order to become *homoioi*. The **sussition** ("common mess") was a common meal group (about 15 members) to which Spartan males were admitted and expected to contribute.

Strange Bedfellows: Spartan Men and Women

Spartan women had, compared to other women in ancient Greece, considerable freedom and extraordinary power. Spartan law permitted women to inherit, so a woman could own family property. Girls were physically trained (naked or scantily clad, which disturbed other Greeks), and they were educated in dancing and choral singing.

Eureka!

Only Spartan men who died in battle and Spartan women who died in childbirth were thought to have deaths worthy of graves marked with epitaphs. All other graves were unmarked or, if marked, anonymous.

Muses

When Gorgo [daughter of King Cleomenes and the wife of King Leonidas] was asked by an Attic woman, "Why do you Spartan women alone rule over your husbands?" she answered, "Because only we are the mothers of men."

—Plutarch, *Sayings of Spartan Women*

Because men were away from home most of the time, either at the *sussition* or in the field, Sparta was unique in its reliance on women to manage household affairs, and it was, apparently, more tolerant of both female homosexuality and female extramarital sex than other Greek states. Even in times of peace, Spartan women wielded private and public influence unheard of in other parts of Greece.

Because the primary role for Spartan women was to bear and raise superior children for the *polis*, girls, unlike boys, were not underfed. (Healthy mothers make for healthy children.) Their secondary role, which they took very seriously, was to validate and support males who embodied Spartan values and goals. Young women ridiculed males who were unmarried or not producing children and, incredibly, Spartan custom allowed woman to engage in *polyandry*, or have multiple husbands or sexual partners. At his wife's request, a husband (presumably one who wasn't keeping up his end of the procreation bargain) could arrange for his wife to have sex with someone else who appealed to her (as a second partner). Other Greeks (at least the men) considered this practice outrageous.

As mothers, Spartan women were famous for being hard and stoic. One mother reportedly killed her son, a deserter, for being an imposter (i.e., "He's not mine. My son was a Spartan"). Another reportedly pointed to her son's shield, just before he went off to battle, and said, "Either [come back] with this [i.e., carrying it], or on it [i.e., as a corpse]."

King of the Hill

After Sparta conquered Messenia, neighboring regions, particularly Argos, held further Spartan expansion in check. In fact, Sparta's defeat by Argive hoplites, under the tyrant Pheidon in 669 B.C.E., may have generated some of Sparta's drastic reforms and the creation of its permanent soldiering class. After narrowly defeating Argos in 546 B.C.E., Sparta solidified its position as the most powerful *polis* in Greece by creating its first major defensive alliance: Sparta and its allies (or, as we now call it, the Peloponnesian League).

Members of the alliance, who included most of the Peloponnesus and *poleis* such as Thebes and Corinth, pledged forces for common defense under Spartan leadership. Members paid no tribute (except in war) and were bound to Sparta (but not to each other) by an oath "to have the same friends and enemies, and to follow the Spartans wherever they lead." Although every member had a vote at their congress, only Sparta could convene the alliance. Thus, even with its isolationist tendencies, Sparta was able to exercise tremendous influence over a vast area of Hellas (and beyond) through its power, wealth, and alliances. In this way, Sparta was able to protect itself, preserve its domination of the helots, maintain stability in the Peloponnesus, and favor stable oligarchies (versus those pesky tyrannies and, later, democracies) in other states. In the meantime, as we'll see in the following sections, Athens was developing in very different directions.

Drifting Toward "Democracy": The Evolving Athenian Experiment

We know little about the Archaic history of Athens. However, we do know that, early on, nine elected magistrates, or *archontes* (*archons*, "rulers") replaced the kings and took over their ancient responsibilities (as well as new functions for the *polis*). The most important magistrates were the *archon basileus* ("king archon"), who had judicial responsibility over important religious matters (such as capital offences), the *polemarch* ("war leader"), originally the chief military officer, and the *eponymous archon* ("the chief executive officer"), who gave his name to the year. Former archons served as an "executive council and senate," the *Areopagus*. Because election to the archonship was restricted to aristocrats alone, this system was firmly in the hands of the aristocracy.

> **Eureka!**
>
> Athenians kept track of years by the names of eponymous *archons*, rather than numbers. In modern terms, under such a system Americans would refer to years by the names of their country's presidents.

As in other *poleis*, aristocratic control led to civil unrest in the seventh and sixth centuries B.C.E. As population and land pressures increased, poor farmers fell into debt and became indentured servants or slaves. More prosperous, but nonaristocratic, citizens found themselves shut out of power.

Tensions among aristocratic factions, combined with pressures from below, set the stage for an attempted tyranny. In c. 632 B.C.E., the Olympian victor Cylon, backed by his father-in-law Theagenes (tyrant of the nearby *polis* of Megara) captured the Acropolis and attempted to seize power at Athens. The coup failed and, although Cylon escaped, his supporters were lured out of the Acropolis and massacred.

Eureka!

The massacre of Cylon's supporters was overseen by Megacles, a member of a rival aristocratic family, the Alcmaeonids ("decendants of Alcmaeon"). This family remained highly influential in Athenian history, but the "curse of the Alcmaeonids," which originated in the massacre, was periodically used against them by their political opponents.

Pressure on the aristocrats continued and, apparently in response, an eponymous *archon* named Draco recorded a law code c. 620 B.C.E. (supposedly Athens' first written code of law). This code was excessively harsh, in that the penalty for almost everything was death, and it is the basis for the term *draconian*, which is used to describe excessively harsh law or administration. Although biased in favor of the aristocrats, the code did limit the power and discretion of the aristocracy by committing the law to writing.

Wise Guy: Solon and His Reforms

By the early sixth century B.C.E., with the situation at a boiling point, the Athenians gave Solon, an eponymous *archon*, executive power to draft the legislation necessary to cope with their civil and economic ills. And here, things began to go differently for the Athenians. In fact, later generations revered Solon as a sage (one of the Seven Sages of Greece) and a founding father of their state.

Eureka!

Solon's four property classes were the *pentakosiomedimnoi* ("500 bushel guys"), *hippeis* ("guys with a horse"), *zeugitai* ("guys with a team of oxen"), and *thêtes* ("serfs"). Although *thêtes* were excluded from offices, these lowest-rung citizens had, probably for the first time, a guaranteed, participatory role in government through the assembly.

Solon changed the nature of Athenian citizenship and politics by grounding the qualifications for political participation in wealth, rather than birth or land ownership, and he created four property classes.

Archons were elected from the top class (still dominated by the aristocracy) by an assembly of all citizens, and minor officials were elected from the top three classes. Solon also created a special "appellate court" (the *Heliaia*) to review the decisions of the *Areopagus* ("senate"), and he (probably) instituted another council, the *boulê*, as a counterbalance to the *Areopagus*.

Through his reforms, the lowest classes received citizenship and a participatory role in the state, and the *dêmos* (people of the territory) received an official presence in governing. Moreover, Solon took action to set the Athenian state on firmer economic footing. He cancelled debts, rescinded the laws that allowed bankrupt farmers and their families to be sold into slavery, and limited the amount that landlords could charge tenant farmers. He also invited craftsmen, traders, and their families to settle in Athens with offers of citizenship.

Not everyone agreed with Solon's legislation. However, he used writing (poetry) to defend and explain his ideas and reasoning. Substantial fragments of his didactic and moralizing poetry remain, and he is remembered both as the first great Athenian statesman and as a literary figure.

> **Muses**
>
> I gave the *dêmos* just the right amount of honor, neither overly reducing nor adding to its privilege. As for the powerful, who were admired for their wealth, I made sure that they, too, had no disgrace. I took my stance and covered both, protecting them with my strong shield and did not allow either to triumph unjustly.
>
> —Solon, Fragment 5

Highlander! The Tyranny of Peisistratus and His Sons

Even with Solon's reforms in place, tensions between the lower classes and the aristocracy, who maintained a firm grip on the *polis*, remained. These tensions were exploited by a talented and affable aristocrat from the hills, Peisistratus (or Pisistratus), a kinsman of Solon. Peisistratus pitched himself as the protector of the common man and convinced the assembly to provide him with a bodyguard (to guard against aristocratic rivals), which he used to take control of the city in 561 B.C.E. Driven out and brought back twice by 556 B.C.E., he eventually returned with mercenaries and defeated his enemies at Pallene c. 546 B.C.E. He ruled for the next 19 years and, like other tyrants, he attempted to make his city great.

Peisistratus exiled some of his rivals and confiscated their lands, which he redistributed to the poor and to his supporters in the *dêmos*. However, he kept Solon's reforms (although his supporters received the top posts), which gave them time to take hold. He created public works projects, promoted Athens' ceramic industry, developed rich silver mines at Laurium (in southwest Attica), and secured steady grain shipments from the Black Sea. Moreover, he developed or enlarged city festivals that celebrated the new Athens, such as the *Panathenaia* ("All-Athens Festival") and *City Dionysia* ("City Festival of Dionysus"). These festivals and their competitions were instrumental in creating an Athenian identity that rested firmly on, and with, the *dêmos*.

Eureka!

The Panathenaic Festival featured many competitions, including recitation of Homer, which probably necessitated the creation of the first official texts of the *Iliad* and *Odyssey*. The centerpiece of the City Dionysia was three days of dramatic competitions, for which the great tragedies and comedies of the Classical period were written.

By the time Peisistratus died peacefully in 528/7 B.C.E., he had transformed Athens from a minor *polis* into a prominent political, economic, and cultural center. His son, Hippias, ruled in his place, and together with his brother, Hipparchus (known collectively as the Peisistratids), Hippias continued Athens' cultural and economic development. Hipparchus was murdered in 514 B.C.E., in a personal revenge killing (later cast as a patriotic political assassination), whereupon Hippias became paranoid and autocratic. His excesses gave home support to the aristocratic factions exiled by Peisistratus, which were led by a certain Isagoras. Isagoras prevailed on Sparta's king Cleomenes to drive Hippias out of Athens in 510 B.C.E. and to make Athens a part of the Peloponnesian League.

Under Peisistratus, Attic pottery became preeminent and moved from black figure into the red figure style.

(Photos by Eric Nelson)

Hippias fled to Persia, and the exiles, with Isagoras elected *archon* in 508 B.C.E., seemed to be back in control of the city. Isagoras moved to revoke the citizenship of those who had received it under Solon and Peisistratus, but quickly found himself opposed by an Alcmaeonid, Cleisthenes. Cleisthenes seemed to have both the program and the pedigree for another tyranny—he was the grandson of a Sicyonian tyrant, also named Cleisthenes, and he took a populist stand.

Isagoras booted Cleisthenes and brought in the Spartans once again, but they underestimated the depth of opposition. When the Spartan king Cleomenes attempted to institute an oligarchy, the Athenian populace rose in opposition, and besieged the small Spartan force in the Acropolis. The Spartan army was forced to surrender (a humiliation), and it was sent packing (along with Isagoras). Cleisthenes returned to Athens and seemed ready to become the next tyrant.

Cleisthenes and the Foundations of Athenian Democracy

But it didn't happen quite that way. Instead, Cleisthenes moved to finish what Solon had begun (possibly unintentionally) and Peisistratus had encouraged, which was breaking the aristocratic hold over Athenian politics. By tradition, Athenians voted by local tribes, over which aristocratic families exerted control in their respective regions. Cleisthenes redrew Attica into 30 subregions (10 city, 10 coastal, and 10 inland) called *trittyes* ("threes"), and recombined them into 10 new tribes (each made up of one city, one coastal, and one inland *trittys*). However, he drew the *trittyes* in a manner designed to maintain the *dêmoi* ("precincts"). This arrangement not only broke regional control, but also combined citizens from various areas in a way that required cooperation and common ground at the level of the *dêmoi*, rather than the level of the *aristoi*. Moreover, it gave new citizens (enrolled by Solon and Peisistratus) a common identity with others. This commonality was further secured by military reorganization: each tribe elected its own *taxiarchos* ("infantry commander"), *hipparchos* ("cavalry commander"), and *stratêgos* ("general").

Moreover, Cleisthenes reorganized the *boulê* ("council") to include 500 men, 50 men from each new tribe. These representatives were elected by lot to proportionately represent the *demes* of the tribe. Each tribe was in charge of the *boulê* for one month, in which the members were called *prytaneis* ("presiding officials"). The

> **CAUTION**
>
> **Labyrinths**
>
> Although Cleisthenes' reforms were radical, it's important to keep an overall perspective. Cleisthenes would have been unable to carry out his reforms without a good deal of consent from the upper classes. And, as with modern redistricting, the reforms involved political favoritism (in this case, particularly to the Alcmaeonids) and compromise.

Lexica

The *ekklêsia* was the full assembly of citizens of the *dêmos*. Its business was regulated by the *boulê* (executive council). Its monthly business was run by *prytaneis* (presiding officials) made up of 50 men from a tribe drawn from the *dêmoi* of each *tryttys*. Confused? See Chapter 14.

head and secretary of the *prytany* changed every day, by lot. The *boulê* was given power to oversee, audit, and impeach magistrates, to prepare business for the *ekklêsia* (assembly of citizens), and to manage affairs of state.

Cleisthenes' reforms, artificial as they might have been, transformed Athens by solidifying its democratic foundations. No group, individual, or class could dominate politics as they once had. Power lay with the *dêmos*, and appeals to the *dêmos* (in addition to the traditional means) were necessary to achieve influence. And Athens would need the support of all of its citizens in the opening years of the next century, because Hippias was coming back with a different solution to political instability, and his idea involved a lot of soldiers.

The Least You Need to Know

- As the hereditary aristocracies lost power, three different power structures emerged: oligarchy, tyranny, and democracy.

- Spartan freedom and independence were maintained through absolute commitment to military strength and a disciplined adherence to their unique social and political organization.

- *Spartiatai* were full Spartan citizens; *perioikoi* were "half-citizens" who served in the army and had limited legal and property rights; and helots were Spartan serfs and the object of systematized subjugation.

- Solon was revered by later generations of Greeks as a sage (one of the Seven Sages of Greece) and a founding father of the Athenian state.

- By the time Peisistratus died in 528/7 B.C.E., he had transformed Athens from a minor *polis* into a prominent political, economic, and cultural center.

- Cleisthenes' reforms, artificial as they might have been, transformed Athens by solidifying its democratic foundations.

Part  The Height of the Classical Period and the *Polis*

If you've studied anything about ancient Greece, you're probably familiar with the fifth century (500–400) B.C.E., the height of the Classical period and of the *polis*, or "city-state." Literature, drama, philosophy, science, architecture, art … it's all there in an explosion of creativity unmatched in much of (documented) human history. And, of course, during this time we also see the development of Athens' famous democracy.

However, you'll discover that these achievements took place in times of chaos and upheaval. The Greeks' stunning victory over the Persians, early in the century, gave Athens an empire and set the stage for 30 years of vicious and bloody warfare (the Peloponnesian War) between Athens, Sparta, and their respective allies at the end of the century. Revolutions and counter-revolutions—in the state, the mind, the soul, and on the stage—brought about explorations and examinations of human experience that substantially changed the course of the centuries that followed.

Chapter 13

The Persian Wars

In This Chapter

- ◆ Athenian involvement with Persia
- ◆ The Ionian Revolt to the Battle of Marathon
- ◆ The heroic Greek defeat at Thermopylae, and victories at Salamis, Plataea, and Mycale
- ◆ Athens rises to power as leader of the Delian League

In Athens, Cleisthenes' dramatic reforms were in place, but strong opposition remained, both at home—among those who supported Isagoras' policies—and abroad—among the Spartans who supported Isagoras' oligarchic party. Moreover, Isagoras had enrolled Athens as a member of the Peloponnesian League, which put Athens, at least in Sparta's eyes, in a consensual relationship under Spartan leadership. It was necessary, therefore, for the new Athenian state to look elsewhere for support and allies, and they went, in 507 B.C.E., to the only power conceivably stronger than the Spartans and their allies: the Persians.

When the Athenian ambassadors arrived in the western Persian capital of Sardis seeking an alliance, they were completely perplexed by the Persian court, as was the court by them. The Persians had no idea who the Athenians *or* the Spartans were, but they offered their form of an alliance:

They admitted Athens into the Persian king's dominions as part of the empire, and they required submission to the king. When the satrap asked for "earth and water" (symbolic offerings of unconditional submission to the Persian monarch), the Athenian ambassadors gave them. When the ambassadors returned to Athens, however, the assembly rejected the terms. But it never sent a representative back to Sardis with an explanation, which left Persia to believe that Athens was a willing addition to the empire and the Athenians to believe that they had rejected the deal. This set of circumstances didn't bode well for the future of Athenian and Persian relations.

This diplomatic *faux pas* may have contributed to the events of the next century. In this chapter, we'll chart the growing tensions between Persia and Greece that erupted into a massive conflict called the Persian War. This war temporarily united the Greeks against an ancient superpower. Miraculously, the Greeks won. The victory galvanized Greek (especially Athenian) self-confidence, and brought Athens power and prestige that rivaled Sparta's.

Who Wears the Pants? The Rise of Persia

As mentioned in Chapter 6, the Persians, under Cyrus the Great (ruling 560–530 B.C.E.), conquered the Lydian Empire of Croesus (ruling 560–546 B.C.E.) and subjugated the Ionian Greek city-states (already under Lydian domination), where they installed tyrants loyal to Persia. By the time of Cleisthenes' reforms, the Persian monarch Darius I (ruling c. 522–486 B.C.E.) controlled a vast empire stretching from Ionia to India and into Egypt, millions of subjects, and unimaginable wealth and resources.

Persian Expansion Toward Greece

Labyrinths

The Persians (people from the area of modern Iran) were not Semitic or Arabic peoples. Their origin and language is Indo-European. This means that they have an ancient ancestry with the Irish and East Indians (not the Iraqis).

In 512 B.C.E., Darius crossed the Hellespont and began to campaign against the Thracian and Scythian tribes that had been disrupting his northern frontier. Here, although he was largely unsuccessful against the Scythians, he subjugated both Thrace and the Macedonian kings, who had seen it coming anyway. Now, other Greek *poleis* ("city-states") and *ethnê* ("tribes") saw it coming, too. After conquering Lydia, Egypt, India, and the Middle East, what possible threat could the small and politically divided Greek *poleis* pose? Darius' empire, now on European land, extended to the northern borders of Greece, and included the Greek city-states of the eastern Aegean and Black Sea.

Whether to acquiesce willingly (and, thereby, get the best terms) or resist became a major Hellenic preoccupation. Parties favoring one course of action or the other led the discussion, although most citizens tried to straddle the fence until it became clear which side to jump down on. Those who favored cooperation with Persia came to be called "medizers" (the Greeks called the Persians "Medes"). The most influential medizer was the Pythian oracle at Delphi. Delphi had close ties to the Ionian Greeks and a lot to lose from being conquered rather than co-opted. Oracles consistently favored submitting to Persia and disparaged resistance.

The Ionian Revolt

In 499 B.C.E., Aristagoras, the Ionian tyrant of Miletus, persuaded the Persian satrap of Sardis to attack the Greek island of Naxos. The attack failed, which emboldened several Ionian states, and they attempted to throw out their Persian-installed tyrants. Aristagoras, who saw that his own jig was up, suddenly turned freedom fighter. Laying his tyranny aside, he went to Greece to ask for assistance in freeing Ionia. In Sparta, king Cleomenes took one look at where the Persian capital was located— three months' march from Ionia—and declined. However, Eretria (on Euboea), which had long historical ties with Ionia, and Athens, which feared getting Hippias—the former Athenian tyrant who had fled to Persia—back if the Persians got the upper hand, voted to send forces. Initially successful, the Greeks sacked and burned Sardis. But the Persians counterattacked, the Ionians fell into disunity, and the Athenians and Eretrians returned to Greece. When Darius gained the upper hand again in Ionia, he had the satrap in Sardis install democracies instead of tyrannies in the resubjugated states. In the Persian War, many of these states fought on the side of the Persians against the mainland Greeks, and were forever tainted by their cooperation.

Now remember, the Persians may have considered Athens to be part of their empire. Darius cleaned up the Ionian opposition by 493 B.C.E., but his eyes were always on the rebellious Athenians. According to Herodotus, he had a slave say to him, "Sire, remember the Athenians," three times at every meal, just in case the little *polis* happened to slip his mind. He even sent envoys throughout Greece to demand earth and water, both to reaffirm the empire's claim over Athens and to make other Greeks an offer they couldn't refuse. Many bought in, but the Athenians tossed the Persian ambassadors into the brig. (The Spartans, ever direct and polite, tossed them into a well, saying that there was plenty of water and earth down there.) To Darius, there was only one option left: Send in the troops and make examples out of Eretria and

Athens. Then Darius could put his good friend Hippias, who had been hanging around with the perfect resumé, back in charge of Athens.

Hippias' Quick Run at Regency: The Battle of Marathon

Darius first sent a Persian force along the northern Aegean in 492 B.C.E., but most of the fleet was wrecked in a terrible storm off the Mt. Athos peninsula. He then tried the direct route. An expedition of around 20,000 troops, with Hippias along, landed (after burning down Eretria) near the village of Marathon, which is, as we all know, about 26 miles from Athens. Athens was in trouble. Big trouble.

> **CAUTION**
>
> **Labyrinths** _____
>
> The modern marathon is taken from a tradition that claims that a runner sprinted 26 miles back from Marathon to Athens, announced *"Niki!"* ("Victory!") to the shocked crowd, and died. However, this tradition appears to be false and, besides, very few marathoners die crossing the finish line these days, (although some may feel like they're going to).

Time and numbers were on the Persian side. Athens needed help from the Spartans, but, unfortunately, Sparta was 140 miles away. An Athenian runner, Pheidippides, became famous for racing from Athens to Sparta in under two days to ask for help. The Spartans were sympathetic, but they were unable to mobilize in time because of a festival (perhaps a good excuse to stay out of what looked like a losing battle?). Only a few hundred forces arrived from the nearby village of Plataea to join the Athenians, who numbered about 9,000, and face the Persians across the plain at Marathon. Datis, the Persian commander, stalled for several days and, then, leaving the land forces to face the Athenians, sent his fleet toward an unprotected Athens. Check and mate? Not quite yet.

Charge!

The 10 Athenian *stratêgoi* ("tribal generals") weren't eager to attack this richly and strangely arrayed force, which was twice their size, especially because the Persian archers, who were particularly deadly, would rain arrows down on their slowly advancing phalanx of hoplites. One general, Miltiades, convinced them to attack. The Greeks spread their forces out (to match the larger enemy's formation) and— for the first time in Greek military experience—charged an enemy at a dead run to minimize the time that the Persians had to form up and pick them off. The Greeks' center flank, without the support of additional ranks, gave way to the Persian line, but the wings won. Instead of pursuing their opponents, however, the two wings formed up into one unit and blindsided the Persian center.

The Greek hoplites were much better armed and trained for close combat, and they routed the Persians, forced them into a marsh, and slaughtered them. In the end, about 7,000 Persians lost their lives, but only 192 Athenians were killed. The Greeks then had to quick-march back to Athens in order to head off the Persian fleet. When they arrived, the Persians departed, taking Hippias with them and leaving Athens a great victory. Two thousand Spartans eventually showed up to assist the Athenians, but by then it was too late. The victory belonged to the Athenians and the Plataeans.

Confidence in, and commitment to, the Athenian democracy surged after the victory at Marathon. After all, the Persians were supposed to be invincible (even though they wore pants, which Greek men found odd and a bit effeminate). For the next generation, being a "fighter at Marathon," was an Athenian's (of any class) proudest boast. Both the poet Aeschylus and his brother (who lost his life) fought there, and the Athenian general Miltiades dedicated his helmet to Olympian Zeus in gratitude for his great victory (you can see it today at the museum at Olympia).

"I'll Be Back": Darius and Xerxes' Invasion of Greece

Marathon didn't please Darius. Oh no, not at all. It wasn't that the defeat threatened the Persian Empire. It was personal. He marshaled forces from the empire for a massive invasion of Greece. Darius was a great builder and organizer, and he carefully planned the logistics of the invasion. He died, however, before his plans were completed and his son, Xerxes (ruling c. 486–465 B.C.E.), took over command.

Xerxes' army, as well as its approach, was supposed to awe his opponents. He created a pontoon bridge over the Hellespont (now known as the Dardanelles) to move his army into Europe, and cut a canal through the Mt. Athos peninsula to avoid losing another fleet around the treacherous tip. Greek tradition held that the army was so large that it took seven days and nights for it to march across the Hellespont, and it drank whole rivers dry. Herodotus estimated the army at 5 million, but it was probably between 150,000 and 300,000 men (depending upon whom you include in the army), accompanied by a fleet of about 600 ships. Regardless of exaggeration, when compared to the size of citizen armies and navies of the *poleis*, it must have seemed enormous.

"The Persians Are Coming! The Persians Are Coming!"

Xerxes' force, commanded by his general Mardonius, began its advance about 480 B.C.E. across Thrace. Many of the states in northern Greece (such as Macedon and Thessaly), whose territory stood between Xerxes and Athens, capitulated to the Persians as the only reasonable thing to do. In central and southern Greece, however, the 31 states of the Peloponnesian League, with Sparta at the head, decided to make a fight of it.

Lexica

The **trireme** was a warship measuring about 120 feet long and 15 feet wide and powered by 170 rowers in three ranks. It was armed with an underwater ram at the bow for ramming and sinking enemy ships. The trireme originated in Corinth in the seventh century B.C.E., and became the standard Athenian warship in the fifth century B.C.E.

Eureka!

Themistocles (c. 528–463 B.C.E.) was the architect of Athens' naval supremacy, and a brilliant and ambitious general, strategist, and politician who foresaw Athens' upcoming struggle with Sparta. Themistocles was eventually ostracized, and he ended his days exiled from Athens and, ironically, as an advisor to the Persians.

From the Persians' tactics at Marathon, the Greeks knew that they had to be capable of defending themselves by land and by sea, and that the Persian army depended upon support and supplies from its navy. However, no Greek fleet could match the Persian fleet, which included forces from Phoenicia, Cilicia, Lycia, Caria, and Greeks from Ionia and the islands. But, in 483 B.C.E., Athens had opened a particularly rich vein of silver in its mines. The Athenians debated whether to parcel out the money in the form of a tax break or use it for some other common purpose. An influential Athenian, Themistocles (who had been one of the generals at Marathon), convinced the Athenians to spend the money building state-of-the art warships. They built 200 *triremes*, which gave Athens the largest navy of any Greek city. This work was completed in time for the Persian army's advance into Greece in 480 B.C.E.

As the Persians made their way through Thessaly, the combined Greek fleet sailed north to meet the Persian fleet near Artemision, and an allied Greek force of about 5,000 hoplites, under the command of the Spartan king Leonidas, marched north to Thermopylae (which means "hot gates," because of the hot-springs near the pass). If the Greeks could hold the Persians at Thermopylae and disable their fleet, they might have a chance. In the meantime, most of the Athenians evacuated their beloved city and waited off the island of Salamis.

A frieze of Persian archers from the reign of Darius, now in the Louvre.

(Photo courtesy of Rochelle Snee)

Head 'em Off at the Pass! Thermopylae and the Invasion of Attica

At first, things went well for the Greeks. The Persian fleet was damaged by a storm, and the narrow pass at Thermopylae kept Xerxes' larger forces from becoming an advantage. Herodotus tells a vivid tale of how the Great King was perplexed, both by the mentality of people who would dare oppose such overwhelming numbers and, particularly, by the behavior of the Spartans, who were doing calisthenics and combing their long hair in preparation for battle. It was only after two Persian assaults were repelled with great losses that Xerxes began to worry. However, a Greek traitor, hoping for a reward, offered to show the king's elite forces, called the "Immortals," a path around the defenders, which would allow the Persians to either surround the Greeks or bypass them.

Muses

One of the most famous quotes of the war comes from Herodotus (7.22). A Melian tells the Greeks before Thermopylae that the Persians have so many archers that their arrows, when shot, block out the sun. Dienices, a Spartan, turns to the group and sneers, "Hey guys, good news: We're gonna fight in the shade!"

When news came that the Persians were making their way around, the Spartan king and commander Leonidas courageously decided to retain only the Spartan force of about 300 soldiers, along with some others (the Spartans' armor-bearing helots, Thespians, and Thebans), at the pass. Apparently, his object was to cover a retreat by the other forces to the Isthmus of Corinth, where the rest of the Greeks were constructing defenses. Retreating to a knoll, about 1,000 hoplites fought a fierce and desperate battle, surrounded on all sides, to the last man. Thermopylae, at which the entire Spartan force and its king fought to the death, has been immortalized as one of the most heroic battles of all time. Even today, there is an epitaph at Thermopylae, attributed to the lyric poet Simonides, for the dead soldiers who were buried where they fell: "Traveler, go tell the Spartans that we lie here, obedient to their word."

The same day, the Athenian and Peloponnesian fleets fought the Persians, and both sides suffered heavy losses. But when news arrived that the pass was taken, the fleet sailed back to join the rest of the Greeks at the isthmus, leaving Athens to be sacked and burned by the invading Persians. The Boeotians (Thebes) went over to the Persians, and the Persians now held all of northern and central Greece, with only a narrow strip of isthmus between them and the Peloponnesus.

Turning the Tide: From Salamis to the Persian Retreat

Eureka!

Delphic Oracles concerning the Persian War are particularly interesting. One conceded that a "wooden wall" (thought by Themistocles to symbolize the Athenian navy) might save Athens and, another, that the death of a king would be the only chance for Sparta (perhaps helping to explain Leonidas' desperate stand at Thermopylae).

On the other side of the isthmus, the Greeks debated what to do next. The Peloponnesians were inclined to hold out behind the isthmus, or just give up altogether. Themistocles feared that the Peloponnesians would cut a deal—one that would leave Sparta in charge of the Peloponnesus by abandoning Athens to Xerxes. Themistocles sent false information to Xerxes, in order to lure the Persian fleet in. With the Persian fleet in place, the Greeks were trapped behind the island of Salamis and unable to disperse. Xerxes then made the ill-fated decision to force a battle in the narrow straits between Salamis and the mainland.

Eureka!

If you're interested in the Persian War, read the original (and still the best!) history of the events, people, and circumstances: *The Persian War* (or *History*), by Herodotus. Herodotus is an excellent storyteller, and his famous history is full of wonderful tales, insights, and observations, far too many to quote here. He is also the first historian to hypothesize a fundamental cultural difference between East (Asia) and West (Europe).

Victory at Sea: Salamis

The naval battle took place in front of the Greeks, including the Athenian refugees, on one side of the straits, and the assembled forces of Xerxes, who sat on a throne, on the other. By using the straits to their advantage, the Greeks were able to outmaneuver the more numerous Persian vessels, box them in, ram them, and sink them. By the end of the day, nearly 200 Persian ships had been destroyed. For the most part, the Persian crew members (unlike the Greeks) couldn't swim, but even when they didn't drown, they were slaughtered as they pulled themselves out of the water.

Suddenly, everything had changed. Persia's imperial army was without the naval support it needed to survive, and it was a long, long way from home. Xerxes hurried to Persia with sea and land forces (to keep the Greeks from severing his route), leaving his general Mardonius to retreat into Thessaly with the remaining forces (perhaps 60,000) for the winter. The Greeks waited for another attack, but it didn't come. Themistocles urged the Greeks to pursue: If they could capture and destroy the bridge at the Hellespont before the Persians could cross it, then they could isolate and destroy the entire army. The Spartans, however, who held the command, believed that it made better sense, and would be far safer, to leave the back door open for a Persian retreat.

> **Eureka!**
>
> Xerxes' disastrous and unforeseeable reversal of fortune is the subject of a tragic drama by the Athenian playwright Aeschylus. *The Persians* was produced in 472 B.C.E., perhaps with props taken from war spoils. In it, a hubristic Xerxes is humbled by fate, justice, and the Athenian victory at Salamis.

Victory on Land and Sea: Plataea and Mycale

It's doubtful that the Persians could have won the war after their defeat at Salamis. Greece was probably too rough for them to conquer and hold without controlling the sea. But if Athens, which did control the sea, could be pried away from the Peloponnesians, then the Persians would be back in control and they could go after Sparta. The Persian general Mardonius made an offer to Athens, but the Athenians refused, with a bit of hedging.

Now it was Sparta's turn to feel the pressure. Suddenly, driving the Persians out of Attica—and fast—seemed like the best plan. The next year, 479 B.C.E., the largest force of Greeks ever assembled (perhaps 50,000 to 60,000), under the command of Pausanias (nephew of Leonidas and the regent for his son), marched north. The Persians, together with their Theban allies, met them at Plataea. After several days of maneuvering, Mardonius attacked. Waiting out the archers, the Peloponnesians attacked the main force at a run, routed them, and killed Mardonius himself. The rest of the Persian army fled for home, leaving Hellas once again in the hands of the Hellenes. The Theban commanders who had sided with the Persians were executed without trial, and the Greeks were left to marvel at the spoils. To commemorate Plataea, the 31 allies set up a monument at Delphi of three intertwined, bronze serpents balancing a golden bowl on their heads. In the fourth century C.E., the Roman emperor Constantine moved this remarkable monument to Constantinople (Istanbul), where it now stands in the Spina (Hippodrome), though without the golden bowl, which was lost in antiquity.

> ### Muses
>
> Pausanias entered Mardonius' tent, with its gold and silver settings and rich drapery, and he ordered the cooks to serve up a meal just as they would for Mardonius … When he saw the lavish layout, he was amazed. Then, for fun, he commanded his own servants to prepare a Laconian meal [the Spartans ate a brackish soup that the other Greeks found inedible]. When it was ready (and what a contrast!), he broke out laughing. He sent for the other Greek generals and pointed out the two meals, saying, "Men of Greece, I've summoned you to demonstrate the stupidity of the Medes' leader. Look: he ate meals like *this* [the Persian feast] every day and came to conquer *that* [the Spartan meal] from us."
>
> —Herodotus, 9.82

In the meantime, the Greek fleet had crossed into Ionia, with assurances of assistance from the islands of Samos and Chios. Landing on the mainland across from Samos at Mycale (Dilek Dagí, Turkey) in late August, a Greek force under the Spartan king Leotychides attacked the Persian garrison and the remainder of the Persian fleet. The Persian Ionian allies deserted, the Persians fled, and the fleet was destroyed.

Row, Row, Row Our Boat

What happened next helps to illustrate the differing Spartan and Athenian mentalities, ambitions, and approaches that would soon turn allies into enemies and tear apart the Hellenic world.

The Athenians wanted to expand, to press on, and to liberate the rest of the Greek cities. The Spartans, who were not expansionist, were not so inclined. And although the Spartans were perfectly happy to have Athenians serving under their command, they were not happy about Athens' new power and prestige. Using an argument that is curious even for the Spartans, they insisted that no city north of the Peloponnesus should have walls (such a city, they argued, could become a fortified hold for the Persians, should they invade again), and they pressured the Athenians to refrain from rebuilding the long walls that linked their city with their port. Athens, on the other hand, had no intention whatsoever of compromising its new position or future plans. Using diplomatic maneuvers, Themistocles held off the Spartans until the wall, which safeguarded the Athenian fleet, could be rebuilt.

Meanwhile, the Greek fleet, under the Spartan commander Pausanias, was busy consolidating Greek power in the Aegean. Pausanias, however, began to eat, dress, and act like an oriental despot (apparently, he no longer found the Persian commanders laughable), and his behavior alienated both the allies and the Ionians. During the siege of Byzantium in 478 B.C.E., things got progressively worse, and the allies asked Athens to take over leadership of the fleet. Sparta sent another commander to replace Pausanias, but the Greeks remained unmoved in their insistence upon Athenian naval command. In the years to come, many allied states would come to regret this decision.

Ancient NATO? The Delian League

In 477 B.C.E., Athens and other maritime *poleis*, about 150 in all, met on the sacred island of Delos and formed what we now call the Delian League. League members bound themselves to Athens and to Athenian leadership, just as the Peloponnesian League's members bound themselves to Sparta and to Spartan leadership. Athens agreed to respect the internal affairs of the states, while each state agreed, according to its size, to contribute either monies or ships as obligatory dues for ongoing operations against Persia.

The treasury, held on Delos, would be administered by the Athenians and policy, although voted on by the common assembly (one vote per state), would be executed by the Athenian leadership. Because the power of the Delian League was concentrated in Athenian hands, the stage was now set for the division of Hellas into two rival powers. Sparta and the Peloponnesian League were grounded in land power and conservative oligarchy, and Athens and the Delian League were grounded in sea power and an expansionist democracy.

Odysseys
The sacred island of Delos is the mythological birthplace of Apollo and Artemis. It was an important shrine to Apollo (second only to Delphi) from the ninth century B.C.E., a place of pilgrimage, and the political and religious center of the Aegean. Today the island is an uninhabited archeological site, but its superb monuments continue to draw thousands of visitors.

The two major powers of Hellas, Athens and Sparta, which had combined to defeat the Persians, would, over the next century, wage an ongoing battle that, in many ways, was made possible by their former enemy.

The Least You Need to Know

- The Persian Wars began as a diplomatic misunderstanding between the Athenians and the Persian monarch Darius.

- The Battle of Marathon, in which the Athenians and Plataeans defeated the Persian army sent by Darius, took place in 490 B.C.E.

- The major Persian invasion of Greece occurred under Xerxes in 480 B.C.E. The main battles took place at Thermopylae, Salamis, and Plataea.

- The Greeks' victory over the Persians led to Athens' rise to prominence, its leadership of the Delian League, and its rivalry with Sparta.

Chapter 14

Democracy Is Coming: Athens at the Helm

In This Chapter

◆ Athens and Sparta's relationship after the Persian War

◆ The Delian League becomes Athens' empire

◆ The rise and fall of Cimon

◆ The reforms of the radical democrats Ephialtes and Pericles

◆ How Athenian democracy worked

The Greeks' decisive victory over the Persians did more than save them from being incorporated into the Persian Empire. It also gave them a sense of common identity and an enthusiastic confidence in the superiority of Greek ways. Instead of looking outward for models upon which to build their new world, the Greeks looked inward, to themselves. Many of the artistic and intellectual achievements of this period were driven and colored by this confidence and bias. Moreover, once Persian domination was eliminated, the wealth of Thrace, Ionia, and the Black Sea was available for Greek domination. Without these resources, the political, artistic, and intellectual achievements of this period would have been impossible.

In this chapter, we'll begin to examine what is sometimes called the "Golden" or "Great" Age of Greece, namely the 50 (or so) years from the Greek victories at Salamis and Plataea (480 B.C.E.) to the outbreak of the Peloponnesian War in 431 B.C.E. During this period, many of the familiar hallmarks of the Classical period—such as Athenian democracy and the tragedies of Aeschylus and Sophocles—came into being. We'll discuss the development of Athenian democracy here, and we'll cover the rest of the century in Chapters 15 through 17.

Athens and Sparta in the Wake of the Persian War

The Greeks' victory over the Persians put them on the threshold of a new era. For the first time in history, the Hellenes had dominant territorial control of significant portions of the Mediterranean and Black Sea. To maintain and extend their gains, however, the Greeks needed new kinds of political structures to unify (or at least provide for the common defense of) Hellenic interests, cities, territories, and trade. Sparta, as the preeminent power in Greece and the leader of its most powerful alliance, was the logical candidate to provide new leadership. However, Sparta's drastic social and political structure, which was barely capable of maintaining control over the helots and immediate neighbors, was unable and—frankly—unfit to handle the job. Spartan kings, such as Pausanias, were notoriously bad out of the Spartan box: They alienated other Greeks and dismayed Spartans at home (who tried, largely unsuccessfully, to rein them in). In addition, the Spartiates were much more concerned about keeping order in the Peloponnesus than about becoming entangled in foreign affairs.

> **Eureka!**
>
> Democracy was a rare form of government for the Greeks prior to the growth of Athenian power and influence. Gradually, democracies sprang up around Greece (mainly, but not exclusively, in the areas of Athenian dominance) until, by the end of the fifth century B.C.E., democracy was the prevalent form of government in areas outside of Spartan control. Its spread, however, was contained by Athens' defeat in the Peloponnesian War.

So it was Athens—whose naval fleet allowed it to protect and extend Hellenic control—who stepped into this vacuum and provided leadership. From its role in the Ionian Revolt; the battles of Marathon, Salamis, and Mycale; and the siege of Byzantion, Athens had gained enough prestige (and enough muscle) to take charge of the newly formed Delian League. Athens' connections (economic and social) with Thrace and the Black Sea aligned its interests with those of the Ionians and other

Greeks who needed sea power to maintain their freedom. Moreover, Athens had an outward-looking, innovative, expansionist character, which permeated its history (from Solon onward), citizenry, and foreign policy, and which distinguished it sharply from Sparta. Whereas Sparta rejected foreign involvement, Athens depended on it. Whereas Sparta tended to fear and avoid outside influence, Athens tended to expand its own influence and control over the people and resources upon which it depended for prosperity. It's no surprise, then, that these two very powerful states, so different in outlook and culture, would soon come to conflict.

Partners or Antagonists? Athenian Leadership Under Themistocles and Cimon

Tension between Athens and Sparta had been part of Athenian politics for a long time (think Cleisthenes and Isagoras, or Sparta's absence at Marathon, or Sparta's opposition to Athenian refortification after the Persian War), and with the foundation of the Delian League Athenians continued to differ in their opinions concerning the roles and relationship of the two states. Some citizens, like Themistocles, believed from the outset that Sparta was a threat to Athenian interests. Such citizens tended to favor more radical forms of democracy, which, they hoped, would undermine aristocratic and oligarchic power (in the tradition of Cleisthenes), both at home and abroad. Others, like Cimon (the son of Miltiades, the general at Marathon), envisioned a cooperative relationship between Sparta and Athens, including joint leadership of Hellas. These citizens tended to favor a more conservative and traditional blend of political power (in the tradition of Isagoras). They leaned toward oligarchy or a moderate democracy, in which only aristocrats and hoplites would share political power.

Although Themistocles had been the architect of Athenian naval power, including the fortification of the port of Piraeus, his personal ambitions and self-aggrandizement made the Athenians nervous, and they voted to *ostracize* him in 471 B.C.E. From Athens, Themistocles headed into the Peloponnesus to encourage cities such as Argos to become thorns in Sparta's side. Meanwhile, the Athenians turned to Cimon, a rich, affable, pro-Spartan aristocrat. Cimon referred to Sparta and Athens as "yoke partners," or as states whose individual leadership of the Peloponnesian and Delian Leagues should serve joint

Lexica

Ostracism allowed Athenian citizens to temporarily exile individuals thought dangerous to public welfare. Each year, if the *ekklêsia* voted that an ostracism was necessary, each citizen inscribed a name on a "potsherd" (*ostracon*) as a secret ballot. The person with the most votes had to leave town in 10 days, without loss of property or citizenship, for 10 years.

interests. He even named one of his sons Lacedaimonius (Spartan) as a public gesture of support for Sparta.

Cimon's popularity and authority came from his background (he was a wealthy and well-connected aristocrat), his character (he was well respected for his integrity), and his performance. He was a brilliant general and statesman who led the Delian League through expansion and revolts, and whose forces crushed the Phoenician fleet and Persian army at the river Eurymedon sometime between 469 and 466 B.C.E. This victory was, in military terms, the greatest of the Persian War, for it ended Persia's ability to exercise power in the Aegean (for the time being). His downfall, however, came a few years later and resulted from his pro-Spartan policies. In 462 B.C.E., he persuaded the Athenians to send troops to Sparta to help them—at their request—quell a helot revolt. But when the Athenians arrived, the Spartans, who apparently found the Athenian hoplites a bad influence (too democratic and possibly sympathetic to their enemies), sent them home.

> ### Eureka!
>
> The Spartans had trouble with a loose cannon of their own, the king Pausanias. The Spartans and Athenians eventually united against Pausanias and Themistocles, accusing them of conspiring with the Persian king and the helots. Themistocles fled to Asia. Pausanias took refuge from arrest inside the temple of Artemis, but the Spartans walled it up and starved him to death.

※ —PERSIAN WARS/ATHENIAN EMPIRE— ※

Making a Delian You Can't Refuse: The Athenian Empire

In the meantime, the Delian League was becoming less of a league and more of an Athenian empire. Some members believed that, because the league was providing for the common defense against Persia, all Greeks who benefited from league activities should contribute to it. However, compulsory membership in a voluntary association is a contradiction in terms. Besides, states wanted the ability to withdraw if they determined that their interests were no longer being served. In particular, tension surrounded the fact that there was no real end game (or what we might call an "exit strategy"), or provision for determining when the Persian War, and the need for the league, was over. Without such a provision, the task of determining the league's necessity fell to the people who most benefited from the continued existence of the league: the Athenians. After Cimon's victory at Eurymedon, it became more difficult to justify the need for a league, but by then it had become too important to Athens to disband it.

Your Presence Is Required

Cimon established several important precedents that helped shape both the future of Athens' relationship with the other Greek states and the future of the Delian League. For example, on Scyros (an island off Euboea) he expelled and enslaved pirates, and he established a kind of colony called a *cleruchy*, in which Athenians retained their Athenian citizenship. Cleruchies became an important mechanism of Athenian domination, by allowing loyal citizens to be placed around the developing empire as garrisons.

Lexica

A **cleruchy** (from *kleros*) was a special kind of Athenian colony, in which citizens of the cleruchy retained their Athenian citizenship and rights. Cleruchies served as outlets for disenchanted or poor citizens, and as garrisons for the Athenian empire.

Shortly after the cleruchy was established on Scyros, the Delian League forced the Euboean city of Carystus to join and pay dues. As a result, other nonmember states realized that they had to ally themselves either with Athens or with other states that could help them maintain their freedom. Then the island of Naxos attempted to withdraw from the league. The Athenians attacked it, destroyed its walls, and confiscated its fleet. Now, without ships to contribute, the Naxians were assigned monetary dues to pay, which drained them of independent military and economic resources and kept them from being autonomous. Thus, the league established a policy of forced membership.

Similar events took place on the island of Thasos. Thasos wanted to control silver mines that were located across the channel in Thrace. The Athenians, however, also had long-standing interests in this area. To give Athens control over the mines, Cimon attempted to found a colony near them. The Thracians drove the colony out, and the Thasians tried to withdraw from the league. After a two-year siege, Thasos surrendered to Cimon, gave up both the mines and its ships, and agreed to pay league dues in money rather than ships. It was now apparent that Athens would use the league to protect and further its own interests, even when they conflicted with the interests of league members.

Show Me the Money: Contribution Becomes Tribute

Following the incidents on Naxos and Thasos, the league steadily shifted away from its original means of funding and equipping the alliance. For the most part, states had originally joined the league as autonomous partners, and they had contributed forces and ships to an alliance under Athenian leadership. Only small states, which couldn't afford ships or crews, contributed money. However, an increasing number of members—whether willing or unwilling—came to contribute the actual monies or financial resources necessary to fund league activities ("outsourcing," so to speak, their defense). These funds were administered (for the league's own good, of course) by Athens. However, league proceeds not only provided Athens with the means to increase its naval supremacy, but also with the means to expand its own economical and political interests. Simultaneously, league obligations deprived member states of the means to either resist the league or thrive independently. As a result, other states became increasingly dependent upon Athens.

> **CAUTION**
>
> **Labyrinths**
>
> The record of member contributions to the Delian League, known as *phoroi* (literally, "brought" or "contributed" resources), was inscribed on stone tablets. Because the dues became mandatory, we call these lists "tribute (not "contribution") lists."

The Ship of State: Democracy and the Tensions of the Fifth Century

Cimon favored aristocratic and pro-Spartan policies, and, at most, a moderate democracy in which aristocrats shared power with hoplites. Themistocles' earlier policies, however, in combination with the transformation of the Delian League into the Athenian empire, had changed Athenian perspectives, politics, and military requirements on the ground and on the sea. Militarily, Athens no longer depended exclusively on hoplites, or on those men who could afford hoplite armor. Now, it depended on rowers (a lot of rowers!). And whereas rowers, like hoplites, needed training and discipline, as well as a strong sense of loyalty to one another, their leaders, and their state, they didn't need expensive armor. Rowers, unlike hoplites, needed only two good arms and a strong back, and these requirements could be met by members of the lowest property classes. Thus, the *thêtes* (the fourth and lowest class in the Solonian census) became integral to Athens' military success.

So pressures to include the lower classes in political affairs—similar to those that were brought to bear by and on behalf of the hoplite classes in many Archaic *poleis*—were created in Athens. Generally, people upon whom the state depends want a political voice, and, however begrudgingly, the state is often forced to give it to them—at least to some extent. Now, as the Athenian ship of state gained power and wealth, the lower classes wanted a voice and a vote in where they were rowing it. In many ways, the lower classes had been held back by a coalition of the hoplite and upper classes, but the situation could be radically altered if the hoplites allied themselves with the lower classes. And Sparta's rejection of the Athenian hoplites offered more radical democrats, and their leaders, the opportunity to make an abrupt change in Athens' political course.

> **CAUTION**
>
> **Labyrinths**
>
> There was no such thing as political parties in Athens. Certain individuals, especially those elected general, wielded personal influence.

Ephialtes and Pericles: Breaking Aristocratic Holds

Sparta's dismissal of the Athenian hoplites, which was an enormous slap in Athens' face, provided an opening for citizens who supported a more radical democracy and opposed pro-Spartan policies. Public embarrassment and anger turned squarely on Cimon. Led by Cimon's political enemies, Ephialtes and his young comrade Pericles, the enraged *dêmos* ostracized Cimon in 461 B.C.E and forged an alliance with Argos (Sparta's enemy). Completing what Cleisthenes had begun, Ephialtes and Pericles shifted the balance of political and judicial power from propertied classes toward a broad-based citizenry. However, they also helped redefine and restrict this citizenry in ways that created profound political and social tensions.

Courting Reforms: The Areopagus

Ephialtes proposed transferring the judicial powers of the Areopagus (the Archaic council and senate), except for trials involving murder and sacred matters, to the *boulê, ekklêsia,* and *hêliaia.* Although his legislation maintained some of the dignity of the ancient aristocratic institution, it completed the process (begun under

Cleisthenes) of placing power in the hands of the *dêmos* rather than the *aristoi*, both in fact and in appearance. These reforms, which had significant implications for the Athenians' conception of their *polis*, were the subject of intense debate and turmoil. In fact, Ephialtes was assassinated the following year by opponents of his reforms. Shortly afterward, the great playwright Aeschylus created a trilogy of tragedies (known as the *Oresteia*) that sought to affirm and sanctify the Areopagus' role in the new state by giving it an august mythological place in Homeric (i.e., aristocratic) tradition.

With Ephialtes' murder, leadership of Athens fell to Pericles, possibly the most famous name in Classical Greece. Pericles was an Athenian imperialist and visionary who became the foremost architect of Athenian policy and strategy. He was, in terms of a metaphor, the preeminent helmsman and captain of the Athenian ship of state during the Classical period. Elected (with the exception of two years) *stratêgos* from 461 B.C.E. to his death in 429 B.C.E., Pericles exercised such influence that Thucydides refers to him as a democratic king, and later historians often refer to the fifth century B.C.E. as the "Periclean Age" of Athens.

Who's Yo' Mama (*and* Yo' Papa)?

In 451 B.C.E., Pericles convinced the Athenians to limit citizenship to those who could prove that both of their parents were Athenian citizens. This legislation was intentionally aimed at aristocrats, who married among themselves and often married aristocrats from other *poleis*. (Under these laws, Cleisthenes, Miltiades, Themistocles, and Cimon—and their children—would have failed to qualify as citizens.) The legislation had a profound impact on the social and political structure of the Athenian *polis* and on Athenian democracy.

How Did the Radical Democracy Work?

Chapter 13 described Cleisthenes' democratic reforms. However, it is with the reforms of Ephialtes (judicial) and Pericles (citizenship) that the "radical" democracy, for which Athens is famous, fully emerged.

Before laying out the particulars of Athenian democracy, however, it is important to note two of its most striking general features. One is the extent to which it was organized to avoid the interference of wealth and bribery in civic and judicial affairs. The other is the extent to which ordinary citizens were entrusted with managing the affairs of a city of roughly 200,000 inhabitants. Ordinary citizens, chosen by lot, were entrusted with everything from acting as city and port commissioners to managing an annual Delian League income equivalent to $200,000,000. This arrangement bespeaks a kind of confidence in the common citizen that has never been entirely duplicated.

Citizen (*politês*), Precinct (*dêmos*) and Tribe (*phylê*)

To be a citizen (*politês*), one had to be born into a free Athenian *oikos* ("household," headed by a free Athenian male citizen) or be granted citizenship by decree. After Pericles' citizenship law of 451 B.C.E., only children born of a citizen mother and a citizen father were eligible for citizenship. Citizen males were eligible to participate in civic affairs at 30 years of age.

An Athenian *oikos* was a part of a *dêmos* ("territorial precinct"). Children with the appropriate qualifications could be enrolled in the *dêmos* at 18 years of age. Each *dêmos* belonged to a *trittys* ("third of a tribe"). Three *trittyes*, one from each geographical demarcation (city, inland, and coastal), made up 1 of the 10 *phylai* ("tribes"). The *phylê* ("tribe") was the voting block by which Athenians voted for military officers (such as the tribe's *stratêgos*) and other magistrates (such as archons), and were enrolled in bodies such as the *prytany* and *hêliaia*.

The *Dêmos* at Work: The Assembly (*ekklêsia*), Executive Council (*boulê*), and Presiding Officials (*prytaneis*)

The *ekklêsia* (sovereign assembly) was composed of all citizen males 30 years and older. It met as needed (which by the mid-fifth century B.C.E. meant about three times a month), rain or shine, hot or cold, in the open air on a hill adjacent to the Acropolis, the Pnyx. At least 6,000 citizens were needed to complete a quorum for decisions on serious issues such as whether to hold an ostracism. Decisions of the *ekklêsia*, usually conveyed by a show of hands, were final: It was the last word in all matters.

Drafting motions and preparing the agenda for the meeting was the task of the 500-member *boulê* ("executive council"). Fifty members of each tribe were chosen by lot to serve in the *boulê* annually. The *boulê* oversaw the day-to-day running of the state (public finance and utility, port authority, foreign relations), audited the books of outgoing officials, and acted as a jury of impeachment for officials charged with misconduct. To carry out its role, it had the right to collect information, summon witnesses, and take citizen input. Each tribe was in charge for one tenth of the year and, during this time, its 50 members became *prytaneis* (presiding officials) of the *boulê*. The chair and secretary of the *prytaneis*, who held the keys to the treasury, each changed daily (again, by lot) among presiding members. The *prytaneis* had the sole right to call and preside over the *ekklêsia*.

Motions for consideration by the *ekklêsia* were posted five days in advance of the meetings, to give citizens the opportunity to consider their positions. Meetings began early and usually finished by early afternoon, to make time for the meeting of the *boulê*. At assemblies, the *prytaneis* brought motions to the floor for consideration, according to the agenda. Citizens were free to speak their minds, propose amendments, or revise the motions. Generals had the right to speak first, followed by other citizens in order of age (usually, those 50 years and older went first). Some people delivered prepared speeches, some spoke extemporaneously, and others never spoke at all. Debate was vigorous, and speakers could expect interruptions from both supporters and hecklers. And style counted, big time. Because the decision of the *ekklêsia* was final, the ability to sway the majority of citizens toward (or away from) a particular position was critically important and highly valued. Even a cursory look at such a system makes it easy to see that the Greeks' fascination with rhetoric and persuasion was born, at least in part, of necessity.

Eureka!

Only about 10 men were ostracized over the course of the fifth century B.C.E. (The practice fell out of use by the fourth century B.C.E.) *Ostraca* have been excavated from the Athenian agora with names of three of the men: Themistocles, Aristeides, and Cimon. Others with the name of Pericles have been found, but Pericles somehow avoided being voted out of town.

The Elect and the Select: Generals (*stratêgoi*), Magistrates (*archontes*), and Public Services (*liturgies*)

The most important officials elected by the tribes were the tribal military officials (*stratêgoi*, *taxiarchoi*, *hipparchoi*), elected annually. Because these officials could be reelected, military positions became, over the fifth century B.C.E., a career choice for some Athenians, independent of politics. The *stratêgoi*, however, as chief commanders of the tribe with the right to speak first in the assembly, remained powerful political and military positions. Pericles, for example, held the office of *stratêgos* every year except two from about 461 B.C.E. to his death in 429 B.C.E. Most other magistrates, such as the *archontes,* as well as the various boards that oversaw everything from port dues to city sewage, were appointed annually by lot. Some of these, like the office of archon, were linked to classifications of wealth.

One particularly interesting public duty was the *liturgy. Liturgies* were costly public services (about 60 in number) that were apportioned to wealthy citizens as expensive, but significant, responsibilities and honors. The most costly and prestigious *liturgies* were the *trierarchia and chorêgia.* The *trierarchia* was a year-long responsibility to maintain, equip, and command a *trireme* (warship). The state supplied the hull, mast, and sails. The *trierarch* supplied all the rest of the equipment for the boat (including a crew of 170 to 180 men and its training) and commanded the vessel for a year. (Imagine an indirect system of taxation whereby the yearly maintenance and command of a navy frigate or aircraft carrier was assigned to a private citizen, and you'll get the idea!) The *chorêgia* was the responsibility to provide a chorus (hire, costume, train, and feed) for one of the lyric or dramatic competitions. In this way, the Greeks were able to fund lavish tragic and comedic plays.

Other liturgies included the *architheoria* (funding a sacred embassy to one of the pan-Hellenic festivals) and *gymnasiarchia* (recruiting and training one of the 10 teams that competed in the torch race at the Panathenaic festival).

We'll Be the Judge of That! The *Dēmos* and the Courts

Under Cleisthenes, Ephialtes, and Pericles, the *hêliaia* evolved from an appeals court alone to an appeals court and body of sovereign jurors (that is, a body of jurors whose decisions were final). Trials were conducted under the administration of magistrates (such as an *archon*) before juries of anywhere from 200 to 1000 men, depending upon the case. These jury courts, known as *dicasteries* (from *dikasteria*), were selected by lot, at the last minute, from the 10 tribes.

The last-minute element, the large number of jurors, and the fact that Athenian court cases were decided in one day discouraged bribery. Because the jury was acting on behalf of, and in the stead of, all the people, most decisions could not be appealed. Pericles introduced payment for service (starting at two *obols*, and increasing after 425 B.C.E. to three *obols*), which made jury service a viable option for the poor, the infirm, and the aged. In this way, the weight of the judicial system could remain firmly grounded in the lower classes.

CAUTION

Labyrinths

Not all judicial proceedings took place before the *hêliaia* or the dicasteries. Minor cases (fines under 10 drachma) were handled by magistrates without trial; murder cases were heard before the Areopagus; and state trials of magistrates were conducted before the *boulê* or *ekklêsia*.

There were two kinds of court actions: private cases brought by one private party against another (a *dikê*), and public cases brought by a private party on behalf of the community (a *graphê*). There were no state prosecutors. Although substantial rewards could be earned by bringing public prosecutions (for example, receiving a share of monies recovered from magistrates who abused their privileges, or simply increasing one's personal reputation), there were fines for dropping cases or for failing to win at least one fifth of the jurors. Such penalties generally discouraged entirely frivolous suits.

At a trial, each party spoke for an equal length of time, measured by a "water clock" (*klepsydra*). The accuser spoke first, followed by the defendant. Parties spoke for themselves, either extemporaneously or using prepared speeches, and they called their own witnesses. Live testimony from women, children, or slaves was not permitted, on the grounds that it was unreliable, but written testimony from tortured slaves was admissible!

The jury then deliberated, and subsequently voted for either conviction or acquittal by placing ballots (shells, pebbles, or bronze discs) in urns. In cases involving harsher penalties, another trial segment took place, in which various penalties were proposed and voted on by the jury. In other cases, the magistrates imposed the fines.

Born to Be Riled: Democrats, Demagogues, and the Winds of Public Opinion

Athenian citizens, as civic participants in the *ekklêsia* and as jurors, held unprecedented political, judicial, and civic power. This meant that the ability to manipulate and influence public opinion in the assembly and before the court was critically important to political and judicial success. Speakers who became particularly adept at persuading and leading the *dêmos* became known as demagogues (*dêmagoges*). But, without strong and stable leadership, and without the keel of precedent, demagogues often veered the Athenian state from one extreme to the other. Indeed, by the end of the century, many people had come to doubt whether a democracy could avoid being manipulated by the powerful and eloquent.

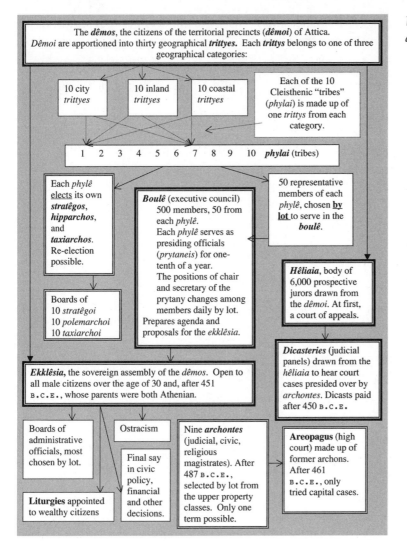

We the People: Athenian democracy in action.

The **dêmos**, the citizens of the territorial precincts (**dêmoi**) of Attica. **Dêmoi** are apportioned into thirty geographical **trittyes**. Each **trittys** belongs to one of three geographical categories:

10 city *trittyes*

10 inland *trittyes*

10 coastal *trittyes*

Each of the 10 Cleisthenic "tribes" (*phylai*) is made up of one *trittys* from each category.

1 2 3 4 5 6 7 8 9 10 *phylai* (tribes)

Each *phylê* elects its own **stratêgos**, **hipparchos**, and **taxiarchos**. Re-election possible.

Boulê (executive council) 500 members, 50 from each *phylê*. Each *phylê* serves as presiding officials (*prytaneis*) for one-tenth of a year. The positions of chair and secretary of the prytany changes among members daily by lot. Prepares agenda and proposals for the *ekklêsia*.

50 representative members of each *phylê*, chosen **by lot** to serve in the **boulê**.

Hêliaia, body of 6,000 prospective jurors drawn from the *dêmoi*. At first, a court of appeals.

Boards of 10 *stratêgoi* 10 *polemarchoi* 10 *taxiarchoi*

Dicasteries (judicial panels) drawn from the *hêliaia* to hear court cases presided over by *archontes*. Dicasts paid after 450 B.C.E.

Ekklêsia, the sovereign assembly of the *dêmos*. Open to all male citizens over the age of 30 and, after 451 B.C.E., whose parents were both Athenian.

Boards of administrative officials, most chosen by lot.

Ostracism

Final say in civic policy, financial and other decisions.

Nine **archontes** (judicial, civic, religious magistrates). After 487 B.C.E., selected by lot from the upper property classes. Only one term possible.

Areopagus (high court) made up of former archons. After 461 B.C.E., only tried capital cases.

Liturgies appointed to wealthy citizens

The Least You Need to Know

◆ The Persian War led to Hellenic dominance of much of the Aegean and a crisis of leadership between Athens and Sparta.

◆ Athenian policy initially favored a cooperative relationship with Sparta, but turned antagonistic.

◆ Athens' leadership of the Delian League transformed the league into an Athenian empire.

- Cimon's ostracism gave Ephialtes and Pericles the opportunity to institute dramatic judicial and citizenship reforms.

- Athenian citizens exercised a tremendous amount of power in the assembly and the courts, through citizen participation in offices, and on civic boards.

Chapter 15

The Peloponnesian War

In This Chapter

- ◆ The First and Second Peloponnesian Wars
- ◆ Pericles' strategy and the Athenian plague
- ◆ Personalities of the age: Pericles, Cleon, Nicias, and Alcibiades
- ◆ Athens veers between dominance and disaster until its final defeat
- ◆ The 400 oligarchs and the Thirty Tyrants

With the ascendancy of Ephialtes and Pericles, Athenian politics were once again driven by an anti-Spartan approach to Athenian expansion. As Athenian military and commercial power grew and extended into central Greece and parts of the Peloponnesus itself, Sparta and its allies became increasingly determined to check Athenian expansion as a threat to their own stability, autonomy, and economic interests.

Under Pericles, however, the Athenians saw their city as the center and engine of a new Hellenism. Within this perspective, they also saw expansion as integral to their own economic and political interests and, in many ways, as their right or prerogative. And the Athenian views were not entirely unjustified. In this chapter, we'll trace the escalating hostilities between the Athenian and Spartan spheres of influence—first, through a phase of periodic conflict (the so-called First Peloponnesian War) and, second, into a period of protracted and bitter warfare (the Second Peloponnesian War), which engulfed the Hellenic world and ended with Athens' defeat. Then, against this backdrop, we'll discuss the culture of this period in Chapter 16.

Problems with Peloponnesians: The First Peloponnesian War

The name *First Peloponnesian War* (460–c. 455 B.C.E.) describes the period in which Athens gained and lost dominance in parts of central Greece and the Peloponnesus. Although Sparta participated in some direct confrontations with Athens, it was primarily Sparta's allies—Corinth, Megara, Aegina, and Thebes—that attempted to check Athenian expansion. Meanwhile, under Pericles, Athens continued to pursue its interests on two fronts and against two potentially formidable enemies: the Peloponnesians in Greece and the Persians in Egypt. Maintaining two fronts proved impossible and, when one collapsed, the Athenians found themselves in serious trouble on both.

Making the Most of Megara and Central Greece

Since the sixth century B.C.E., Athens and the powerful city of Corinth had been commercial rivals. Corinth jealously guarded its control over the trade that came through the Corinthian Gulf from the west, as did Sparta, who depended on Corinth as a trading partner and naval power. However, a series of events provided Athens with the opportunity to undermine Corinthian control on the gulf. First, between Athens and Corinth, on the north coast of the gulf, lay the city of Megara, which, caught as it was between rivals, became a flash point of conflict in both Peloponnesian Wars. Shortly after Ephialtes' death, Megara, also under a democracy, allied itself with Athens against Corinth, giving the Athenians an ally on the gulf. Then a massive earthquake on the Peloponnesus provided the helots with an opportunity for revolt. Unable to overcome a rebel stronghold on Mt. Ithome, the Spartans allowed the rebels to leave. The Athenians settled the rebels at Naupactus (also on the gulf), giving Athens another base of operations and further undermining Corinthian control.

> **Labyrinths**
>
> The Peloponnesian War usually refers to the famous conflict of 431 to 404 B.C.E., described by the historian Thucydides. However, historians identify two separate conflicts between Athens, Sparta, and their respective allies, and so the famous war is, technically, the Second Peloponnesian War.

In 459 B.C.E., Corinth and Aegina (Athens' long-standing naval rival) allied against Athens and Megara, but the Athenians were able to defend both themselves and Megara successfully. The Spartans entered the growing conflict in 457 B.C.E., to help Thebes maintain control over Boeotia, but by 456 B.C.E. Athens dominated much of Boeotia and had installed (or encouraged) democracies there. In addition, Athens added Aegina, the lands east of Thebes (Phocis and Locris), and the cities of Troezen and Achaea (in the Peloponnesus itself) to the Delian League. The Athenian empire had now reached its greatest expanse.

Overexpansion in Egypt Bursts the Bubble

Meanwhile, the Delian League hadn't forgotten the Persians. League activities against Persia continued in Cyprus (against the Phoenician fleet) and in Egypt (in support of a protracted rebellion against Persia). During this time (454 B.C.E.), the Athenians transferred the treasury of the Delian League from Delos to Athens, on the grounds that the treasury was vulnerable to attack. (The threat to the treasury seems a convenient exaggeration, however.) Following an 18-month siege of the Nile Delta island of Prosopitis, the Persian commander, Megabazus, diverted and drained the waters around the island. With the Athenian fleet grounded, he marched across and slaughtered the Athenian force. The Persians also defeated the relief force in 453 B.C.E., inflicting both military and morale losses on the Athenians.

Eureka!

Historians use the transfer of league funds from Delos to Athens in 454 B.C.E. to mark the transformation of the Delian League into the Athenian empire. By this time, only the islands of Lesbos, Chios, and Samos (out of, roughly, 150 members) remained autonomous enough to supply warships instead of tribute. Within a decade, inscriptions refer to "the cities ruled by the Athenians" rather than "the Athenians and their allies."

During Athens' involvement in Egypt, the Persians tried to convince the Spartans to attack Athens to draw Athenian forces out of Egypt, but the Spartans refused. Following their defeat in Egypt and fearing that the Spartans might reconsider, the Athenians were amenable to working things out with Sparta. When Cimon (the ostracized Athenian statesman and general) returned to Athens in 451 B.C.E., he negotiated a five-year peace treaty between Athens and Sparta. A crucial part of the negotiations involved severing the alliance between Argos and Athens and instituting a 30-year treaty between Argos and Sparta. When Cimon died fighting the Persians in Cyprus in 450 B.C.E., the Athenians also appear to have negotiated a settlement with Persia (the so-called *Peace of Callias*) to further cut their losses.

Labyrinths _____

The **Peace of Callias** is named for Cimon's former brother-in-law, who supposedly negotiated the settlement after Cimon's death. There is no hard evidence for this treaty (other than the fact that Athens and Persia stopped fighting), however, until the next century, and some historians doubt that it occurred at this time, if at all.

Nonetheless, things fell apart quite suddenly. In 448 B.C.E., Locris and Phocis abandoned the league; the Athenians were driven out of Boeotia by the Thebans; Euboea revolted and, while Pericles was trying to quell this revolt, Megara revolted and slaughtered the Athenian garrison. To make matters worse, when Pericles hurried back from Euboea to deal with Megara, he found that the Spartans had invaded Attica. Through a great deal of diplomacy involving promises and, probably, bribes, Pericles convinced the Spartans to return home, and, by agreement, Pericles returned to Euboea. Although Pericles recovered Athenian control of Euboea, Athens lost Boeotia to an antidemocratic Thebes, and Megara reverted to the Peloponnesian League.

Long Peace with a Short Half-Life: The 30 Years Peace with Sparta

Although Athens was in trouble, Sparta was unwilling to expend the resources necessary to finish the fight. So in 445 B.C.E., the two sides reached an agreement and signed a 30-year truce that divided Hellas into two major spheres of influence. Athens gave up its land empire (except Plataea and Naupactus, and, in violation of the truce, Aegina) to Spartan control, and Sparta acknowledged Athens' maritime empire. Both sides agreed not to interfere with one another's affairs or allies, to allow treaties with neutral states, and to settle disagreements by arbitration. No allies were permitted to switch sides, and each leader could use force within its own alliance to resolve internal conflicts.

Eureka! _____

In reorganizing the imperial finances and collection of tribute, Pericles appointed Sophocles (the famous tragic poet) the chief treasurer in 443 B.C.E. Sophocles also served as *stratêgos* a few years later and put down the revolt of Samos.

With matters apparently settled with both Sparta and Persia, Pericles undertook the joint tasks of firming up Athenian control over the allies and carrying out his earlier proposal for using league funds to complete a massive building program in Athens. This program included rebuilding and restoring civic buildings on the Acropolis (such as enlarging the Parthenon) and elsewhere. In addition, Pericles enhanced Athens' maritime security by linking the port of Piraeus with Athens by means of long walls (thus making the city and port one fortress), and by employing Hippodamus of Miletus to both reconstruct Piraeus on an efficient grid plan and enlarge the port. These projects met with opposition from conservatives, who claimed that Pericles was acting as yet another tyrant, but when their leader Thucydides (not the historian) was ostracized in 443 B.C.E., Pericles was in firm control of the city.

The Parthenon, one of the monuments to Pericles' reconstruction of Athens.

(Photo courtesy of Norita White)

Prelude: Commerce and Conflict

In the ensuing years, Athens concentrated on its alliance and on trade in the east, and it was involved only to a limited extent in the west. (It did found a colony, Thurii, in southern Italy in 443 B.C.E.) League tribute, in combination with the city's annual income, filled public coffers and built up, by design, enormous reserves.

In 440 B.C.E., Athens crushed potentially disastrous revolts in Samos and Byzantion, and in 427 B.C.E., it founded an important colony, Amphipolis, at a strategic location on the Strymon River in Thrace (where Cimon's colony had been wiped out 30 years before). Moreover, Pericles made a grand trip around the Black Sea to plant colonies and promote Athenian interests in areas upon which the city increasingly depended for food, raw materials, and trade goods. However, political and economic tensions remained in the increasingly bipolar Hellenic world. These tensions were easily ignited by conflicts between small, independent states, which were often caught between the Athenians and the Peloponnesians, and which often appealed for assistance to one side or the other. When just such a situation involved Corinth and Athens, the Thirty Years Peace came to an abrupt end.

Odysseys

The Athenian colony of Thurii (southeast Italy, near Taranto) became the home of the historian Herodotus. Although the colony was founded in Corinth's sphere of influence, the whole matter seems to have been handled with uncharacteristic diplomacy. Just three years later, the Corinthians even cooperatively blocked the Peloponnesians from attacking Athens during the revolt of Samos (in 440 B.C.E.), citing the stipulations of the Thirty Years Peace. Events at Corcyra and Potidaea would soon alter the dynamics, however.

Things Begin to Fray: Corcyra and Potidaea

In 433 B.C.E., the Corinthians intervened in a war between the city of Epidamnus and the island of Corcyra. The Corcyrans appealed to Athens. Athens half-heartedly sent 10, followed by 20, ships to help. When the Corinthians mistook the 20 Athenian reinforcements for their entire fleet, they panicked and withdrew. Then, trouble erupted in Potidaea, on the Chalcidic peninsula (northern Greece). Potidaea was a Corinthian colony, with close ties to its mother city, but it was also a member of the Delian League. The Athenians ordered the Potidaeans to sever all ties with Corinth and to tear down their own defenses. A revolt, instigated by the Macedonian king Perdiccas and supported by Corinthian and Peloponnesian "volunteers," was put down by Athens only after a long and costly siege.

Megara, Yet Again, and the Outbreak of the War

The Athenians retaliated against the Peloponnesians and against Megara (who had sided with Corinth against Corcyra) by imposing an empire-wide trade embargo against Megara. Because Athens controlled virtually all seaports and sea trade, and because the decree banned Megarian merchants from all Athenian ports, the embargo was devastating to Megara. Although imposing the embargo didn't *technically* violate the letter of the truce (that is, the Athenians claimed to be regulating their sphere of influence only), it violated the spirit of the truce in a manner that could not be ignored.

In 432 B.C.E., the Corinthians denounced the Athenians at the Peloponnesian League congress at Sparta and, against the advice of the Spartan king Archidamus, the Spartans voted to go to war with Athens. Most of the Greek states, as Thucydides makes clear, were rooting for the Peloponnesians at the outset of the war, for they saw the Spartans as the defenders of independence and freedom from Athenian rule. In an attempt to avoid direct conflict, the Spartans demanded concessions (rather unrealistic ones), but both sides were entrenched. Pericles refused to give up the Athenian empire or rescind the Megarian decree. Finally, in 431 B.C.E., an impatient Thebes made a provocative attack on Athens' ally Plataea, and the *Pentakontaetia*, the period between the Persian and (Second) Peloponnesian Wars, was over.

Lexica _____

Thucydides calls the period between the Persian and (Second) Peloponnesian Wars the *Pentakontaetia,* or "50-year period." Although it was, strictly speaking, about 47 years, the name stuck and remains in use today.

Part I: The Archidamian War (431–421 B.C.E.) Through the "Peace of Nicias" (421–416 B.C.E.)

The first phase of the Peloponnesian War is known as the Archidamian War, after the Spartan king Archidamus (under whom the Spartans repeatedly invaded Attica). During this period, Pericles' defensive strategy, despite a devastating plague (which killed Pericles in 429 B.C.E.), was largely successful. On the offense, Athens established a base of operations in the Peloponnesus at Pylos, which threatened Sparta's hold on its own territory, and demoralized Sparta by taking nearly 300 of its elite troops prisoners of war. But Athens overplayed its hand. A dramatic march into Chalcidice by Archidamus' brilliant and eloquent successor, Brasidas, seriously threatened Athenian interests there. At this point, both Sparta (which had no desire to either draw out the war or overly empower its kings outside of Sparta) and Athens (which was on the defensive) paused for an uneasy and unworkable peace, framed by the Athenian Nicias in 421 B.C.E. In the meantime, there were shocking examples of the brutalities of war, civil strife, and imperial subjugation, which were recorded by Thucydides as illustrations of his general theory of human conflict. In the following text, we discuss the events in more detail.

Pericles' Intramural Strategy, the Plague, and the Base at Pylos

From the beginning, Pericles knew that to win Athens only needed to achieve a draw. That is, Athens didn't need to capture territory to win the war; instead, it needed to wear down Sparta's patience and reserves and, by so doing, force Sparta to agree to the status quo. Pericles' strategy, therefore, was defensive: Athens would resist direct engagement with the Peloponnesians' superior land forces and rely on both its substantial reserves and its ability to conduct its affairs over the sea lanes. Instead of marching out to meet the Peloponnesian forces, Pericles convinced the Athenians to abandon Attica to the invaders (who would eventually have to head home) and let them do their worst. In the meantime, the livestock would be sent to Euboea, and the rural population would camp within the long city walls.

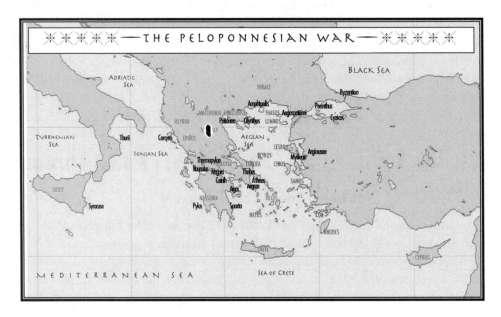

Although this strategy was tormenting to rural citizens, who watched as their farms and olive trees were razed by the Peloponnesian army, it was initially successful. However, a devastating plague struck the cramped city in 430 B.C.E., continued for a year and half, and reoccurred in 427 B.C.E. By the time it was over, Athens had lost about one fourth of its population (roughly 50,000 people), its substantial advantage in manpower, and its leader, Pericles, who died of the plague in 429 B.C.E.

Eureka!

Thucydides' horrific description of the Athenian plague (he contracted it, but lived to tell the story) and its social consequences is particularly famous. Because the reported symptoms don't accurately describe any known disease, scholars have proposed various diseases—from influenza to typhus to ebola—as candidates for the plague. Other scholars have speculated that Thucydides' description is more literary than medical, making a definitive diagnosis impossible.

Tan Their Hides: Cleaning Up with Cleon

After Pericles' death, Athens entered a period of aggressive offense under the leadership of Cleon (a tanner and demagogue) and Demosthenes (an innovative general). Cleon advocated a hard line against both Sparta and rebellious allies. For example, when Mytilene (an important Athenian ally) revolted and was subdued in 428–427 B.C.E., Cleon convinced the *ekklêsia* to massacre the adult male population and sell the women and children into slavery. The debate, along with the assembly's change of heart (it decided to execute only 1,000 Mytileneans), is described by Thucydides in a very famous passage.

> **Muses** _____
>
> I have often been convinced that democracy is incapable of empire, and never more than now concerning your change of heart regarding Mytilene … completely ignoring that your empire is a despotism over unwilling participants, whose compliance is guaranteed, not by your insane concessions, but by a superiority given you by strength and not their loyalty!
>
> —Cleon, from the "Mytilenean Debate," Thucydides 3.27

In 425 B.C.E., Demosthenes succeeded in establishing a base of operations in the Peloponnesus itself, at Pylos in Messenia. Panicked that the Messenian helots would revolt, Sparta recalled the army that was ravaging Attica and sent in its best forces. But the Athenians cornered and, eventually, overran 420 Spartans on the island of Sphacteria. They took 292 Spartan prisoners of war (nearly one half of them Spartiates), which was a devastating blow to Sparta. Although Demosthenes engineered the victory, Cleon, who had been elected general that year, arrived in time to take credit for it. Seeing victory within their grasp, the Athenians rebuffed Spartan peace overtures and pressed on toward a complete victory (at Cleon's urging). They redoubled their efforts … and the tribute.

Brasidas' Brassy Gambit and the Troubled "Peace" of Nicias (421–416 B.C.E.)

Things didn't go according to plan for Athens. Athenian attempts to retake Boeotia failed, and a brilliant, charismatic Spartan general, Brasidas, made a surprise march north into Chalcidice. There he convinced several Delian allies to revolt and, in a move that stunned the Athenians, he made a nighttime attack and took the city of Amphipolis before Athenian reinforcements could arrive. Interestingly, the historian Thucydides, an Athenian general at the time, had been offshore at Thasos when the disaster occurred. Subsequently blamed by the *dêmos* for the loss of Amphipolis,

Eureka!

In 416 B.C.E., during the Peace of Nicias, Athens forced the neutral island of Melos to join its alliance by massacring the men and enslaving the women and children. Thucydides (5.84–116) composes a disturbing conversation (the "Melian Dialogue") between unnamed Athenian and Melian representatives, which illustrates power politics in a bipolar world and the threat posed to both sides by independence.

Muses

Alcibiades was the nephew of Pericles. Ambitious, reckless, licentious, and charismatic, the young aristocrat became one of the pivotal characters of the Peloponnesian War and one of antiquity's most famous personalities. You can get a portrait of him—drunk, salacious, and seductive—in Plato's *Symposium*.

Thucydides was exiled by the angry *ekklêsia* and spent the rest of the war in Sparta composing the history for which he is famous.

Now Athens had a major problem. A new front had opened up within its own territory, threatening both its northern trade routes and its revenues from silver mines in the region. Brasidas continued to encourage revolts, despite Spartan demands that he stop while negotiations proceeded. Cleon led an expedition north, but the inexperienced commander was caught in a skirmish with Brasidas, and both were killed.

With the two hawkish leaders dead, Sparta and Athens reached an agreement, negotiated by Nicias (a cautious and careful general and politician). Each side allowed the other to maintain its own hegemony but, because none of their concerns were addressed, the Peloponnesian allies furiously excluded themselves from the treaty. Corinth, Megara, and Boeotia refused to sign. Several cities allied with Argos (whose peace treaty with Sparta had expired) in 420 B.C.E., but they were defeated by Sparta in 418 B.C.E. at Mantinea. Among their forces were hoplites from Athens, whose participation had been encouraged by Alcibiades, the political enemy of the cautious Nicias. Amphipolis refused to rejoin the Delian League. Athens refused to give up Pylos. Clearly, the Peace of Nicias only slowed the pace of a continuing war.

Part II: Acropolis Now: The Sicilian Expedition (415–411 B.C.E.)

A turning point in the war occurred in 415 B.C.E. when the Athenians, at the request of the Sicilian city of Egesta and at the urging of Alcibiades, decided to launch a massive invasion of Sicily. Sicily was rich in grain and cities, and Syracuse, its chief city, was an ally of Sparta and Corinth. If Syracuse and Sicily could be brought under Athenian control, the Peloponnesians would be cut off from the west and surrounded.

Command of the enormous force (roughly 260 ships, 6,400 soldiers, and 20,000 crewmen) was balanced between the impetuous Alcibiades, the level-headed Nicias (who opposed the expedition), and an experienced general, Lamachus.

Dismemberment Has Its Rewards: The Mutilation of the Herms

Just prior to the start of the Sicilian expedition, someone vandalized the *herms* ("statues of protection and good luck") in Athens. An uneasy public viewed this act as an ill omen and the work of sacrilege. Suspicion turned on Alcibiades and his young compatriots, who had developed a reputation for unruly conduct, religious mockery, and antidemocratic (i.e., pro-oligarchic) sympathies.

Although Alcibiades argued that a trial should take place immediately, his enemies made sure that he (and his supporters) had sailed before formal charges wre pressed. When summoned back to Athens to face these charges, Alcibiades fled to Sparta. There he advised the Spartans to send a general to Syracuse to keep the Athenians from conquering the island (and the entire Greek world, for that matter). Eventually, Alcibiades was in trouble in Sparta as well (over an affair with the king's wife), and he fled to Persia. There he acted as an advisor to the Persians (that is, he gave advice on how Persia could best turn the Peloponnesian War to its own advantage), and he began to engineer his own comeback. He advised Persia to let both sides play themselves out and then pick up the pieces.

Lexica

A **herm** is a representation of the god Hermes, showing his face and erect phallus on a pillar. These pillars were used to demarcate property and to provide protection and good luck.

Disaster in Sicily: Spartan Momentum and Persian Involvement

During the Sicilian expedition, if something could go wrong for the Athenians, it did go wrong. The generals couldn't agree on an attack strategy and, while they wasted nearly a year on trivial endeavors, Syracuse gained strength and Spartan reinforcements, led by Gylippus, arrived. Alcibiades fled and turned traitor; Lamachus was killed in 414 B.C.E.; and Nicias' cautious personality became a distinct disadvantage.

In sole command and ailing physically, Nicias proved entirely incompetent. The Spartans turned Nicias' siege against him, and the Athenians were forced to beach their ships on an exposed shore, where they could be trapped by the Syracusan navy. Athenian reinforcements arrived in 413 B.C.E., led by Demosthenes, but, when their attempt to take the city failed miserably, Demosthenes urged Nicias to set sail for home. However, cowered by an eclipse and his own superstitions, Nicias balked. The delayed departure was precisely what his enemies needed. The Syracusans blocked the harbor and defeated the remaining Athenian fleet. Now with the entire force trying to retreat overland, they surrounded the Athenians and either massacred them or took them prisoner. Both Nicias and Demosthenes were executed. As prisoners of war, the Athenians were tossed into rock quarries in Syracuse, where most died before being ransomed. It was a stunning defeat: Nearly 50,000 Athenians were killed, wounded, or taken prisoner; and 173 ships were lost.

> **Odysseys**
>
> You can still visit the impressive quarries in Syracuse where the Athenian prisoners—about 7,000 of them—languished and died after their defeat in Sicily.

To make matters worse, during the same year, Sparta established a permanent base of operations at Decelea, only 13 miles from Athens. Just as the Athenians had used Pylos to threaten and demoralize the Spartans, the Spartans used Decelea to threaten and demoralize the Athenians. The outpost cut off Athens from its own countryside, it drained Athenian resources, and it served to foster rebellion and defection among the underclass and slaves. In fact, nearly 20,000 slaves escaped over the course of the war.

Infused with new confidence and funded by Persia, Sparta began to construct a fleet of its own. It hoped to drain the Athenian bathtub, so to speak, by attacking Athenian interests in the Hellespont and Black Sea and by encouraging Athenian allies to revolt. In return for Persia's assistance, Sparta allowed it to reclaim the Greek cities it had lost in the Persian War. Athens broke into the emergency funds and scrambled to get new ships in the water.

Part III: The Ionian War and the End of It All (413–404 B.C.E.)

Remarkably, during the last nine years of the war, Athens held on and snatched victory from the Spartans a few mores times. Even more remarkably, they held on through increasingly antagonistic and violent tensions at home.

Athenians were now divided between two camps: those who supported the radical democracy and those who supported a return to a more oligarchic state. The latter, who argued that the radical democrats had done enough damage already, insisted that a change in government was necessary to preserve and restore Athens. The democratic faction was primarily supported by, and composed of, Athenian sailors, and the oligarchic faction was primarily supported by, and composed of, the propertied citizens who remained in Athens. In the years following Athens' defeat, these factions would come to civil war and set the stage for the execution of Socrates.

When the Fleet's Away, the Oligarchs Will Play

When the Spartan fleet hit the water, virtually every major Athenian ally jumped ship. In the eastern Aegean, only Samos remained loyal, and this island became the base for Athenian operations to recover the alliance.

In 411 B.C.E., while the fleet was in Samos, a faction of powerful Athenian citizens (favoring oligarchy) used murder and intimidation to induce the Athenians (in Athens) to vote the democracy out of existence. The city was placed under the jurisdiction of the Four Hundred (that is, a council of 400 men that replaced the *boulê*), who, in time, would supposedly give way to a governing body of 5,000. The fleet on Samos, however, which refused to recognize the oligarchs' "ancestral constitution," set up its own democracy in exile on the island. Then, *voilà*, it recalled Alcibiades (who was in contact with both sides, and who might have been helping the Four Hundred) as a commander.

When the Athenian fleet (that is, the Four Hundred's fleet) was defeated by the Spartans off Euboea, the Four Hundred were discredited, overthrown, and replaced by the Five Thousand. When the Five Thousand began cooperating with the fleet-in-exile, the stage was set for both Alcibiades' official return as one of the reinstated exiles (indeed, as the commander of the fleet) and the eventual restoration of the Athenian democracy. Sparta, on the defensive, requested a peace treaty (at the current status quo) in 410 B.C.E., but the overly-confident *dêmos* refused.

Fleeting Victories and Final Defeat

Under Alcibiades, the Athenian fleet began scoring victories, with major ones at Cynossema, Cyzicus, and Byzantion. The fleet ravaged the coast of Asia Minor, raising money from war booty. In 407 B.C.E., Alcibiades was dramatically recalled to Athens to receive extraordinary powers of command, and for a little while, he was king of the hill. Then, discredited by the performance of a subordinate in battle and by reports that he had fortified a private getaway on the Gallipoli peninsula, Alcibiades was not reelected general. Afraid for his life, Alcibiades retired to his estate on the Hellespont, never to see Athens again.

Athens was running out of resources, money, men, and luck. It offered freedom to slaves who would join the fleet and, newly manned with slaves, the Athenian fleet defeated the Spartan fleet off the Arginusae islands. When a storm prevented picking up the Athenian survivors (who drowned in the rough waters), the Athenians recalled the generals (including the young Pericles) and executed them. Finally, Lysander, Sparta's new powerful and ambitious commander, surprised and captured (the now irreplaceable) Athenian fleet while it was ashore at Aegospotami, across from his base at Lampsacus. Athens was cut off from everything. With Lysander bearing down on it by sea, and Peloponnesian soldiers at its walls, the starving city capitulated in 404 B.C.E. The Peloponnesians wanted to treat the Athenians precisely as the Athenians had treated the Melians: death to the men and slavery to the women and children. But Lysander refused. Athens agreed to the destruction of the long walls and the fortifications at Piraeus; they surrendered all but a dozen ships; they formed an alliance under Spartan control; and they agreed to the return of the exiled oligarchs.

> **Eureka!** _____
>
> The trial and unconstitutional execution of the commanders at Arginusae remain a puzzling and deeply disturbing act of a desperate city. It was opposed by the chair of the *ekklêsia* on that day—the philosopher Socrates—who, at great personal risk, finally walked out on his frenzied fellow citizens.

Although much of Hellas celebrated the destruction of Athens' walls as a day of freedom, the Spartan wake was scattered with ill omens and garrisons. Lysander had forced various cities to accept oligarchies loyal to Sparta, backed by Spartan garrisons, and Sparta had given over the Ionians to the Persians. In Athens, Lysander appointed 30 men to oversee the state, among whom was Critias—one of the former Four Hundred, a pupil of Socrates, an Athenian intellectual, a fervent antidemocrat, a close relative of Plato, and a man who would order numerous murders. Under Critias, the Thirty Tyrants engaged in a reign of terror, which finally resulted in civil war and, with Sparta's assistance, both the restoration of the democracy and the first recorded amnesty in history (403 B.C.E.). Chapter 18 covers this period.

> **Eureka!** _____
>
> In the end, and wanted by both victorious Spartans and Athenian sympathizers, Alcibiades fled to the Persians, who sided with his enemies. In bed with a courtesan, Alcibiades awoke one night to find the house on fire. Taking a sword in one hand and wrapping a cloak around the other as a shield, Alcibiades made a "Butch Cassidy and the Sundance Kid" charge into the night and was cut down by

The Least You Need to Know

◆ The "Peloponnesian War" usually refers to the Second Peloponnesian War (431–404 B.C.E.), which Athens lost.

◆ The Athenians, under Pericles, used Delian League funds to increase Athens' civic and military greatness.

◆ The Athenian plague (430–27 B.C.E.) and the Sicilian Expedition (415–411 B.C.E.) were major turning points in the war, and both contributed to Athens' defeat.

◆ After the Sicilian Expedition, Athens was increasingly divided between democratic and oligarchic factions.

◆ Athens' defeat resulted from a complex mixture of disease; self-serving, but powerful, personalities; overconfidence; poor governing decisions; and repeated refusals to accept favorable peace terms with Sparta.

Chapter 16

Classical Culture

In This Chapter

- ◆ Life in the Greek *oikos*
- ◆ Citizens, resident aliens, and slaves
- ◆ The hidden lives of women
- ◆ Greek economy, trade, and travel

In the fifth century B.C.E., cultural advancements and adaptations accompanied, and were often in response to, the political and social tensions of the times. Although most historical overviews of the Classical period highlight its cultural and intellectual achievements, some fail to note the connection between Classical culture and the extraordinary pressures of the period. As we go through the next two chapters, then, it will be important to remember that Classical culture existed and developed within a context of social and political upheaval, the devastation of war and disease, and numerous kinds of economic pressures.

It will also be important to remember that, although we can discuss the lives of women and slaves, the sources for our information are male writers (that is, citizens and resident aliens) and artisans. Neither women nor slaves speak to us in their own voices and, although the lives of women are portrayed on vases, the artisans who painted the scenes were male. So, very unfortunately, we cannot speak to the internal lives of women, or to their thoughts, feelings, or dreams. Such things must be surmised, by each reader individually, from male accounts of the lives of women. However, in this chapter we will step into the worlds of both men and women as we know them, and in the next (Chapter 17), we will look at the remarkable intellectual, artistic, and literary achievements of the fifth century B.C.E. Because most of our cultural information comes from Athens, we will focus on Athenian culture here. For more on Spartan culture, see Chapter 12.

It's a Man's World

In Classical Greece, as in other cultures of the period, there was an overall division between the dominant spheres, personal lives, and daily activities of men and women. Respectable women of the time lived predominantly indoors—sheltered and shadowed away from the outside world and civic involvement—and they were responsible for managing domestic affairs, raising children, and overseeing the household slaves. In contrast, men lived civically engaged and public lives, often holding political office, serving in the military, attending civic gatherings, and interacting with fellow citizens. Male citizens and, to a lesser degree, "resident aliens" (*metics*) were awarded civic and political responsibilities, and males who shunned these obligations, or who avoided public interaction, were often regarded with deep suspicion.

> **Muses**
>
> Man is by nature a political animal. And he who by nature and not by mere accident is without a state [i.e., *polis*] is either a bad man or above humanity; he is like the tribeless, lawless, heartless man, whom Homer denounces. The natural outcast quickly becomes a lover of war and he is like an isolated piece in [the game of] draughts.
>
> —Aristotle, *Politics*, 1.2

All in the Family: Life in the *Oikos*

The Greek *oikos* ("family" or "household") was the primary unit of both production and reproduction, and it consisted of family members and slaves. When a baby was born into a family, the decision to raise or expose it (that is, abandon it to die) was left to its father. Although accounts differ on the degree to which infants were exposed by the fifth century B.C.E., we can be fairly confident that male infants had a better survival rate than female infants. Family lineage was perpetuated through males (females would eventually belong to their husbands' families), male labor was valuable to the family, and males generally took care of their aged parents (including burial expenses and family tombs). However, it was common to raise the first-born child, regardless of sex.

For an Athenian male, entry into the *dêmos* came through membership in his father's *phratry* ("brotherhood"). A father enrolled his son in his *phratry* and vouched for his paternity (that is, claimed the boy as his biological child and the biological child of an Athenian mother). For males, membership in a *phratry* was a desirable, and possibly necessary, step to becoming an Athenian citizen, and, for both sexes, membership in an *oikos* was essential to becoming an accepted member of the *dêmos*.

> ### Eureka! _____
>
> An intact nuclear family was the exception rather than the rule in Classical Athens. The average age of death for females was 36 years, and the average age of death for males was 45 years. Of the children born, only about half survived infancy. Women were often widowed through war; men lost wives in childbirth; divorce was rarely stigmatized (unless it involved scandal); males without sons often adopted male relatives to continue their family lineage; widows and divorced people often remarried. So, "blended families" are not a modern invention!

Within the Greek household, space was divided between the males and the females, and each group had its own quarters. Entertainment took place in the male's quarters, and visitors to the home rarely saw the women. Women produced clothing, supervised the household slaves, and managed the domestic affairs. However, because shopping required a visit to the *agora* or "marketplace," male family members or slaves generally purchased groceries and household items. With the exception of festivals or funerals, respectable women confined themselves to their houses or interior courtyards, and only extreme circumstances could compel them to work outside of the home.

For most male citizens, agriculture was the preferred method of production and income. In the democracies, farms tended to be small, and they were worked by male family members and, to a lesser extent, their slaves. Farmers grew fruit trees, vines or olives, and sometimes grain, and farms often included sheep and goats. The Greek diet was simple—consisting mostly of fruit, vegetables, bread, cheese, olives, and wine, supplemented with fish and meats—so farmers could often produce the basic necessities of life. Also, until the latter part of the fifth century B.C.E., when warfare became all-consuming, armies tended to fight in the summer months only, which left the remainder of the year for production.

Boys' Night (and Day) Out: A Citizen's Life in the *Polis*

The various tasks of governing and defending the state fell to male citizens. Only male citizens had property and political rights and, although *metics* paid special taxes and were recruited for military service, each *polis* depended upon the political and civic involvement of its citizens (see Chapter 14). Indeed, some of things over which modern states claim rights and responsibilities were in the hands of individuals in ancient city-states. For example, individuals, rather than the state, owned property (with the exception of some forests and grazing areas) and mineral deposits (state-owned mines were leased to individuals, and privately owned mines were taxed), and, by taking on liturgies (public services), wealthy individuals relieved the state of many large expenditures. However, in Athens, the state paid some citizens for their political involvement, such as the members of the *boulê* (who received a drachma per day) and the members of the jury (who eventually received two or three obols daily). And, although care of the aged and infirm fell to family members, jury service provided a kind of pension for elderly jurors.

Business transactions often took place at the various "marketplaces" or *agoras*, which were provided by the state and, in large cities, different vendors could be found at separate marketplaces (for example, fish vendors at one and grain merchants at another). Shops in the *agora* were rented from the state, and the state provided "officials" (*agoranomoi*) to keep order, collect rents, and enforce fair prices and measures. During the day, a great deal of bargaining, socializing, political and civic activity, and the exchange of news and gossip took place. In addition to housing temporary shops and banker's tables, the Athenian *agora* also housed permanent public buildings, law courts, shrines, and alters. In Athens and other large port cities, *deigmata* (literally, "sample"), or specialized market halls, were set up by the state to allow foreign vendors to display samples of their wares. These markets were predominantly wholesale markets, where vendors could sample merchandise prior to purchasing it for resale.

In the evening, men could enjoy formal and informal dinner parties, participate in clubs and associations, or attend public feasts or banquets. Symposia were a particularly popular form of evening entertainment for the wealthy. A "symposium" (*symposion*) was a private drinking party, to which only men were invited as guests, which followed an evening meal. *Hetairai* (female "companions") might be present for entertainment, music was often provided by a female flute player (sometimes accompanied by other musicians), and the entertainment might include jugglers, dancers, or acrobats. For the meal, the guests reclined on couches and were served by slaves. Afterward, they drank wine, conversed, sang songs, or played games. A symposium might include everything from intense philosophical conversation to drunken revelry—depending, in part, on the guest list. To step into an ancient male drinking party, and to meet people as interesting as Socrates and Alcibiades, pick up Plato's *Symposium*.

The Athenian Agora.

(Photo courtesy of Norita White)

Meticulous Distinctions: Resident Aliens and Slaves

In the city-states, many of the inhabitants were noncitizens. For example, although the Greeks didn't take a census, reasonable estimates of the Athenian population include 150,000 citizens, 35,000 *metics*, and 80,000 slaves (including men, women, and children in each category). Indeed, both *metics* and slaves had a substantial impact on the economy and development of the city-states. However, although we know that *metics* lived in many *poleis* besides Athens, most of our information pertains to Athenian *metics*.

"Resident aliens," or *metics*, were foreigners (both Greek and non-Greek) who resided permanently in a particular city, and who had greater privileges and responsibilities than temporary residents. In Athens, after a *metic* enlisted a citizen to be his "sponsor" (*prostates*), he was required to register in a *dêmos*, pay an annual "poll tax" (*metoikion*), and undertake some of the duties of a citizen (such as serving in the military and accepting liturgies).

Although *metics* enjoyed full civil and social status, they had no political or voting rights, were barred from owning property or houses, and forbidden to legally marry citizens. However, *metics* socialized comfortably with citizens, and some of Athens' most prominent and distinguished intellectuals were *metics* (such as the philosophers Aristotle and Anaxagoras, and the rhetorician Gorgias). Most *metics* in Athens engaged in commercial or industrial activities, and many were quite wealthy. When freed, slaves became *metics* rather than citizens.

> **CAUTION**
>
> **Labyrinths** _____
>
> Athens did control some semi-independent communities (such as Plataea), which were similar to the Spartan *perioikoi*, but these were exceptions. They also controlled the Scythians, a few hundred slaves who made up the police force for the city and surrounding countryside. We know relatively little about this police force.

Although Sparta had state-owned slaves (helots), most of the slaves in Athens were owned by individuals. Even poor families generally owned at least one or two household slaves, and wealthy families often owned a large number of slaves.

Within the households, and under the supervision of the wife, slaves performed domestic chores, such as childcare, food preparation, and the manufacture of clothing. In agriculture, although the extent to which slaves participated is the subject of debate, we know that slaves assisted in the fields.

In nearly all cases, masters and slaves worked side by side, and their living and working conditions were similar. Moreover, a large number of slaves were employed as craftsmen and laborers, and they could receive the same pay as citizens and *metics* (although part of their pay was often given to their owners). Their jobs tended to be gender specific and, whereas men manufactured swords, shields, pottery, and other such items, women generally worked in textile-related industries.

Many slaves eventually purchased their freedom, or were granted their freedom, and became *metics*. Another group of slaves, however, were not as fortunate. In the ancient quarries and mines, slaves were often treated miserably and, quite literally, worked to death. Also, household slaves could be forced to serve the sexual needs of their masters, and they were, at times, restricted in their own choice of partners.

Slaves were often non-Greeks, acquired as war booty or purchased through slave dealers. Although some slaves were Greek, the practice of enslaving Greeks became progressively controversial, as the idea of natural capacities began to be investigated. For example, philosophers such as Aristotle began to call into question the morality of enslaving individuals who possessed the full range of human intellectual capacities. In other words, if all Greeks had the same natural capacities, then the practice of enslaving Greeks would be morally unjustified. In contrast, the practice of enslaving members of "inferior" (that is, barbarian) races would be morally justified, because they were, by nature, physically and intellectually fit only for servitude. Either way, the institution of slavery would exist in ancient Greece, as it did elsewhere, for a long time to come.

> **Muses**
>
> For he who can foresee by the exercise of mind is by nature lord and master, and he who can use his body to put such foresight into effect is a subject, and by nature a slave; hence master and slave have the same interest. Now, nature has distinguished between the female and the slave ... But among barbarians no distinction is made between women and slaves, since there is no natural ruler among them, and they are a community of slaves, male and female.
>
> —Aristotle, *Politics*, 1.2.

The Hidden World of Women

In fifth-century B.C.E. Athens, although women were granted technical citizenship, they received none of the political and civil rights of citizenship. They had extremely restricted property, inheritance, and business rights, and they had no voice in government whatsoever. All of a woman's business was conducted for her by her father or husband, and her marriage was arranged by her father or male guardian. In the case of a divorce, the children generally resided with the father, and the laws of inheritance were through the male line. The position of women depended on their social status and, although very little was written about any women, we know more about wealthy women and those who lived in Athens.

From Girl to *Gynē:* A Citizen's Wife

Generally, Athenian men married around age 30 and Athenian women married around age 15 and, for respectable women, there was no real alternative to marriage. After the age of five, a woman's father arranged her betrothal. At the formal betrothal, her father gave her to the bridegroom, in the presence of a witness, to "sow" for the purpose of producing legitimate children. After the bridegroom accepted, he entered into negotiations with the bride's father concerning her dowry. The bride's dowry (generally cash and portable property) and the bridegroom's contribution (often land, the house, and most of its contents) made up the economic foundation of the *oikos*.

Marriages to close relatives (for example, first cousins) were common and, at times, women were expected to marry a close relative of their father, in order to perpetuate his *oikos*. In such a case, a father without sons would give his daughter in marriage to one of his relatives—even if one or both were already married and had to divorce their spouses. A son of this union would become the heir of his maternal grandfather. Although most Greeks of this period had only one spouse at a time (Macedonians were an exception), a sexual double standard permitted husbands to have additional sexual partners of either sex.

Upon her marriage, a woman went to her husband's home and become part of his *oikos*. The veiled bride was escorted into the home by the groom's mother, and the couple would retire to the bedroom to consummate their marriage, while young men and girls sang the wedding song outside the bedroom door. Although religious rituals could be included in marriage ceremonies, the marriage itself was a civil contract, which could be dissolved by either party. However, whereas a marriage was easily dissolved by the male, females often found the process more difficult, because the male would have to repay her dowry.

Labyrinths

In Athens, a favorite time for marriages was the full moon in the month of Gamelion (from *gamos*, "marriage"), our January, when agricultural work was slow. At the ceremony, a sacrifice was made to the appropriate gods, such as Zeus and Hera, and the bride could dedicate a lock of her hair. The bride and groom each took ritual baths, and a banquet was held at the groom's father's home. In the evening, the bride was taken to the groom's house in a torchlight procession.

Running the Domestic Show: Women of the *Oikos*

All women (including female slaves) slept in the women's quarters. When strangers or nonrelatives were in the house, the women would retire to their quarters, and if they were discussed by the guests (which would be highly unusual), they would not be mentioned by name. Women rarely left their homes and, even then, they would be accompanied by female slaves. Women occasionally shopped or fetched water from the well, but, whenever possible, these tasks were performed by slaves. Older women and widows had more freedom, as did Spartan wives, and poor women sometimes worked outside the home (selling goods in the market, spinning, acting as a wet nurse) or alongside their husbands.

Women were responsible for the domestic affairs of the *oikos*, and if a young wife did not enter marriage prepared for her duties, her husband would provide further instruction. These duties included the supervision of slaves, care of children and the elderly, tending to the sick, cooking, cleaning, making clothes (from spinning the wool to completing the garments), and safely storing the household goods (to ensure an adequate supply of food and clothing). Many of these tasks were performed by slaves, under the supervision of the wife, but, ultimately, it was the responsibility of the wife to see that the agricultural products provided by her husband (for example, wool, fruits, vegetables, and grain) were transformed into edible food and wearable clothing.

In Athens, the average woman bore 4.3 children, 2.7 of whom survived infancy. Childbirth took place at home, with all of the household women (and possibly a mid-wife) in attendance, and, in case of problems, a male doctor might have been called in. The mortality rate for women during and after childbirth was probably quite high, and gynecological treatises comprise a large portion of the Hippocratic Corpus. If the father chose to raise the child, a "purification ceremony" (*amphidromia*) took place on the fifth or seventh day of life.

Although contraception was ineffective, it was practiced (for the most part by poor women and prostitutes). Contraceptive devices included barriers soaked in such things as vinegar, cedar resin used as a prophylactic, and herbal preparations. Abortion was induced by means of instruments and physical exercise, and it was sometimes practiced as a form of contraception.

> **Eureka!**
>
> Athenian parents could not only name their sons, they could also delete their names from the registry and disinherit them. Fortunately for the sons, this act didn't result in a loss of political status.

Stepping Out: Priestesses and *Hetairai*

Within religion, women did have important roles, including dominant roles at funerals, weddings, and a number of public festivals. Moreover, there were many priestesses and, because both priests and priestesses usually enjoyed an elevated legal and social status, priestesses could often act on their own behalf and without the intervention of a male guardian. Priestesses, like priests, were entitled to a portion of sacrificial animals and sometimes to housing. In fact, the priestess of Demeter at Eleusis was given a private house. In general, gods were served by priests and goddesses by priestesses, but there were exceptions. Some cults had both priests and priestesses, and some cults of Apollo were served by priestesses, such as the Pythia at Delphi.

The term *hetairai* ("female companions") was used for women who traded in sex. Generally, these women were foreigners, slaves or former slaves, and abandoned girls, who became prostitutes or courtesans. *Hetairai* were often extremely accomplished courtesans, and common prostitutes called *pornai* were widely available on the streets and in brothels.

Many *hetairai* entertained (as professional dancers and musicians) at men's symposia, and others, such as Aspasia, became the highly regarded mistresses of men such as Pericles. Although *hetairai* were not found in Sparta, "common prostitutes" (*pornai*) were quite numerous in port cities like Piraeus and Corinth. In general, *hetairai* enjoyed more liberated lives than women of an *oikos*, and they may have been able to own property. They paid taxes and, in some cities, they were granted legal protections.

Labyrinths

Coins of the fifth century B.C.E. were normally double sided, with the head of a deity on one side and a related design on the other. Athenian coins, which showed the head of Athena on one side and an owl (a symbol of Athena) on the other, retained their Archaic design, with very few changes, until the Roman period.

Odysseys

Although a visit to Greece might be spent on rough, rocky, mountainous terrain, it is unlikely to be spent in the cool shadows of great forests. Indeed, as early as the fourth century B.C.E., Plato (in the *Critias*) speaks critically of the massive deforestation, the resulting soil erosion and runoff, and the destruction of richly productive lands.

Show Me the Money: Greek Economy

Athenian male citizens had a general disdain for indoor manual labor, being subjected to the commands of another person, and work that was not afforded some degree of traditional nobility. For this reason, Greek citizens who could choose their occupations tended to engage in farming. This is not to say, of course, that all craftsmen and industrial workers were *metics* and slaves, or that all indoor manual labor was shunned. Indeed, some craftsmen—both citizens and *metics*—became renowned for their skills and quite wealthy. However, agriculture formed the economic basis of the entire region in the fifth century B.C.E.

Let It Grow, Let It Grow, Let It Grow

Considering the importance of agriculture, it is surprising that Greek farmers of the fifth century B.C.E. were still learning the value of crop rotation. During this time, half the land was often allowed to lie fallow in alternate years, which contributed to the poverty of small farmers. Generally, small farmers produced only enough to feed their *oikoi* and to sell at local markets. However, in areas that produced more than was needed locally, individual farmers or cooperatives had to arrange for export, because the interests of many Greek states extended only to timber and grain. This lack of state-supported exportation applied to industry as well, and in areas other than the main industrial centers, only a small percentage of manufacturing was geared toward export.

Ahoy, Matey! Commerce and Trade

Nonetheless, the exchange of goods was facilitated by the widespread use of coinage and, in time, coins of the great industrial centers (like the "owls" of Athens) were widely circulated. Although the rough Mediterranean terrain made travel by road extremely difficult, Greek ships traveled in all directions. Among other things, they brought back silk from the East; grain, papyrus, ivory, slaves, and exotic animals from Egypt; textiles from Carthage; bronzework and boots from Etruria; purple dye and dates from Phoenicia; pigs, grain, and cheese from Sicily; and grain, hides, cattle, slaves, and iron from the Black Sea region. For these items, the Greeks traded olive oil, wine, pottery, and other items. Although Greek sailors were willing to cross open seas, they preferred to hug the shoreline whenever possible to facilitate navigation. Piracy, both private and state-sponsored, often interfered with commerce, but, during this period, Athenian triremes virtually cleared the sea of pirates.

> **CAUTION**
>
> **Labyrinths**
>
> There were no passenger ships per se. People who wanted to travel by sea had to find a merchant ship that was sailing to their destination. Once on board, passengers lived on deck or under tentlike shelters, and they brought their own food. Passengers were allowed to use the galley to cook food, but most had slaves prepare and serve their meals. Water was generally provided for passengers, but lifeboats were not.

Visiting Friends and Foes

Although some people, like Socrates, never left the confines of their cities (except to engage in warfare), others traveled widely. Moreover, there seemed to be a general willingness among Greek (and even Persian) aristocrats to offer one another both class-related and personal hospitality. For example, the Athenian dramatists Agathon and Euripides spent their final years in Macedon; Alcibiades lived with both the Spartans and the Persians, who were, ostensibly, his enemies; Plato visited the Sicilian tyrant Dionysus I; and Aristotle, who was born in Stagira (in the Chalcidice), lived in Athens, on the islands of Assos and Lesbos, and in Macedon.

The Greek language was divided into various dialects, but many of the dialectical differences were small enough to allow speakers of one dialect to be understood by speakers of another. However, because the Greeks also seemed quite capable of communicating with speakers of other languages, such as the Persians, we must surmise the availability of translators, at least prior to the conquests of Alexander the Great in the fourth century B.C.E. and the widespread use of a common Greek "dialect" (*koinê*).

The Least You Need to Know

◆ In Classical Greece, there was an overall division between the dominant spheres, personal lives, and daily activities of men and women.

◆ Resident aliens, or *metics*, were foreigners (both Greek and non-Greek) who resided permanently in a particular city.

◆ In many city-states, even poor families generally owned at least one or two household slaves, and wealthy families often owned a large number of slaves.

◆ Agriculture formed the economic basis of the entire region in the fifth century B.C.E.

◆ The exchange of goods was facilitated by the widespread use of coinage, and Greek ships traveled extensively, exporting some items and importing a wide range of others.

Chapter 17

Methods from the Madness? Intellectual, Artistic, and Literary Developments of the Fifth Century B.C.E.

In This Chapter

◆ The Sophists, Socrates, and questions of the age

◆ The cultural roles of theater (tragedy and comedy)

◆ History and medicine as a part of the intellectual landscape

◆ Architecture and the visual arts

The fifth century B.C.E. was a period of remarkable intellectual, artistic, and literary development. Although it would be a vast oversimplification to attribute all of these developments to one cause or intellectual chain of events, it is nonetheless important to note a few of the questions and concerns that influenced multiple disciplines. One of these questions involved the relationship of *nomos* ("convention" or "law") and *physis* ("nature") to the origin and authority of values, traditions, and moral codes. For example, if moral values and cultural standards are determined by our nature as humans, or by nature itself, then we might be able to claim that they have an inviolable status and firm authority over our conduct. On the other hand, if moral values and cultural standards are merely the result of diverse traditions and customs, then they are situational, relative to particular places and times, and subject to judgment, revision, and rejection. Such questions and concerns place the status of dearly held "truths" at stake, and the conversation is rarely comfortable or entirely civil.

In this chapter, we will look briefly at (among other things) the roles of *nomos* and *physis* in the intellectual, artistic, and literary developments of the Classical period. Keep in mind, however, that the intellectual and artistic flowering of the fifth century B.C.E. resulted from a complex combination of factors, rather than from one overarching or isolated cause.

The Examined Life: Greek Philosophy

Chapters 3 and 10 discussed the Presocratic philosophers and left you with a few of their fragments to mull over. Although the Presocratic pluralists Anaxagoras (c. 500–428 B.C.E.), Empedocles (c. 484–424 B.C.E.), and Democritus (c. 460–370 B.C.E.) worked in the fifth century B.C.E., we're going to focus here on the sophists and Socrates (also discussed in Chapter 3). For more information on the trial and execution of Socrates, see Chapter 18.

The Price of Success: The Sophists

In several works, Plato criticizes the methods, qualifications, and knowledge of the sophists, and in the *Apology* (Plato's rendition of the defense of Socrates), Socrates argues against the suggestion that he is a sophist. Due to such criticisms, the sophists are often characterized as clever con artists, or as men of questionable moral character who capitalized on the growing importance of rhetorical skills to Athenian citizens. And, certainly, some of the sophists were unqualified or unscrupulous profiteers. However, it is important to note that Plato's criticisms have their own context. First, both Socrates and Plato were highly skeptical of the ability of average citizens to govern successfully, and they feared that democracies would be open to manipulation by powerful, persuasive, and tyrannical demagogues. Moreover, they argued that true knowledge is absolute and unchanging and that, although knowledge can be ascertained by human reason, it cannot be created or destroyed by human endeavors. Given these philosophical approaches, Socrates and Plato would have been rightly suspicious of men who promised to teach young aristocrats the precise arts necessary to manipulate a democracy, and who taught (for the most part) that knowledge is situational or relative.

For their own part, the sophists differed in both their object (practical arts and control over one's life) and their method (empirical observation and extrapolation) from the Presocratics and from philosophers such as Plato and Socrates. Although earlier (and later) Greek philosophers certainly engaged in empirical observation, they tended to focus on speculation (to identify objective principles) and deduction (to explain particular phenomena in terms of those principles). Yet, as the Greek world became more internationalized, and as the Greeks became increasingly familiar with diverse cultures, Greek objective "truths" (scientific, mythological, and moral) were, quite naturally and expectedly, called into question. Indeed, in light of cultural diversity, the Greeks were faced with the question of whether their own particular ideas and ideals were based on mere "convention" (*nomos*) or grounded firmly in "nature" (*physis*).

The sophists, whose methods tended to emphasize observation and induction, developed theories about knowledge, the origins of civilization, and moral behavior that largely emphasized the role of "convention" (*nomos*). For example, Protagoras of Abdera (c. 490–420 B.C.E.), a renowned sophist who moved to Athens around 450 B.C.E., is well known for his saying, "Man is the measure of all things—of things that are, that they are, and of things that are not, that they are not." Here Protagoras is suggesting that truth is determined by (rather than discovered by) human experience and judgment, and that it is, therefore, relative. Such a suggestion, which calls many religious and objective "truths" into question, can be deeply threatening or frightening.

Muses

Darius ... called together some of the Greeks ... and asked them what [price] they would take to eat their dead fathers. They said that no price in the world would make them do so. Afterwards, Darius summoned those of the Indians called Callatians, who *do* eat their parents, and, in the presence of the Greeks ... asked them what price would make them burn their dead fathers with fire. They shouted, "Don't speak of such horrors!" ... I think Pindar is right when he says, "Custom is the king of all."
—Herodotus, *History,* 3.38

Moreover, with the spread of democracy, political success depended upon the ability to speak well, and the political "virtues" became highly prized and sought after. Although affluent Greeks were often suspicious of people who charged a fee, and although poorer Greeks often resented the sophists for providing a service that they could not afford, all economic classes required well-trained and well-spoken political representatives. And, although it was difficult to gauge the qualifications of self-proclaimed rhetoricians, the rhetorical skills were in enough demand to justify the financial risk.

On the darker side, however, it became clear to many citizens (not merely to Socrates and Plato) that rhetorical skills could be used to advance personal causes, attack beloved traditions and values, and distract audiences from principles of justice and fairness. Thus, although the sophists claimed to teach various "virtues," many Greeks feared that there was no limit to what the sophists would use rhetoric to defend. One of the most famous rhetoricians and sophists, Gorgias (c. 483–376 B.C.E.) of Leontini (Sicily), visited Athens in 427 B.C.E. as part of an embassy that hoped to involve Athens in Sicilian affairs. In a famous piece, Gorgias defends Helen against the charge of causing the Trojan War by accompanying Paris to Troy.

There is little doubt that some sophists taught the art of making the weaker argument appear to be the stronger, that some were deeply skeptical of received values and traditions, and that some championed the rights of the strongest (especially Thrasymachus in Plato's *Republic*). However, the sophists were also an important educative force in ancient Greece.

Gadfly of the Age: Socrates

Socrates was born around 469 B.C.E., and although we know little about his early economic circumstances, we know that, during adulthood, Socrates served as an Athenian hoplite. During the Peloponnesian War, Socrates distinguished himself for bravery at Potidaea in 431–430 B.C.E. and again at the defeat of the Athenians by the Boeotians in 424 B.C.E. Physically, Socrates appears to have been a bit, well, unattractive, and his appearance is often ridiculed in literature. For example, in Plato's *Symposium*, Alcibiades says that he has the face of a satyr and, in the *Clouds*, Aristophanes says that he strutted like a waterfowl.

However, we know that Socrates was physically robust, with enormous powers of endurance. He wore the same garment year-round, walked barefoot (even during a winter military campaign), and had an extraordinary ability to endure fatigue and hunger. He had recurring periods of abstraction (the *Symposium* tells of one that lasted a full day and night), which have been variously interpreted as mental concentration, seizures, or ecstasies. From childhood onward, Socrates received warnings from his personal *daimonion* or "divine voice," and during his defense at trial, he mentioned that his *daimonion* did not warn him away from the proceedings (saying, in effect, that no harm would befall him, even if he was convicted and executed).

Socrates' early interest in natural philosophy progressed into an intense search for wisdom, knowledge, and virtue. This search was precipitated by a famous occurrence at Delphi. Chaerephon, a dear friend of Socrates, asked the Delphic Oracle if any living man was wiser than Socrates. The Oracle answered "No." Socrates did not believe that he possessed great

> **Eureka!**
>
> Socrates married a woman named Xanthippe, who is best known for her shrewish character. However, the story of her behavior just prior to Socrates' death (in Plato's *Phaedo*) paints another picture altogether. Here, although Xanthippe is clearly grieved by their parting, Socrates appears entirely indifferent. Together they had three children.

wisdom, but did believe that the oracle was incapable of lying. Thus he concluded that the god could mean only one thing: Socrates was the wisest man because he recognized his own ignorance. From here, Socrates saw his mission as one of seeking true wisdom and knowledge, of enlisting the assistance of men who would listen to him, and of exposing ignorance and falsehood.

However, as mentioned earlier, Socrates never wrote a thing. Our understanding of his life and philosophical approach comes largely from his pupil, Plato. Our other sources include Xenophon's Socratic works (*Memorabilia* and *Symposium*) and various references in Aristotle. Because each author characterizes Socrates' philosophical interests and character in a different manner, our sources can raise as many questions as they answer. Moreover, although Plato is generally regarded as the most authoritative source for the historical Socrates, he uses Socrates as a literary character and places his own ideas (as well as Socrates' ideas) into the mouth of Socrates. Thus we cannot avoid some degree of uncertainty as to where one philosopher ends and the other begins. For this reason, we will examine Plato's philosophy in Chapter 20, and we will look at the method of Socrates here.

Socrates is famous for his method of "conversation" (*dialektos*) and "cross-examination" (*elenchus*). To begin, Socrates would profess his ignorance of what, say, piety or virtue is, and ask another man (often an expert) to teach him. After his interlocutor offered a definition (often with supreme confidence), Socrates would express his gratitude, but point out that the definition was problematic (and perhaps remark upon the other man's reluctance to teach him). Then, by asking questions, Socrates would control the direction of the conversation and, eventually, show the inadequacy of the original definition. The interlocutor would offer a new or revised definition and the process would begin anew. Although certain definitions were ruled out (e.g., mere examples of, say, virtue), the process rarely resulted in an acceptably universal definition (e.g., what virtue is per se). Although Socrates' dialectical method often angered or embarrassed his interlocutors, it was extremely popular with the young men who congregated around him. However, as Socrates pointed out, he did not teach per se. Instead, he allowed others to listen to his conversations and he encouraged them to care for their souls (that is, to study philosophy and acquire virtue) above all else. He referred to his method as "midwifery," to emphasize his attempt to get each man to recognize truth with his own mind and to care for his own soul.

All Life Is a Stage

Just as the fifth century B.C.E. saw the development of philosophy, it also saw the development and decline of tragedy and Old Comedy. And although there appears to be a link between these dramatic forms and the time period, the tragedies and comedies of ancient Greece are (quite rightfully!) still renowned and influential today. For the Athenians, theatrical events were much more than entertainment. They were large-scale religious, social, and civic events, and audiences expected to be both entertained and edified. The intellectual and cultural tensions of the time were played out in various guises on the stage, and the audience actively engaged the material. For example, the response of the audience (acclamation or disappointment), along with the verdict of the judges, would proclaim which artist had best performed his dramatic task of improving the *dêmos*. More importantly, because virtually all Athenians attended the performances, the plays became part of an ongoing communal dialogue.

The following sections describe the theater itself, delve a bit into tragedy and comedy, and discuss the roles that drama played in the turbulent fifth century B.C.E. For an overview of both drama's origin in religious festivals and the major Athenian playwrights (Aeschylus, Sophocles, and Euripides for tragedy; Aristophanes for Old Comedy), see Chapters 2 and 12. To read about the liturgies that funded the plays, see Chapter 14. However, we must begin with an important caution: It is impossible to reduce Greek drama to a few pages without giving an incomplete and potentially misleading picture! In fact, ever since the fifth century B.C.E., great minds have wrestled with tragedy's dramatic, religious, and philosophical breadth, as well as with the power of its poetic language. So consider our discussion a springboard for further exploration!

Looking down on the Theater of Dionysus from the Athenian Acropolis.

(Photo by Eric Nelson)

The Greek Theater

Greek theater was an outdoor affair. Spectators sat in a semicircle upon wooden or stone seats set into a "hillside" (the *theatron*). They looked down on a (roughly) circular flat area called the *orchestra* ("dancing place"), where the chorus sang and danced in rhythm and some of the action took place. Side "entrances" (*eisodoi*) led into the *orchestra* for players to come and go. Opposite the audience, there was a raised platform, backed by a building with central and side doors, called the *skênê* (hence, "scene"). Most of the action took place on the raised platform, with the *skênê* serving as both a backdrop (e.g., a palace, or decorated as a forest) and a changing room for actors. In some plays (such as Aeschylus' *Agamemnon*), actors were placed on the roof. To show interior scenes (such as an indoor murder or the inside of a temple), a platform on low rollers, called the *ekkyklêma* (roughly "the rolling-out thingy"), could be rolled out of the central doors with performers placed on it. Finally, a crane, called the *mêchanê* ("machine"), could raise and lower actors (portraying gods or other flying characters) in and out of the action. This device was used humorously by Aristophanes to, quite literally, place Socrates' head in the clouds (the *Clouds*).

Eureka!

In some of his plays, Euripides used the *mêchanê* to bring in a god to provide an unexpected or improbable resolution. Today, we retain the expression *deus ex machina* (Latin for "god from the machine") to indicate an implausible solution, created to get a character out of a jam (such as the aliens who swoop down and accidentally pick up Brian in Monty Python's *Life of Brian*).

To avoid unfairly stacking a particular play with talent, actors were allocated to playwrights. Actors, extras, and chorus members (12 for tragedy, 24 for comedy) were male, and they wore full-head masks made of cork or molded mache. Only the aulis players (the aulis was a kind of oboe), who provided the musical accompaniment, were unmasked. Therefore, actors could not use facial expressions to convey emotions and reactions. Instead, they had to rely on language and tone, accompanied by movement or gestures. Some costuming was particular to the burlesque dramas: satyrs wore tails and phalluses, and comic actors who played men wore leather phalluses and padding on their stomachs and buttocks. Comic masks might be caricatures of the actual persons being played (e.g., Socrates, Cleon, or Lamachus). Different dramas also had particular linguistic and musical styles: tragedy and satyr plays were performed with grandiose language and music (or a mockery of it), whereas comedy tended to use more colloquial language and music.

The No-Win Scenario: Greek Tragedy and the Tragic

In tragic plays, larger-than-life characters experience and participate in deep, inordinate, and compelling suffering. Modern readers often seek to affix blame (*x* or *y* is at fault, or *x* should have done *z*) and, thereby, miss the essence of tragedy: in tragedy, suffering is brought on by circumstances beyond human control (fate, absurdity, divine caprice, accident) or beyond the characters' capacity to apprehend (through the limitations of knowledge, unpredictable consequences, or secondary effects).

In tragedy, as in life, suffering is inevitable—even *when* or even *because* someone does the *right* things according to religious, social, and moral codes. And suffering often occurs because of deep-seated tensions between religious, philosophical, personal, and civic codes that cannot be either resolved or reduced to blame. To explore such tensions and to find meaningful responses to them requires us to delve deeply into questions of religion, personal accountability, human nature, ethics, the moral (or amoral) nature of the universe, and the meaning of both success and failure within those systems. In addition, such an endeavor takes a great deal of courage, and it is an enduring credit to the Athenians that they participated in it as a public body. Perhaps tragedy (rather than democracy) should be seen as ancient Greece's highest vote of confidence in the overall potential of humankind.

For the most part, playwrights used the grand, august, or heroic characters of myth as subjects. However, their plays also confronted the questions and concerns of the times, and they reflected contemporary intellectual, political, and ethical developments. For example, whereas earlier plays gave predominant roles to the dictates of fate or divine principles of "justice" (*dike*), later plays gave such roles to "chance" (*tuchê*), capricious gods, or the power of rhetoric. Sometimes, as with Aeschylus'

Oresteia, references to the current political situation (Ephialtes' reforms) were specific; in other cases, as with Euripides' *Trojan Women* (after Melos), the references were less obvious. In any case, tragedy explored essential tensions, ones that have never been absent from the human condition, and, thanks to the genius of the Athenian playwrights, the plays have remained relevant and insightful through the ages.

We're Not Laughing with You, We're Laughing *at* You: Old Comedy and Aristophanes

Some comedy resolves discomfort and restores order; some creates discomfort in order to force change. Athenian Old Comedy falls into the latter camp. It originated in festivals, in which groups of performers could momentarily expose social and cultural pretensions and ridicule various elements of society, including the powerful, to express grievances, employ shame, and advocate change. In pre-Classical Greece, these performances were called *komoi* ("revels"), and the word *comedy* means "song of the *komos.*"

Old Comedy was something like a song and dance version of *Saturday Night Live* or *Doonesbury* on steroids. Comic playwrights brought contemporary problems to the stage, and then pummeled them with satire (often farcical and obscene), until both the problems and the solutions (as they appeared to the playwrights) were exposed to the *dêmos.* Direct criticism of the *dêmos* at large, however, was not permitted. Instead, playwrights created comic heroes (fictitious members of the *dêmos*), who would invent fantastic solutions to real problems and foil the resistance of their antagonists (real Athenians, who were often sitting in the audience!).

> **Eureka!**
>
> Cleon twice sued Aristophanes for defamation. During his trial, Socrates alluded to his appearance in the *Clouds,* while objecting to being characterized as a natural philosopher or a sophist. Aristophanes himself appears as a character in Plato's *Symposium,* where he speaks about love's attraction and the desire to be complete.

Old Comedy included two elements that allowed playwrights to make their points clear: the *parabasis* (where, about mid-play, the chorus leader stepped out of character and spoke a message from the playwright directly to the audience) and the *agôn* (a contest, usually rhetorical, between the comic hero and his chief antagonist). Only 11 plays survive, all written by Aristophanes (the most famous Old Comedy writer), but they provide us with a (sometimes viciously) provocative picture of the city and its prominent citizens. They also offer what appears to be an aristocrat's disparaging view of Athens' new intellectual and political elite.

Muses

In Aristophanes' *Clouds*, the comic hero Strepsiades makes it into Socrates' "Thinkery," in order to learn how to wriggle out of his debts, only to find Socrates hanging aloft in a basket, staring into space:

Strep.: Yoo-hoo, Socrates ... O Socratidikins!

Soc. (Torn from contemplation): Do you, measly mortal, address me?

Strep. (Distracted from his original purpose): Gazing at gods from a basket? Why don't you do that down here?

Soc. (Waxing theoretical): I could never really discover celestial phenomena without elevating my mind and mingling its subtle essence with the like-minded air. [Seeing he needs to continue] Contemplating the heavens from down there would be fruitless, you see, for earth's natural force draws thought's subtle moisture to itself. [No luck; he tries an analogy] The same process occurs with lettuce.

Strep.: Huh? Thought makes lettuce moist?

Making Connections: A Systematic Approach

Contemporary problems, views, and approaches were also the subject of systematic, reasoned inquiry. The Greeks' application of reason to causal explanations (see Chapter 3), along with their examination of what exists by nature as opposed to convention, provided a broad framework for various kinds of human inquiry. For example, the emphasis on reasoned, natural explanations for natural phenomena influenced many Greeks' approach to human affairs, communication, and well-being and health. However, rhetoric complicated (and some would argue improved) these approaches, by providing both the argumentative tools necessary to establish and promote competing theories and disturbing examples of how argumentation, rather than truth, could influence human affairs and reason.

Nothing Divine in Disease: Hippocrates and Greek Medical Science

We see just such a systematic and natural approach at work in Greek medicine of the period. For example, itinerant practitioners in northern Greece and Thessaly began to make case books (now called the *Epidemics*), from which physicians could make predictions and analogies based on Presocratic theories. This led, in turn, to theoretical explanations of disease that situated both disease and human beings within the natural world, and to theoretical confrontations with healing traditions that were based on superstition, religion, and magic.

Physicians, who competed for business and reputation with both traditional healers and one another, turned to argumentation and rhetoric to convincingly set out and publish their views. The most famous of these physicians, Hippocrates of Cos (c. 460–377 B.C.E.), became famous, in part, by arguing that health and disease were natural, not divine, phenomena that had to be treated with therapies appropriate to their natures.

Making a Science of the Past: Greek History

Philosophy, rhetoric, and medicine all had an impact upon the emergence of history as a science or discipline. As we know from Chapter 3, both Herodotus and Thucydides sought to preserve events, explain their causes, and provide rational explanations that were based on reliable (or supportable) evidence. Herodotus drew on epic and tragedy to give his work depth and grandeur, but he also utilized ideas of *nomos* ("convention" or "law") and *physis* ("nature") to explain divergent cultural standards and practices (see the *Muses* sidebar in this section).

Thucydides turned even further toward a naturalistic approach. He used speeches and rhetoric to show that accepted "truths" were often merely conventions, which could be adapted, revised, or rejected. He also used rhetoric to show that, even within such conventions, the meanings of critical terms, such as "justice," often differed significantly (as Socrates also pointed out).

Borrowing from contemporary medicine, Thucydides postulated that human "nature" (*physis*) is the constant that underlies human conventions. With a constant in place, he could develop case studies (events that placed human beings and human society under stress), which could be analyzed to develop a set of symptoms (the predictable behavior of individual and collective humans under stress). This set of symptoms could be used to diagnose past/present events and predict future events.

> **Muses** _____
>
> Rival leaders, trumpeting the finest phrases (like "political equality" and "moderate aristocracy"), sought their own gain amid the public they pretended to cherish. Sparing no means, they committed gross excesses to win and went even further in vengeance once they did. They didn't stop at what was just or good for the state, but pressed each opportunity to the fullest; they were equally ready to condemn a verdict as unjust or to claim a needed demonstration of strength—whichever served their momentary animosities. And so religion was cherished by both parties—but only as a means of using fine phrases to achieve wicked ends. In the meantime, the moderate citizens perished, either because they wouldn't join the extremists, or because envy would not allow them to escape.
>
> —Thucydides 3.81.7

> **" " Muses**
>
> Words changed their customary meanings to suit the times: "Reckless daring" became "loyal courage" and "prudent hesitation" became "veiled cowardice"; "moderation" became a drape for "unmanliness" and "the ability to consider" for "the inability to act." The zealot was most trusted, his opposite most suspected. To plot successfully was to be shrewd, to ferret out a plot still shrewder, but to conduct oneself so as to have to do neither was to betray one's party and fear one's enemies.
>
> —Thucydides, 3.81.4

Architecture and Art in Periclean Athens

During this time period, we also see an artistic focus on realism and naturalism. Pericles intended to make Athens the capital of Hellas, in terms of its strength and its beauty, and, for the most part, his building project was supported by the Athenians. Moreover, the scale of his plans encouraged Athenian support for the empire, because league tribute was necessary to finance the lavish public monuments. Although Pericles' rivals denounced his use of league funds, and suggested that he was little more than a petty tyrant, the rivalry itself increased Pericles' power and prestige. In 443 B.C.E., the Athenians indirectly voted for the building project by ostracizing Thucydides (not the historian), its fiercest opponent.

> **Eureka!**
>
> The new Parthenon (dedicated in 438 B.C.E.) became a Christian church in the Middle Ages and, in the fifteenth century, with the coming of the Turks, the church was turned into a mosque. In 1687, the Parthenon was nearly destroyed when Venetian bombardment exploded the Turkish arsenal stored there and, in the 1800s, Lord Elgin brought many of its sculptures to London, to reside in the British Museum.

Big Plans: The Project of Pericles

The Athenian Acropolis held the most important—and the most beautiful—buildings in Athens. One of those buildings was the temple of Athena Parthenos ("the virgin"), known as the Parthenon. The Persians destroyed the structure in 480 B.C.E. In 447 B.C.E., Pericles hired the architects Ictinus and Callicrates, along with the sculptor Pheidias, to rebuild the temple on the site of the older Parthenon.

The new Parthenon was a blend of Doric and Ionic elements (see Chapter 3, for more information) built mostly of Pentelic marble (with the exception of the timber roof and doors). It had 8 columns on the front and back, and 17 on the sides, and it measured approximately 100 by 230 feet. A sculptured frieze, which ran around the top of the exterior wall of the *cella* ("inner shrine"), commemorated the Panathenaic procession (celebrated every 4 years) and the presentation of a new robe (*peplos*) to the goddess, and featured the 12 Olympians, humans, horses, and sacrificial animals. The east pediment (the triangular frame, above the entablature, at either end of the temple) showed the birth of Athena, and the west pediment showed the struggle between Athena and Poseidon over primacy in Athens. Pheidias' magnificent gold and ivory statue of Athena stood inside the temple.

After dedicating the Parthenon in 438 B.C.E., during the Panathenaic festival, Pericles authorized construction of a new entranceway to the Acropolis, at the western end. Between 437 and 432 B.C.E., the Propylaea (monumental entrance gates) were built from the designs of Mnesicles. About 423 B.C.E., the temple of Athena Nike ("Victory") was built by the architect Callicrates on the bastion in front of the Propylaea. At the end of the century, a marble parapet, adorned with figures of the Victories, was placed along the edge of the bastion.

Construction of the most elaborate building on the Acropolis, the Erechtheion, began in 421 B.C.E. and, after being interrupted by the Peloponnesian War, was completed about 406 B.C.E. This temple, sacred to Poseidon Erechtheus, consisted of three Ionic porches, and its most striking feature was the south porch, or the Porch of the Maidens (Caryatids), which used the figures of six maidens (instead of columns) to support the roof.

The Porch of the Maidens, Erechtheion.

(Photo by Eric Nelson)

In addition to those described above, the Acropolis housed many other buildings, temples, and statues. In the fifth century B.C.E., their sculptural features were painted in bright colors (mainly blue and red) and often adorned with gold leaf.

Seeing Is Believing: The Visual Arts

Although the stiff, unnatural poses that characterized artwork of the Archaic period could still be found in some paintings and sculptures of the Classical period, many other works showed an increased focus on realism, naturalism, and movement. Although vase painting was constrained by the shape and size of the vessels, and although bronze and marble did not lend themselves easily to fluid naturalism, Greek art of the Classical period included a strong sense of movement, extraordinary presentations of mythological stories, and evocative depictions of ordinary human life.

Vase paintings of the Classical period are centered on human beings, and they provide us with a unique window into the lives of the ancient Greeks. Numerous scenes depict daily activities, domestic affairs, work and play, sex, and warfare. The figures are generally portrayed in action and engaged in their own affairs (that is, they are not posing for the artist). Unfortunately, Greek wall painting of the Classical period has not survived.

Relief sculpture adorned temples and grave stelai and, although temple sculpture often dealt with mythological scenes, funerary relief provides us with another glimpse into the lives of ordinary Greek citizens. For example, one well-preserved funerary relief of the Classical period shows a young girl holding some doves. This memorial to a dead child stands in stark contrast to the temple scenes of gods and mortals engaged in battle, and to the scenes of half-animal, half-human mythological figures.

Odysseys

To see the remarkably well-preserved sculpture from the Temple of Zeus at Olympia, visit the Archaeological Museum at Olympia. The central hall houses sculpture from the Temple of Zeus, and the corner room houses exhibits pertaining to the Olympic Games. The museum also houses collections from prehistory through the Classical period, to the Romans.

The Temple of Zeus at Olympia, completed between 470 and 456 B.C.E., held Pheidias' enormous gold and ivory statue of Zeus, which was considered to be one of the wonders of the ancient world. Beginning in 1876, excavations of the temple unearthed remarkable sculptures from the pediments. The metopes depicted the Twelve Labors of Heracles. The west pediment showed a battle between the Centaurs (creatures who were half-human, half-horse) and the heroes Peirithoos and Theseus, at the wedding of Peirithoos and Deidameia. From the east pediment, which depicted a complicated story involving Agamemnon's ancestor Pelops, a wonderfully detailed statue of an elderly seer has survived.

The elderly seer from the Temple of Zeus at Olympia.

(Photo by Eric Nelson)

The Least You Need to Know

◆ In the fifth century B.C.E., multiple disciplines were influenced by a growing interest in nature versus convention, argumentation, empirical evidence, and the nature of truth.

◆ The sophists and Socrates generally disagreed as to whether truth is relative (sophists) or objective (Socrates), and the sophists, unlike Socrates, taught skills necessary for public success.

◆ For the Athenians, theatrical events were more than entertainment: by publicly engaging the social and political tensions of the times, tragedy and comedy were integral to the well-being of the *dêmos*.

◆ Fifth-century B.C.E. Athenian architecture flourished under Pericles' ambitious building programs, and artwork had an increased focus on realism, naturalism, and movement.

Part 4

The Breakdown of the *Polis* to the Death of Alexander the Great

The end of the Peloponnesian War was not the end of Athens, or of the city-state. Not by a long shot. It took another half-century of conflict and jockeying for position—among old foes such as Sparta, Athens, and Corinth, and new powers such as Thebes and Pherae—to show that the *polis* was incapable of sustaining a stable order among the Greeks. In this section, we follow the demise of the city-state and chart the rise of a new power, Macedon, under the rule of Philip II. Philip's conquest of Greece was in preparation for an invasion of Persia. Although he never got to carry out his long-range plans, his son Alexander the Great did. Alexander's conquests far exceeded his father's wildest dreams, and by the time we bury both Alexander *and* the Classical period (for his death in 323 B.C.E. and the death of Aristotle in 322 B.C.E. mark its end), the world will never be the same.

In some ways, a transformation of the ideas and ideals of the city-state also takes place during this time, and traditional thought is synthesized with new political and cultural ideas. While we begin the century with the Athenians' angry execution of Socrates within the *polis*, we end 70 years later with the remarkable achievements of Plato, Aristotle, and other theoretical thinkers that far transcend the *polis*.

Chapter 18

Political Cutthroat: Shifting Dominance

In This Chapter

- ◆ The rise and fall of Sparta
- ◆ The Thirty Tyrants and the trial of Socrates
- ◆ Shifting alliances, chaos, and war among the city states
- ◆ The Theban hegemony

The Peloponnesian War was followed by a period of instability and intense rivalry. In the face of Spartan incompetence and arrogance, old foes forged new alliances, and Athens briefly regained power in what historians call the Second Athenian Confederacy. Thebes, under the charismatic leadership of Epaminondas, briefly replaced Sparta as the foremost power in Greece by defeating Sparta in war and by liberating Messenia from Spartan domination. But Thebes, like Sparta, would prove incapable of sustained dominance.

During this period, Hellenic affairs also became further internationalized, and they involved both Persia and Macedon in ways that would eventually alter all of Greece and Asia Minor (see Chapters 19 and 20). Eventually, Macedonian involvement with Theban and Athenian interests would result in the domination of Greece by Philip II of Macedon, and the Greeks' involvement with Persia would set a precedent for Philip's plans to attack Persia (a plan carried out by his son, Alexander the Great).

Peloponnesian Epilogue

The Peloponnesian War exhausted and depleted Greece. Athens and Attica, which had been ravaged by Peloponnesian armies for nearly 30 years, were particularly devastated. However, as the dust settled in 404 B.C.E., neither vanquished nor victor had much left except the ravages of war, diminished populations, disrupted economy and trade, and bitter political factions. Indeed, the Peloponnesus, which had been economically isolated from the rest of Greece by Athens' maritime supremacy, was about 30 years behind the times. Throughout Greece, the war had initiated profound social changes, as farmers were forced to leave the countryside and become laborers, mercenaries, and other nonagricultural workers. In turn, these changes produced an ever-increasing gap between rich and poor, which was complicated by political factions and "civil strife," or *stasis*, within the *poleis*.

> **Lexica**
>
> **Stasis** (a "stand") indicates a polarization of factions within a *polis* (such as democratic or oligarchic).

Spartans Rule!

Although Sparta emerged as victor, it was (still) ill equipped for widespread leadership. Only about 2,000 Spartiates survived the war, which left Sparta with few human resources to draw upon. Moreover, Spartan character, which had proved so noble in defeat, proved unbearably arrogant and myopic in victory.

> **Lexica**
>
> **Hegemony** indicates a dominant power, especially one state over another. It comes from the Greek *hêgemôn*, the "leader" (either individual or state) of a league of states.
>
> A **decarchy** is an executive board of 10 men in control of the state.

Sparta appeared to have one answer to Greek instability: replicate itself. Thus, in cities taken from Athens, it gave oligarchies loyal to Sparta the power to crush opposition. Under a new imperial outlook championed by Lysander, Sparta moved quickly to establish *hegemony* over Greece and, thereby, to preclude other states from doing what Athens had done.

The Spartan commander Lysander replaced democracies with oligarchies, each under the control of a *decarchy* ("a board of 10 oligarchs"), backed by Spartan garrisons. The decarchies were brutal to their political enemies, murdering opponents and confiscating property, and their brutality created a backlash that, within a few years, resulted in the restoration of numerous democracies hostile to Sparta. We know little about these political transformations, but, by analogy, we imagine that they were similar, though smaller in scale, to the rule of the Thirty Tyrants in Athens and the restoration of the Athenian democracy (see below).

The Dirty Thirty

In Athens, a board of 30 men, led by Critias, was installed to draft a new law code in accordance with oligarchic values and Spartan interests. However, after convincing Lysander to give them a Spartan garrison as backup, the Thirty Tyrants and their private police force of 300 "whip bearers" began a violent cleanup of the state. They dismantled the democracy, but they did not establish the "ancestral constitution" as expected. Instead, they abolished the democratic *boulê* and law courts in favor of a new aristocratic council and a citizen roll of Three Thousand, whose members would be entitled to trial by a new *boulê*. Those people not on the list were even forbidden to enter Athens.

By restricting the citizenry to the Three Thousand, the Thirty were free to execute others with impunity and to confiscate their property. At first, when the tyrants persecuted only war profiteers and informants, the general population wasn't overly alarmed. However, the Thirty soon went after their political opponents, their suspected political opponents, the supporters of their suspected opponents, wealthy metics, suspected wealthy metics, and so on. Moreover, the Thirty removed uncooperative citizens from the roll of Three Thousand, making it possible to kill them with impunity. In addition, they attempted to make members of the Three Thousand complicit in their reign of terror by forcing them to round up noncitizens for execution. When Socrates (who was a member of the Three Thousand) received orders to round up some noncitizens, he acted just as he had in the face of the conviction and execution of the generals at Arginusae: He went home.

Eureka!

Theramenes, one of the Thirty Tyrants himself, fell victim to the suspicions and tactics of his fellow leaders. Fearing that the moderate might lead a revolt, the Thirty brought him to trial before the *boulê*. When it became apparent that he might prevail, Critias struck his name from the Three Thousand and had armed supporters drag him off for execution. Theramenes reportedly toasted Critias' health with the last drops of hemlock, the poison by which he was executed.

Due to the political upheaval, many Athenians went into exile. Although Sparta had forbidden neighboring states from harboring Athenian refugees, Thebes and Megara, fed up with Sparta's heavy-handed ways, provided refuge to a growing army of exiles. From Thebes, the exiles mounted a campaign to retake their city (404–403 B.C.E.). Led by the democratic general Thrasybulus, they seized a fort on the Athenian side of the Attic/Boeotian border, moved down into Piraeus (always a hotbed of democratic sentiment), and finally, with their numbers growing, established themselves on the heavily fortified Munychia Hill. There the Thirty and their supporters made an unsuccessful uphill charge, in which Critias was killed. Rejecting Thrasybulus' offer of peace, the Thirty fled to a prepared refuge at Eleusis (prepared, in part, by the murder of 300 Eleusinian males and the confiscation of their property) to await Spartan assistance.

> **Odysseys**
>
> Munychia Hill (modern Kastélla) remains a popular tourist attraction in Athens. But, unlike Critias, you won't die trying to scale it. Now a tram will whisk you to the top!

Amnesty: Lest We Not Forget

Spartan assistance, however, never materialized. Many Spartans, including the kings Agis and Pausanias, were uncomfortable with the violent imperialism of Lysander and his supporters. So, instead of helping the Thirty, Pausanias marched into Attica and brokered both a reconciliation of the various Athenian political parties and the first recorded *amnesty* in history. Under its terms, only the Thirty and their chief officers could be prosecuted for crimes that occurred before 403 B.C.E. All other complaints and grievances had to be renounced. The Athenian democracy was restored by the autumn of 403 B.C.E., and individual members of the Thirty were executed thereafter.

> **Lexica**
>
> **Amnesty** comes from the Greek *a* ("not") + *mnês* ("remember"). An *amnêstia* is an agreement to "not remember" irreconcilable wrongs of the past in order to try to bring about peace in the present.

Sock It to Socrates! The Democracy Swats Its Gadfly

Even though the Athenians attempted to abide by the terms of the amnesty, at least for the most part, their tempers and nerves were frayed. The loss and devastation of the war, the political bloodshed, and even the amnesty itself had left the Athenians with unanswered questions and unassigned blame. What had undermined the Athenian democracy and left the city so vulnerable to attack and manipulation? Why had the gods turned against Athens? Who had created such monsters and megalomaniacs as Critias and Alcibiades?

Three Athenians—Anytus, Meletus, and Lycon (representing Athenian craftsmen and politicians, poets, and rhetoricians)—turned their anger and suspicion on the eccentric, 70-year-old philosopher, Socrates. Here was a man who had great influence over affluent, potentially powerful young men, and who held questionable political ideals. Indeed, Socrates' pupils included (at least) two of Athens' most infamous citizens, Alcibiades and Critias, and he openly criticized democracy. Moreover, Socrates engaged in an exasperating practice of argumentation, publicly confuting the claims of men who were known for their knowledge or expertise. And, by refusing to participate in the trial and execution of the generals at Arginusae, Socrates had embarrassed many of the citizens responsible for those acts.

Although the amnesty prohibited Socrates' accusers from charging him with inciting his pupils to treason, it did not prohibit them from bringing two other, fairly unusual, charges against him. Brought to trial in 399 B.C.E., Socrates was charged with, and convicted of, impiety (i.e., not believing in the gods of the state and teaching new gods) and corrupting the youth. Socrates' extraordinary and wildly nonconciliatory defense was later recorded by Plato (who, at 29 years old, was present at the trial) in the *Apology*.

Although Socrates persuaded nearly half of the jury (he was convicted by about 30 votes), his suggestions during the penalty phase (mainly, that, rather than death, he be given free meals for life as the beneficent gadfly of Athens) seem to have angered the jury. They voted for execution, and Socrates was imprisoned. His final day and his death by hemlock are recorded in Plato's *Phaedo*. It is probably fair to say that that the execution of Socrates is one of the most serious blemishes—if not *the* most serious blemish—on the ancient Athenian democracy.

Uncomfortable Companions: The New World Disorder of the Fourth Century B.C.E.

Spartan tactics increasingly concerned and alienated other Greek states, and patience was wearing thin. Sparta was willing to use garrisons and heavy-handed pressure to establish puppet governments and pro-Spartan oligarchies, which, by itself, was a potentially explosive problem. To make matters worse, Lysander carried out his policies in a brutal and arrogant manner, and Spartan imperialists had both a volatile relationship with Persia and a general willingness to abandon the Asiatic Greeks to Persia. When the Spartan king Agis died and Lysander engineered the succession of his close friend, the king's brother Agesilaus, many states (in particular Athens, Corinth, Thebes, and Argos) began to find common ground in their opposition to Spartan hegemony.

Meanwhile, in 404 B.C.E., Lysander's Persian ally, Cyrus, became involved in a struggle with his brother Artaxerxes for the throne. With the assistance of more than 10,000 Greek mercenaries, Cyrus' army was victorious at Cunaxa (near Babylon) in 401 B.C.E., but Cyrus was killed attempting to slaughter his brother. This turn of events left the Greek mercenaries in a precarious position. Their leader was dead, they were in the heart of the Persian Empire, and they had just attempted to overthrow the Persian king. They elected an Athenian, the (soon to be) historian Xenophon, as one of their leaders.

Xenophon's account of their remarkable march (the *Anabasis*) through 1,500 miles of hostile territory is an entertaining source of information and an enduring example of tactical retreat. The Greek mercenaries eventually sailed home, and their experience showed that Persia was vulnerable. With both Cyrus and the hopes of an alliance with Persia now dead, Agesilaus invaded Persia. Eventually, hoping to stir up enough trouble in Greece to get Agesilaus sent home, Persia offered Sparta's enemies what they most needed to mount armed opposition to Sparta: money.

Muses

Xenophon describes the moment the Greek mercenaries reached the sea:

As soon as the advance guard reached the top of the mountain, a great shout went up and Xenophon, in the rear guard, thought that they were under attack … but the din grew louder as they approached and he could see men running forward to join the growing numbers who kept shouting and shouting, so he knew that it must be something extraordinary. Taking his horse and the cavalry, he rode forward to help and suddenly they all heard men cheering, "The sea! The sea!" Then everyone, rear guard, cavalry, baggage horses—everyone—broke into a run for the summit. There, both men and generals tearfully embraced each other.

—Xenophon, *Anabasis*, 7.4.21–25

The Corinthian War (395–387 B.C.E.) and the King's Peace

It worked. Although Lysander and the Peloponnesians initially won minor victories over the coalition of Athens, Corinth, Thebes, and Argos, Lysander was killed in 395 B.C.E. and Agesilaus was recalled from Persia. Then the Persian fleet, under Conon (an Athenian who was now an admiral in the Persian fleet) and primarily manned by Greeks, won a decisive victory over the Spartan fleet at Cnidus in 394 B.C.E.

The following year, Conon returned to Athens and, funded by Persia (with contributions from Thebes and other sympathetic states), his crews rebuilt both the fortifications at Piraeus and Athens' long walls. As a revitalized power in Greece, Athens recovered Scyros, Imbros, and Lemnos, and renewed its alliance with several Aegean states.

The costly war dragged on until, at the urging of Sparta, the Persian king Artaxerxes enforced a common peace, known as the King's Peace (387 B.C.E.). This peace applied to all states and it was based (in Greece) on the principle of autonomy. In it, Persia regained control over the Greeks in Asia Minor and on the islands of Clazomenae and Cyprus. All other Greek states (except Scyros, Imbros, and Lemnos, which belonged to Athens) were to remain or become autonomous (that is, free to govern themselves). These terms forced Athens to give up its maritime alliance, Thebes to grant independence to its Boeotian allies, Corinth and Argos (who had attempted an experimental union during the war) to separate, and Greece to surrender its Asiatic cities to Persia.

When Thebes attempted to sign the treaty on behalf of all Boeotia, the Spartan king Agesilaus refused and, insisting upon autonomy for all Boeotian cities, he began assembling forces. Deeply embittered, but under threat of attack, Thebes, a rising military power in its own right, signed the treaty. Ironically, Sparta, whose wanton disrespect for the autonomy of other Greek states was the original catalyst for the war, was given the task of enforcing the peace—and it embraced this task with renewed brutality and vigor.

During the Corinthian War, the Athenians gained a significant advantage by employing light-armed support troops, including archers, slingers, and, especially, javelin throwers (called peltasts, from their light wicker "shield," the *peltê*). Although Demosthenes had developed light-armed troops in the Peloponnesian War, it was the Athenian general Iphicrates who mastered the use of these troops and used them with deadly efficiency against the Spartans in the Corinthian War. Light-armed troops not only disadvantaged Sparta, which seemed incapable of adjusting, but, because of the lower cost of the arms, they also made it possible for the poor to support themselves as mercenaries.

The Kinder, Gentler, Second Athenian Confederacy

In the years that followed, Sparta used its peacekeeping role to dominate and intimidate its rivals, which resulted in confrontations with both Thebes and Athens. In Thebes, which was divided between pro-Spartan and pro-Athenian factions, a Spartan force occupied the acropolis (called the Cadmea) and helped install a pro-Spartan government. After fleeing to Athens, the Theban rebels (i.e. the anti-Spartans) staged a movielike comeback. Disguised as women, seven of them were taken to the pro-Spartan magistrates, ostensibly for the magistrates' enjoyment. Instead, the rebels drew hidden weapons and promptly assassinated the magistrates.

Although Athenian support was informal, two Athenian regiments assisted in the removal of the Spartan garrison from Thebes. Then, the Spartan commander in Boeotia attempted a secret attack on Piraeus. When it failed, Athens formally allied with Thebes and pressed ahead with its plans for a new naval confederacy, which historians call the Second Athenian Confederacy.

Initially, the new confederacy, which had 60 to 70 members (including about 35 from the former Delian League), was set up on an egalitarian basis, and its purpose was to safeguard the common peace of 387 B.C.E. Athens was specifically prohibited from acquiring territory in allied states, and all members were granted both their own autonomy and freedom from tribute. League decisions and policy had to be ratified by both the Athenian *ekklêsia* and a "corporate body" (*synedrion*) of member states. Although no tribute was specified, league operations were financed by a system of "contributions" (*syntaxeis*).

The confederacy was initially successful against Sparta and, in 375 B.C.E., the Spartans signed a "common peace" with Athens, which recognized its new league. This not-at-all-common peace was soon shattered, however, by renewed fighting. In 371 B.C.E., during another attempt to negotiate a common peace, the situation deteriorated further. This time, because the Spartans once again refused to recognize Thebes' hegemony over Boeotia, the Thebans walked out.

Over time, the allies became less willing to participate in the confederacy. Athens appears to have reverted to some of its former ways, establishing cleruchies and interfering in the internal affairs of some states. Finally, under the prodding of the Carian king (and Persian satrap) Mausolus, the Athenian allies Cos, Rhodes, Chios, and Byzantion revolted in 357 B.C.E. Historians call this the Social War (from the Latin *socius*, "ally"). When the Athenians were unable to recover their lost allies (due, in part, to Persian threats), more states withdrew, and the Second Athenian Confederacy was left toothless.

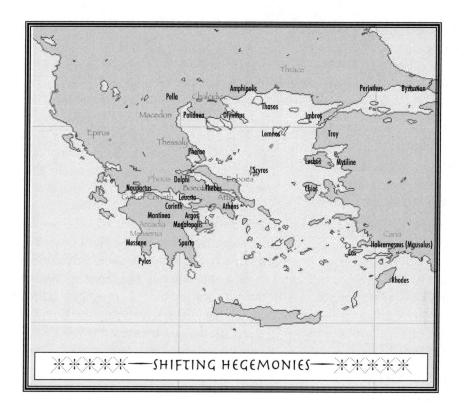

✳✳✳✳✳ ——SHIFTING HEGEMONIES—— ✳✳✳✳✳

The Theban Hegemony

Thebes' growing antipathy towards Sparta was matched by its own growing militarism and imperialism under two charismatic leaders and intimate friends, Epaminondas (c. 410–362 B.C.E.) and Pelopidas (c. 410–364 B.C.E.). Epaminondas and Pelopidas brought about a brief period known as the Theban Hegemony, during which Sparta was eliminated as a major military power and the seeds of Macedonian imperialism under Philip II were sown.

Muses _____

Many, indeed, think their strict and entire affection dates from the battle at Mantinea [385 B.C.E.], where [Epaminondas and Pelopidas] both fought … Pelopidas, having been wounded seven times … fell upon a heap of slain friends and enemies. But, Epaminondas, although he thought [Pelopidas] past recovery, advanced to defend him and his armor, and alone he fought a multitude, resolving to die rather than forsake [him]. Now, [Epaminondas was] in distress and wounded himself … and Agesipolis, the king of the Spartans, came to his aid from the other wing, and beyond hope delivered both.

—Plutarch, *Lives*, "Pelopidas."

Rows upon Rows at Leuctra

As the Theban representative, it was Epaminondas who walked out of the peace negotiations of 371 B.C.E., and the Spartans, under King Cleombrotus, retaliated. With an allied force of about 10,000 men, the Spartans invaded Boeotia, and they were met by Epaminondas, Pelopidas, and a force of about 7,000 men at Leuctra. Here, Epaminondas unexpectedly arranged the Theban hoplite forces 50 rows deep on the left wing (normally the weaker side), and he placed the famous *Sacred Band* at the fore. He used this overwhelming force to attack the Spartan right wing (traditionally 12 rows deep) at an oblique angle, rather than head on, to maximize the impact. The elite Spartiates were mown down, the left wing scattered, and the era of Spartan invincibility was over. Of the roughly 700 Spartans present, 400 of them, including the king, lay dead. Altogether, the Spartan-led army lost about 1,000 men, and the remainder, mostly allies, withdrew. Thebes lost 47 men. Now, the total number of Spartan hoplites numbered a meager 1,000.

> **Lexica**
>
> The **Sacred Band** was the Thebans' elite military force composed of 150 pairs of male lovers. Formed by Epaminondas c. 378 B.C.E., this famous brigade was instrumental in Theban military supremacy until it was wiped out by Philip II at Chaeronea in 338 B.C.E. Both Plato (*Symposium*) and Plutarch (*Pelopidas*) discuss the theory that lovers, fighting side by side, would rather die than act in a base or cowardly manner.

The End of Spartan Supremacy

After his victory at Leuctra, Epaminondas took the fight into the Peloponnesus, which was anxious to shake off Spartan domination. Invading in 370–369 B.C.E. with a force of over 40,000 men, Epaminondas destroyed Sparta's base of power. Although he was unable to take the city of Sparta itself (the *perioikoi* remained loyal), he liberated Arcadia and founded a new capital, Megalopolis ("Big City"). Most importantly, he freed the Messenian helots and established the new capital of Messene on Mount Ithome.

It wasn't long, however, before Theban imperialism got out of hand. In the north, Thebes had a deteriorating alliance with its ambitious ally, Jason, tyrant of Pherae in Thessaly. Briefly, Jason unified Thessaly and attempted to make it into a major power, but he was assassinated in 370 B.C.E. Now, if Thebes could take Thessaly and challenge Athenian naval supremacy with a fleet of its own, it could, possibly, extend its hegemony over all of Greece. However, although Thebes did build a fleet and win over a few allies, its plans were never clearly formulated and never fully realized.

Pelopidas was killed in battle in Thessaly, and Thebes was unable to maintain its costly fleet. Theban allies became disillusioned and distrustful, and when Sparta tried to regain its territory in 362 B.C.E., some of the "liberated" Peloponnesians allied with Sparta against Thebes. The Thebans met the alliance at Mantinea. Although the Thebans were victorious, Epaminondas was mortally wounded and, with his dying words, advised his fellow soldiers to make peace.

In the end, the legacy of Theban hegemony is marked by one outstanding disadvantage. By eliminating Sparta as a military power, Thebes also eliminated Sparta's ability to help Greece protect itself from further imperial domination, or from Philip II of Macedon. Indeed, Thebes helped train and prepare Philip for his future conquests.

Eureka!

When King Amyntas III of Macedon died, he left three sons: Alexander II, Perdiccas III, and Philip II. To improve relations with Thebes, Alexander sent his 13-year-old brother Philip to Thebes as a hostage. From 369 to 367 B.C.E., the young prince witnessed Epaminondas and Pelopidas' military innovations, learned Greek tactics, and acquired a sense of Hellenic culture. As the ruler of Macedon, Philip used his training to create a new Macedonian state and to achieve hegemony over Greece.

Meanwhile, Way out West: Dionysus I of Syracuse

In the aftermath of the Athenian defeat in Sicily, Syracuse established itself as the most powerful and influential city on the island. When the Carthaginians attempted to invade the island, Dionysus I, an aristocratic general, manipulated events to become tyrant of the city. Firmly backed by a mercenary force of 10,000 to 20,000 men, whom he kept loyal through lavish generosity (well, he confiscated land and estates, sold the original owners into slavery, and gave the estates to his mercenaries), Dionysus controlled most of Sicily, parts of southern Italy, Corsica, and Elba until his death in 367 B.C.E. Throughout, he maintained good relations with both Athens and Sparta, and a crushingly heavy hand on his own dominions.

Dionysus was a keen innovator, a patron of the arts, a civic builder, and a ruthless despot. In fact, Plato, who stayed briefly in Syracuse, unsuccessfully attempted to turn him into a philosopher king. Dionysus did not embrace the philosophical life, but, under his watch, Syracuse developed the most sophisticated siege equipment and complex military organization of the time.

The Least You Need to Know

♦ The Peloponnesian War was followed by a period of instability and intense rivalry.

♦ In Athens, the Thirty Tyrants' reign of terror ended with the restoration of the Athenian democracy (403 B.C.E.) and the first recorded amnesty in history.

♦ In Athens, Socrates was convicted of impiety and corrupting the youth and executed in 399 B.C.E.

♦ Athens temporarily regained power and formed the Second Athenian Confederacy.

♦ The Theban hegemony resulted in the elimination of Sparta as a military power.

The Man with the Silver Spear: Philip II of Macedon and the Conquest of Greece

In This Chapter

- ◆ The Macedonian kings leading up to Philip II

- ◆ Philip's reorganization of the Macedonian state and army

- ◆ Philip's ongoing conflict with Athens and his conquest of northern and central Greece

- ◆ The formation of the League of Corinth and Philip's plans to invade Persia

Mired in conflict, Sparta, Athens, and Thebes struggled their way to an exhausted stalemate by the mid-fourth century B.C.E. Although Sparta tried to recover some of its lost status and territory in the Peloponnesus, Thebes was bogged down in an unresolved conflict with Phocis and Pherae. In the Social War instigated by Mausolus (the ruler of Caria), Athens was losing its grip on the confederacy. Meanwhile, a young and Hellenized Macedonian king, Philip II, was transforming Macedon into the next world power. A former hostage of the Macedonian royal house to Thebes, Philip would utilize his Theban training to great effect.

In this chapter, we'll spend time with Philip II of Macedon—a remarkable man, brilliant (albeit shifty) strategist, and important historical figure. Often overshadowed by his famous son, Alexander the Great, Philip deserves careful attention in his own right. Indeed, even in his own time (and thereafter!), the hard-drinking, hard-living, and hard-fighting warrior king elicited strong and conflicting reactions. To Demosthenes, his chief opponent in Athens, Philip was a tyrannical despot and an enemy of freedom. To Isocrates, also in Athens, Philip was a potential savior, who could unify the Greeks and lead them to greatness over Persia. Theopompus (a historian and pupil of Isocrates) notes Philip's remarkable crimes and excesses, but Polybius (the historian, writing two centuries after Philip's death) characterizes him more favorably.

The Making of Macedon

To appreciate and understand Philip, some background information is necessary. Since early antiquity, the Macedonian kings faced four enormous obstacles to a unified and secure kingdom. First, they had to control the clans in the mountainous highlands, tame their own nobility, and bring the Macedonian lowlands and highlands together under one rule. Second, they had to establish stable and secure borders in a land that was surrounded by aggressive and hostile enemies. Third, they had to control a portion of coastline to engage in trade and commerce. Lastly, they needed revenue, which could come from grain and timber (if Macedon could access coastal ports) and silver or gold (if it could control the mines). Although Philip's predecessors each attempted to address these obstacles, only Philip overcame them all simultaneously.

> **⚠ CAUTION**
>
> **Labyrinths** _____
>
> As noted in Chapter 6, in both ancient and modern geopolitics there is a question of whether the Macedonians are Greek. The royal family claimed Dorian heritage, but the sources are scanty and ambiguous enough to keep nationalist debates ardently polarized, perhaps indefinitely.

Kings Before Philip

In the sixth century B.C.E., under king **Amyntas I,** the Macedonian royal line (the Argeads) made an alliance with Persia. This alliance took on historical significance during the Persian War and the rule of **Alexander I** (c. 495–450 B.C.E.), son of Amyntas I. Although Alexander claimed Greek heritage and introduced Hellenic customs and culture into Macedon, he also maintained the Macedonian alliance with Persia. Perhaps unsurprisingly, then, Alexander seems to have played both sides during the Persian War. For instance, although Alexander served with the Persian forces, he secretly advised the Greeks. For his assistance, he became known as the "Philhellene" (lover of Greek things), was admitted to the Olympics, and was recognized at Athens as a *proxenos* ("ally of the city"). Nevertheless, during the main invasion, he smoothed Persian progress through Thessaly and, after Salamis, he attempted to convince Athens to surrender to Persia on generous terms (which would have split the Greek alliance). In the wake of the Persian retreat, Alexander captured silver mines and became the first king to issue a Macedonian coinage. His further expansion was restricted by Athenian power.

Perdiccas II (c. 454–413 B.C.E.) attempted to keep any formidable city-state or league from establishing territory on the Macedonian borders. Both Athens and Macedon wanted control over the cities of the Chalcidice, which provided access to rich mines and to the northern Aegean trade routes. Perdiccas was drawn into the Athenian and Corinthian conflict at Potidaea, as was his chief northern enemy, the Thracian king Sitalces (who also wished to control the area). Perdiccas encouraged the cities around Chalcidice to establish their own league, centered on the city of Olynthus, and he helped this area revolt from Athens.

Archelaus (413–399 B.C.E.), son of Perdiccas II, had friendlier relations with Athens, providing timber for its fleet and bringing the tragic poets Euripides and Agathon to his court (both remained there until their deaths). Archelaus began to centralize Macedonian power by building roads for commercial and military travel, establishing forts and garrisons to control the hinterland, and establishing the capital (with Athenian help) at Pella. He also began to spar with his southern neighbors in Thessaly, where conflicts would, in succeeding years, create conditions favorable to Philip's invasion of Greece. Archelaus' death ushered in a period of regional instability, in part because other regional powers were taking shape in the wild northern areas.

> **Eureka!**
>
> Although we don't possess any of Agathon's tragedies, he appears as a character in Greek literature. Plato's *Symposium*, for example, is a banquet in honor of his first victory (416 B.C.E.), and he is caricatured in Aristophanes' *Thesmophoriazusae.*

Amyntas III (c. 392–370 B.C.E.), father of Philip II, barely held on to the country. The Illyrians, under king Bardylis, expanded into Macedon and Epirus, but they were driven back by the Macedonians and the Spartans (in Epirus) with great difficulty. The neighboring Thessalians became unified under Jason of Pherae and, allied with the Molossians and Thebans (for a while), they threatened southern Macedon. And, as always, the Macedonians had to contend with cities such as Olynthus, Methone, and Amphipolis in the northwest.

A Stable Instability

Amyntas' death in 370 B.C.E. might have spelled disaster for Macedon, and, indeed, two of his sons (Alexander II and Perdiccas III) had short and violent careers. But the other powers in the region were also reeling. Sparta had been crippled at Leuctra in 371 B.C.E., and Jason of Pherae was assassinated in 370 B.C.E. Athens reasserted its claim to Amphipolis after Leuctra, and Pelopidas was called in by the Thessalians to intervene in their battle with Macedon and Pherae (369 B.C.E.). However, Pelopidas was bogged down in the protracted conflict and eventually killed (364 B.C.E.). When Epaminondas was killed two years later at Mantinea (362 B.C.E.), Thebes was left without either of its charismatic leaders. Alexander II of Macedon was murdered in 368 B.C.E., and Perdiccas III (along with about 4,000 Macedonian troops and numerous Macedonian aristocrats) was killed in battle with the Illyrians (360 B.C.E.). Following their victory, the Illyrians and Paeonians prepared to invade Macedon, and both Athens and Thrace supported pretenders to the Macedonian throne. So, when Philip took the throne in 359 B.C.E., he took control of a very shaky kingdom in the middle of an unstable, but potentially rich and powerful, region.

> **CAUTION Labyrinths** _____
>
> Because no Macedonian texts survive, ancient histories of this period are told from distinctly Greek perspectives. How might the story have been told by the Macedonians—people who, for the most part, saw themselves as one people, rather than as citizens of particular city-states? In retrospect at least, a Macedonian history might have attempted to chronicle and explain the successful rise of the first nation-state in European history.

Philip's Military Machine

To establish Macedonian security, Philip needed military supremacy. Although Macedon always had a fine cavalry, organized among the nobility, it lacked a powerful and effective infantry. To establish Macedon as a military power, Philip needed to challenge the modern hoplite armies (supported by light-armed troops and cavalry) and, like his father, he needed a highly mobile force that could move back and forth between borders. In addition, because establishing control over the coast and the (silver and gold) mines required attacking heavily fortified cities, he needed the ability to take and control these sites without engaging in protracted sieges.

Won't You Be My Companion?

Philip created a professional, royal Macedonian army by reorganizing the cavalry and infantry into a force closely allied with the king. He recruited and enlisted new cavalry members, both Macedonian and Greek, who served with status as the "king's companions." He also recruited and enlisted the best foot soldiers from among the peasants, and gave them the title of "foot companions." Sons of the nobility served the king as royal pages, received their education at his court, and were later recruited as officers. Through this reorganization, Philip increased the cohesion of Macedon as a state and secured the loyalty of its soldiers to their king.

Eureka!

Both Philip and Alexander the Great strengthened their bonds with their armies by living, carousing, and fighting alongside their "companions." These personal bonds were intense and, during Alexander's invasion of Persia, Macedonian soldiers reacted furiously to Alexander's inclusion of new, non-Macedonian "companions" (as though Alexander had "cheated" on them).

A Prickly New Phalanx with All the Options

Combining what he had learned in Thebes with his own inventions, Philip transformed the hoplite phalanx (see Chapter 9) into a compact, mobile, and deadly formation. Philip armed each soldier with a 15-foot, two-handed spear called the *sarissa*, a light shield that hung over the left arm from around the neck, and a short sword.

Philip's innovations made the Macedonian phalanx twice as mobile (by increasing the space between men) and twice as powerful (soldiers could close into the open spaces and fight two to one) as the former version. And it was much deadlier. With four rows of spear points protruding from the front ranks, the phalanx *was* capable of striking an enemy before it could get close enough to utilize traditional swords.

Lexica

The **sarissa** was a 15-foot-long pike, weighted heavily at the butt end, invented by Philip II for his new phalanx. The new weapon allowed Philip's armies, arranged in a compact formation, to attack with four rows of spear points protruding from their ranks.

Moreover, Philip added archers and slingers as auxiliaries and made a tactical distinction between his two wings (that is, one offensive and one defensive). Such a formation relied on intense training and discipline, and Philip drilled and exercised his new troops into shape, along with the light-armed troops and cavalry (both heavy and light) that both protected the phalanx and took advantage of its offensive power. Philip adroitly used his intellectual, human, and financial resources to, in the words of a Pythian oracle, "fight with silver spears."

From Tearing Down Walls to Tearing Across Country

To effectively lay siege to and storm cities, Philip adapted recent advancements in mechanics (such as those pioneered by Dionysus I). Developing the use of arrow-shooting catapults and siege towers, the Macedonian army could storm cities that were previously protected by their heavy fortifications. Also, because Philip used long, forced marches as a training exercise, a fully equipped Macedonian army could move from one front to another with amazing speed and dexterity—gaining experience, loyalty, and confidence all along the way.

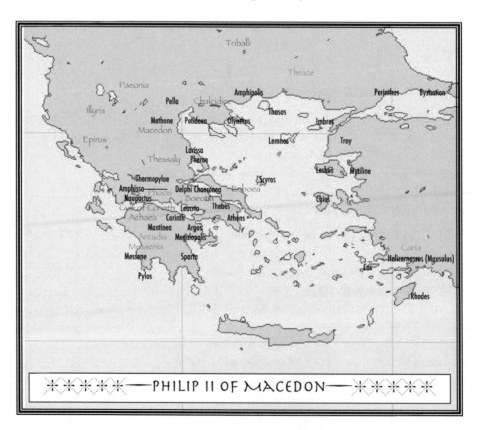

✳✳✳✳✳✳ ——PHILIP II OF MACEDON—— ✳✳✳✳✳✳

So ... Let's Get Busy

Philip was neither a slow learner nor a slow starter. His early campaigns focused on regaining Macedonian control over the western and northwestern regions of Macedon. To do this, he subdued both the Illyrians and the Paeonians, and formed an alliance with the Molossians in Epirus. In the east, he took Amphipolis by surprise (357 B.C.E.), which gave him control of the gold mines just over the Thracian border. These mines brought him about 1,000 talents a year (in Greek currency, 1 talent = 60 minae = 6,000 drachmae) and constituted the financial basis of his operations.

Although the Athenians declared war on Philip when he took Amphipolis, the Social War and their own financial difficulties kept them from sending troops or ships to oppose him, even when he took the cities of Potidaea (356 B.C.E.) and Methone (354 B.C.E.). Philip's control of these coastal cities further increased his revenues through trade and port taxes, and allowed him to build the ships necessary to interfere with Athenian commerce.

> **Odysseys**
>
> Methone (modern Modon) was where Philip, besieging the rebellious city, was struck in the eye by an arrow.

> **Eureka!**
>
> In Macedonian culture, polygamy was a socially-accepted practice, and Philip pursued diplomacy through marriage. He had seven wives, and only one of them, his last, was Macedonian. In 357 B.C.E., Philip married his fourth wife, Olympias, a noblewoman from Epirus, which gave him an important alliance in the west. The next year, Olympias bore Philip a son, Alexander.

The Silver Spears Head South

Macedonian involvement in central Greece began when Thebes and Phocis became embroiled in a battle for control of Delphi and the Amphictyony (the council that oversaw the shrine and the Pythian Games). Phocis was allied with Pherae, and Thebes with Thessaly. In 356 B.C.E., Thebes and her allies declared a Sacred War (the Third Sacred War) on the Phocians. Overmatched in forces, the Phocians seized Delphi, confiscated its enormous treasuries, and hired a large mercenary force. The Phocians' use of the Delphic treasuries, which included melting down vast repositories of dedications and statues, is one the world's great artistic disasters, but it allowed Phocis to hire a powerful army. Together with Pherae, the Phocians were able to drive out the Thebans and extend their dominance into Thessaly.

> **CAUTION**
>
> **Labyrinths** _____
>
> The Delphic Amphictyony fought four "sacred" wars to liberate (i.e., control) Delphi. In the First Sacred War (c. 601–591 B.C.E.) it took control of Delphi by defeating the neighboring city of Crisa. In the Second (448 B.C.E.) and Third (356–346 B.C.E.) Sacred Wars, it regained control from the Phocians. The Fourth Sacred War (339 B.C.E.), against the Locrians, gave Philip (leading the Amphictyony) his pretext to intervene decisively in central Greece.

Thebes and its Thessalian allies appealed to Philip and, although Phocian forces defeated Philip twice in 353 B.C.E., the tide began to turn. But, Philip had no intention of increasing Theban power. While fighting on the side of Thebes, Philip opened secret negotiations with Phocis. In return for surrender, Philip offered to forego the customary penalty for sacrilege (death to all males of military age) in lieu of repayment to Delphi, reorganization of Phocian territory, and the transfer of Phocis' votes in the Amphictyony to him (which gave him a majority). In 346 B.C.E., after having its forces crushed at Thermopylae, Phocis accepted the terms. That same year, Philip became the first Macedonian king to preside over the Pythian Games.

Demosthenes' Fears

In the meantime, Philip's power, ambitions, and accomplishments made him the subject of great debate in Athens. Athenians were split between two factions: one fiercely anti-Macedonian (led by the young orator Demosthenes) and one favoring constructive engagement (led by the orator Aeschines and the chief statesman of the day, Eubulus). In speeches that became known as the *Philippics*, Demosthenes denounced Philip's pernicious influence and imperialistic ambitions, and he repeatedly advised the Athenians to commit their resources to the creation of a force capable of both checking Philip and protecting their interests in the north Aegean. However, at the time, Athenian finances were restrained by Eubulus' creation of the *Theoric Fund*, which redirected surplus revenues to Athens' civic programs and to the poor. Although Demosthenes' assessment of the situation may have been correct, it is unlikely that—without the support of a united Greece—his proposed solution would have been successful.

> **Lexica** _____
>
> The **Theoric Fund** was created by Eubulus and held Athenian surpluses, which were used for public works and distributed to the poor. Besides easing civic tensions in Athens, the fund tended to make expensive military adventures less appealing to the lower classes.

Nonetheless, Athens did offer occasional—and mostly ineffectual—resistance, and it did send a large force to Thermopylae in 352 B.C.E. to block Philip's advance in the Third Sacred War. Even so, it wasn't until Philip attacked the city of Olynthus in 348 B.C.E. that Athenians glimpsed what might be their own future. When Olynthus grew fearful of Philip and abandoned its alliance with him, it sought to make peace with Athens. Olynthus sent desperate appeals for help to Athens, but, although Athens declared war on Macedon (again), it didn't have the resources to provide adequate or timely support. Philip razed Olynthus, sold its citizens into slavery in Macedon, and disbanded the Chalcidic (Olynthian) League. Philip now securely held Macedon, Northern Greece, Epirus, and the Chalcidice. Athens, still technically at war with Macedon, needed peace.

> **Eureka!**
>
> In 346 B.C.E. the Athenian orator Isocrates published *Philippus* (*Address to Philip*), a pamphlet that called on Philip to unite Greece in a military campaign against Persia. Although we don't know whether this work paralleled or inspired Philip's own designs, we do know that Philip began to make plans to invade Persia shortly thereafter.

The Peace of Philocrates ... or Not

In 346 B.C.E., the Athenian statesman Philocrates negotiated a lopsided peace treaty with Philip (the Peace of Philocrates). Each side agreed to the status quo, particularly as it pertained to their allies, but with very important exceptions. Athens gave up its longstanding claim to Amphipolis, and it permitted Philip to continue his battle with the Phocians, who were Athenian allies. Oddly enough, the Athenians seemed to believe that Philip would neither attack their Phocian allies nor intervene in central Greece. However, it was just after signing the treaty that Philip marched into central Greece and finished off the Third Sacred War.

After crushing the Phocian forces at Thermopylae, Philip negotiated the Phocian surrender, received their two votes in the Delphic Amphictyony, and enjoyed the honor of hosting the Pythian Games. Both Athens and Sparta refused to attend. Support for the Peace of Philocrates evaporated, and accusations of conspiracy with Philip were brought against Aeschines and Philocrates. In fact, Demosthenes brought Aeschines to trial in 343 B.C.E. and the speeches are famous examples of Greek rhetoric.

> **Labyrinths**
>
> Aeschines appears to have been the recipient of Philip's lavish generosity, both in Macedon and at the Pythian Games, where he was Philip's guest. Although it might be easy to condemn Aeschines' behavior in retrospect, we often accept the fact that modern dignitaries are frequently treated to banquets, private suites at sports stadiums, and other lavish gifts and perks.

Although Aeschines was acquitted by 30 votes, pro-Macedonian leaders were now in disrepute.

The End of the *Polis* as We Know It

Although his peace with Athens was disintegrating, Philip turned his attention to Thrace (342 B.C.E.), where he gained control of the northern Aegean coastline to the Hellespont. However, in 340 B.C.E., his siege of Perinthus was undermined by assistance from the Athenians and their allies (who were determined to keep the Macedonians from the Hellespont) and the Persians (who were anxious to keep the Macedonians from crossing it). Philip finally declared war on Athens, and Athens responded with yet another war declaration of its own. Although other operations prohibited Philip from engaging in open warfare with Athens for the next year, he captured the entire Black Sea grain fleet, which Athens depended on for food, sending Athens into a panic.

In 339 B.C.E., Philip received an invitation to enter central Greece and he leapt at the opportunity. The Delphic Amphictyony had declared war on Amphissa (in Locris), for cultivating ground that was consecrated to Apollo, and they offered command to Philip. Within a few months, the Amphictyony had defeated Amphissa, Philip's army was entrenched in Phocis, and the final showdown was imminent. Demosthenes attempted to form a pan-Hellenic alliance but, in the end, only Thebes, Corinth, Megara, Messenia, and a few other cities stood with Athens against Philip. Sparta, embittered by its degrading defeat at the hands of the other Greeks, spurned the call and turned its back.

The Battle of Chaeronea and the League of Corinth

The final (and only) battle took place in the summer of 338 B.C.E., at Chaeronea (in Boeotia). Roughly 37,000 Greeks met roughly 32,000 Macedonians in a battle that would, as it turns out, alter the course of history. Using tactics reminiscent of Leuctra (see Chapter 18), Philip brought his phalanx against the Greeks at an oblique angle, and then staged a feigned retreat of his right wing. When the overeager Greeks responded and gaps appeared in their lines, the Macedonians counterattacked.

Alexander, who was now 18 years old and in command of the left wing, led a decisive cavalry charge against the isolated Sacred Band and wiped it out. One thousand Athenians were killed and another 2,000 were taken captive.

Philip was now in charge of Greece. He treated Thebes harshly. However, because Athenian support would further his overall interests, he treated Athens leniently and with respect. The Athenian dead were sent back to Athens with an honor guard, led by Alexander and the general Antipater. Philip even allowed his opponent Demosthenes (who fought at Chaeronea) to deliver the funeral oration. In 337 B.C.E., Philip called the Greek states together at Corinth to learn of his future plans. Only the Spartans refused him.

> ### Muses
>
> When Philip saw the bodies of the Sacred Band and learned that it was a band of lovers, he shed tears and said, "Perish any man who suspects that these men either did or suffered anything that was base" (Plutarch, *Pelopidas*). A magnificent stone monument, the Lion of Chaeronea, was placed over their remains. The Lion (which once again watches over the grave) and 254 skeletons (laid out in 7 rows) were excavated in 1881.

Big Plans for Greece and Persia: The League of Corinth

At Corinth, Philip proposed an alliance of all Greeks, with a twofold purpose: to maintain a common peace among the Greeks and to retaliate against Persia for its hostilities against the Greeks. Although this alliance (known as the "League of Corinth") legitimized Philip's domination of Greece, it also established Greece as a federation and set the stage for Alexander's future conquests. Members agreed to maintain a common peace and to support one another against aggression, and to allow a "council" (*synedrion*) to pass binding decrees, settle disagreements by arbitration, and try individuals accused of betraying the league.

With Philip elected as *hêgemôn*, or "leader," the league looked toward an invasion of Persia. These plans, which so closely resembled Isocrates' earlier solution to Greek instability, were well timed to take advantage of Persian instability. When the Macedonian general Parmenio led an advance force across the Hellespont in 336 B.C.E., various Greek cities in Asia Minor revolted and allied with Philip, and preparations were made for a massive land assault of Persia.

For Whom the (Wedding) Bell Tolls

But Philip never made it to Persia. In 338 B.C.E., Philip had married Cleopatra, a Macedonian princess. Although his fourth wife, Olympias, had borne Philip's designated heir, Alexander, and although she had always ruled over his other wives, this marriage threatened the planned succession, and Olympias and Alexander went into exile. However, when Cleopatra bore a daughter, Europa, Philip and Alexander were reconciled. (Olympias remained in exile.)

> **Odysseys**
>
> In 1977–1980, archeologists working in Vergina (northern Greece) uncovered two enormous, treasure-filled Macedonian tombs that dated to the fourth century B.C.E. The cremated remains appear to be those of Philip II (the skull shows signs of an injured right eye socket) and Alexander's assassinated son, Alexander IV.

Even with the reconciliation, family problems remained. Pausanias, a male relative of Cleopatra, had been brutally raped and abused by the servants of Cleopatra's uncle, Attalus. Apparently, Pausanias had slandered a young relative of Attalus (because Philip had chosen him as a lover), and the young man had been killed. Pausanias despised Philip for failing to halt the abuse. Although Philip tried to placate him by promoting him to a "king's companion," Pausanias took his opportunity for revenge at the marriage of Philip's daughter in 336 B.C.E. As Philip led a grand procession, Pausanias leapt from the crowd and stabbed Philip to death. Thus, Philip's plans were left to his son and heir, Alexander, whose even grander plans would take him all the way to the Himalayas.

The Least You Need to Know

- In the second half of the fourth century B.C.E., a young Macedonian king, Philip II, transformed Macedon into the next world power.

- Philip reorganized Macedon's army, weaponry, and military strategy, and created a formidable fighting machine.

- Philip gained control of Macedon, Northern Greece, the Aegean coastline, Chalcidice, and Epirus before conquering central Greece.

- In 338 B.C.E., Philip defeated a combined Greek force at Chaeronea to take control of Greece.

- As leader, Philip united the Greek states in the League of Corinth, and prepared to invade Persia, but he was murdered in 336 B.C.E., before his plans could be realized.

Life, Literature, and Culture in the Twilight of the *Polis*

In This Chapter

- Changes in the life of the *polis*
- Comic tensions in Menander
- Plato and Aristotle on reality and knowledge
- The emerging roles of rhetoric

The fourth century B.C.E. saw the end of the *polis* as an independent, autonomous political entity. By Alexander's death (323 B.C.E.), the *poleis* were relatively insignificant members of a new world state dominated by Macedon, and the transformation was neither easy nor smooth. Thebes was destroyed and Sparta faded to a relic. However, Athens retained its cultural and intellectual vigor, along with some of its former stature, even though it opposed Macedon.

Although the fourth century B.C.E. was a period of political instability, it was also a period of intellectual and artistic growth and maturation. Rhetoric, art, philosophy, and the sciences all developed in scope, depth, and complexity. In addition, as the Classical *poleis* underwent political changes, their underlying social structures were forced to change as well. In this chapter, we will examine some of the cultural and intellectual developments that mark the turbulent transformation from the Classical to the Hellenistic period. Once again, our information about this period comes primarily from Athenian sources.

The Times They Are A-Changing

Philip and Alexander created new, overarching political structures that, for the most part, eliminated the potential for armed conflict between, and internal meddling among, the major *poleis*. Until these structures were in place, however, stasis and political instability were commonplace throughout Greece. In many cities, the economic devastation of the Peloponnesian War resulted in factions of "democratic" under classes pitted against upper class, wealthy "oligarchic" factions. The factional struggles for power—which were exacerbated by internal and external pressures and competing Athenian, Spartan, Theban, and Macedonian interests—drained and diverted the internal vitality of the *poleis*.

Meanwhile, the broad social fabric of both the *oikos* and the *polis* were altered by the widespread dislocation of families, the loss of male heads of households to war, and pervasive civil strife. In general, both individuals and families became alienated from the larger social structures and ideologies that had nurtured, supported, and controlled them. Many citizen men, forced out of traditional agricultural work, became mercenaries; others became increasingly dependent upon the state; and still others moved into manufacturing jobs or trades traditionally held by *metics*. Citizen women were more frequently forced to work outside of the home (e.g., as nurses, weavers, and so on), as the traditional structures of the *oikos* became weakened and less able to economically sustain the households. Overall, at every level of Classical society and culture, rigid traditions and cultural boundaries were blurring and breaking down. Although this trend allowed for the possibility of individualism, it was also accompanied by personal isolation and loss of control. Moreover, Macedonian political and military domination not only undercut the already weakened civic and political structures, it eliminated the need for city-states to produce and train citizen-soldiers as well. This, in turn, led to a kind of identity crisis for both states and citizens. If the purpose of the citizen was not to defend and support the *polis* (in war and by having legitimate children) what was it? If the *dêmos* was not sovereign, what could be gained by taking an active role in the *polis*? Yet, Athenian politicians and playwrights continued to affirm the value of legitimate citizens, democratic *poleis*, and the relationship between the two.

From Satire to the *Simpsonidae:* Moving Toward Menander and the New Comedy of Everyman

The changing dynamics of the *polis* and *oikos* were reflected in the progression from the "Old" comedies of Aristophanes (c. 450–385 B.C.E.) to the "New" comedies of Menander (c. 344–292 B.C.E.), one of the most famous writers of antiquity. Although we don't possess any of the comedies that were written in the interim between these two playwrights, we know that Athenian comedy became something of an export in the fourth century B.C.E. In the process, it moved beyond the largely topical confines of Athens to confront issues of concern to a wider Greek audience. For example, Menander's plays were social situation comedies, filled with representative fathers, sons, wives, slaves, doctors, hookers, and soldiers, all caught in troubles of their own making that modern audiences would easily recognize from contemporary sitcoms.

Whereas Aristophanes' comedies encouraged the *dêmos* to make changes in the world, Menander's comedies encouraged individuals to return to traditional structures (i.e., an *oikos* of a democratic *polis* based upon citizen birth). This return was not advocated as a means to defending the state, however, or to making peace with Sparta, or even to becoming conscious of world affairs. Instead, it was advanced as the means to personal happiness and fulfillment, usually in the form of reuniting lovers and families within their "proper" context. Audiences watched and laughed at the personal foibles, illicit ambitions, and inappropriate quirks of misguided individuals who would eventually recognize the error of their ways.

> ## Muses
>
> Menander's plays, like those of Shakespeare, provide us with hundreds of pithy sayings and proverbs. Many of them survived the loss of his plays in lists of one-liners (*Monostikoi*) and quotations. Here are a few:
>
> "Bad company ruins good morals." (*Thais*)
>
> "He whom the gods love dies young." (*Double-deceiver*)
>
> "I call a fig a fig, a spade, a spade." (Fragment)
>
> "Riches cover a multitude of woes." (*Lady of Andros*)
>
> "He who runs may live to fight again." (*Monostikoi*)

Thus, although Menander's plays were not political in the manner of Aristophanes' plays, they can be seen as comedic reactions to the breakdown of Classical social and political structures. In the meantime, two preeminent Classical philosophers, both working by the dying light of the *polis*, were formulating complex philosophical theories concerning the nature of reality, knowledge, and the good life for humans.

Asking the Big Questions: Plato and Aristotle

Both Plato and his most illustrious student, Aristotle, were deeply interested in (among other things) ethics and politics. However, before they could answer questions about living well or governing well, they had to address questions about the nature of reality and knowledge. For example, how can one *know* what is good or just if one is unable to distinguish between knowledge (which is absolute and unchanging) and opinion (which can be erroneous, unreliable, or poorly informed)? Moreover, how can one distinguish between knowledge and opinion if one cannot explain what knowledge *is*, what things humans can have knowledge of, and how humans gain knowledge? Worse yet, how can one explain any of these things without addressing the nature of reality (that is, what exists, what remains constant, what changes, whether our senses provide us with accurate and reliable information, and so forth)? See the problem?

In addressing these questions (and many others!), Plato and Aristotle took different pathways to very different conclusions. For example, in several allegories (especially in the *Republic*), Plato divided reality into the intelligible (i.e., that which we can apprehend with our intellect) and the sensible (i.e., that which we can experience with our senses), and he argued that we can have knowledge only of the intelligible, unchanging aspects of reality. Aristotle, on the other hand, who was a scientist as well as a philosopher, grounded his approach to reality in both the natural world and philosophical speculation.

In the following sections, we will look briefly at the lives and thoughts of both Plato and Aristotle. However, a very large caution is in order! Because of their complexity, depth, and breadth, it is impossible to encapsulate the works of Plato and Aristotle. Indeed, it takes years of reading and study to gain a comprehensive understanding of these philosophers, and scholars still discuss their voluminous texts at length. So here, we will give you only a glimpse of their different approaches to the nature of reality and knowledge. For more information on Plato and Aristotle, see Chapter 3.

CAUTION

Labyrinths

Although many high school and college students read Aristotle's *Nicomachean Ethics* (his primary ethical treatise), it is difficult to comprehend Aristotle's ethical approach without also reading his *Politics*, *Metaphysics*, *Physics*, *Rhetoric*, and *De Anima* (*On the Soul*). Still, it's better to read only one text than none at all!

Pi in the Sky: Plato

Plato was born c. 428 B.C.E. to aristocratic parents. Given his aristocratic family, Plato was surely expected to take an active (and perhaps prominent) role in Athenian politics. In fact, he was invited by the Thirty Tyrants (some of whom were friends and relatives) to join them. However, in his *Seventh Letter* (written when he was over 70 years old), Plato tells us that the rule of the Thirty "made the former constitution seem like a golden age by comparison." The policies of the Thirty, in combination with their demand that Socrates bring in a fellow citizen for execution, made Plato reluctant to participate. When the democracy was restored, Plato once again (but quite hesitantly this time) considered a life in politics. However, after the trial and execution of Socrates, Plato gave up all political aspirations—though he never gave up considering ways to improve and reform the constitution itself. Thus, Plato turned from public affairs to philosophy, and he eventually founded the Academy in Athens, which was probably the first European university, and in which philosophy, mathematics, politics, psychology, and aesthetics were studied. He died in 348–347 B.C.E. at the age of 81, and his influence on the development of philosophy, religion, and human inquiry cannot be overstated.

Eureka!

At 40 years old, Plato traveled to Italy and Sicily. In Sicily, he befriended Dion, the brother-in-law of Dionysus I, tyrant of Sicily. This friendship, and Plato's influence on Dion, angered Dionysus. As the story goes, Dionysus turned over Plato to be sold into slavery! Plato was rescued from the slave market and returned to Athens. Apparently, Plato made another trip to Sicily, after the death of Dionysus I, to instruct the tyrant's adult son, Dionysus II.

It is well known that Plato was influenced, personally and philosophically, by Socrates. However, as a philosopher, he was also influenced by Cratylus (a follower of Heraclitus and Plato's long-time acquaintance), Parmenides (whose follower, Eucleides, Plato appears to have known), and Pythagoras (whose followers he might have visited in Italy and Sicily). (See Chapters 3 and 10 for more information on Heraclitus, Parmenides, and Pythagoras.)

Heraclitean philosophers believed that everything is in a state of flux, or ever-changing. And Plato himself argued that sensible objects and qualities (i.e., things that are perceived by the senses) are mutable and in flux, which makes them unsuitable as sources of knowledge. But, if this is the case, what is the basis for knowledge? And if things such as virtue and justice are also in flux, how can there be ethical knowledge?

Plato answered these questions by suggesting that there is a stable, unchanging realm of reality, the intelligible realm, which is separate from the ever-changing world that our senses reveal to us. On this view, knowledge is of the intelligible forms of things, rather than of sensible objects and their characteristics. But, if this is the case, how do we know the forms, how do we define them, and how do they give determinate being to sensible objects?

Plato argued that we know the forms through recollection. On this theory, our souls have contact with the forms (and, thus, with knowledge) prior to birth; however, we forget the knowledge when our souls are embodied at birth. Through education, study, and dialectical conversation, we "recollect" knowledge, rather than learn it. We gradually come to understand that sensible objects "participate" in the forms by resembling them (as imperfect copies that have additional, but superfluous, qualities and characteristics). For example, although a tabletop might participate in the form "rectangle," it will also have sensible qualities such as color and texture that are not part of the form "rectangle."

Because definitions of the forms could not involve these sensible characteristics, Plato (following Pythagoras) looked toward precise mathematical terminology (e.g., numbers and ratios) for the purposes of definition. For example, because the ratios that underlie the relations between successive notes in the enharmonic, harmonic, and chromatic scales had been discovered, might it be possible to discover the ratios that underlie other relations (and to frame definitions in terms of these mathematical properties)? In any case, knowledge for Plato is apprehended by pure reason, and it is of the universal and unchanging concepts that exist in the intelligible realm of reality.

Down in the Dirt: Aristotle

Aristotle was born in 384 B.C.E., in Stagira, of a wealthy family, which had connections to the Macedonian royal court. At around 17 years old, Aristotle was sent by his family to study at Plato's Academy. He remained there, as a pupil and teacher, for the next 20 years. During his adulthood, Aristotle tutored Alexander the Great, founded the Lyceum in Athens, and worked prodigiously. Only about one fifth to one quarter of Aristotle's works survive, and these texts are his lecture notes and working drafts. Although ancient sources describe Aristotle's (now lost) published works as eloquent and literary, his surviving texts are difficult, compact, and occasionally incomprehensible.

Following the death of Alexander the Great, Athens became hostile to residents with Macedonian connections, and Aristotle was accused of impiety—the same charge leveled at Anaxagoras and Socrates. He left Athens, reportedly saying that he would not allow Athens to sin twice against philosophy. He died at the age of 62 in 322 B.C.E. in Chalcis, a Macedonian stronghold and the birthplace of his mother.

Aristotle had a profound interest in knowledge of all kinds, and he is the father of botany, zoology, physics, linguistics, logic, and literary criticism, to name a few. Many of his ideas on ethics, politics, logic, and literary criticism remain highly relevant today, and for the breadth of his work, the depth of his intellect, and the scope of his influence (on philosophy, science, and religion), he is quite possibly without equal in the history of human inquiry.

> **Eureka!**
>
> Aristotle married Pythias, the niece and adopted daughter of Hermias, ruler of Atarneus (on Assos). After Pythias died in Athens, Aristotle began a relationship with Herpyllis, also a native of Stagira, but they apparently never married. Their son, Nicomachus (named for Aristotle's father) edited Aristotle's treatise on ethics, the *Nicomachean Ethics*, which bears his name.

As we said, Aristotle was both a scientist and a philosopher, and he combined features of both empiricism and rationalism to examine topics as diverse as the physiology of crustaceans and the principle of non-contradiction. Depending upon the nature of his investigation, (whether, for example, he was discussing a theoretical or a practical science), he emphasized either speculation (and deduction from axiomatic first principles) or observation (and induction from particulars to first principles, or universals). In addition, Aristotle carefully reviewed the theories of his predecessors—especially the Presocratics and Plato—and retained, usually with considerable revision, some aspects of their opinions or accounts.

To describe the natural world, Aristotle sought to identify the entities that exist independently, and to separate them from mere qualities or characteristics of such entities. In a highly complex theory, Aristotle claimed that independently existing entities are called "substances." Primary substances are individual specimens (e.g., a human being, a horse, or a tree), and secondary substances are the species to which individual specimens belong. For example, an individual man is a substance, but so, too, is his species, *Homo sapiens*. In fact, because all individual entities are made from materials that could have been combined into any number of things, each individual entity of a specific kind must be a combination of both materials and form (a blueprint of sorts, or universal principle, which is not separate from its material instantiation). So, it is by way of form and matter that a human is a human rather than, say, a chimpanzee. For example, in modern terms, we could say that although human beings and chimpanzees share roughly 99 percent of their DNA and numerous chemicals (materials), they are, nonetheless, separate species (by way of their form and the arrangement of their matter). In contrast to substances, qualities and traits (such as color and courage) do not have independent existence; there is no such thing for Aristotle as disembodied "whiteness" or courage.

In addition, for Aristotle, a complete explanation of something—whether an object or an action—that undergoes change will include all four of its "causes": its formal cause (universal principle), material cause (the stuff of which it's made), efficient cause (the source of change), and the final cause (its end or purpose). For example, a house has a formal cause (the design or structure given in its plan), a material cause (wood, nails, and so forth), an efficient cause (the builder), and a final cause (giving shelter).

Moreover, in the natural world, all things have an end goal or purpose (final cause). For example, by their nature as humans, all persons seek *eudaimonia* (usually translated as "happiness"), or living well and flourishing. In like manner, other living creatures have purposes that are internal to them (generally, thriving as a specimen of a particular species), although artifacts have purposes that are external to them, in the sense that the purpose of an artifact is determined by its inventor or manufacturer. Thus, although Aristotle's natural universe is teleological (from *telos*, "end, goal, or purpose"), it would be an error to identify all final causes or purposes with internal, conscious intentions.

This discussion is just the tippy-top of a very large iceberg! Even a summary of Aristotle's view of the nature of reality could fill every page of this book! But in short, for Aristotle, understanding the nature of reality (and, thus, knowledge) requires both speculation and observation, a correct approach to the subject matter at hand, and sophisticated systems of classification. Although comprehending mathematical axioms, for example, which are unchanging, requires speculation, achieving human excellence requires virtue, practical judgment, and experience.

Speak Up! The Age of Orators and Rhetoricians

As the influence of comedy and tragedy waned within the *polis*, the power and influence of rhetoric—as a medium through which to explore and confront issues of immediate public concern—grew in their place. Rhetoric emerged as a tool of communication through which ideas and aspirations could be effectively expressed and hopefully realized. From the wide range of orations left from this period, we know a great deal about actual events and the lives of real people. Here, we will focus on the practice of and approach to rhetoric of three famous rhetoricians.

> **CAUTION** **Labyrinths** _____
>
> Greek rhetoric distinguished between three kinds of oratory: "deliberative" (*sumbouleutikon*), for making decisions (such as in the assembly); "forensic" (*dikanikon*), for establishing guilt or innocence (in court); and "epideictic" (*epideiktikon*), for bestowing praise or blame (in a more general venue). Examples of each can be found in the orators and all three kinds are discussed by Aristotle in the *Rhetoric*.

The Practice of Persuasion

The literature of the fifth century B.C.E. shows a growing awareness and use of rhetoric and the techniques of argumentation. In part, rhetoric developed in response to the practical necessities of individual participation in the courts and political life of the *polis*. In this sense, rhetoric came to be seen as a practical tool that was vitally necessary to both individual citizens and the *polis*. Additionally, as a result of increased literacy in the late fifth and fourth centuries B.C.E., orators' speeches were compared and analyzed, often with an eye to the aesthetics of rhetoric as an art. Here we focus on three great orators, whose influential works came to represent three rhetorical styles. For more information on Greek rhetoric and rhetoricians, see Chapter 2.

Lysias (c. 445–380 B.C.E.) was a wealthy Athenian *metic* from Syracuse, whose family was invited by Pericles to move to Athens. Lysias and his brother Polemarchus were among the first victims of the Thirty Tyrants. Their property was confiscated, Polemarchus was executed, and Lysias barely escaped to Megara, where he helped the Athenian exiles. Once he returned to Athens, he became a speechwriter, famous for capturing the personality and character of his clients in highly effective speeches, such as the one he wrote for a crippled man, who was defending his state pension. His own speeches, such as his prosecution of Eratosthenes for the murder of his brother, are works of passion and genius. Lysias' brilliant, clear, and understandable orations came to represent the "simple" or "plain" style of rhetoric.

Isocrates (436–338 B.C.E.) followed the sophists in advancing rhetoric as a practical tool of political success. The long-lived orator knew Socrates, studied with sophists such as Gorgias, and lived to see Philip conquer Greece. Like Lysias, Isocrates fled the Thirty Tyrants, but later returned to Athens. There, he wrote speeches for clients and opened a school for highly select pupils (who were to be the future leaders of Greece). The school was, in a way, the West's first combination Think Tank and public relations firm. Isocrates considered himself a teacher of philosophy—but philosophy of a practical nature, which was concerned with contemporary affairs and problems—and he taught rhetorical composition in combination with practical

Muses

Isocrates and Lysias are discussed in Plato's dialogues, and both knew Socrates. Socrates predicts a bright future for Isocrates in the *Phaedrus* (and claims that Isocrates has a greater genius and finer character than Lysias), and the *Republic* takes place in Cephalus' (Lysias' father's) house in Piraeus, with Lysias in attendance. Lysias' brother Polemarchus and Cephalus are two of the first speakers to engage Socrates.

moral and political theory. Both Isocrates and the alumni of his school worked to promote their own interests—such as a unified Greek campaign against Persia—and they became very successful and influential. Because Isocrates was a poor speaker, he focused on highly polished literary orations (such as the *Archidamus* and *Philippus*), which were circulated as persuasive pamphlets. These fluid and rhythmical speeches came to represent what was later known as the "middle" or "smooth" style of rhetoric.

The orator and statesman **Demosthenes** (384–322 B.C.E.) was (and is) the most famous Greek orator. Demosthenes, who overcame a speech impediment, wrote speeches for clients, and became the chief spokesman (sometimes the only spokesman) against Philip II. Like Isocrates, Demosthenes published polished speeches that were intended to influence public opinion and enhance his reputation. Demosthenes was a master of adapting and blending various stylistic elements in order to create forceful and provocative speeches. This style became known as the "grand" or "high" style. Unlike Isocrates, however, Demosthenes considered himself an orator rather than a philosopher, and a patriot rather than a pragmatist. While Macedonian forces were hunting down and executing anti-Macedonians, Demosthenes fled Athens and committed suicide. As the story goes, he drank the poison that he always carried in his pen.

Rhetoric and the Search for Truth

The application of theory to rhetoric took place alongside, and in conjunction with, other sciences and practices. We know from Plato's writings that there were fifth century B.C.E. handbooks that explained how to compose effective court or assembly speeches, and the sophists provided rhetorical training that was largely focused on practical success in these same areas. Isocrates approached rhetoric as, primarily, a tool of civic discourse, whose effectiveness depended upon the skill and character of the craftsman. He wrote on the practical techniques of composition, and his approaches—such as the stages of invention, arrangement, and style (revision)—still form the

Labyrinths

Isocrates' teachings on education had a greater influence on the practice of western education from the Hellenistic period until the eighteenth century than did the works of Plato and Aristotle.

bedrock of most college English composition courses. Aristotle completed a much more comprehensive formulation of the function of rhetoric and the modes of persuasion in his work, the *Rhetoric*.

Despite its practical uses, rhetoric and argumentation were also used to present and promote scientific and philosophical theories, and these uses suggested that it was (or could be) a tool of discovery and a means of finding truth. Nonetheless, the amoral and immoral uses of rhetoric (e.g., making the weaker argument appear stronger, or successfully promoting an unjust cause) disturbed many Greeks, including Socrates, Plato, Isocrates, and Aristotle. Their shared dissatisfaction, however, led them in different directions. For example, in dialogues such as the *Gorgias* and *Phaedrus*, Plato argued that rhetoric must be grounded in philosophy, so that the soul may be led in the proper direction. Isocrates rejected this approach, and asserted that immediate public affairs should be the philosopher's primary concern. To Isocrates, the use of rhetoric should not, and could not, depend on either the lumbering search for truth or the souls of the audience. In some ways, Aristotle's approach lay between these two extremes. Aristotle recognized and addressed rhetoric's practical uses (including the fact that, although rhetoric should be used virtuously, it was often used otherwise), and he formulated a theory of rhetoric that incorporated reason, emotion, and character as modes of persuasion.

Even today, the tensions between these approaches to rhetoric and argumentation are evident in education, politics, and the media.

The Least You Need to Know

- By Alexander's death (323 B.C.E.), the *poleis* were relatively insignificant members of a new world state dominated by Macedon.

- As the *poleis* and *oikoi* underwent significant changes, citizens became alienated from the larger social structures and ideologies that had nurtured, supported, and controlled them.

- The changing dynamics of the period were reflected in the progression from the "Old" comedies of Aristophanes to the "New" comedies of Menander (c. 344–292 B.C.E.).

- Plato and Aristotle took different pathways to very different conclusions, but both had a profound effect on the future of philosophy and religion, and, in the case of Aristotle, science.

- Rhetoric emerged as a tool of communication through which ideas and aspirations could be effectively expressed and hopefully realized.

21

Boy Wonder: Alexander the Great and His Conquests

In This Chapter

- ◆ Alexander's early life and conquests
- ◆ The conquest of the Persian Empire
- ◆ Troubles and trials in Bactria and India
- ◆ Alexander's vision for himself and his empire

Although Alexander III of Macedon came to be known as Alexander the Great, even the title "the Great" is insufficient to describe a life, legend, and personality that blur the borders of fact, fantasy, history, and myth.

Even the barest outline of Alexander's life suggests an extraordinary individual. For example, as an adolescent, Alexander was tutored by Aristotle; from youth onward, he rode the legendary horse Bucephalus; at the age of 16, he became a battlefield commander and achieved his first victory; at age 20, he was crowned king of Macedon; and, by the age of 32, he had conquered a significant portion of the world. Even in his own lifetime, people struggled to distinguish fact from fiction and metaphor from megalomania, and, to this day, we remain uncertain as to whether these distinctions were clear in Alexander's own mind.

The search for the historical Alexander is complicated by the fact that the sources for his life—the *Alexander Romance* (authorship uncertain), Plutarch, Diodorus, Pompeius Trogus, Quintus Curtius Rufus, and Arrian—were writing long after his time. Arrian is probably the most reliable source, because his account is based, in part, on the lost memoir of Alexander's general, Ptolemy. In contrast, the *Alexander Romance*, which was enormously popular even into the Middle Ages, embellished basic facts with elaborate fantasy.

Whereas Alexander's father, Philip II, was (and is) often seen as a man of personal and professional excesses, cunning disloyalty, and brutal violence, Alexander's own life was (and is) often viewed through a filter of admiration and wonder. Yet, in many ways, Alexander was his father's son. Both men took advantage of all available means to achieve adventure, conquest, and victory. Both possessed the ability to blend and mold traditions, and both met challenges with creative and decisive action. And both men led lives that were characterized by excess. By living on the edge, and by continuously challenging the boundaries of physical, social, cultural, and personal norms, both men contributed to their untimely deaths. So, in this chapter, we'll try to capture both the legend and the life of Philip II's son, Alexander the Great.

Early Alexander

By the time of Philip's assassination, Alexander had already led a remarkable life. Born in 356 B.C.E., the son of Olympias (Philip's fourth wife), Alexander was Philip's designated heir (except for a brief period when Philip's marriage to Cleopatra, a Macedonian, placed the succession in jeopardy). In addition to his cavalry training, Alexander was tutored by one of the world's greatest philosophers, Aristotle. In 343 B.C.E., Philip called Aristotle—whose father, Nicomachus, had served as court physician to Philip's father, Amyntas III—to teach his 13-year-old son. For about three years, Alexander studied political science, ethics, science, and literature under Aristotle, and he gained an appreciation of Homer. Indeed, it is said that Alexander always slept with Aristotle's annotated copy of the *Iliad* and a knife under his pillow.

Alexander also gained a strong sense of his own connections with his mythological ancestors, Achilles and Heracles. (Alexander's mother was a member of the royal house of Epirus, which claimed Achilles as an ancestor; Alexander's father was a member of the

> **CAUTION**
>
> **Labyrinths**
>
> It is reported that, during his campaigns in Asia, Alexander sent plant and animal specimens to his former tutor, Aristotle, to assist his botanical and zoological studies. Beyond these stories, however, we have little evidence of Aristotle's influence on Alexander, and no record of Aristotle's reaction to Alexander's execution of Callisthenes—Alexander's official field historian and Aristotle's nephew.

royal Macedonian family, which claimed descent from Heracles.) These legendary heroes—one, the preeminent Greek warrior against Troy, and the other, the explorer and tamer of wild lands beyond the Greek horizon—had a profound impact on Alexander's conceptualization of himself and his place in history. Although Aristotle discussed such things as ethics, colonization, and monarchy with Alexander, we are left to wonder whether these teachings made much of an impression upon the young prince. For comparison, imagine a 13-year-old boy, descended by tradition from J.R.R. Tolkein's Princes of Gondor or Elves of Rivendell. Then give him a copy of Tolkein's trilogy *The Lord of the Rings* and a textbook on political science and see which one leaves a greater mark.

> ### Eureka!
>
> Bucephalus ("Ox-brow") was Alexander's famous war horse. According to tradition, when Philip's trainers were unable to tame the fierce black stallion, Alexander (about 10 years old) asked to try. To everyone's astonishment, the horse allowed Alexander to approach and mount him. Bucephalus carried Alexander into every major battle until, in 326 B.C.E., he was killed in battle at the Hydaspes River. Alexander erected an enormous tomb and founded a city, Bucephala, in his honor.

In 340 B.C.E., at the age of 16, Alexander became Macedonian Regent (ruling representative) while Philip was besieging Byzantion, and he began commanding a wing of cavalry (he remained a cavalry commander throughout his career). He was victorious against a Thracian rebellion and, two years later at Chaeronea, he helped defeat the Greeks. When Philip was assassinated in 336 B.C.E., Alexander was the heir apparent, but his position was far from secure. Besides having to cope with pretenders to the throne, Alexander was surrounded by hostile regional forces, which hoped to take advantage of any instability.

Getting a Grip

Alexander's decisive movements in the first year of his rule both secured his place as king of Macedon and foreshadowed his characteristically aggressive approach to problem solving. Quickly, Alexander gained the support of Philip's chief general, Antipater, who presented him to the army for acclamation as king. With the allegiance of the army, Alexander had the allegiance of Macedon. He executed the conspirators and returned to Greece before anti-Macedonian forces in Athens and Thebes could mobilize. He replaced Philip as *hêgemôn* of the League of Corinth, archon of Thessaly, and commander of the war against Persia. He then departed to secure the Macedonian borders, campaigning northward to the Danube against the

Triballi, and, barely but decisively, defeating the Illyrians in the southwest. By then, however, trouble was brewing, once again, in Greece.

Rebellion? Not a Good Plan

Fueled in part by rumors that Alexander had been killed (he was, in fact, wounded while fighting the Illyrians), Thebes rebelled. It called on other Greek states to join the rebellion and Athens voted to send military aid. But when Alexander, who had been informed of the events, suddenly arrived at Thebes with his army, the Athenians, along with the rest of Greece, held back.

Just as Philip had once made an example of Olynthus, Alexander now made one of Thebes. When the Thebans refused to surrender, Alexander captured and razed the entire city—except for the temples and the home and descendants of the poet Pindar—to the ground. Roughly 6,000 Thebans were killed and about 30,000 others, mostly women and children, were sold into slavery.

Although other Greek cities had suffered the same fate during earlier wars, the destruction of Thebes was considered an atrocity of enormous proportions. In the wake of such an event, Alexander could afford to be lenient toward the other Greek states. Leaving Antipater behind—in a now pacified Greece—to manage supplies and reinforcements, Alexander departed for Persia (334 B.C.E.) with a combined Macedonian-Greek force of about 32,000 soldiers and 5,100 cavalry, and a train of siege equipment. He would need it all, and more, during the next 11 years.

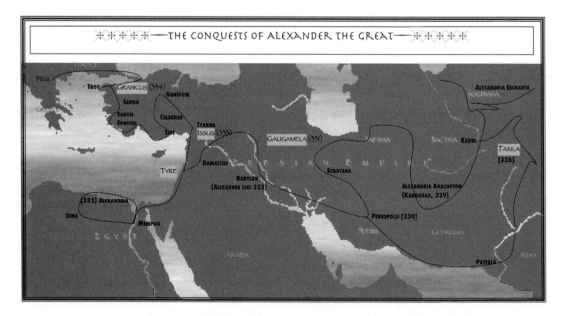

Asia Minor? Knot a Problem

With a dramatic flourish, Alexander first visited Troy to pay homage to his ancestor Achilles and to request that Priam, the ancient king of Troy, pardon him for invading Asia. Then, having defeated a small Persian army at the Granicus River, he took Persian-controlled cities one by one. He maintained administrative control over them, and he made their tribute, formerly paid to Persian overlords, payable to him. In Greek cities, although he eventually supported democratic governments and abolished Persian taxes, he required "contributions" toward his military campaign.

In Caria, he gave civil control to Queen Ada, who adopted him as her son and heir, but he left military control in the hands of a Macedonian commander.

Thus, by 333 B.C.E., when he took Gordium and "solved" the *Gordian Knot*, it was clear to everyone that Alexander intended to do much more than "liberate" (which had taken on a whole new meaning!) the Greeks. Yet, resistance in Greece was stifled by the mobilization of a Persian army, under King Darius III, which was nearly twice the size of Alexander's army. The two armies finally met at Issus (Iskendrun, Turkey).

> **Lexica**
>
> The **Gordian Knot** was attached to the ancient wagon of the legendary King Midas of Phrygia, in the capital, Gordium. Legend claimed that the person who could untie the impossibly intricate knot would rule Asia. Alexander, faced with the conundrum, decisively cut through the knot with a sword.

Guess Who's Coming to Dinner

At Issus, although the Persian army had the upper hand, Darius fled when Alexander and his cavalry charged his position. The remainder of the Persian army lost heart, and those soldiers who weren't slaughtered followed their king. Alexander captured the camp at Issus, in which Darius' wife and family were awaiting his return, and he took the royal family as hostages. Shortly thereafter, he captured the royal treasury at Damascus, which ended his financial concerns, and he rejected the humiliated king's offers of alliance in exchange for his family. However, Alexander is said to have treated Darius' family honorably, and even to have developed a friendship with Darius' mother.

Instead of pursuing Darius, Alexander moved down the Mediterranean seaboard, cutting off resistance and depriving the Persian fleet of its land bases. Most of the Syrian and Phoenician cities submitted, but Tyre, a previously impregnable city, became a major obstacle. The Tyrians rejected Alexander's request to enter the city, and they threw his ambassadors over the walls. Alexander was not amused.

This restored mosaic from Pompeii (now in the Museo Archeologico Nazionale in Naples) probably depicts the battle of Issus; details are enlargements of Darius and Alexander.

(Photos courtesy of Rochelle Snee)

After a brutal and protracted siege, which lasted eight months, Alexander took Tyre, in part, by constructing a huge mole (a jetty, at least 200 feet wide and 20 feet high) to connect the mainland with the island fortress. This engineering feat was a mark of the determination and innovation that characterized Alexander's conquests. However, it was the arrival of about 120 warships from Cyprus and about 80 from Phoenicia that ultimately secured Alexander's victory. For resisting, the Tyrians suffered the same fate as the Thebans. Quite consistently, Alexander made sure that his adversaries could count upon two things: brutal treatment if they resisted and more lenient treatment if they capitulated.

> **Odysseys**
>
> You can still walk upon the famous mole (jetty) that Alexander built during the long siege of 332 B.C.E. to conquer the island city of Tyre (southern Lebanon). However, over the centuries, it has grown into a broad land bridge crowned with buildings.

About this time, ambassadors from Darius arrived with an offer of marriage, complete with dowry. Darius offered Alexander his daughter in marriage, 10,000 talents for the return of his family, all lands west of the Euphrates, and his friendship and alliance. Against the advice of Philip's general, Parmenio, Alexander rejected the offer. After all, he could have most of those things anyway. While Alexander headed for Egypt, Darius continued to raise another army and prepare for what was to come.

The Incredible Journey

From early childhood, Alexander's mother had encouraged her son to develop an exalted self-image by claiming that there was something divine about his birth. And, regardless of what Alexander originally believed about his heritage, he apparently began to conceive of himself as something extraordinary in the model of his semi-divine, mythological ancestors, Heracles and Achilles. With his appearance at Troy, Alexander publicly linked himself with that mythological ancestry.

As time went on, he began to conduct himself like a semidivine hero, with a hero's fate, a hero's parentage, and a hero's destiny. However, scholars disagree as to whether Alexander's vision drove his accomplishments or explained them (even to himself), and as to whether Alexander used it to transcend the limits of both Greek and barbarian traditions or to merely transcend the limits of traditional public relations devices.

 Muses

[Alexander] used to say that, more than anything else, sleep and sex made him conscious that he was mortal because both weariness and pleasure had their common origin in natural weakness.

—Plutarch, *Alexander*, 22.3

Ammonly Human?

Egypt, which was more than happy to be free of Persian rule, fell to Alexander without a fight. Alexander was crowned Pharaoh in 332 B.C.E. (just as the Persian kings had been). He appointed local (Egyptian) governors to rule the country under Macedonian financial and military control (a scheme that was becoming customary), which gave him enormous financial resources.

While Alexander was in Egypt, two significant events took place. Alexander founded the city of Alexandria on the Nile delta, and he traveled across the sands of Libya to the oracle of Zeus Ammon (Zeus in the form of Ammon). Located in the Oasis of Siwah, this oracle was one of the three most sacred (along with Delphi and Dodona) in the Greek world. There, the priests proclaimed Alexander the "Son of Ammon." To the Egyptians, the proclamation might have been customary: All Egyptian kings were probably welcomed to the shrine as sons of Ammon. To the Greeks, who equated Ammon with Zeus, Alexander would have been presenting himself as a Son of Zeus. To Alexander ... well ... no one knows for sure. But from this point on, Alexander more openly embraced models that equated kingship with divinity, particularly in cultures that adopted such models. Soon, the Greeks and Macedonians would find the practices of the Son of Ammon distasteful.

Odysseys

The Oasis of Siwah is about 300 miles west of the Nile in the Libyan desert. Alexandria became the major trade, cultural, and intellectual center of Alexander's emerging empire; under the Ptolemys, its Museum and Library became famous centers of learning. Parts of the old city, which sank under the sea, are being carefully recovered by archeologists.

Burning Down the House

From Egypt, Alexander embarked on a campaign for the rest of Persia. In 331 B.C.E., the main battle took place at Guagamela (just south of Mosul in Iraq). Darius' enormous army included a strong cavalry, a weak infantry, scythe-enhanced chariots, and war elephants. Alexander, whose combined Greek and Macedonian force was greatly outnumbered, relied on a disciplined army and strategy reminiscent of Issus. Although the fighting was fierce and the Macedonian phalanx was struggling, Alexander's cavalry charge once again sent the king fleeing. This time, Darius left central Persia and fled with his kinsman, Bessus, into the mountains toward Ecbatana (modern Hamadan, Iran). Alexander's army declared him king of Asia and, soon, the western capitals of Persia—Babylon, Susa, and Persepolis—all fell, or were handed over, to Alexander.

When Darius fled, he left behind treasuries, administrative centers, and governing satrapies—all for the taking. As the new king of Asia, Alexander usurped and adapted, rather than destroyed, most of these Persian structures. As the satraps surrendered, they were allowed to retain their former positions—in subservience to Alexander and under the watchful eye of a Macedonian-controlled garrison.

> **Labyrinths**
>
> According to one story, Alexander burned down the palaces at Persepolis in a drunken revel and at the instigation of a courtesan. Although drunken revelry might have been involved, Alexander did not act on impulse. Modern excavations suggest that two centuries worth of Persian treasures had been removed from the palaces prior to the conflagration.

In Babylon and Susa, Alexander ordered his troops to respect the population and their property. In Babylon, he further pacified the population by sacrificing to their main god, Marduk, and by ordering the reconstruction of Marduk's ziggurat, Esagila (which the Persians had destroyed long before). Only the royal palaces of Persepolis—which were spiritually and ceremoniously identified with Persian rule and, thereby, the symbolic object of the Greek expedition—were destroyed.

What's a King to Do?

For Alexander, things were looking good. Darius fled farther eastward, leaving the last Persian capital, Ecbatana, and its treasures to Alexander. A Spartan rebellion at home had been crushed. The goals of the League of Corinth had been realized. Alexander triumphantly discharged his remaining Greek troops and ended the original league expedition. And yet, there he was, the king of Asia, with only that pesky king Darius III left to oppose his authority. If Darius could be killed or, better yet, captured, Alexander could ensure a complete transfer of authority and become, unquestionably, monarch of it all. So, with his royal Macedonian army, Alexander furiously pursued Darius. But before they could reach the king, Darius was arrested and assassinated by satraps sympathetic to Bessus (330 B.C.E.). Alexander's advance forces caught up with the king, barely cold, as Bessus (who proclaimed himself king of Persia) and his allies fled east.

The assassination of Darius III not only allowed Alexander to usurp the throne, but it also gave him an unusual item with which to claim royal power and authority: the body of Darius. Stories about Darius' last words circulated, and it was said that, with his dying breath, Darius thanked Alexander for taking care of his family and asked him to avenge his death. Alexander gave Darius a royal burial, and he exchanged his role as avenger of the Greeks to avenger of the Persian royal line (against the rebels and assassins). As the chosen successor to the king, Alexander began to adopt Persian customs and royal dress, which he combined with royal Macedonian dress. Many of the Macedonian troops were deeply troubled by the new Alexander.

Hanging On to the Highlands

From 330 to 327 B.C.E., Alexander struggled to capture eastern Iran and the central Asian steppe. Bactria (Afghanistan) and Sogdiana (Uzbekistan and Tajikistan) were areas with a long history of fiercely independent tribal fighters, shifting alliances, and notoriously difficult terrain. Alexander's lack of familiarity with the politics, peoples, and alliances of the region sparked a brutal rebellion, led by the brilliant guerilla commander and Sogdian noble, Spitamenes, which lasted for nearly three years.

During this time, Alexander's forces suffered some of their most serious military defeats. In 329 B.C.E., Bessus' followers (who now feared for their own lives) exchanged Bessus for both a pardon and a place in Alexander's fold. Bessus was tried and executed by Alexander's Persian supporters. Eventually, Spitamenes was murdered by his allies, and the rebellion ended.

In 327 B.C.E., Alexander married Roxane, the beautiful daughter of a Sogdian noble (who would later bear his ill-fated heir apparent, Alexander IV), which solidified Alexander's political alliances in the region. During the rebellion, Alexander founded garrison cities (all named Alexandria) along his northeast frontier, and Alexandria Eschata (Alexander the Man-This-Place-Is-Remote) by the Jaxartes River on the northernmost border of the Persian Empire.

Troubles in the Trenches

Meanwhile, the Macedonians—who had trudged, starved, and fought their way to an exhausted desire for home—were watching their royal "companion" transform into something strange and alarming.

Although, more than once, Alexander's personal resolve and brave example had kept them going, the Macedonian troops now had a long list of complaints. First, Alexander had married a foreign queen (which precluded a Macedonian heir), and he was recruiting Persian nobles as "companions" and officers. Second, Alexander was adopting Persian customs and granting former enemies their previously held positions and status. Worst of all, Alexander began to require his subjects to observe the Persian ritual of *proskynêsis* ("ritual prostration") as a mark of his divine kingship. Although the Greeks and Macedonians barely tolerated the practice when it was required of the Persians, they were infuriated when Alexander unsuccessfully attempted to impose it on them! Plots and mutinies—some real and some imagined—broke out.

> **Lexica**
>
> **Proskynêsis** is ritual prostration as a sign of subservience to and recognition of divinity.

In response to both rumors and evidence of disloyalty, Alexander censored his troops' communications with home and executed some of his inner guard (including the general Parmenio and his son Philotas) and closest associates (including the historian Callisthenes). Moreover, Alexander personally murdered Cleitus the Black, a man who had saved his life at the Granicus River. Although some of the plots were real, others may have been engineered by Alexander himself to uncover and eliminate disloyalty, and still others may have been nothing more than Alexander's fearful imaginings. Regardless, the bond that had brought Alexander and the Macedonians from Pella to the Punjab was breaking apart. Even though Alexander had eliminated most of his old guard, he pressed on over the Hindu Kush Mountains and into the Indus Valley, and he responded to an earlier appeal from Taxiles, ruler of Taxila (near Rawalpindi, Pakistan) to unseat the neighboring king, Porus.

> **Eureka!**
>
> Taxila was a center of religious thought, and tales of Alexander's encounter there with the *gymnosophists* ("naked philosophers," probably Brahman priests) have fascinated both ancient and modern historians.

We're Definitely *Not* in Kansas: The End at the End of the World

The land of the Indus River (modern Pakistan) was known as "India" to the Greeks and the Persians alike, and it was there that Alexander's campaign passed into a near-mystical realm. Even legendary Greek heroes, like Heracles, had failed to conquer this fabled land of monsters, magic, and terrible tribes. And, in fact, the army had dropped out of the clouds into a subcontinent of vast kingdoms, strange animals, terrible diseases, and the worst weather they had ever seen.

Struggling against the monsoons, Alexander's last, and possibly greatest, victory came against Porus (who had 200 war elephants!) at the flooded Hydaspes (modern Jhelum) River in 326 B.C.E. Following the battle, when Porus asked only to be treated "like a king," Alexander incorporated Porus' kingdom into his eastern dominions, but left Porus in charge as his governor.

However, fear, fatigue, ceaseless rains, and rumors of more war elephants yet to come brought the army to a mutinous and mule-like halt at the river Hyphasis (modern Beas). The men had spent eight and a half years marching over 10,000 miles, and they were not going on to the Ganges. After pleading, threatening, and promising glory all failed, Alexander spent three days sulking (like Achilles) in his tent. Finally, Alexander reluctantly turned west and south and made his way, through heavy resistance and fierce battles, to the Indian Ocean. Along the way, while besieging Malli, Alexander's siege ladder collapsed behind him and he was trapped inside the enemy city. After being hit in the lung by an arrow and bravely rescued, he nearly died.

In 325 B.C.E., while his fleet sailed along the coast, Alexander, his army, their families, and camp followers (perhaps 80,000 in all) staggered through the arid wastelands of Gedrosia (southern Iran), ostensibly to found port cities beside the ocean. It was a disaster. Thousands died, including most of the soldiers' families who were caught in a flash flood, before they finally reached Carmania.

> **Eureka!**
>
> Alexander's legacy in India soon passed into romance and legend. Although he conquered lands and established colonies and garrisons, his hold on India was short-lived. However, his troops and his fleet (who encountered, among other wondrous things, whales that they attempted to frighten away with trumpets) brought back a vivid and valuable picture of India to an astonished Hellenic world.

Reports of My Demise Have Been Greatly Exaggerated

Alexander's return from India was, shall we say, unanticipated by many Macedonian officials and Persian satraps, and it created great turmoil throughout the empire. Some officials, who assumed that Alexander would never return, had begun to exploit the empire for their own personal profit. Others, who could be easily cast into the role of scapegoats, had become the victims of court politics and personal schemes.

Without delay, Alexander deposed some, executed others, and ordered all satraps to disband their private mercenary forces. However, even a divine king has to do *something* with an unemployed mercenary force of roughly 20,000 men, so Alexander ordered the Greek states to receive their exiles back as citizens. The social and economic strain caused by the returning exiles, combined with Alexander's later request that mainland Greeks honor him as a living god, brought Greece to a rebellious simmer.

Divine King or Deranged Despot?

Alexander's attempts to create a unified kingdom of east and west only made matters worse. Many Greeks saw the Macedonians as (barely Greek) conquerors and the barbarians (that is, all non-Greeks) as naturally inferior. The Macedonians saw themselves as Alexander's royal companions and as overlords of the Persians. The Persians and the Egyptians were heirs to advanced and ancient empires that had just been conquered. However, Alexander attempted to encourage and enforce a syncretism of eastern and western cultures and religions under his rule.

To begin, he held a real and symbolic marriage of east and west in Susa in 324 B.C.E. In a huge ceremony, he took two Persian wives (the daughters of Artaxerxes III and Darius III), which gave him control over the royal lineage, and 90 of his officers took noble Persian and Median wives. In addition, he distributed generous financial rewards to 10,000 of his soldiers who followed suit. He incorporated a large number of Persians, who had been trained in Macedonian military tactics, into his army as "successors" (i.e., "future companions") and he attempted to dismiss Macedonian soldiers who were no longer fit for service. Because mixed marriages were one thing and mixed "companions" another, the troops mutinied. Alexander mollified them by explaining that the Macedonians were his *true* "companions." The mutiny ended, but in short order, Alexander dismissed and sent home the roughly 10,000 men that he had originally declared too old or ill for service. He retained their Persian-born children, however, whom he hoped to mold into future soldiers of mixed lineage and one loyalty.

Lexica

Homonoia means "concord" or "being of one heart and mind."

Before he dismissed them, however, Alexander held an elaborate ceremonial banquet attended by political and religious representatives from all over his empire. According to some scholars, participants drew wine from a common bowl and offered a joint libation to the gods, and Alexander prayed for an empire marked by *homonoia* ("concord") and fellowship. However, it appears that only Macedonians drank from the bowl, and, even if Alexander said such a prayer, what did he mean by the words and how did he envision the development of his new empire? No one knows, really. His actual motivations and intentions are buried under centuries of speculation, contradiction, and moral bias. Moreover, even Alexander's actual beliefs, hopes, and plans were undoubtedly influenced by his growing physical and emotional instability. His demands for *proskynêsis* and for recognition as a god, especially by the Greek world, were always doomed to failure. Indeed, even his vision of a single kingdom, united under one divine being, could be seen as the desire of a megalomaniac to reign supreme over all humanity.

Ending Before Beginning

The last year of Alexander's life was marked by frenetic activity, unfulfilled plans, personal tragedy, loss of self-control, and illness. His closest friend and lover, Hephaestion, died from fever and excessive drinking in 324 B.C.E., which sent Alexander into a grief-stricken and drunken frenzy of activity. He executed Hephaestion's physician, ordered an extravagant burial monument for his friend, and returned to Babylon to plan a naval campaign to Arabia and the Caspian Sea.

After a series of omens foretold Alexander's death, Babylonian priests tried desperately to change the course of fate. However, Alexander (who was also drinking heavily) fell ill with a fever. Ten days later, on June 10, 323 B.C.E., he died in Babylon at the age of 33. When asked who should inherit his kingdom, Alexander said "the strongest."

Eureka!

The cause of Alexander's death has been a mystery from the beginning. Although legend claimed that he was poisoned, his death has also been attributed to (among other things) malaria, acute pancreatitis, and West Nile Fever (based on an omen of dead crows). Most likely, the strain of long campaigns, numerous wounds, personal grief, excessive drinking, and relentless activity resulted in illness and a natural death.

Although it took nearly a year for Alexander's funeral procession to make its way from Babylon to Alexandria, where he was buried, the dust never really settled on Alexander's world. In the years to come, Alexander's son and heir would be murdered, and his empire would be broken apart by the generals who served under him. Yet, before the age of 33, Alexander the Great had conquered and ruled most of the civilized world. And, for better or worse, he had changed the course of human history.

> **Muses**
>
> When Asclepiades first brought the news of Alexander's death to Athens, Demades urged the people not to believe it saying, "If Alexander were dead, the whole world would stink from his corpse."
> —Plutarch, *Alexander*, 9

The Least You Need to Know

◆ As the new king of Macedon, Alexander took control of Philip's army, replaced him as *hêgemôn* of the League of Corinth, and led an invasion of Persia.

◆ Alexander conquered the Persian Empire and Egypt, and he reached the Indus Valley before heading back to Babylon.

◆ Alexander's Greek and Macedonian soldiers were displeased when their leader adopted Persian customs and mannerisms and integrated Persians into his army and court.

◆ How seriously Alexander took his role as a divine monarch and leader of a united empire is still the subject of intense debate.

Part **5**

The Legacy of Hellas

This section shows how Alexander's conquests gave a large portion of the globe a connective tissue of Hellenistic culture, language, and learning. It was, however, a fractious mixture. Macedonian dynasties (descended from Alexander's generals), leagues of cities, island powers such as Rhodes, and small eastern kingdoms fought one another until they and their cultural heritage became a part of Rome's dominions.

The Hellenistic kingdoms may not have survived, but Roman conquest ensured that many of ancient Greece's intellectual and cultural achievements remained a vibrant part of the world heritage. In fact, the Roman poet Horace wondered who, in the end, had conquered whom. From Rome to the west, and from Byzantium, Jerusalem, and Alexandria in the east, we trace how "Hellenistic" culture came to have profound influence on Rome, Christianity, Islam, and our contemporary age.

22

Citizens of the World: The *Cosmopolis* and Hellenistic Culture

In This Chapter

- ◆ The convoluted history of the Hellenistic kingdoms
- ◆ Individuals and individualism in the Hellenistic period
- ◆ Philosophy and religion for the *cosmopolis*
- ◆ Hellenistic literature and art

The Hellenistic period—from the death of Alexander in 323 B.C.E. to the conquest of Ptolemaic Egypt by Rome in 30 B.C.E.—will, in some ways, seem familiar to modern readers. For example, within two generations, citizens of small and intensely participatory *poleis* became members of a *cosmopolis* (world *polis*). These individuals lived, traveled, and worked in increasingly pluralistic and culturally diverse societies, and under expansive economic, political, and military systems over which they had little, if any, direct control. Yet, by their very scale and scope, these systems provided increased opportunities for Greek men and women, especially as

Lexica

Lingua franca was originally a medieval pidgin of several languages, which was used by traders and travelers in the eastern Mediterranean. Today the term indicates a language that is used by speakers of different languages for common (usually commercial) communication. Hellenistic *koinê* ("common Greek") was the *lingua franca* of antiquity.

Greek became the *lingua franca* of the new world order. In turn, an education in Greek literature and culture became the means to advancement and the mark of an educated, civilized, and successful individual. In this chapter, we will look at the complicated birth and life of this Hellenistic world.

General Mayhem Following Alexander's Death

Alexander died without naming an heir apparent or specifying a succession plan, and his generals and armies disagreed as to who should rule. Some favored Alexander's half-brother, Arrhidaeus (a half-wit), because he was a full-blooded member of the Macedonian royal line (the Argeads); others favored Roxane's infant son, Alexander IV (a half-blood), because he was Alexander's direct heir. Armed conflict was avoided by way of an odd compromise: Arrhidaeus, as Philip III, and Alexander IV were made co-kings. Perdiccas, the general to whom Alexander, on his deathbed, had given his signet ring, became the regent of Asia and guardian of the kings.

Heir Today, Gone Tomorrow

If we mapped out the events that followed, the result might resemble a cross between a sophisticated flowchart and a complicated board game. However, in brief, the struggle for Alexander's empire—which was complicated by revolts, plots, and political machinations—continued for the next 40 years and tore the empire to shreds. The major players were: Ptolemy, the satrap of Egypt; Antigonus Monophthalmos ("The One-Eyed") of Phrygia and his son, Demetrius Poliorcetes ("The Besieger"); Seleucus of Babylon; Lysimachus of Thrace; and Antipater (whom Alexander had left in charge of Greece) and his son Cassander. These men became known as the *diadochoi*, or "successors."

During this struggle, the kings were used as pawns. In a bid to legitimize his own power, Perdiccas negotiated with Olympias (Alexander the Great's mother and Alexander IV's grandmother) to marry Alexander the Great's sister, Cleopatra. However, in 321 B.C.E., after being defeated in battle by Ptolemy, Perdiccas was assassinated by his own officers. The regency changed hands several times and, when it was eventually contested, the women entered the fray.

In 317 B.C.E., Olympias and Eurydice (the queen of Philip III) led opposing armies. The joint kingship was broken and, after defeating Eurydice in battle, Olympias ordered the execution of both Eurydice and Philip III. Within the year, however, Olympias was also executed. Soon, Cassander (now regent for Alexander IV) shut away Roxane and Alexander IV in Amphipolis, never to be seen again, and attempted to legitimize his own power by marrying Alexander's half-sister, Thessalonice, and producing an heir (Philip IV). Within a few years, the *diadochoi* were all (virtually simultaneously!) proclaimed king by their own armies.

Be Free ... Under Me

Meanwhile, following Alexander's death, several Greek cities revolted, and "freedom for the Greeks" became a rallying cry, particularly at Athens. In the east, the Bactrian Greeks rebelled, and 23,000 of them began the long journey home. After suffering a savage attack, ordered by Perdiccas, the survivors returned to Bactria and eventually created a powerful Greek kingdom.

In the west, the ready supply of mercenary soldiers gave Athens and Aetolia the means to corner Antipater in Lamia (hence the Lamian War, 323–322 B.C.E.). Antipater eventually defeated them, disbanded the League of Corinth, hunted down anti-Macedonian leaders (such as Demosthenes), and dismantled Athens' democratic institutions. In 317 B.C.E., Cassander gained control of Athens and ruled through his governor, Demetrius of Phaleron. Other rebellions followed, encouraged first by Antigonus and his son Demetrius Poliorcetes, and later by Ptolemy. In 307 B.C.E., Demetrius Poliorcetes drove out Demetrius of Phaleron and reinstated the Athenian democracy, and, after seizing Corinth and the northern Peloponnesus, attempted to revive the League of Corinth (under his leadership, of course).

> **Odysseys**
>
> After their revolt, the surviving Bactrian Greeks returned to Bactria and eventually created a powerful and influential kingdom. A hint of its splendor remained in Afghanistan at Ai Khanum, though pre-Islamic sites have recently suffered destruction by the Taliban.

Now We Are Three: The Hellenistic Kingdoms

For a brief time, it seemed that the father and son team of Antigonus and Demetrius would prevail, but their rivals united against them. In 301 B.C.E., at the Battle of the Kings at Ipsus, Antigonus and Demetrius were defeated by the combined forces of Cassander, Lysimachus, and Seleucus. Antigonus was trampled under Seleucus' war elephants, and Demetrius fled. Although Demetrius eventually gained control of

Athens (295 B.C.E.) and Macedon (294 B.C.E.), he was forced to surrender to Lysimachus and Seleucus in 286 B.C.E., and he died under house arrest in 283 B.C.E.

In 281 B.C.E., the forces of Lysimachus and Seleucus (who were once again fighting for control of the empire) met at Corupedium in Phrygia, and Lysimachus, now over 80 years old, was killed in battle. Within a year, however, Seleucus, who was also over 80, was assassinated by Ptolemy Ceraunus ("The Thunderbolt"), an exiled son of Ptolemy. In 279 B.C.E., Ptolemy Ceraunus was killed defending Macedon from an invasion of Gauls, a Celtic people who were busy taking advantage of the instability in Macedon.

> **Eureka!**
>
> The invasion of the Gauls in 279 B.C.E. contributed, in an unexpected fashion, to the evolving political system in Greece. By defeating the Gauls at Delphi and Lysimacheia, both the Aetolians and Antigonus Gonatas ("Knock-knees"), son of Demetrius Poliorcetes, legitimized their respective power and positions. The Aetolians emerged as the protectors of Delphi and foremost power in central Greece, and Antigonus became the king of Macedon.

After 279 B.C.E., three great Hellenistic dynasties settled in: The Ptolemys, who controlled Egypt and, at times, Palestine, Libya, Cyprus and other south Aegean islands; the Antigonids, who controlled Macedon and northern Greece, and overshadowed most of Thrace and the Aegean; and the Seleucids, who controlled varying portions of Alexander's Asian conquests. The Ptolemys and Seleucids ruled in the tradition of Alexander—as combination Macedonian kings and divine monarchs. At the edges of and in the cracks between these empires, city-states such as Athens, islands such as Rhodes, leagues such as the Aetolian and Achaean Leagues, and kingdoms such as Pergamum (Bergama, Turkey) grew and prospered.

Citizens of a Lonely Planet

Although Alexander covered his empire with a Greek veneer, the underlying cultures had very deep roots. For the most part, the Hellenistic kingdoms retained Egyptian or Asian administrative structures under the autocratic rule of the kings and their representatives. Nevertheless, regional citizens—who continued to be more Jewish or Egyptian or Iranian than Greek—found themselves living side by side in the major metropolitan centers.

In these centers, hybrid customs, mixed families, and adapted practices created an eclectic Hellenistic world culture. However, under such circumstances, people often seek to preserve their own traditions and to protect themselves from unwelcome change and foreign intrusion. So, just as in modern cities, there were social prejudices and ethnic segregation, and the Greeks and Macedonians (who were the minority) were resented for occupying most of the positions of power. In addition, both at home and abroad, there were occasional backlashes against the intermixing, as well as attempts (such as by Demetrius of Phaleron in Athens) to maintain strict controls over reproduction and marriage. However, ideologies of purity and tradition rarely became the practice of the day, even among those who professed them.

That Sucking Sound *Is* Hellenism

Greek and Macedonian men benefited greatly from the new Hellenistic world. Indeed, many parts of Greece experienced a population decline and an intellectual drain as men were lured away by the promise of opportunity and adventure. In cities stretching from Afghanistan to Egypt, Greeks came to comprise the majority of lower- to mid-level administrators, teachers, and professionals. Talented artists, poets, and scholars benefited from the patronage of the rich Hellenistic courts. Many others, especially Macedonians, served as mercenaries in the Hellenistic armies and garrisons. All of this, in turn, increased the opportunity for, and the occurrence of, social mobility. Some educated and enterprising slaves, for example, once freed from wealthy masters, went on to successful careers in banking and trade, and became influential participants in politics.

Women and Social Structure

The *cosmopolis* also opened opportunities for women that would have been unthinkable in the Classical period. Although in Classical Athens the lives and worlds of females were strictly regulated and rigidly segregated, such practices were never ubiquitous among the Greeks. In the Hellenistic period, these practices were further eroded by the blending of social and cultural traditions.

A wealth of private and public documents (on papyri, recovered mostly from Egypt) describe a Hellenistic world in which women increasingly engaged in public lives, managed households, became poets, owned property, and even (on very rare occasions) entered the exclusively male worlds of philosophy and public affairs. Just as for men, however, expanded opportunities were far more prevalent among the upper classes.

Nowhere were these changes more apparent than with the emergence of the Hellenistic queens. Beginning with Ptolemy II Philadelphus and his queen Arsinoë II, and lasting through the final Ptolemaic monarch, Cleopatra VII, the Hellenistic queens became deified (i.e., declared as gods) autocrats, political leaders, patrons of the arts, and models for other upper-class women. A particularly famous example is Berenice II (c. 273–221 B.C.E.), the sole heir to the city of Cyrene and wife of Ptolemy III, whose life and rise to power had all the intrigue of a Greek drama. Berenice owned ships and racehorses (which competed successfully in the Olympian and Nemean Games), governed Egypt in her husband's absence, and may have ridden with her troops on the battlefield (she was an accomplished equestrian). She is celebrated in Callimachus' poem, *The Lock of Berenice*, in which a lock of her hair is swept up to take its place among the stars.

Individually Suited: Philosophy and Religion for Citizens of the World

In the face of relentless political and social turmoil, citizens of the late Classical and Hellenistic periods often found themselves adrift in an unfamiliar world, searching for ethical guidance, personal control, and a sense of inner tranquility.

Two preeminent philosophies of the time, Epicureanism and Stoicism, offered explanations for the physical universe, and the place of human beings within that universe, that provided individuals with practical approaches to achieving both a sense of personal control and a state of personal "composure" or "inner quietude" (*ataraxia*). For more on Epicureanism and Stoicism, as well as other philosophical schools of this period (Cynics, Skeptics), see Chapter 3.

What About *Me?* Epicureanism and Stoicism

Epicurus (341—270 B.C.E.), the founder of Epicureanism, established a philosophical community in Athens, known as "the garden," and wrote voluminously—about 300 works in all. However, most of his writings are lost, and his existing work consists mainly of three letters and some fragments. However, a later disciple of the school, the Roman poet Lucretius (c. 94–55 B.C.E.), wrote a long poem (*De Rerum Natura*, or *On the Nature of Things*) on Epicurean philosophy, in which he attempts to liberate humans from the fear of death and of the gods and lead them to a sense of inner tranquility.

Epicurus followed Democritus in arguing that the physical universe is composed of atoms. The material bodies that we experience (including the human body and soul) are composed of atoms and, when the bodies perish and decay, their atoms scatter and recombine into new bodies. Thus, for the Epicureans, death was nothing more than nonexistence, or the absence of all feeling and sensation. There was no immortality to either fear or seek: death ends human existence and the gods neither interfere with nor intervene in human affairs.

Muses

So that the man speaks but idly who says that he fears death not because it will be painful when it comes, but because it is painful in anticipation. For that which gives no trouble when it comes, is but an empty pain in anticipation. So death, the most terrifying of ills, is nothing to us, since so long as we exist, death is not with us; but when death comes, then we do not exist. It does not then concern either the living or the dead, since for the former it is not, and the latter are no more.

—Epicurus, *Letter to Menoeceus*, trans. C. Bailey.

In this life and by their nature, humans seek pleasure (understood as the absence of pain), and it is in reference to pleasure that humans choose some objects and activities and avoid others. Epicurus argued that simple, long-term pleasures (rather than the pleasures that result from satisfying fleeting desires or living extravagantly) lead to tranquility and happiness. Quite realistically, he also argued that humans must often accept short-term pains in order to achieve long-term pleasure. To live pleasantly, then, humans must live justly, honorably, and moderately, with few needs and desires. In this way, they avoid the pains that accompany unethical action, fear, desire, and the disruption of personal tranquility.

Zeno of Citium (c. 336–265 B.C.E.), the founder of Stoicism, was influenced by the teachings of both Socrates and Heraclitus. Around 300 B.C.E., he founded his own school of philosophy in Athens, which takes its name from the Painted Porch (*Stoa Poikilê*), where he lectured. He was succeeded in the leadership of the school by Cleanthes of Assos (c. 331–233 B.C.E.), and Cleanthes by Chrysippus (c. 280–208 B.C.E.). Although Stoicism was extremely appealing to the Romans (Cicero, Seneca, and the emperor Marcus Aurelius all wrote works on Stoic philosophy), we will focus here on the early Stoa of the Hellenistic period.

Odysseys

To visit a Greek Stoic state, travel back in time to Sparta, under kings Agis IV (262–241 B.C.E.) and Cleomenes III (260–219 B.C.E.). Through economic and cultural reforms—which combined "Lycurgan" institutions and Stoic ideals—these kings renewed the strength and vigor of Sparta, and their reforms were praised by Greek intellectuals. However, in 222 B.C.E., just as Sparta was about to dominate the Peloponnesus once again, the Macedonians and Achaean League defeated them in battle.

Like Epicurus, Zeno divided philosophy into logic, physics, and ethics. Unlike Epicurus, however, Zeno argued that the universe is ordered and governed for the good. According to the Stoics, reality includes two material principles: an active principle (known by such names as god, *logos*, or reason), and a passive principle (which is matter). The active principle is not separate from the world, but rather permeates, directs, and connects one, ordered whole.

Because the universe is governed and directed by reason, however, it is determined, and human beings have free will only to a limited extent. On this view, although human beings are free to choose their internal attitudes, emotions, and reactions to external events, the events themselves are determined. In other words, although humans must follow the laws of nature, they are rational beings and, as such, have the privilege of understanding these laws and the freedom of consciously consenting to them. And it is here that we find the key to Stoic ethics. For the Stoics, only virtue is good in the full sense of the word, and living virtuously is living in accordance with the active principle and right reason. To accomplish this, humans require both wisdom (to comprehend their own role) and apathy (to accept, without strong or negative emotions, those things that they cannot change). Some activities and attitudes are morally indifferent, but even so, certain ones are preferable to others. Above all, virtue requires right reason, conformity to nature, and internal composure. Although this state of internal composure was achieved by the Stoics at the expense of strong emotions and deep attachments, it offered individuals a sense of internal freedom and control, regardless of their external circumstances.

CAUTION

Labyrinths

Stoicism appealed to people from many walks of life, because it offered the possibility of inner tranquility under any circumstances. In fact, among prominent Stoics of later periods, one, Epictetus (c. 50–130 C.E.), was born a slave and another, Marcus Aurelius (121–180 C.E.), was a Roman emperor.

Between Me and the Gods: New Individualistic Religions

The Hellenistic period also saw the development and growth of individualistic religions. Previously, religious systems tended to focus on the gods' relationship with a people or a city, and the relationship was mediated through rulers and/or priests. Although individualistic religious cults (such as the mystery and healing cults) did exist previously, the popular appeal of religions that offered direct contact between individuals and the divine grew during the Hellenistic period. Moreover, mixed marriages and geographical mobility encouraged blended religious traditions, as well as increased blending of religious beliefs among the Greek elite, who sometimes worshipped Hellenized forms of foreign gods (such as Isis).

> **Eureka!**
>
> In the second century B.C.E., when Hellenized Jews, backed by Antiochus IV Epiphanes, tried to replace Jewish religious practices in Jerusalem with Greek traditions and practices, a rebellion erupted. Led by the Maccabees, the rebels triumphed, and their victory is celebrated in the Jewish festival of Hanukkah.

Scholars and Scrolls: Alexandrian Scholarship and Hellenistic Arts

Just as Athens was a center of Classical culture, Hellenistic cities such as Alexandria were centers of Hellenistic culture. However, at the start of the Hellenistic period, Hellenes did not conceive of "Greek" culture in the sense that we now understand it. Instead, they had various stories, myths, and histories, often of individuals who were associated with different ancient cities.

It was Alexandrian scholars who assembled Hellenic literature, codified Hellenic learning, recorded Hellenic accomplishments, and sought to perpetrate a Hellenic legacy. Yet, even then, this legacy was primarily centered on what the Greeks saw as their "classical" period. For this reason, although the Hellenistic period was replete with literature, the works of fifth and fourth century B.C.E. Athens became canonized and preserved.

Bibliomania: The Museum and Alexandrian Scholarship

The Ptolemys, especially Ptolemy I and his immediate successors, turned Alexandria into the intellectual and cultural capital of the Greek world. They created a research center, the Museum (Temple of the Muses), where distinguished scholars, intellectuals, and artists (supported by government stipends) lived, worked, and studied. Within this environment, specialized studies—such as astronomy, medicine, mechanics, applied mathematics, and applied physics—developed and emerged as separate disciplines. The greatest Hellenistic poets (e.g., Callimachus, Apollonius of Rhodes, Theocritus), scientists (e.g., Euclid, Ctesibius, Eratosthenes), physicians (e.g., Herophilus and Erasistratus), and textual scholars (e.g., Zenodotus and Aristophanes of Byzantium) were drawn to Egypt.

The Ptolemys supported their work with money and materials—even providing condemned criminals for vivisection by Erasistratus!—and with the establishment of libraries of Greek literature at the Museum and the Serapeum (temple of Serapis). The Ptolemys hoped to obtain a copy of every book written in Greek, and Ptolemy II supposedly ordered the production of the Greek translation of the Jewish Bible, the *Septuagint*. If visitors to Egypt and subject states possessed books that were not yet in the library, their originals were confiscated and replaced with cheap copies. By the first century B.C.E., the Alexandrian Library contained an estimated 700,000 papyrus rolls!

CAUTION
Labyrinths

Several traditions regarding the destruction of the Library at Alexandria variously blame Julius Caesar, the Christians, or the Muslims. The evidence suggests that the royal library itself (including up to 400,000 works!) was accidentally burned when Caesar, besieged in Alexandria (48–47 B.C.E.), set fire to the port. Evidence also implicates the Christians in the intentional destruction of the Serapeum (which housed another large library) and other temples, and the Muslims in the intentional destruction of additional pagan works. The combined loss is historically and intellectually catastrophic.

Short and Sweet: Alexandrian Literature

Alexandrian literature developed in response to the classical models and forms that scholars were studying, and to the massive amounts of literary and cultural data that they were accumulating. Overall, certain tendencies emerged. One was a movement toward concise expression in poetry (as opposed to wordier Homeric and classical forms), and the development of diminutive forms (such as the *epyllion*, or "little epic"). A notable exception was Callimachus' rival, Apollonius of Rhodes, who retold the story of Jason and Medea in a long epic, the *Argonautica*. Another tendency was the use of obscure local myths, facts, and other inside information, which often limited the audience to people "in the know" (i.e., those who could spot and understand the references). The pastoral odes, or idylls, of Theocritus made particularly good use of local legends and rural scenes.

Other poets wrote didactic poems (see Chapter 2) on subjects that ranged from astronomy to history. Finally, Alexandrian poetry had a tendency to focus on personal emotion and the perspective of particular individuals. These various characteristics not only fit the individualism of the Hellenistic period, but were also highly influential on the development of Latin poetry in Rome.

Eureka!

Alexandria's rival library was at Pergamum, founded by Eumenes II. Tradition reports that Egypt placed an embargo on papyrus to keep Eumenes from enlarging his inventory, which forced him to use vellum (hide). But the Ptolemys had the last laugh: The Roman conqueror Mark Antony gave the Pergamum Library (containing roughly 200,000 scrolls) to Cleopatra as a gift.

Individual Standouts: Hellenistic Art and Architecture

Hellenistic art and sculpture followed similar trends by expanding on classical forms to further explore and portray individuals, strong movement, and emotion. Sculpture ranged from grand-scale works to small terracotta figurines of everyday men, women, and children—much like modern collectibles and knickknacks. Likenesses of Hellenistic monarchs on coins—or numismatic portraits—are fascinating studies in state art used as propaganda (e.g., showing monarchs as gods) and portraiture. Caricatures, including grotesques and exaggerations of individual traits, were also popular styles.

A study in relief styles from grand building projects of different periods: the classical Parthenon frieze (British Museum, right) and the Hellenistic Pergamum Altar (Berlin Museum, left).

(Photos by Eric Nelson)

In keeping with the grandiose egos and budgets of the era, the Hellenistic period was also a time of grandiose building projects. Chief among them was the Pharos, Alexandria's 400-foot-high tower crowned by a statue of Zeus Soter ("Savior"). Huge mirrors reflected the light of its beacon fire far out to sea, to guide sailors safely to Alexandria. Other enormous projects included the Colossus of Rhodes (a 110-foot-high bronze statue of Helios astride the harbor entrance), the restored temple of Artemis at Ephesus (the Archaic temple supposedly burned to the ground the night Alexander was born), and the unfinished temple of Apollo at Didyma.

> **Odysseys**
>
> Famous examples of Hellenistic sculpture include the Victory (Nike) of Samothrace at the Louvre in Paris, the statue of Laocoön at the Vatican Museum, and the Pergamum Altar in the Berlin Museum.

The famous Laocoön statue from the Vatican Museum.

(Photo by Eric Nelson)

The Least You Need to Know

- Within two generations, citizens of small and intensely participatory *poleis* became members of a *cosmopolis* (world *polis*).

- After 279 B.C.E., Alexander's empire was divided between three great Hellenistic dynasties: the Ptolemys, the Antigonids, and the Seleucids.

- Hellenistic religion, philosophy, literature, and art all addressed individuals within their changing world context.

- In the Museum and Library at Alexandria, applied science, literature, and scholarship developed and flourished.

Chapter 23

You Will Be Assimilated: Hellenism and the Coming of Rome

In This Chapter

- The rise of Rome
- Rome's intervention in Greece and Macedon
- Rome's involvements and conquests in the East
- The end of the Hellenistic dynasties

In our historical journey, we ended with the establishment of three Hellenistic dynasties (Ptolemaic, Antigonid, Seleucid) in the third century B.C.E. Subsequently, the dynasties all attempted to gain prominence and power, but, whenever one would advance, its rivals would ally to keep it in check.

This game of cutthroat was complicated by a host of players, which we might call "malcontents in the middle." The ancient city-states (such as Athens, Corinth, and Sparta) continued to resent Macedonian domination, and to cling to their own ideals, aspirations, and hopes of regaining past glory. New leagues (such as the Aetolian and Achaean Leagues) became powerful federations, which were capable of maintaining independence and exerting power in ways that the Classical *poleis* could not. And new powers (such as Pergamum, Rhodes, Bithynia, Bactria, Pontus, and Parthia) emerged. Even the minor players helped to keep the Hellenistic world dangerously and unpredictably unstable, by forging temporary alliances with and against both one another and the various dynasties.

The Hellenistic kings focused their attention and efforts on Alexander's empire and the wealth of the east. There was little to interest them in the west, which had long been divided between the Carthaginians, the western Greeks of southern Italy and Sicily, and the Etruscans of northern Italy. However, a new power was emerging in Italy, one unlike anything anyone had ever seen before.

Rome, a city without a history (as the Greeks might have thought of it), and the Romans, a people largely (and rather proudly) uncultured, had been consistently intervening in the affairs of, and dominating, the lands around them. In the third century B.C.E., Rome's outward expansion reached Magna Graecia and Sicily and, eventually, the Hellenistic malcontents sought Roman assistance.

Amidst the chaos, Rome's strategy of *divida et impera* ("divide and rule") worked all too well. Too late, the Greeks learned that Roman protection came at a high cost: The Romans imposed their own order, brutally subjugated and enslaved their subjects, and pillaged cultural treasures. In this chapter, we'll discuss the period during which Rome conquered the Hellenistic world. In the next chapter, *Return of the Trojan Horse*, we'll describe how Hellenic culture influenced Rome, continued in Byzantium, and became a legacy for Christianity, Islam, and the Renaissance.

We Came, We Saw, We Conquered: A (Very) Brief History of Early Rome

Rome began as settlements on the hills above the marshes at the first major ford of the Tibur River. Tradition claims that the mud huts went up in 753 B.C.E., just about the time of Homer and Hesiod. In time, the settlers unified under clans and a king, drained the marshes, and created a central forum. In the sixth century B.C.E., Etruscan monarchs, the Tarquins, developed the civic and commercial aspects of the city, much as the Greek tyrants were developing the emerging *poleis* of Archaic Greece. However, late in the sixth century B.C.E. (509 B.C.E.), the Roman nobility drove out the Tarquins. By replacing the kings with annually elected magistrates, they established the beginnings of the *Roman Republic*.

> **Lexica** _____
>
> The **Roman Republic** refers to the period from 509 B.C.E. to the beginning of the Augustan Principate in 27 B.C.E. "Republic" comes from the Latin *res publica* ("the public thingy"), the name that the Romans gave to their collective political enterprise. The second-century B.C.E. historian Polybius saw the Republic as a balance of the elements of kingship, oligarchy, and democracy.

Frequently Down but Never Out

After the kings were ousted, Rome was repeatedly threatened by neighboring tribes and cities, and by an invasion of Gauls (390 B.C.E.). Even so, by 338 B.C.E., Rome was in control of its Latin neighbors, and it had established a series of direct alliances with conquered cities. This progressive expansion brought Rome into conflict with the Samnites, a fiercely independent tribal people who occupied central Italy and served as a buffer between the Romans and the Greeks of southern Italy. Three hard-fought wars, from 334 B.C.E. to 290 B.C.E., eventually gave Rome control over the Samnites in the south and their Etruscan allies in the north, and made Rome the preeminent power in central Italy. These conquests also brought Rome into conflict with the Samnites' southern neighbor (and former nemesis), the Greek city of Tarentum. And here, we find the conflict that sets the stage for the beginning of the end of the Hellenistic world.

> **Labyrinths** _____
>
> Tradition holds that the Romans traveled to Greece, visited Athens and Sparta, and adapted Athenian institutions to their own use. However, the Roman system of administration and early Roman treaties look to be influenced more by Sparta's political system and arrangements with the *perioikoi* than by Athenian institutions.

Tangling with Tarentum

Tarentum was a powerful city, which jealously guarded its control over the heel of Italy. So, to protect its own interests and colonists, Rome supported and protected Tarentum's rivals along the southern coast. These alliances brought Tarentum and Rome into direct conflict. Tarentum looked across the Ionian Sea to Epirus, and to its ambitious king, Pyrrhus (c. 319–272 B.C.E.), for assistance. Pyrrhus, who had been educated in Egypt and was married to a Ptolemaic princess, had dreams of becoming another Alexander the Great. Seeing Tarentum's call as his opportunity, Pyrrhus made the crossing in 280 B.C.E., with about 20,000 mercenaries and five war elephants.

Pyrrhus fought a series of battles against the Romans, which he won at an exorbitantly high cost (hence the phrase "pyrrhic victory"). In these battles, the Roman legions proved an able match for the Greek phalanx, which they would later face in battles against Philip V and Antiochus III. Pyrrhus, who hoped that Rome's allies would revolt and side with him (a miscalculation later repeated by Hannibal), tried to take Sicily, failed, and eventually returned to Epirus. There, he attempted to conquer Macedon and Greece. He was enjoying some success when he was killed in a most unlikely fashion. During a battle in the city of Argos, a woman threw a pot out of an upper window; the pot hit Pyrrhus on the head and killed him.

After a two-year siege, Tarentum fell to the Romans. Rome now had control of Italy, an influx of Greek slaves, and increased contact with Greek culture. Rome had also become a player in the unstable politics of the Mediterranean.

"Stand Back, I Take Big Steps": The Coming of Rome

After conquering and unifying Italy, Rome moved (mid-third to mid-second century B.C.E.) to conquering the Mediterranean. Initially, what began as interventions—which were designed to counter threats to Roman dominance, maintain stability, and expand Roman commercial interests—ended in conquests. Very quickly, however, conquests came to serve the increasingly imperialistic aims of Rome's ambitious upper classes, which were becoming fabulously wealthy and powerful through the spoils of war and provincial administration.

Pirates and More Elephants

The first great struggles took place in the western Mediterranean, against the Carthaginians (upon whose sphere of influence the Romans had begun to infringe) and the Illyrians (whose pirate kingdoms across the Adriatic were interfering with Greek cities now under Roman control). Through both of these conflicts, Rome became involved with Macedon, and with the murky affairs of Greece and the Hellenistic kingdoms.

The Illyrian Wars (229–228, 220–219 B.C.E.) put Rome on Macedon's doorstep. The Romans initially put a Greek adventurer, Demetrius of Pharos, in charge of the conquests (because he betrayed the island of Corcyra to them), but Demetrius proved to be more of a pirate than the Illyrians. He allied with Macedon and began attacking cities—some now Roman protectorates—down the coast and into the Aegean. When the Romans drove him out, he fled to Macedon, where he advised the young king, Philip V (238–179 B.C.E.), that he had better do something about those Romans … who were just getting into a major conflict with Carthage.

The Romans and Carthaginians fought three Punic Wars (*Punici* is Latin for "Carthaginians"). In the first (264–241 B.C.E.), Rome took Sicily and Sardinia from Carthage and made them into provinces. In the second (218–202 B.C.E.), the Carthaginian general Hannibal crossed the Alps (with elephants), to invade Italy from Spain, and he nearly defeated the Romans on their own turf. (He was eventually forced back to Africa and defeated.) In the third (151–146 B.C.E.), Rome helped engineer a war between Carthage and its other enemies that allowed the Romans to conquer and raze Carthage to the ground.

> **Eureka!**
>
> Hannibal Barca (247–c. 182 B.C.E.) was one of antiquity's great generals. After his bold invasion of Italy failed, he served as an able administrator of Carthage. The Romans continued to hound him and to demand his extradition, and they pursued him when he fled Carthage. After taking refuge with Antiochus III, on Crete, and in Bithynia, Hannibal finally took poison to avoid capture.

Menacing Macedon: The First and Second Macedonian Wars

When it appeared that Hannibal would triumph over Rome, Philip V briefly formed an alliance with Carthage (in the west) and Bithynia (in the east), and attacked Roman interests in Illyria. Rome responded by forming its own alliance with the Aetolian League (in the west) and Pergamum (in the east), and regained some of Illyria before hostilities ceased in 205 B.C.E. However, Philip was mainly interested in securing Antigonid control over Greece and the Aegean.

To offset the opposition of Egypt, the Aetolian League, Pergamum, and Rhodes, Philip allied with the Seleucid king Antiochus III ("the Great"). He was on the verge of achieving most of his aims when Aetolia, Egypt, and Pergamum appealed to Rome for help, and accused Philip and Antiochus of plotting to carve up Egypt.

Resentment against Philip, unwillingness to allow him to gain such power, and the promise of conquest brought Rome to Macedon in 200 B.C.E. The Romans defeated the royal Macedonian phalanx at Cynoscephalae in 196 B.C.E. and, although Philip was permitted to retain his kingdom, he was forced to pay a heavy yearly tribute and allowed only a limited army.

The Roman general Flaminius, who was fluent in Greek and admired Greek culture, made an appearance at the Isthmian Games. In the name of Rome, he proclaimed that the Greek states were free and independent from Macedon. Pandemonium broke out and Flaminius was celebrated throughout Greece. But, if the Romans hoped that Greece would now be stable, they had failed to study history. And, if the Greeks thought that they and the Romans meant the same thing by "free," they had failed to study the Romans.

Attacking Antiochus

Meanwhile, Philip's supposed ally, Antiochus III, had been busy. He had successfully regained a good portion of the Seleucid empire, defeated Egypt, and married his daughter, Cleopatra I, to Ptolemy V. Pergamum, which had been a part of the Seleucid empire, saw the writing on the wall and appealed to Rome. Rome sent Flaminius, fresh from his proclamation, to tell Antiochus to back off. Hannibal also showed up, to tell Antiochus that his only hope of defeating Rome lay in forming an alliance of the Greeks. But his advice fell on deaf ears: Unity through conquest was more Antiochus' style, and willing cooperation among the Hellenistic Greeks was, well, unimaginable.

In 192 B.C.E., the Aetolians (who, remember, called in the Romans in the first place) asked Antiochus to drive the Romans out. Antiochus attacked Greece, but the Romans, allied with Rhodes, Pergamum, Philip, and the Achaean League, easily drove Antiochus back to Asia. There, they defeated him at Magnesia in 188 B.C.E. and, after he plundered a temple in Susa the next year, Antiochus was assassinated. The Romans carved up most of his western kingdom for their allies Pergamum (which became one of their most loyal allies in the east) and Rhodes (which became a major naval and economic power).

> **Odysseys**
>
> Ancient Magnesia is near modern-day Manisa, Turkey, at the foot of Mount Sipylus. Strong earthquakes have left few ancient remains.

Cleaning Up

With the defeat of Antiochus, it was clear that the Romans were becoming the enforcers in the Mediterranean—and that they were also becoming rather fond of the role. In subsequent years, although Macedon and the Seleucid empire attempted to reestablish themselves as major powers, they were checked by Rome and by the continued opposition of other Hellenic states.

In the east, a resurgence of the Seleucids was cut short by the Romans, who intervened to protect Egypt from an invasion by Antiochus IV (168 B.C.E.). In the west, continued rebellions and unrest in Greece resulted in harsh reprisals. And, in the meanwhile, Rome began to intervene in the affairs of Egypt, the last major Hellenistic kingdom. It also received several states as bequests to the Roman state, making its interests in, and direct hold over, the eastern Mediterranean stronger than ever. (For more on these bequests, see the section titled "Take My Kingdom, Please" later in this chapter.)

> **Muses**
>
> Antiochus meets the ever-tactful Roman, Popilius Laenas, outside of Alexandria in 168 B.C.E.:
>
> [Antiochus] met the Romans near Alexandria. When he greeted them politely by holding out his hand to Popilius, Popilius stuck the decree of the Senate in it instead and told him to read it first. After reading it, Antiochus responded that he would convene his friends to consider what he ought to do. But Popilius drew a circle around the king with his stick and demanded, "Give me a reply to take to the Senate before you cross the circle." Taken aback, the king briefly hesitated and finally responded, "I will do what the Senate thinks right." Only then did Popilius extend his hand to him.
>
> —Livy, *From the Founding of the City*, 45.12

The End of Macedon and Greece

Greece used its freedom to generate enough civil strife to nearly tear itself apart. Although this strife was often cast as a battle between rich and poor, it was also a power struggle between factions supported by the Aetolians and factions supported by Macedon. Meanwhile (171 B.C.E.), Philip V's son, Perseus, rebelled against Roman-imposed limitations and went on the attack. The Romans, under Aemilius Paullus, defeated him decisively at Pydna in 168 B.C.E. Perseus was forced to walk, clad in black, in Aemilius' triumphal procession in Rome, and he died a few years later in Roman captivity. In 167 B.C.E., Aemilius ended the potential for problems in Epirus, and secured his financial future, by razing 70 towns and selling 150,000 people into Roman slavery—to his own, and his soldiers, great profit.

In Macedon, the Romans attempted to break the national unity created by Philip and Alexander by abolishing the monarchy and creating four distinct Macedonian provinces. These provinces had direct relations with Rome, but they were denied the rights of independent alliances, intermarriage, and trade with one another. The Romans took control of state mines and resources, and forced the Macedonians to pay such a high yearly indemnity that the Romans could afford to cancel the direct taxes of all Roman citizens. Roman oppression and the longing for a national state led to one more uprising, under Andriscus (who claimed to be Perseus' son), in 149 B.C.E. The Romans defeated Andriscus 148 B.C.E., and made Macedon into a Roman province, which permanently ended its independent political existence.

In Greece, the Romans imposed a similarly terrible order. In Aetolia, Roman troops assisted in brutally eradicating Macedonian sympathizers. In addition, the Romans discovered, among private papers that Perseus had failed to destroy, the names of 1,000 leading citizens in Achaea. They deported these citizens, without trial or hearing, to Italy for internment (among them was the historian Polybius). By the time the hostages were released, 16 years later, only about 300 of them were still alive.

In 146 B.C.E., to punish both Corinth and the Achaean League for rebelling, the Romans, under Lucius Mummius, razed Corinth to the ground. After killing most of the males, Mummius made his fortune by selling most of the women and children into slavery and by shipping Corinth's art treasures back to Italy for resale. Rhodes, which had tried to negotiate between Perseus and Rome, was stripped of territory, power, and income. Rhodes could no longer afford to support its full navy, and piracy once again flourished in the Aegean.

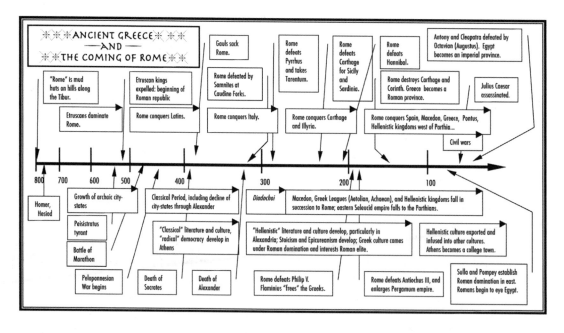

To preclude collective Hellenistic enterprises in the future, the Romans disbanded the Greek leagues, replaced democracies with oligarchies loyal to Rome, and gave each city separate relations with Rome (under the watchful eye of the governor of Macedon). Later, after the desperate Greeks sided with Mithridates (88 B.C.E.), the famous Roman general and dictator Sulla ravaged Greece and looted Attica (86 B.C.E.). Finally, the Roman emperor Augustus converted Greece into the province of Achaea in 27 B.C.E.

Take My Kingdom, Please

Interestingly, in the period after 146 B.C.E., several small kingdoms, which might otherwise have been swallowed up by their rivals, took the tactic of preserving themselves (after a fashion) by giving themselves to Rome. For example, in 133 B.C.E., Attalus III, who had no heir, bequeathed Pergamum to the Roman people. Ptolemy Apion, the ruler of Cyrene, bequeathed Cyrene to Rome in 96 B.C.E., and King Nicomedes IV of Bithynia, also without an heir, bequeathed his kingdom in about 75 B.C.E. As dynastic struggles continued in Egypt, a will was produced in about 80 B.C.E. that claimed Egypt itself had been given to Rome. This claim was not pursued until about 65 B.C.E., when Crassus (a fabulously wealthy and ambitious Roman aristocrat) suggested that Egypt be annexed, and not settled until Cleopatra's suicide in 30 B.C.E.

That Messy Middle East

Roman "possessions" in the Middle East provided Rome with both the interests and the excuse to intervene directly in the affairs of the area, and this intervention alarmed the kingdoms that saw Rome as a threat to their own aspirations and autonomy. The two greatest challenges came from kingdoms on the fringes of the Seleucid empire: the kingdom of Pontus, which grew along the shores of the Black Sea, and the Parthian empire, which had taken over most of the Seleucids' eastern possessions.

The Romans' first direct confrontation was with the wily and ruthless king of Pontus, Mithridates VI (134–63 B.C.E.). Mithridates and Bithynia (a Roman protectorate) were at odds, and when the Romans encouraged Bithynia to attack, Mithridates struck back, hard. Posing as a liberator of the Greeks against the barbarian Romans, he encouraged a widespread revolt. He sent representatives to various Greek cities to gain support for his cause, and he ordered the execution of nearly 20,000 Italian merchants and slave dealers on Delos. In cities such as Athens, pro-Roman oligarchies were driven out, and Mithridates was welcomed as an ally.

This initial conflict was brought to a standstill by Sulla in 85 B.C.E., but reignited when Nicomedes IV of Bithynia bequeathed his kingdom to Rome. In 74 B.C.E., Mithridates occupied Bithynia to keep it from the Romans, igniting an 11-year war with the Roman generals Lucullus and Pompey the Great. Pompey's victories over the Mediterranean

> **Odysseys**
>
> Finally cornered, Mithridates killed his family and ordered his own execution. His body was given to Pompey, who enhanced his own reputation by returning the body for burial in the royal tombs of the kings of Pontus at Sinope (modern Sinop, Turkey, on the southern shore of the Black Sea). Sinope was also the home of the famous Cynic philosopher Diogenes.

pirates (66 B.C.E.) and Mithridates (65 B.C.E.), in combination with his conquest and settlement of the Middle East (66–62 B.C.E.), extended Rome's dominions to the Euphrates River. By organizing these areas into provinces and client kingdoms, Pompey established the political framework of the area for centuries to come.

Pompey's power, wealth, and prestige fueled the aspirations of other ambitious Romans. In 65 B.C.E., Marcus Crassus hoped to annex Egypt, by force if necessary, but his plans were foiled by his political opponents. Eventually (55 B.C.E.), Crassus, cooperating with Julius Caesar and Pompey, received an eastern command as governor of Syria. In 53 B.C.E., Crassus attempted an invasion of Parthia, but the Parthians defeated and massacred his army (only 10,000 of the original 40,000 returned), killed Crassus, and captured his legionary standards (that is, the banners and emblems of Crassus' legion, the silver eagles) at Carrhae—a stinging mark of shame for Rome. Years later (20 B.C.E.), the emperor Augustus got the treasured standards back, along with the surviving Roman captives (from Carrhae and afterward).

> **Eureka!**
>
> In Crassus' overly ambitious attack upon Parthia, he literally lost his head: the Parthian court used it as a stage prop in a production of Euripides' *Bacchai.*

Cleopatra's Gambit and the End of the Hellenistic Age

Meanwhile, dynastic struggles for control of Egypt placed the last Hellenistic kingdom squarely into Rome's orbit. Externally, the Ptolemys were engaged in a struggle against the Seleucid empire and, internally, they were engaged in a battle between the male Ptolemys and a female line of powerful and resourceful Cleopatras.

As was customary in Egypt, the Ptolemys engaged in *endogamy* (the marriage of close relatives, in this case brother-sister), to preserve their dynastic lineage. However, in Alexandrian Egypt, these marriage alliances were often fraught with strife and accompanied by violent uprisings. Sulla had forced Cleopatra Berenice to marry and share the throne with her stepson, Ptolemy XI (c. 100–80 B.C.E.). However, when Ptolemy murdered Berenice 19 days after the wedding, he was killed by the Alexandrians, which left only an illegitimate son, Ptolemy XII Auletes (c. 116–55 B.C.E.), and a (probably false) will that bequeathed Egypt to Rome.

Rise of Cleopatra

Ptolemy XII married his half-sister, Cleopatra V, and they had at least three children, Ptolemy XIII, Cleopatra VI, and Cleopatra VII. Ptolemy XII was driven out of Egypt by the Alexandrians and fled to Rome, but, with the help of the Romans, he was restored to his throne in 55 B.C.E. He bequeathed his throne to his son, Ptolemy XIII, and his daughter, Cleopatra VII, who were married as joint rulers.

In 48 B.C.E., after Ptolemy XIII had forced Cleopatra out of Egypt, she returned with an army to reclaim her position. As the armies prepared to engage, Pompey (who had been defeated by Julius Caesar in the Roman Civil War) landed in Alexandria, where he hoped to raise another army. As he came ashore, Pompey was murdered. In an attempt to gain favor with Caesar, Ptolemy's advisors beheaded Pompey and pickled his head in brine. Caesar, who was pursuing Pompey, arrived a few days later and he was, apparently, disgusted by his gift. When Caesar attempted to restore Cleopatra to the throne, he was besieged in Alexandria by Ptolemy's forces for several months. (This is when he set fire to the port and, it appears, accidentally burned the Library at Alexandria.) In the end, Caesar prevailed and Ptolemy was killed (47 B.C.E.). By this time there was a "little Caesar"—Caesarion (which means "Little Caesar")—around the palace, and Cleopatra was in firm control of Egypt.

Labyrinths _____

Cleopatra VII was descended from the marriage of Egyptian and Seleucid royal households, beginning with Ptolemy V and Cleopatra I (daughter of Antiochus III) in 193 B.C.E. Her own parents were Ptolemy XII Auletes and his sister, Cleopatra V.

Eureka! _____

Cleopatra was a remarkable woman. She spoke several languages, was highly educated, witty, ambitious, wily, and attractive. Next to Hannibal, she was Rome's most-feared enemy, and she nearly succeeded in conquering Rome with a Roman (first with Julius Caesar, then with Mark Antony). Had she prevailed, she would have exceeded the achievements of Alexander and given us a markedly different world.

Not long afterward, as part of a division of spoils with Octavian (Caesar's adopted heir and the future emperor, Augustus), Mark Antony (Caesar's lieutenant) received the eastern part of the Roman empire. He summoned Cleopatra to Taurus in 41 B.C.E. They became intimate companions and co-conspirators, who hoped to achieve domination over both Octavian's and Alexander's former empire.

Antony married Cleopatra in 37 B.C.E. and, despite growing fear of a foreign empress ruling Rome, Antony made her "Queen of Queens" of the east. However, they lost the decisive sea battle with Octavian at Actium (31 B.C.E.), and, subsequently, Antony committed suicide. Shortly thereafter, Cleopatra also committed suicide, by means of an asp, and passed on to the realms of the sun-god, Ra.

Octavian had Caesarion, now 16 years old, executed, and he made Egypt his personal province. With its riches, Octavian set the tottering Roman state on firmer footing and ensured its survival for the next several centuries. Thus ended the last Hellenistic dynasty and, with it, the Hellenistic period.

The Least You Need to Know

- From its humble foundations in the eighth century B.C.E., Rome came to dominate Italy and Magna Graecia by the third century B.C.E.

- Roman intervention in the Hellenistic world in the third and second centuries B.C.E. was precipitated by regional instability and encouraged by competing factions and powers.

- The Hellenistic period ended with the suicide of Cleopatra VII in 30 B.C.E. and the transformation of Egypt from a Hellenistic kingdom into a Roman province.

Chapter 24

Trojan Horse? The Greek Legacy from Rome to the Renaissance

In This Chapter

♦ The influence of ancient Greece on the Romans

♦ The rebirth of Greek culture and literature in the "Second Sophistic"

♦ The rise of the Byzantine Empire, Christianity, and Islam

♦ The return of Greek language and learning to the west

Rome's conquest of the last Hellenistic kingdom in 30 B.C.E. did not put an end to the influence of ancient Greece. For at least 300 years prior to this conquest, the Romans had been profoundly influenced by Greek literature and culture and, afterward, Hellenic culture and education continued to be cultivated by elite Romans. Although the western half of the Roman empire remained Latin, the sphere of indirect Hellenic influence continued to widen. The early Christian Church received, suppressed, and adapted the Hellenic legacy and, through the chaos of the early Middle

Ages and the division of the eastern and western churches, this fragile legacy often hung by a thread, an individual, or a single manuscript.

In the east, the Romans maintained the Hellenistic administrative framework, and they provided enough regional stability to allow for a resurgence of Greek culture in the second century C.E. These developments, in turn, helped to establish the eastern Roman empire as essentially Greek. Here, although Christianity was hostile to the pagan past, it both fused with Roman/Greek administrative structures and was infused with a sense of Greek identity. The tensions that were created by such strange bed fellows worked to preserve (at least some of) that same past in cities such as Constantinople, Antioch, and Alexandria. In this chapter, we'll follow the trail of ancient Greece's direct and indirect legacy through Rome, Byzantium, and Islam, and back to the west.

Captured by the Captive: Romans and Greek Culture

In large measure, the Romans saw themselves as pragmatic people who had little time for (or patience with) cultural nuances and niceties. However, as they came into contact with Greek cities, and as Rome itself developed in size and scope, the Romans found that the Greeks had developed a few useful things. For example, the Greeks had history to record and preserve their achievements, rhetorical training to advance their public aspirations, drama to entertain themselves, and some really nice statues.

At first, the Romans acquired these things in the traditional Roman manner: they conquered the people who had them. This way, the Romans could make use of both the people themselves (as slaves) and their possessions (as war booty). However, exposure to Greek culture came at a price: Many elite Romans came to embrace the poetry, literary culture, and intellectual aspects of Hellenism. Other Romans, of course, saw these Hellenistic imports as dangerous, softening, and foreign.

Hellenism in the Republic

Although the Romans had long been in contact with Greek cities such as Cumae and Neapolis (Naples), as well as with the partially Hellenized Etruscans, it was after the Roman conquest of Tarentum (272 B.C.E.) that history begins to trace the development of Greek influence on Rome. Among the captives brought back to Rome from Tarentum was Livius Andronicus, who translated the *Odyssey* into Latin verse, taught Latin and Greek grammar, and wrote plays in Latin. Soon other writers (mostly from southern Italy) were translating Hellenic literature into Latin and writing Greek-style literature of their own. By the turn of the century, Greek plays, such as those adapted by the famous Umbrian playwright Plautus, were entertaining Italian audiences, and Rome had its first patriotic epic, the *Annales*, written by the Calabrian poet Ennius (239–169 B.C.E.).

As Rome conquered Macedon and "freed" Greece, Roman elites such as Flaminius and the general Scipio Aemilianus (son of Aemilius Paullus and adopted grandson of the famous Scipio Africanus) encouraged tolerance toward

Muses

The Roman poet Horace (65–8 B.C.E.) described Rome's acquisition of Greek literature and culture this way: *Graecia capta ferum victorem cepit et artis intulit agresti Latio* ("Captive Greece captured its wild conqueror and brought its arts into rustic Latium").

Greek culture. Aemilianus patronized a circle of intellectuals (such as the historian Polybius, the Stoic philosopher Panaetius, and the comic playwright Terence), and the heads of three philosophical schools visited him in Rome (155 B.C.E.). The Athenian philosophers created a buzz among the Roman youth, but cultural conservatives, such as the censor Marcus Porcius Cato the Elder, spoke out against them. Indeed, Cato the Elder passed legislation that prohibited philosophers from living and teaching in Rome, and he wrote works that he considered suitably Roman.

Eureka!

Roman moralists identified the influx of wealth and Hellenic culture (from the conquest of Syracuse, Carthage, and Macedon) as a cause of moral decay and Roman decline. Cato the Elder (234–149 B.C.E.), who called philosophy "plain gobbledygook," made various luxuries (e.g., imported foods and beautiful slaves) illegal or subject to high luxury taxes. Other writers complained that young Romans had begun to pick up vile Greek habits, such as having music at banquets.

Although Roman distrust of foreign ways persisted, by the end of the first century B.C.E., Roman poets and intellectuals had created vibrant Latin literature, based mainly on Hellenistic models, and many elite Romans (such as Cicero) were sending their sons to Athens and Rhodes to study rhetoric and philosophy at their old alma maters.

The "Library of Celsus" (left) at Ephesus, dedicated by a freedman in 120 C.E. (Note the double walls to keep the manuscripts safely cool.)

(Photo by Eric Nelson)

Return of the Wise Guys

Two centuries of relative stability, which followed Rome's conquests, allowed the former Hellenistic world to grow and develop. Moreover, Hellenistic culture appealed to emperors such as Nero (54–68, who made a grand tour of Greece in 66 and competed at the major Greek games), Hadrian (117–138, who visited Athens on three separate occasions and helped rebuild the city), and Marcus Aurelius (161–180, who adopted Stoicism and wrote his famous *Meditations* in Greek). Also, wealthy Roman expatriates lived in the east, and freedmen (i.e., Greeks formerly enslaved by the Romans) returned to, or patronized, their own cities.

In this environment, Hellenic culture and literature experienced a renaissance, sometimes called the Second Sophistic, in which Greek writers sought to reaffirm the values and virtues of their Classical past. Plutarch's (c. 45–120) voluminous works (such as the "Parallel Lives," in which he compares famous Greek and Roman statesmen), Athenaeus' (c. 200) *Deipnosophistai* (*The Learned Banquet*, in which historical and fictitious characters engage in intellectual party conversation), and Diogenes Laertius' (c. 200–250) compendium of Greek philosophy (from the Presocratics to Epicurus) all exemplify this trend.

Meanwhile, Greek literature was becoming available to the general populace, in romance novels and through the transformation of Greek rhetoric into a performance art. Greek novels, such as *Chaereas and Challirhoe*, were both popular and, in many ways, as predictably formulaic as modern romance novels: boy meets girl; someone, usually girl, suffers from lovesickness; boy loses girl to pirates; boy proves his true love through many adventures; boy gets girl back.

In addition, since the fourth century B.C.E., students had been composing and delivering practice orations as a part of their political and civic training. However, at this time, gifted speakers had no practical outlet for their training except public entertainment. Some Greek rhetoricians, such as Dio "Golden-mouth" Chrysostomus (c. 40–115), became famous lecturers (much like modern "motivational speakers"). Others, such as Herodes Atticus (101–177), Philostratus (c. 170–220, who coined the term *Second Sophistic*), and Aelius Aristides (117– or 129–89) performed extemporaneous orations (mostly on Classical themes and subjects) to packed crowds. Such speakers even had the ancient equivalent of modern groupies and fan clubs! Yet rhetoricians and intellectuals consistently sought to develop (and even speak) a "pure" Classical Attic style, in an attempt to recover the language, if not the reality, of past glory. The widespread nostalgia for the past increased tourist travel to Greece, and tourists were assisted by Pausanias' (c. 150) traveler's guide, *Description of Greece*, which helped travelers appreciate the ruins and avoid the tourist traps.

At the same time, more serious work was taking place in other areas. For example, Galen, the great medical writer and physician, came to Rome from Pergamum, became Marcus Aurelius' physician, and wrote works that dominated western medicine until the 1800s. Ptolemy of Alexandria, the greatest astronomer of antiquity, wrote the *Megalê Suntaxis* (based on observations c. 121–151), and carried out experiments in optics from which he attempted to develop a theory of refraction. The reintroduction of the *Megalê* into western Europe in the twelfth century revolutionized European astronomical knowledge, and it was eclipsed only by Nicolaus Copernicus' "Copernican revolution" in the early sixteenth century.

> **Eureka!**
>
> The Arabs rendered the *Megalê Suntaxis* as *al-Majisti*. When their copies were translated into Latin in the twelfth century, it became the *Algamest*, the name by which Ptolemy of Alexandria's greatest work is best known.

Twilight of the Gods: The End of Antiquity

Yet even as Greek literature and culture were reaching their zenith within the Roman empire, dark clouds were looming over the Greco-Roman world. Along the northern borders of the empire, invasions and migrations, which would eventually contribute to the collapse of the western Roman empire, were beginning. Within the empire itself, Christianity, which was emerging from both its early formative stages and sporadic state persecutions, was on its way to becoming the official Roman state religion and the dominant religion of the western world.

Breaking Up Is Hard to Do

After Marcus Aurelius, the Roman empire entered a century of progressive instability. Emperors (such as the Severi, who came from Leptis Magna in modern Libya) ruled from the provinces and arose from the armies. At times, there were so many of them that it seemed the empire would be torn into several kingdoms, just as Alexander's empire had been. Plagues, Gallic rebellions, Gothic invasions, and even the capture of a Roman emperor (Valerian, 253–260) by the Persians threatened to complete the breakup.

But the emperor Diocletian (284–305) held the empire together, and he attempted to reform the imperial system by splitting the empire into two administrative halves. These halves were unified by an imperial cult that recognized the emperor as a divinely appointed *dominus* ("lord and master"). Christians who were serving in the military and the civil service resisted, and Christian persecutions increased. However, shortly thereafter, Constantine the Great (312–337) made Christianity the official state religion and established a new capital, *Nova Roma* ("New Rome," soon known as Constantinople and, eventually, as Istanbul), on the site of Byzantium (325).

> **Labyrinths**
>
> Although our term *Byzantine* indicates the distinctive civilization that continued after Justinian, the Byzantine emperors and citizens saw themselves as—and called themselves—*Romanoi*, or "Romans." Western Europeans often referred to the Byzantines as, simply, "the Greeks," in recognition of the empire's Greek character and language.

The two halves of the empire, Greek in the east and Latin in the west, had separate destinies. The west continued to spin out of control through wave after wave of invasions, and, in 476, the last western emperor was deposed (although Justinian, 527–565, briefly reasserted control). The Greek east continued, in what we call the Byzantine Empire (565–1453), through the sacking of Constantinople by the Crusaders (1204), until the Turks sacked the city (1453). Facing the latter invasion, Byzantine refugees fled to the west, bringing their language and learning to fuel the emerging Italian Renaissance.

The Triumph of Christianity and the End of the Classical World

Christianity's early rise to power was marked (and fueled!) by tensions with the pagan world, disagreements among Christians, and sporadic persecutions. The publication and dissemination of early Christian documents in Greek (including the letters of Paul, the gospels, and most of the early patristic writings), and the progressive adoption of Christianity by Hellenized peoples, led to sharp tensions and divisions. Many influential Christians rejected the legacy of ancient Greece, and they characterized

Greek ways and practices as demonic, worldly, and dangerous. At the same time, however, Christians adopted Greek rhetorical tools and philosophical ideas (particularly Stoic and Neoplatonic ideas), and utilized them to both formulate Christian doctrine and defend their faith. When Christian writers (such as Augustine, Clement, Justin, and Origin) had to confront and explain such complex matters as the foundations of knowledge, time (i.e., the infinite and the finite), good and evil, and the nature of reality itself, they looked to Athens almost as often as they looked to Jerusalem.

Muses

Beware lest someone capture you with philosophy's empty deceptions, based on human tradition and the elemental spirits of the world, not on Christ.

—Paul, *Letter to the Colossians* 2.8 (first century)

I pray and strive to be seen as a Christian not simply because Christ's teachings differ from Plato's. Plato's views are no more similar in all respects to Christ's than are those of the Stoics, the poets, or the historians. But these people spoke the truth in proportion to each one's innate share of divine reason ... [and so] whatever has been truthfully said by anyone belongs to us Christians.

—Justin, *Apology,* 2.13.2 (second century)

Surprisingly, perhaps, Constantine's decision to convert the Roman state to Christianity contributed to the preservation of the Greek past, at least in the east. For example, heresy now posed a threat to the unity and stability of both church and state. Thus, theological debates gained additional importance and urgency, and a series of councils (beginning with the Council of Nicea in 325, over which Constantine himself presided) were convened to establish orthodox doctrine and arrange for its enforcement. These debates and councils required the use of classically grounded philosophical argumentation and rhetoric. Moreover, administration of the empire depended on educated bureaucrats and on the continuation of educational systems (including the formation of universities). Because possessing a classical education was the hallmark of an educated person, the curricula included classical texts and an artificial Attic dialect.

In contrast, in the west, political and cultural instability left classical language, learning, and literature devoid of political and cultural support, and Greek was lost to the west. When the philosopher Boethius (c. 480–524) was executed, he had completed Latin translations, with commentaries, of some of Aristotle's works (and he wrote *The Consolation of Philosophy* from his jail cell). But his planned work to translate, with commentaries, all of Aristotle and Plato's works could not be completed by anyone else. With his death, the west was devoid of Latin speakers who also had a comprehensive knowledge of Greek and, for centuries thereafter, the west (or, those few people in the west who could read) had access to the legacy of ancient Greece only as it was already preserved in Latin texts.

As the west declined, Byzantium's increasing isolation, inward-looking character, and growing antipathy toward the Latin church contributed to its preservation of its Greek (albeit pagan) past, both as its distinctive heritage and as its treasured mark of superiority.

Islam and the Classical World

Just as Christianity (and Judaism) uncomfortably embraced and integrated various parts of their Hellenic heritage, so, too, did Islam. Islamic philosophy, science, and medicine were profoundly influenced by the Islamic conquests of parts of the Byzantine Empire. As Muslims conquered Syria, Palestine, Alexandria, and Sicily, and took over their administration, they acquired the works of antiquity that were housed there. Some of these works were intentionally destroyed as un-Islamic, but others—especially philosophical and scientific works—were translated into Arabic, and they contributed to what has been termed the "Islamic Renaissance" (eighth through eleventh centuries).

Islamic centers of learning produced some of the greatest minds and scholars of the period. These include the philosopher Ibn Sina (known in the west as Avicenna, 980–1037), whose metaphysical and religious theories drew, sometimes loosely, on both Neoplatonic and Aristotelian ideas; the great physician and scientist al-Raze (known in the west as Rhazes or Razis, 865–925), who wrote works on philosophy, chemistry, religion, and medicine (e.g., the massive *al-Hawi*, translated into Latin in 1279); and the great Aristotelian commentators Ibn Rushd (known in the west as Averroës, or, simply, as "the Commentator," 1126–1198) and Moses ben Maimon (known as Maimonides, 1135–1204), a Jewish physician (to Saladin) and philosopher. Averroës, who maintained that truth can be reached by either reason or revelation, had a profound influence on the west, particularly on the development of the empirical sciences and the study of Aristotle at the University of Padua in the thirteenth century. By using Aristotle (and a bit of Neoplatonism), Maimonides sought to harmonize Greek philosophy and Jewish Law, and he formulated proofs for the existence of god.

However, the synthesis of Hellenic and Islamic learning was accompanied by conflicts between faith and reason, and between paganism and true faith. Within Islam, the synthesis was restrained by such philosophers and theologians as the influential al-Ghazali (1058–1111). Al-Ghazali argued that humanity could not attain truth and avoid the punishments of hell through reason, unless reason was guided by (and subservient to) the superior and authoritative truths revealed in the Koran. Nonetheless, Islam's philosophical and scientific achievements helped to influence European intellectual development in the direction of reason, empiricism, and secularization in ways that would shake Renaissance and Reformation Europe.

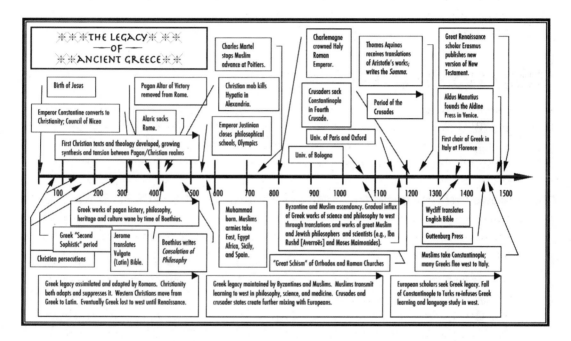

The "Rebirth" of Greece in the West

The divide between the eastern and western churches was deepened by the progressive estrangement of the popes (who saw themselves as the apostolic leaders of the Roman Catholic Church) and the Greek Patriarchs (who, as heads of the Orthodox Church, believed that the popes were under their jurisdiction). Cut off from the east, the popes turned to Frankish kings (beginning with Clovis, 466–511) to defend them from hostile invasions in the north, and, later (Charles Martel, 688–741), to defend western Christendom against Islamic invasions.

Eventually, the Frankish king Charlemagne (768–814) was crowned Holy Roman Emperor by Pope Leo III on Christmas Day, 800. This act (which, apparently, came as a surprise to Charlemagne) ushered in a new power block, one that could claim papal rule over the former Byzantine territories in central Italy and that could claim an emperor equal in status to the Byzantine emperor. Indeed, Charlemagne even called his capital at Aachen *Roma Secunda*, or "The Second Rome."

The institution of the Holy Roman Empire, in combination with Charlemagne's encouragement of classical learning in Latin (the so-called Carolingian Renaissance), set the stage for the reintroduction of Greek to the west in the high Middle Ages (1100–1500).

Eureka!

Under Charlemagne, educated monks of the Carolingian age copied manuscript after manuscript, in the hopes of preserving the entire heritage of ancient Latin and early Christian cultures. Due to the work of the monks, almost no works that survived to 800 were subsequently lost, and over 90 percent of the works of ancient Rome, which we know today, exist in their earliest forms in Carolingian manuscripts (and these manuscripts form the basis of most modern editions).

Bloody Brothers: The Transmission of Learning Through the Crusades

Europe's growth during the tenth, eleventh, and twelfth centuries was accompanied by increased learning and literacy among scholars and members of the clergy, and by an increased interest in rhetoric and logic (stimulated, for the most part, by the works of Boethius). It was also accompanied by increasing trade and interchange between the European, Byzantine, and Islamic worlds.

In the universities, European scholars were eager to get their hands on the works of antiquity (especially the works of Aristotle and Galen, and those of Roman law), which their Byzantine and Muslim colleagues possessed. But European scholars not only lacked the works themselves, they also lacked the means to read them in either their original language or Arabic. The scholars were inadvertently assisted when the Europeans launched a series of holy wars (1095–1249), which were intended to reclaim the Holy Lands for Christendom. In addition to horrific conflict and long-standing hatreds, these European "crusades" created prolonged intermixing and exchange between Europeans, Byzantines, and Muslims (in the Holy Lands, Sicily, and Spain), and between crusaders and Greeks (in Constantinople and the Venetian maritime empire (c. 1200–1670). As this occurred, Latin translations of texts, commentaries, and works of science, which had been made from the Arabic versions in Sicily and Spain (Toledo), began to make their way into Europe in the twelfth century.

> ### Odysseys
>
> The European crusaders set up "Crusader States" after their conquests, which were both centers of prolonged conflict and sources of cultural exchange. These states left an enduring mark upon the subsequent history and architecture of the entire region. They include the following areas:
>
> The County of Edessa (1098–1149), the Principality of Antioch (1098–1268), the Kingdom of Jerusalem (1099-1291), and the County of Tripoli (1102–1289), created in the First Crusade.
>
> The Kingdom of Cyprus (1189–1489), conquered in the Third Crusade by Richard I of England and ruled by the ousted descendants of the kings of Jerusalem.
>
> The Empire of Romania (1204–1261), the Kingdom of Thessalonica (1204–1224), the Duchy of Athens (1205–1456), and the Principality of Achaea, or Morea (1205–1460). These states were created out of the Byzantine Empire after the Fourth Crusade, in which Constantinople was conquered and an attempt was made to establish Latin rule.

The Rediscovery of Greek in Europe

Among the first Greek works to arrive in Europe from Islam in the thirteenth century were those that European scholars sought most desperately: works of science, such as Ptolemy's *Almagest,* and works of Aristotle. Indeed, Aristotle was held in such esteem in Europe that he was referred to simply as "the Philosopher."

The texts sparked a heated debate among scholars and the church, which concerned, in particular, the authority of the Bible and the authority of the Philosopher. The church responded to these debates by banning the works of Aristotle: the study of any Aristotelian work (including Boethius' translations) was banned in Paris in 1210, and, from 1231 to 1263, papal commissions and decrees either allowed only selected (and censored) Aristotelian works to be taught or banned them altogether—to no avail.

St. Thomas Aquinas (1225–1274) wrote massive works, in which he attempted to reconcile Aristotelian and Christian thought, and he argued that there is no conflict between the teachings of philosophy and those of theology. Although his works were briefly banned by the church, his *Summa Theologica* became a foundational part of the philosophy and doctrine of the Roman Catholic Church. In fact, as recently as 1879, Pope Leo XII commended the study of Aquinas' philosophy. In England, Robert Grosseteste (chancellor of Oxford and Bishop of Lincoln, 1168–1253), and his follower Roger Bacon (1220–1292), argued that students of either the Bible or Aristotle should be able to read the original texts and compose their own translations. This philological approach to text and individual study had a significant influence on pre-Reformation theologian and translator John Wycliffe (c. 1330–1384) and on the coming Reformation.

More Greeks Bearing Gifts: The Renaissance

By the fourteenth century, conditions in Europe (particularly in Italy) were conducive to the reintroduction of Greek texts, learning, and language. Threatened by the Turks, Byzantium increased its economic, diplomatic, and cultural connections with Italy, and a growing number of Byzantines migrated to the west. Interests in science, *Roman law*, philosophy, medicine, and the church fathers (whose works could *also* be used to defend classicism) remained strong. Also, among the upper classes—who supplied members of the clergy, diplomats, and university professors—there was a renewed interest in the literature, mythology, and history of the classical world.

Lexica

Roman law, as recognized since the Middle Ages, was based on the *Corpus Iuris Civilis* ("Body of Civil Law") codified by the emperor Justinian in the sixth century. Roman law governs most of Europe, Scotland (originally), South America, Quebec, and Louisiana. Along with Islamic Sharia and Anglo-American "common law," Roman civil law forms one of the three major legal systems prevalent in the world today.

The influential humanist Francesco Petrarch (1304–1374) engaged Leonzio Pilato as a translator of Homer and Euripides, and Petrarch's friend, Giovanni Boccaccio (1313–1375), helped establish him at Florence (1360) as the first professor of Greek in the west since the fall of the western Roman empire.

In 1396, Florence secured the services of the Byzantine diplomat Manuel Chrysoloras (c. 1350–1415), who became the preeminent teacher of Greek in the early Renaissance. His successive appointments as professor of Greek at Florence, Bologna, Venice, Paris, Rome, and Constance (Germany) brought him into contact with some of the finest minds of the early Renaissance, and further increased the need for texts, critical editions, commentaries, and translations of classical works. Chrysoloras' comprehensive Greek grammar (the *Erotêmata*), his excellent instruction, and his emphasis on lucid translation are largely responsible for the return of Greek classics to their foundational place in western education—at the dawn of the Renaissance and just prior to the fall of the Byzantine Empire.

The Least You Need to Know

- After the Roman conquest of Tarentum (272 B.C.E.), history begins to trace the development of Greek influence on Rome.

- Greek language and learning were lost to the west shortly after the fall of the western Roman empire (476).

- Classical culture and works contributed to the development of the Byzantine Empire and to what has been termed the "Islamic Renaissance."

- Classical works returned to the west, from Islam, in the thirteenth century, and contributed to the Italian Renaissance.

Radical, Romantic, and Revolutionary: Ancient Greece from the Renaissance to Today

In This Chapter

- The Renaissance and Reformation
- The Enlightenment and Romanticism
- Radicals and Revolutionaries
- The very least you need to know!

With the dawn of the Renaissance, we arrive at the legacy of ancient Greece in the modern West. Yet, just as we opened this book with one broad overview, we must close it with another. A comprehensive examination of the legacy of ancient Greece—as it was expressed and developed in each historical period (e.g., the Renaissance), or as it influenced each movement (e.g., Romanticism) or prominent figure (e.g., Johann Winckelmann)—would require thousands upon thousands of pages! Worse yet, because the legacy of ancient Greece pervades the foundations of Western art, literature, science, and philosophy, it is discernible virtually everywhere. From da Vinci to Dali, Descartes to Derrida, Fontenelle to Freud, Galileo to Gould, Nietzsche to Nussbaum, and William of Ockham to E.O. Wilson, the scientific, artistic, and intellectual history of the West is intertwined with, and part of, the legacy of ancient Greece. Thus, this chapter is not a last word. Instead, it is an introduction to, and an invitation to further explore, a very expansive topic.

To rein in this broad subject a bit, we've chosen to organize and discuss it under several topical R's (Rebirth, Reform, Reason, Romance, Radical, Required). Each topic includes a few representational illustrations and examples, which will, we hope, open the door and point the way to new and fascinating territory!

Rebirth: The Renaissance

The very term *renaissance* (or "rebirth") suggests that a culture that has been stagnant or suppressed is revived or reawakened. In Europe, the Renaissance was a period of unprecedented cultural, scientific, and intellectual development. For a renaissance to occur, however, there must be *something* to revive and, in this case, the revival often involved, or was assisted and accelerated by, Greek literature and learning.

As you know from the previous chapter, the intellectual and cultural groundwork for the Renaissance had been laid over a long period of time, and Greek texts had been slowly filtering into the west since the late twelfth century. Thus, it would be an over-simplification to suggest that the beginning of the Renaissance was a distinct moment in time, or that the Middle Ages could be accurately termed the *Dark Ages*. However, imagine a voracious desire for texts (accompanied by a mad and competitive scramble for manuscripts), which is suddenly fed by the invention of the western printing press (c. 1450). Now, at long last, mass publication of texts and translations could become both possible and profitable, and centuries of accumulated knowledge could be accessed and studied.

Moreover, such a desire and search for classical texts suggests a sense of confidence, at least on the part of humanists and scholars, in both the intellectual traditions of the past and their relevancy to the present. In this, Renaissance scholars were similar to both their ancient predecessors and to those of us who still find the ancient world more relevant than it is remote. Very interestingly, however, although European interest in the works of ancient Greece initially focused on the recovery of scientific knowledge, it shifted from the content of the texts to the method of inquiry. In time, the Renaissance became a profound celebration of ancient Greece's less-tangible accomplishments: an approach to knowledge that emphasized individual observation and study, an exploration of the human condition in human terms, and a profound sense of aesthetics. Indeed, it was during the Renaissance that artists became elevated to the status of philosophers (i.e., those who can capture and convey essential truths), and that painting, sculpture, and architecture became part of the liberal arts, rather than simply professions.

Reform: The Reformation

The Renaissance was also a period in which intense study of theology and the New Testament took place. Reformers began as Renaissance scholars, whose classical educations and confidence in individual study and human reason enabled them to challenge the teachings and authority of the church. Such early reformers include Thomas Linacre (c. 1460–1524) and John Colet (c. 1467–1519) in England, the great Dutch scholar Desiderius Erasmus (c. 1466–1543), the German reformer Martin Luther (1483–1546), and the Swiss reformer John Calvin (1509–1564). In addition, because discrepancies arose between the Latin Vulgate (the New Testament in Latin) and the Greek New Testament, reformers published textual criticisms and critical editions of the Greek New Testament (e.g., Erasmus' 1516 edition, which was based on new manuscripts and included both commentary and a new Latin translation).

The reformers' confidence in education, individual study, and human reason also led them to translate the Bible into modern languages (e.g., Luther's German translation, which he made from Erasmus' edition), and to advocate for public education. Such measures were intended to make both education and the Bible accessible to the common people. Previously, only those who could read Greek or Latin (or had access to John Wycliffe's, c. 1328–1384, handwritten English manuscripts) had been able to read and study the Bible themselves!

However, profound differences arose between reformist scholars and between reformist movements. Among other things, they disagreed on the degree to which classical (pagan) works could be of value to Christians, on the limits of human reason (within their own, individual understandings of scripture and doctrine), and on the authority of textual scholarship (once their own versions of scripture, including both books and translations, had been canonized). As the debates became increasingly polarized, scholars like Erasmus found it difficult to define and hold any middle ground, particularly without infuriating both sides. Not surprisingly, similar differences concerning faith and reason, the purposes of education, and the authority of scholarship and textual criticism are still vigorously discussed by Christian scholars and theologians today.

> **Muses**
>
> "Either the Greek original is not the Gospel … or we [i.e., who use the Latin] are not Christians.
>
> —Thomas Linacre
>
> The Romanists claim that Paul says [Ephesians 5:31–2], "The two shall become one flesh; this is a great sacrament" … [but] where the Vulgate uses "*sacramentum*," the Greek texts read "*mystêrion*" … That is how they came to understand marriage as a sacrament … which they would not have done if they had read the Greek.
>
> —Martin Luther
>
> I don't want you to imbibe pagan morals together with pagan writings. You will, however, find many things in them which assist in living a holy life, and you shouldn't reject the good precepts of a pagan author.
>
> —Erasmus

Reason: The Enlightenment

Although human reason remained linked, or subservient, to faith or revealed truth within the Reform movement, it broke free in the "Enlightenment," a self-named movement of the seventeenth and eighteenth centuries. Enlightenment scholars argued that humans live in a fundamentally rational universe, one that can be fully apprehended only through empirical observation and the application of reason.

On this view, because truth is ascertained through experience and reason, none of the various religions or traditions could claim authority on the basis of revealed "truths" alone, because authority must be grounded in truth and truth is not revealed. Moreover, because reason can make connections between, organize, and unify disparate pieces of information and knowledge, some Enlightenment scholars argued that all things, including humans, could be studied and understood as part of the natural world. This confidence in a unified theory of knowledge can be found today in the writings of such prominent theorists as the Harvard naturalist and Pulitzer Prize winner E.O. Wilson. In the arts, classical (i.e., Greek and Roman) models, which expressed (in writing) or demonstrated (in form) the serene rational order and harmony of the universe, became *canonized* (a movement

> **Lexica**
>
> A **canon** is a body of rules, principles, or books that are considered (by the authorities) to be authoritative and fundamental to a study or field. The canon of English literature would, for example, include Shakespeare. In Christianity, various books (e.g. Revelation, the Apocrypha) are considered by various sects to be "outside the canon" of scripture.

known as Neoclassicism). Poets, from John Milton (1608–1674, whose *Paradise Lost* is a Christian epic) to Alexander Pope (1688–1744, possibly the acme of English classicism), relied upon classical educations and texts.

In the natural sciences, European discoveries and advancements (such as those by Galileo, 1564–1642) exceeded those of the past, which led some scientists to consider the past irrelevant to enlightened rational minds. However, with the rediscovery of Epicurean philosophy, the theory of atoms became influential on Enlightenment scientists, like Isaac Newton and Robert Boyle, and in the development of the calculus, through the work of Newton and philosopher and mathematician Gottfried Wilhelm Leibniz (1646–1716).

Labyrinths

After receiving a superb education, René Descartes (1596–1650) concluded that neither ancient philosophy nor modern science contained the kind of wisdom he was seeking, and he claimed to offer a unique philosophical and scientific approach. He is identified with the phrase *"cogito, ergo sum"* ("I think, therefore I am"), which claims that, if something is thinking and doubting, then it must exist. However, Descartes' works show the influence of both Plato and Aristotle, and his most famous claim (namely, that you can't doubt *unless* you exist) had already been explored by St. Augustine (354–430) in *Against the Academicians,* and anticipated by Avicenna (980–1037), who argued that the soul can conceive of itself apart from a body.

Humans themselves became part of the Enlightenment project, as natural subjects with rational capacities, which could be understood and improved. History, it was thought, recorded humanity's "progress" from its childlike and imaginative responses to the world (displayed in "primitive" religion, myth, superstition, and poetic texts), through successive phases, to its mature and "enlightened" adulthood (exemplified by western European males, science, and "rational" religion). A scholarly interest in this process resulted in the beginnings of mythology (the study of the meanings, functions, and origins of myth) and the study of national folklore, and involved such famous scholars as Bernard de Fontenelle (*On the Origin of Fables,* c. 1724), David Hume (*The Natural History of Religion*), and Christian Heyne (1729–1812, who coined the term *myth*).

In other areas, Greek classics served as resources for the development of human and political science. Thucydides' history, for example, was influential on the work of Thomas Hobbes (1588–1679, who claimed that life, for primitive humans, was "solitary, poor, nasty, brutish, and short"). Hobbes, who studied to become a classical

" " Muses _____

Enlightenment is man's emergence from his self-imposed immaturity. Immaturity is the inability to use one's understanding without guidance from another. This immaturity is self-imposed when its cause lies not in lack of understanding, but in lack of resolve and courage to use it without guidance from another.

—Immanuel Kant, _What is Enlightenment?_

scholar, published a famous translation of Thucydides in 1628, before he published the _Leviathan_. In his political philosophy, Hobbes rejected democracy in favor of a social contract that was backed by absolute authority and based on the laws of nature. Other political philosophers, notably John Locke (1632–1704), also argued for social contract theory, but incorporated equality (for males) and educational safeguards.

During the Enlightenment, there appeared to be two major impediments to progress on a grand scale: the church (primarily the Roman Catholic Church in France) and hereditary aristocracies (which were developing into absolutist monarchies in France, Prussia, Austria, and Russia). Both were seen as dangerous relics of Europe's primitive beginnings, and as impediments to progressive maturation and improvement. However, in a time of colonialism, "improvement" often included forcing European ways and beliefs upon "primitive" people, who were still in the childhood of humanity. In this sense, "progress" contributed substantially to the subjugation and "improvement" of indigenous persons, so that each might develop, as the philosopher and political theorist Jean-Jacques Rousseau (1712–1778) put it in _The Social Contract_, from "a stupid and unimaginative animal" to "an intelligent being and a man." This exportation and imposition of religious, political, and economic systems (for the good of the "backward," "primitive," or "immoral" people, of course) remain one of the West's most shameful tendencies and legacies.

Romance: Romanticism

The self-assured, monolithic, and scientific approach to humanity and the cosmos that characterized the Enlightenment, combined with the social and cultural affects of the Industrial Revolution, inspired a counter-reaction, called Romanticism. Romanticism's roots lay in Rousseau's "noble savage"—a phrase that indicates humankind as unencumbered and unfettered by civilization and, in such a state, as naturally good. For Romantics, the Enlightenment and the industrial revolution had attempted to constrain the human spirit within rationality and mechanization. Human expression and meaning, they argued, could not be found in the rationalistic or mechanistic conquest of the natural world. Instead, they thrived in the emotional and artistic connection to nature that was found in "primitive" cultures. (Think of the _Star Wars_ cycle and you have a movie epic of a Romantic hero struggling against an Enlightenment empire.)

Romanticism emphasized nature, emotion, passion, and internal freedom from the constraints of contemporary society. It sought release in the primitive, the imaginative, and the mystic. For this reason, the Romantics were fascinated by primitive cultures, whose folklore and mythology, they believed, conveyed their own national characters. Their enthusiasm was fanned by the decipherment and translation of Sanskrit (the classical language of India), the discovery of the Norse *Edda* (1753) and other epic works of poetry, and the collections of national folklore (such as by the Brothers Grimm).

The Romantic Movement was particularly strong in Germany, where it evolved, in part, in response to French cultural domination and an emerging German national identity. It originated in the ardor of art critic Johann Winckelmann (1717–1768), who claimed that the essential and sublime perfection of Greek art emanated from the social and even physical perfection of the Greeks themselves, and that such perfection could only be attained by studying and appreciating the Greeks. Since this time, Hellenism has been a driving source of intellectual energy and scholarship in Germany. From Lessing to Goethe and Schiller, Heyne to Nietzsche, Hegel, and Heidegger, and Freud to Jung and beyond, the influence of Germanic Hellenism on the modern world cannot be overstated.

Germany's higher educational system was reorganized around the study of ancient Greece in the late eighteenth and early nineteenth centuries, and its ideals inspired both educational reforms and a Romantic movement in England. British Romanticism is primarily associated with William Wordsworth (1770–1850), Samuel Taylor Coleridge (1772–1834), and Lord Byron (1788–1824), who died assisting the Greeks against the Turks.

> **Odysseys**
>
> Byron carved his initials in several evocative places, as evidence that he had visited. One of the most famous is the magnificent temple of Poseidon at Cape Sounion (a day trip from Athens). But don't try to leave your initials there: Such vandalism *isn't* romantic and it carries a huge fine!

Hellenic Radicals

From the Renaissance to Romanticism, Rome and Latin symbolized, for the most part, the prevailing order and the established institutions of church and state. Greek literature and "Hellenic" ideals (often self-defined) served as radical alternatives to what scholars, clerics, political theorists, and revolutionaries perceived as "Roman."

In this respect, western Hellenism has been, since the Renaissance, a cultural insurgency against "Roman" order (of whatever definition). However, it is a cultural insurgency that more frequently changes and modifies the prevailing order than overthrows it, and that seems most comfortable when it is confined within that order.

Eureka!

The identification of Rome with oppressive state power appears in the popularization of Marianne (the symbol of the French Revolution) in her Phrygian cap—the mark of a freed Roman slave—during the revolution, and in later personifications of Liberty (such as in Delacroix' *Liberty Leading the People*, 1830). As revolutionaries became respectable members of their own republics, Liberty's symbolic opposition was constrained a bit. In France, Marianne sometimes appears in a diadem (rather than her seditious cap), and on the American "Liberty Dime," where Liberty appears in her winged cap (symbolizing freedom of thought), Roman fasces (symbols of ultimate state authority and power) appear on the other side of the coin.

For example, even though the American and French revolutionaries adopted (in some quarters) an anti-Roman stance, they ultimately placed more faith in Roman civil liberty than in Hellenic-style democracy. In America, the Roman federalism of John Adams held sway over more radically democratic ideals borrowed from Greek, Anglo-Saxon, or Native American traditions. However, comparisons between America and Rome are often the subject of anxiety and denial, particularly in light of America's status as a world power. After all, thick irony would attend the notion that, after gaining its own independence from an oppressive state, America became history's most powerful "New Rome."

Unsurprisingly, then, the comparisons between America and Rome have encouraged a new kind of Hellenism. Both liberal and conservative elements have emphasized their (often vaguely formed) "Greek" ideals and rejected (or ignored) their more Roman characteristics. Even twentieth-century "Western Civ" curriculum, for example, focused almost entirely on the "glories" of ancient Greece. However, when faced with the realities of ancient Greece, both sides often shrink away, for the ancient Greeks rarely provide us with clean and easy ideals. Sometimes, we all prefer our Hellenism to be served up within a Roman banquet.

The legacies of ancient Greece remain inspirational and controversial. The murals, "The Twelve Labors of Hercules" (Labors 7–12 shown), created by Michael Spafford for the Washington State House of Representatives in 1981, were covered by a curtain for nearly 20 years, as offensive, and then removed. Today they are housed at Centralia College's beautiful Corbet Theater (Centralia, Washington).

(Photo courtesy of Don Frey)

Required

As we complete this book, fresh comparisons between America and Rome, and between America and Greece, come from within American and from without. The world recently celebrated the Olympic Games in Athens, and scientists are making comparisons between Epicurean atomism and quantum theory. Neurobiologists are producing modern support for Aristotelian theories, and psychologists are reexamining Plato's version of the soul. The movies *Troy* and *Alexander* are hitting the big screen, and Islamic and Christian worlds, both with roots in Hellenism, are talking in terms of "crusades" and "holy wars." Reformulated Aristotelian and Stoic theories of virtue, with their focus on human character and development, are competing with prominent moral theories (i.e., consequentialism and deontology). So it's fairly obvious that ancient Greece and Hellenism are relevant today! However, as we said in the beginning of this book, there is often a gap between ideals and reality, and between what we merely imagine and historical fact. Our hope is that, in the spirit of Hellenism, you will continue to seek out ancient Greece for yourselves. In addition, we hope that you have come to realize that a full understanding and appreciation of modern intellectual, artistic, and literary history depend upon a knowledge of (or at least a familiarity with) ancient Greece. Without some knowledge of Homer, the historians, the philosophers, and the tragedians, you will miss modern allusions to, or adaptations of, ancient texts and contexts. Whether you are reading Victor Davis Hansen's or Chalmers Johnson's editorials, looking for meaning in James Hillman's

The Soul's Code, or watching Agamemnon meet his (decidedly nonclassical) demise in *Troy*, without some grounding in the classics, numerous details and dimensions will remain unrecognizably "Greek" to you. And so, here, we encourage you to read at least one original work (translations are fine!) to see what all the fuss is about!

Finally, as we have noted, the history, literature, and legacy of ancient Greece has been, at least for the most part, written and interpreted by males, about males, for males (and, generally, only certain kinds of males at that). The perspectives and voices of non-Athenians, women, people of color, gays and lesbians, and the lower classes are either absent or selectively filtered and interpreted. Today, however, a new generation of scholars, writers, philosophers, and intellectuals—who come from diverse backgrounds and perspectives—are turning to ancient Greece. They are bringing fresh eyes to formerly accepted scholarship, challenging or confirming textual and physical evidence, and discovering entirely new approaches and applications. Yet, whether they contest or confirm accepted traditions and truths, they will become part of the inquiry and the discussion. We invite you to join in!

Sometimes good ideas take time. The Corinth Canal (constructed 1882–1893) was about 2600 years in the making! The Corinthian tyrant Periander (c. 602 B.C.E.) would be proud! He initiated the first attempt, cut the first turf himself with a golden pick, and carried the dirt on his back (apparently the precedent for the dignitary "ground-breaking" ceremony).

(Photo courtesy of Norita White)

The Least You Need to Know

- The return of Greek literature, language, and learning to the West helped to initiate and fuel the intellectual, artistic, literary, and scientific developments of the Renaissance.

- Reformers began as Renaissance scholars, whose classical educations and confidence in individual study and human reason enabled them to challenge the teachings and authority of the church.

- Enlightenment scholars argued that humans live in a fundamentally rational universe, one that can be fully apprehended only through empirical observation and the application of reason.

- From the Renaissance to Romanticism, Rome and Latin symbolized, for the most part, the prevailing order and the established institutions of church and state, to which Greek culture provided radical alternatives and approaches.

- A full understanding and appreciation of modern intellectual, artistic, and literary history depend upon a knowledge of (or at least a familiarity with) ancient Greece.

Your Own Odyssey: Reading, Surfing, and Travel Itineraries in Ancient Hellas

If you've developed special interests, or if you just want to find out more about ancient Greece, take a look at the following resources. Each book lists further resources, and each website is a gateway to the ancient world. So let the games begin!

The Greeks in Print

For inexpensive translations of ancient authors that feature good introductions, begin with the Penguin Classics. For secondary sources, start here and then head to your local library or bookstore.

The Oxford History of Greece & the Hellenistic World, John Boardman, et al., Oxford University Press, 2002 (ISBN 0192801376).

Women in Ancient Greece, Sue Blundell, Harvard University Press, 1995 (ISBN 0674954734).

Myths of the Ancient Greeks, Richard P. Martin and Patrick Hunt, New American Library, 2003 (ISBN 0451206851).

The Ancient Olympics: A History, Nigel Spivey, Oxford University Press, 2004 (ISBN 0192804332).

Warfare in Ancient Greece: A Sourcebook, Michael M. Sage, Routledge, 1996 (ISBN 0415143551).

Alexander of Macedon 356–323 B.C.: A Historical Biography, Peter Green, University of California Press, 1992 (ISBN 0520071662).

Gateways to the Greeks

Classicists, philosophers, and other scholars have established comprehensive websites, where you will find such things as texts in both ancient Greek and translation, maps, photos of art and architecture, archeological sites, lexicons and encyclopedias, search tools, and links to all things Greek. Begin here:

Perseus Digital Library (www.perseus.tufts.edu) is housed at Tufts University and is the most comprehensive Classics website available. For information of every kind, this is the place to begin!

The Stoa (www.stoa.org) is a consortium for electronic publications in the humanities. Among its many features, the Stoa includes a photographic archive of the archeological and architectural remains of ancient Athens, Metis (where you can find interactive, panoramic views of numerous sites), and Diotima (where you can learn about women of the ancient world).

Internet History Sourcebooks Project (www.fordham.edu/halsall) is edited by Paul Halsall, and features collections of public domain and copy-permitted historical texts from numerous eras and locations.

Didaskalia, Ancient Theater Today (http://didaskalia.open.ac.uk) is an electronic resource and journal dedicated to the study of ancient Greek and Roman drama in performance.

On the Road to Ruins

If you're interested in seeing both sites and artifacts, begin with well-placed archeological museums. Below are a few; for a full list, visit the Hellenic Ministry of Culture at www.culture.gr/2/21/toc/museums.html.

The Archeological Museum at Olympia houses collections from the sanctuary of Olympian Zeus in Olympia and the Olympic Games.

The National Archeological Museum of Athens and the **Acropolis Museum** are only two of the numerous museums in Athens.

The Archeological Museum of Delphi sits in the ancient sanctuary and houses offerings and other finds from Delphi.

The Archaeology Museum of Thessaloniki houses the contents of the tomb of Philip II of Macedon, including his bones.

The Graeco-Roman Museum in Alexandria houses collections of Hellenistic, Roman, and Christian artifacts.

The Antiquities Museum in the Alexandrine Library is part of the new Library at Alexandria and highlights Alexandria through the ages.

Glossary

agôgê ("path, education") The 13-year training program that Spartan boys (except for royal sons) received in order to become *homoioi* ("full Spartan citizens").

agon A struggle (hence "agony") in contest for an *athlon* ("prize"). Those who competed came to be called athletes.

agrarian Refers to organizations based on farming and agriculture.

aitia (or *aetia*) The Greek word for "reason/cause," as in (a)etiology, the study or history of cause and effect.

allegory An approach to mythology in which it is thought that myths are, or contain, symbolic elements that must be interpreted metaphorically in order to be correctly understood.

amnesty (from the Greek *a* "not" + *mnês* "remember"). An *amnêstia* is an agreement to "not remember" irreconcilable wrongs of the past in order to try to bring about peace in the present.

anachronism (from the Greek *ana* "back" + *chron* "time") The error of placing a person, object, or way of thinking back into the wrong time. Also the error of imposing modern ideas or attitudes onto peoples, cultures, or beliefs that existed prior to the emergence of such ideas or attitudes.

anthropomorphic A term that means "created or represented in human form."

archon (plural *archontes*)   A term for political leader or ruler.

aretê   Greek term meaning "excellence," often translated as "virtue."

athlon   A prize awarded in competitive games.

B.C.E.   Contemporary international scholarship uses **B.C.E.** (Before the Common Era) in place of B.C. (Before Christ), and **C.E.** (Common Era) in place of A.D. (*anno domini*, "The year of our Lord").

black figure   A pottery technique where the figures were painted in black silhouette and the details cut through them into the red clay. Red figure was the opposite: The figures were left red against a black background with details painted in with a fine brush.

boulê   ("council") Along with the assembly (*ekklêsia*), one of the two primary governing bodies of the Greeks. In Classical Athens, the *boulê* was composed of 500 men, chosen by lot, and it prepared business for the assembly.

canon   A body of rules, principles, or books that are considered (by the authorities) to be authoritative and fundamental to a study or field. The canon of English literature would, for example, include Shakespeare.

chryselephantine statues   Monumental statues made of ivory (for flesh) and gold (for drapery) over a framework of wood.

cleruchy   A special kind of Athenian colony, in which citizens retained their Athenian citizenship and rights. Cleruchies served as outlets for disenchanted or poor citizens, and as garrisons for the Athenian empire.

cosmopolis   world *polis* (city-state).

cult   A term used to indicate an organized system of traditions and ritual used in religious worship of any god or deity.

Cycladic   Name that refers to the islands of the central Aegean (e.g., Paros, Delos, Naxos).

dactylic hexameter   The meter of epic poetry. It is based on "six measures" (*hexa meter*) of dactylic (long-short-short) "feet."

decarchy   An executive board of 10 men in control of the state.

deify   To make something or someone into a god or divine being.

dêmos (plural *dêmoi*)   A territory and the people (sometimes connoting the free males) who live in it. Although the term came to be used by aristocrats (probably in the seventh century B.C.E.) as a term for "commoners" or "the masses," it retained its more inclusive sense (i.e., "the whole people") in legal inscriptions.

dendrology   The study of woody plants. Evidence that corroborates the dating of events that impact climate changes can be found in such things as tree rings.

dialektos   ("conversation") This Greek term describes a process of synthesis and analysis used to derive understanding. It became associated with logical argumentation with Aristotle and with logic itself in the medieval period. Hegel and Marx used "dialectic" to describe how we transcend logical contradictions inherent in our ways of understanding.

didactic   Tending or intending to teach.

earth and water   Symbolic offerings that indicated willing and unconditional submission to the Persian monarch.

ekklêsia   ("assembly") One of the two primary elements, along with the council (*boulê, gerousia*), of Greek government. In Athens, the full assembly of citizens of the *dêmos*.

elenchus   ("cross-examination") Socrates called his method (using questions and answers to draw out logical inconsistencies) *elenchus*.

ephoroi   ("overseers") In Sparta, an annually elected board of 5 adult citizens, each over the age of 30. Ephors had executive political and judicial power over the *gerousia*, "assembly," and kings in order to maintain adherence to Spartan laws and customs.

eponymous   (from Greek *epi* "upon" + *onym* "name") A personal name from which another term originates (e.g., the mythical King Aegeus for whom the Aegean Sea is named, or George Washington for whom Washington State is named).

ethnos (plural *ethnê*)   A group of people who share a common identity and territory, such as a tribe.

euhemerism   An approach to mythology in which myths are thought to contain historical facts that have been amplified and exaggerated in an historical process of transmission.

feminist scholarship   Although there is no single feminist approach to scholarship, feminist scholars tend to agree on some core ideals of feminism (e.g., that males and females should have equal political, economic, and social opportunity, voice, and value).

freestanding statues   Statues finished on all sides.

gender   A conception, composed of social and cultural assumptions and expectations, regarding what male or female persons, behaviors, and roles are and should be. Sex is a biological distinction (male or female).

gerousia ("body of elders") In Sparta, the *gerousia* was a council of 28 men, each over 60 years old, and the 2 kings. Election to the *gerousia* was for life, and it was the highest honor for a Spartan.

Gordian knot The knot attached to the ancient wagon of the legendary King Midas of Phrygia in the capital, Gordium. Legend claimed that the person who could untie the impossibly intricate knot would rule Asia. Alexander the Great, faced with the conundrum, decisively cut through the knot with a sword.

hegemony A dominant power, especially one state over another. It comes from the Greek *hêgemôn*, the "leader" (either individual or state) of a league of states.

Hellenes The word *Greek* comes from Latin. Ancient and modern Greeks call themselves Hellenes after a mythological ancestor, Hellen, son of Deucalion. Words with this base (e.g., Hellenic, Hellenism, Hellenistic) indicate "Greek" in a broad sense.

helot (from the Greek word for "capture") Spartan serfs and the object of systematized subjugation.

herm A representation of the god Hermes, showing his face and erect phallus on a pillar. These pillars were used to demarcate property and to provide protection and good luck.

heterogeneous (from the Greek *hetero* "other" + *gen* "created") This term means having dissimilar characteristics or origins.

heuristic This term pertains to general formulas or sets of rules that guide investigation of complex subjects or help to solve complex problems.

hieroglyphic script A script that uses pictures, or pictographs, to represent words, like the bumper sticker "I [heart] my [picture of a breed of dog]." If the symbols are syllabic, they represent syllables such as "ba" or "po."

historia Greek term for "research" or "investigation," first applied to the events and causes (*aitia*) of what we now call "history" by Herodotus.

Homeric Question The question of whether one author (known as Homer) created the *Iliad*, the *Odyssey*, both, or neither.

homogenous (from the Greek *homo* "same" + *gen* "created") This term means having the same (or very similar) characteristics or the same origin.

homoioi ("equals") Full-rank Spartan male citizens of age.

homonoia "Concord" or "being of one heart and mind."

hoplites   Specialized heavy infantry who fought in a disciplined formation, the *phalanx*.

hubris   This term means wanton arrogance. Hubris often manifests in grossly inappropriate (and often violent) actions or attitudes.

idiosyncratic   The Greek term *idiotes* means "private individual," and *syncrasis* means "mixture." *Idiosyncratic* indicates a mixture of (eccentric) characteristics that are unique to a particular individual (or group). The negative connotations of *idiot* come from its use for people who are just a bit *too* unique.

Keftiu   This may be the ancient name (or at least the Egyptian name) for "Minoan." However, the name might pertain to certain kinds of traders (of which the Minoans would have been a substantial part), rather than exclusively to the Minoans of Crete.

kleros (plural *kleroi*)   An allotment of farmland, passed on through the male line, which was generally sufficient to support a family.

koinê   This is the "common" Greek dialect of the late Hellenistic and Roman imperial world. Both the Jewish Septuagint and the New Testament were written in this dialect.

kouroi   Monumental (life-size or larger) statues of men (*kouroi*) or women (*korai*).

krypteia   ("secret society") A secret police force in Sparta, which identified and assassinated subversive (or potentially subversive) helots. All Spartan youths were enrolled in this society for a time.

Linear A   The system of writing on clay tablets used by the Minoans c. 1800–1450 B.C.E.

Linear B   An adaptation of Linear A by the Mycenaeans to their own language c. 1450–1200 B.C.E.

lingua franca   Originally a medieval pidgin of several languages, which was used by traders and travelers in the eastern Mediterranean. Today the term indicates a language that is used by speakers of different languages for common (usually commercial) communication. Hellenistic *koinê* ("common Greek") was the *lingua franca* of antiquity.

matrilineal   A bloodline that is traced through the mother, not the father. Through the father is *patrilineal*.

matronymic   A term indicating that one uses one's mother's name to keep track of one's birth (e.g., Susan Priscillasdaughter, Eric Bettysson).

megaron   A large interior hall, with a large, circular, raised hearth and a chimney vent in the center. Megarons have a portico entrance at one end, a small anteroom at the other, and four pillars around the hearth to support balconies and the roof.

metropolis   The "mother-city" of the colony. The leader of the colonists and "founder" of the colony was called the *oikistês* (Greek term), or oikist (common English term).

misogynistic   (from Greek *miso* "hatred for" + *gyn* "woman, wife") Hatred for or toward women.

Nemean Lion   The Nemean Lion's skin was impregnable, but Herakles (Hercules) used his great strength to strangle and kill the beast (one of the Twelve Labors). He then skinned it with its own claws and wore the hide and head as a cloak.

ode   A general term for a poetic song, which appears in such words as *episode* and *monody*.

oecumene   Indicates the world inhabited by humanity, often under a divine being.

oikos   The Greek work for "household," which included the family, property, real estate, slaves, and animals.

omnipotent   All-powerful.

omnipresent   Everywhere at once.

omniscient   All-knowing.

orthodoxy   (from Greek *ortho* "right" + *dox* "opinion") Religious focus that places emphasis on correct belief.

orthopraxy   (from Greek *ortho* "right" + *prax* "action") Religious focus that places emphasis on correct ritual action.

ostracism   A practice that (possibly instituted by Cleisthenes) allowed Athenian citizens to temporarily exile individuals thought dangerous to public welfare. Citizens wrote one name on a potsherd, as a secret ballot, and the person who received the most votes had to leave Athens in 10 days, without loss of property or citizenship, for 10 years.

paleobotany   The study of ancient vegetation.

palynology   The study of pollen.

pastoral   Refers to organizations based on herds (such as cattle and goats) and herding.

patriarchy   (from Greek *patr* "father" + *archy* "rule") The human social interaction and organization that results from consciously and unconsciously conceiving of and ordering human affairs to privilege males and male authority.

Pentakontaetia   Thucydides calls the period between the Persian and (Second) Peloponnesian Wars the *Pentakontaetia*, or "50-year period." Although it was, strictly speaking, about 47 years, the name stuck and remains in use today.

perioikoi   ("dwellers-around") Term used to describe neighboring peoples who are subordinate to a dominant *polis*. It is often applied to the non-Spartan inhabitants of Laconia and Messenia who retained local autonomy, but who were nonetheless obligated to serve in the Spartan military and pay taxes to Sparta (although they were not granted full citizenship).

phalanx   A tightly packed fighting formation of shoulder-to-shoulder hoplites arranged in ranks, usually about eight deep.

polis (plural *poleis*)   City-state.

polyandry   The culturally sanctioned practice of having multiple husbands or sexual partners for one wife. (Polygamy usually refers to multiple wives for one husband.)

polytheistic   Having or pertaining to many gods.

primary source materials   These have a direct link to their objects of study, whereas secondary source materials are a step removed from their "primary" sources. For example, critical editions of Plato's works in classical Greek are considered primary, and translations of and commentaries on Plato are secondary.

project (scholarly)   Scholars use this word as a term to encapsulate the primary purposes, concerns, and intentions of a particular person's work or intellectual endeavor.

proskynêsis   A ritual prostration as a sign of subservience and recognition of divinity.

prytanis (plural *prytaneis*)   A term for a presiding official or magistrate.

Ptolemaic   The period of Greek rule over Egypt is known as Ptolemaic from the line of Macedonian pharaohs established by Alexander the Great's general Ptolemy, who controlled Egypt after Alexander's death. The Ptolemaic dynasty ended with the death of Cleopatra in 30 B.C.E.

pyrrhic victory   Named for the "victories" of King Pyrrhus of Epirus over the Romans, a pyrrhic victory is a victory won at excessive cost, or one that involves staggering losses (and, possibly, eventual defeat).

Pythian   This term comes from the serpent Pytho, which Apollo killed in order to found the shrine at Delphi. ("Pythian Apollo" refers to Apollo in conjunction with the Delphic shrine.)

red figure   Red figure was a pottery technique where the figures were left red against a black background with details painted in with a fine brush. Black figure was the opposite: The figures were painted in black silhouette and the details cut through them into the red clay.

relief sculpture   Sculpture that projects from, but is not free from, the background from which it has been cut.

rhetoric   A systematic approach to communication and persuasion. Greek rhetoric distinguished between three kinds of oratory: "deliberative" (*sumbouleutikon*), for making decisions (such as in the assembly); "forensic" (*dikanikon*), for establishing guilt or innocence (in court); and "epideictic" (*epideiktikon*), for bestowing praise or blame (in a more general venue).

Roman Republic   This description refers to the period from 509 B.C.E. to the beginning of the Augustan Principate in 27 B.C.E. *Republic* comes from the Latin *res publica* ("the public thingy"), the name that the Romans gave to their collective political enterprise.

Sacred Band   The Thebans' elite military force, composed of 150 pairs of homosexual lovers. Formed by Epaminondas c. 378 B.C.E., this famous brigade was instrumental in Theban military supremacy until it was wiped out by Philip II at Chaeronea in 338 B.C.E.

sarissa   A 15-foot-long pike, weighted heavily at the butt end, invented by Philip II for his new phalanx. The new weapon allowed Philip's armies, arranged in a compact formation, to attack with four rows of spear points protruding from their ranks.

satrap   The name for an Assyrian or Persian province under the rule of a governor, or satrap.

sex   A biological distinction (male or female). Gender is a conception, composed of social and cultural assumptions and expectations, regarding what male or female persons, behaviors, and roles are and should be.

sexual relationships (heterosexual and homosexual)   The English terms *heterosexual* and *homosexual* have Greek roots. To describe sexual relationships, they are used in the customary sense: **heterosexual** (from Greek *heter* "other") refers to male-female relationships and **homosexual** (from Greek *homo* "same") refers to male-male and female-female relationships.

Spartiatai   Full Spartan citizens. Spartiates were barred from all professions except soldiering.

stasis   (a "stand") A polarization of factions within a *polis* (such as democratic or oligarchic).

sussition   ("common mess") A common meal group (about 15 members) to which Spartan males were admitted and expected to contribute.

syncretism   (from Greek *syn* "together" + *cret* "mix") The process of blending different cultural beliefs and customs into a synthesis that incorporates elements of each.

synoikism   (from the Greek *synoikismos*, "having *oikoi* together") The process of forming disparate communities into one political unit.

Theoric Fund   Created by Eubulus, this fund contained the Athenian surpluses that were used for public works and distributed to the poor. Besides helping ease civic tensions in Athens, the fund tended to make expensive military adventures less appealing to the lower classes.

thêtes   The fourth and lowest class in the Solonian census.

tholos   A monumental stone burial chamber, cut into a hillside in the shape of a conical "beehive" (*tholos*). It had a processional entrance with huge bronze doors.

trireme   A warship, about 120 feet long and 15 feet wide, powered by 170 rowers in 3 ranks, and armed with an underwater ram at the bow (for ramming and sinking enemy ships). The trireme originated in Corinth in the seventh century B.C.E. and became the standard Athenian warship in the fifth century B.C.E.

Index

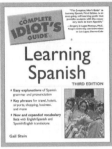